Dennis Barker is the a... of non-fiction books ... human study of the B... ...g On, and a portrait of a great aristocratic estate, *One Man's Estate*. He has worked as a reporter, feature writer, broadcasting correspondent and columnist for the *Guardian*. He has also been a frequent broadcaster.

Dennis Barker

RULING *the* WAVES

An Unofficial Portrait of the Royal Navy

SPHERE BOOKS LIMITED

SPHERE BOOKS LTD

Published by the Penguin Group
27 Wrights Lane, London w8 5tz, England
Viking Penguin Inc., 40 West 23rd Street, New York, New York 10010, USA
Penguin Books Australia Ltd, Ringwood, Victoria, Australia
Penguin Books Canada Ltd, 2801 John Street, Markham, Ontario, Canada l3r 1b4
Penguin Books (NZ) Ltd, 182–190 Wairau Road, Auckland 10, New Zealand

Penguin Books Ltd. Registered Offices: Harmondsworth, Middlesex, England

First published 1986 by Viking
Published by Sphere Books Ltd 1988

Made and printed in Great Britain by
Richard Clay Ltd, Bungay, Suffolk

CONTENTS

6 · *Contents*

INTRODUCTION

It should have been done before. This is a book about the men, women and ships of the Royal Navy as a largely unseen and unsung (until the Falklands) strand of British contemporary life. Rudyard Kipling tried it around the time of the First World War with a series of human documentary books about the Fleet, in which patriotic feeling understandably, in view of the period, sometimes deputized for calm reportage. Britain and the Royal Navy have both changed drastically since then.

For almost half a century now, the Royal Navy and most of the British public have been mutually invisible. As a layman writing for other laymen as well as members of the service, I have tried to portray the atmosphere and *feel* of the Senior Service and its people rather than attempting an encyclopaedic description of the Royal Navy's forbidding and diverse tasks and technologies. I choose this approach partly because people rather than technology provide the continuing historical thread and partly because complicated technologies are changing so fast that much that was written one year would be out of date by the next. And (apart from the fact that I happen to find people more interesting than machines) there is already a deep enough chasm in the sense of public misunderstanding of the Navy's role without deepening it any further with complex technological descriptions.

It was the red-faced anger of one Royal Navy officer that, for me, emphasized the width of the chasm. I knew I had offended the spirited, incisively competent and widely experienced officer by not knowing in advance the complex details of his particular operation, about which I had gone to see him, as a detached but not unsympathetic taxpayer, in the hope of learning. Who the blazes was this civilian who didn't understand as much about the workings of the Royal Navy as he and his fellow officers did? I would have to pull my socks up. That was the clear message that came across. I retained my politeness with some effort. Some days later, though I had in any case regarded myself as having been a guest in the mess, I received two mess bills for wine I hadn't consumed. I didn't pay them. It was the only difference of opinion in the course of researching this book which had real asperity.

We all tend carefully to edit our behaviour in major matters and reveal ourselves in apparently minor ones. I recount this little incident not to score off any individual or group (I had some sympathy with the officer's irritation), but because I think it may be illustrative of a fairly wide band of opinion in the Royal Navy: that if civilians don't understand the need for, and function of, the Royal Navy in today's conditions, they must be idiots on whom little time need be wasted. This attitude is a dangerous one, doubly so in an era when organizations of far less importance than the Navy are becoming increasingly sophisticated in putting their case to the general public.

Practically every naval man I spoke to believed that the Royal Navy was not sufficiently understood and appreciated by the public; but only some realized that part of the answer must be in their own attitudes at each and every level, in each and every contact with civilians. However unpalatable it may be to some officers of the Royal Navy, today's voters are used to having things explained to them in their own terms.

The Royal Navy consists of some 70,000 people, including 7,500 Royal Marines, about the same number in the Fleet Air Arm, and 3,500 members of the Women's Royal Naval Service: in all, about a third of the size of the coal industry. Fifty-three frigates or destroyers, four aircraft/Marine carriers, including the new £320 million HMS *Ark Royal*, four Polaris nuclear submarines, fifteen hunter-killer submarines, fifteen remaining diesel submarines, about thirty minesweepers or patrol boats, two assault landing ships, thirteen survey vessels and a number of training craft. And the Royal Navy is still all around the world. It has a constant or frequent presence in the Persian Gulf, the West Indies, Hong Kong and the Far East, and the South Atlantic around the Falkland Islands.

All this is real enough. But, subjectively for most of the British nation and electorate, there is no longer a Royal Navy, any more than there is still a sea around Britain. *They never see either.* It is a boring wait at two airports, and a flight in a metal tube, that separates the average holidaymaker from the Costa Brava or Tenerife, not the sea. Unless he is a poor student or a rich playboy on a world cruise, he never sees the vastness of the oceans. And unless he lives in a Navy town like Portsmouth, Plymouth or Rosyth, he never sees the Navy. If someone wants to make defence cuts in the Navy, why should he care?

Of course, objectively, he should care. He should care very much. Over 95 per cent of essential supplies still come to the United Kingdom by sea. In war, an enemy who could knock out the Royal Navy in the English Channel, the North Sea and the North Atlantic could effectively bring a starving nation to its knees in a matter of weeks; and the United States' nuclear umbrella would in itself offer no infallible protection, since it is unlikely that any great power would precipitate mutual nuclear destruction by using nuclear weapons in support of a starving Britain. All the lessons of the past forty years – since the atomic bomb was first used in circumstances where only one side had it – have been that aggressive armed conflict is undertaken with conventional weapons and has to be answered with them, nuclear weapons being held back as a last resort.

In short, the Navy is as necessary today as it was in Nelson's and Kipling's times. The life-blood of Britain and the West flows only with its protection.

That is why ideally, *all* unmilitary civilians like myself should be able to journey through the Navy more or less at will, as I was able to do, to observe a Navy very different from the time of Nelson and the Battle of Trafalgar, when some boys entered at the age of eight, ships often carried women as well as men, rotten salt beef drove men to delirium by forcing them to drink foul water and the penalty for 'talking back' to an officer was being 'gagged' – put in irons with an iron bolt across the open mouth.

I hope that in this book readers can make the trip vicariously. The Royal Navy of today could hardly be more different – a high-technology force that is still interesting in human terms, even if some naval people find it almost as hard as computer programmers to talk in simple and winning terms to the average civilian.

The Royal Navy allowed me a great deal of freedom. True to naval tradition, they left me largely to my own devices in painting this naval portrait. I was not oppressively taken over by any public-relations machine, and this had its good, as well as occasionally inconvenient, side. I was able to sail on ships during sea trials and mock battles; talk to aircraft handlers on the noisy decks of aircraft carriers; see the life and crucial importance of post-colonial Gibraltar in the Navy's present-day strategy; spend some time with the Royal Marines, in snow holes during their training in or near the Arctic Circle, where temperatures are often as low as forty degrees below freezing, or under canvas in a Devon wood; and sample life in a submarine carrying Polaris nuclear missiles.

The result is a contemporary portrait of the Royal Navy as seen through the eyes of an interested civilian. I had all necessary and feasible help from the Royal Navy itself. But, as with my corresponding book on the British Army, *Soldiering On*, the finished work remained my own, the only condition being that it should be subject to correction on points of fact and security. I am indebted to officers and ratings at all levels, men and women, who spoke courteously and frankly to me on the understanding that they would be quoted by rank but not by name. The final portrait remains my responsibility. It is, as far as I am aware, the only one of its type since the far-off Kipling era.

I am grateful to Mrs R. Kloegman for typing my civilian's eye view of a largely invisible service. I am also, of course, grateful to that irate officer for illustrating how easy, excusable and potentially disastrous it is to brush civilians up the wrong way in what is, for good or ill, a populist age: an age as different from Kipling's as the Royal Navy is different.

PART I

WAYS OF LIFE

I

THE VERBAL FRONT LINE

'Why have we got this terrific phobia about the tremendous Russian navy when the Americans have also got an enormous navy in the Mediterranean? They must be as repressive as the Russians?'

– Civilian questioner at Royal Navy Presentation
Team civic meeting, East End of London.

'There is general sympathy for the Navy. The audience is almost exclusively and extraordinarily pro-Navy, whether or not they are pro other things, like the government, Cruise and Trident.'

– Lieutenant-commander, member of the Royal Navy
Presentation Team, Gravesend, Kent.

'Do Wrens sleep in hammocks?'

– Civilian questioner at Royal Navy Presentation
Team meeting.

There had been only one previous question from the audience when the lady with the white woolly cardigan and the inquiring spectacles tried to shoot down the role of the Royal Navy as a protective force for Britain.

'If it came to war with Russia,' she asked, 'wouldn't the Navy find that there is very little left of Britain to defend – or any of the West, for that matter? They would just wipe us out with a few nuclear missiles, and there would be nothing to defend.'

'Perhaps,' replied the Royal Navy captain equably, 'you have missed a point of the argument. The whole point of having nuclear weapons is *not* to use them. They are not particularly attractive items, so perhaps we turn the existence of them to some form of advantage. You have got to make it not worthwhile for the other side to use them. I don't believe the Soviets want to start a nuclear war, and we don't.'

But, said the captain, the Soviets had an enormous maritime potential and capability, and had shown they were prepared to use it to 'nibble away' at the West. Hence the value of conventional forces, especially the Navy, in its defence of our vital routes for incoming food and raw materials and outgoing exports.

The lady was plainly not convinced. The whole atmosphere was by now not the most favourable for the Royal Navy or any other military force.

In a civic hall next to the swimming baths in Bethnal Green, part of the highly Left-wing London Borough of Tower Hamlets in London's East End, an audience of 110 people less than half filled the available seats. Anoraks, blousons, scuffed tennis shoes and CND sympathies had been cautiously in evidence at the Royal Navy's sherry reception.

'Most people who *work* in a London borough like this, if they are the sort we are trying to reach – of all professions and classes – probably don't *live* there,' said the captain who was leading the Royal Navy Presentation Team in one of its September-to-March public meetings in which the work of the Navy is explained to the public. 'Perhaps they commute to somewhere else in the evening. We normally get a bigger audience than this – around four hundred. Usually we send out invitations to double the number of people we actually hope to get. For this one we sent out 900 invitations to get 110. I wouldn't say it was an entirely satisfactory session.'

There are two Royal Navy Presentation Teams, one led by the captain – whose next job would be commanding HMS *Illustrious*; an evident high-flyer. The captain's audiences are the large civic and industrial ones. Another team, directly under a commander, talks to clubs, societies, and smaller organizations. Each team does an average of four presentations a week, and on Friday is usually in its London office, located on the Thames South Bank, to discuss the past week's experience and the coming week's plans.

Before the questions at Bethnal Green, there was the stock fifty-minute briefing from the captain. He stood on the stage behind the Navy's own portable lectern, one of the two props that go around with the team. The other is the gilt-lettered, white-painted Royal Navy lifebelt which is displayed in the foyers of the buildings visited.

The captain reminded his audience of Britain's dependence on the sea; how our continued free use of the sea might be threatened; and then discussed the ways the Navy was prepared to meet such a threat. Then he said, 'Recently there has been an upsurge of interest and concern over defence. The activities in the South Atlantic in 1982 focused great attention on the Royal Navy and the Royal Marines. The conflict with Argentine forces made many people realize the need for a well-balanced conventional Navy and the requirement to retain the flexibility to deploy this seapower worldwide.'

The audience listened to all this politely enough, as they did to the statistics illustrating the stranglehold an enemy could put upon Britain if she did not control the surrounding seas: 95 per cent of the weight of our entire trade was still carried in ships. The United Kingdom and other countries of Western Europe could not survive without a minimum of a thousand shiploads every month of essential food and critical raw materials. On any one day there were over three hundred ocean-going merchant ships and a further four hundred smaller vessels loading or unloading their cargoes in ports around the United Kingdom. Our Merchant Fleet had contributed over

£1,000 million towards our balance of payments last year, despite two thirds of Britain's trade now being carried by foreign ships.

It was when the captain switched the subject matter of the audio-visual presentation to the Russian Navy, its size and its activities, that the audience audibly started to polarize. There was some muttering when the captain pointed out that Russia spent twice the proportion of its gross national product on defence as any NATO country; and that Russian fear of invasions, such as there had been in the past, could not justify the extent of Soviet power generally and the development of the Soviet Navy in particular. It was easy to see – or, rather hear – that part of the audience thought this to be predictable Soviet-bashing. But a larger section of the audience drew in deep breaths when the illustrations of ships of the Russian Navy came up on the screen: the 'Kiev' Class of aircraft carriers (the fourth under construction at the time); the recently introduced nuclear-powered cruiser *Kirov* (the largest surface warship, apart from aircraft carriers, to be built by any nation for thirty-five years); the latest amphibious ship, the *Ivan Rogov* (more than twice the displacement of any previous Soviet amphibious ship); the largest (450) submarine fleet in the world, nine times the size of the German submarine fleet at the start of the Second World War, and soon to be reinforced with the largest submarine in the world, the *Typhoon*, as big as an aircraft carrier and more than five thousand tons heavier than HMS *Invincible*.

'It is sometimes argued,' said the captain, 'that Russia is a world power whether we like it or not and that, as such, she pursues her interests legitimately by this traditional exercise of seapower; and that provided we don't challenge her, she won't interfere with us. The last contention cannot be guaranteed. The Soviet Fleet exists; it is a fact, and even though the Russians may not intend to challenge us today, once capabilities exist, intentions can change overnight. History has repeatedly shown that the temptation to use armed force for national ends can often prove irresistible.'

The captain explained how NATO ground forces in Europe – including the 55,000 men of the British Army of the Rhine – were outnumbered by the Warsaw Pact forces and would need reinforcement in time of emergency: 'Such reinforcement would require over one million American servicemen, nine million tons of equipment and ammunition and fourteen million tons of fuel to be transported across the Atlantic. Five hundred shiploads a month would be needed to sustain these reinforcements. And this is in addition to the shiploads required each month to support the basic economic and civilian needs of Western Europe. An evident ability to reinforce and re-supply Europe from the United Kingdom and, particularly, from the United States is a key factor, both in maintaining an effective deterrent to Russian military adventures in Europe, and in sustaining the confidence of America and of the West European nations in NATO itself. If the Russians ever thought that they could successfully cut Europe off from the United States in war, and that they would have to deal only with "in-place" forces, they might be much more ready to try their hand.'

Then came the explanation of how the Navy would react to a threat by sweeping mines; hitting enemy submarines with the twelve – soon to be more – nuclear-powered attack submarines, or the sophisticated missile Ikara, which homes in on its target; deploying the Sea Harriers; and using the weapon that proved its value all too well in the Falklands war – the Exocet missile. Britain, with the exception of France, had more Exocets than any other Western navy, said the captain.

The density of this material was not easy to digest on a fairly warm spring evening in London, even assisted by the couple of sherries consumed by most members of the audience on their way in. The intellectual indigestion caused one of two broad reactions in the question-and-answer period: a reluctance to believe that preparing against the supposed Russian threat would mean anything in practice, or a rather tensely earnest preoccupation with the minutiae of British ships and equipment and their effectiveness in a real war.

The latter school of thought asked the first question. A youngish man with a moustache and a junior-executive blue suit got himself involved in a numbers tangle by asking about the effectiveness of some of the Royal Navy's ships, the Type 22 in particular. The captain thought that he possibly meant Type 42, because the *Sheffield* had received the most criticism, and also possibly the Type 21, where it had also been suggested we had had problems with the aluminium used in the super-structure, because it would burn.

'The *Sheffield* and *Coventry* were Type 42,' said the captain. 'There were some misinformed comments about the use of aluminium. Yes, these do make some use of aluminium, but we don't use as much as the Soviets or the United States do. It was a very tightly designed ship with a very great top weight – ten tons of special equipment like radar, practically on top of the mast. But aluminium doesn't burn, it melts at 700 degrees. It was 1,000 degrees when the Argentine Exocet hit and didn't explode but kept making heat with its propellant, which kept on cooking. The ship didn't sink for another thirty-six hours. The aluminium didn't get badly scorched.'

The audience heard this rather long technical tête-à-tête out in polite silence. Then it was the turn of the lady in the woolly cardigan and the prim glasses. She got one or two murmurs of agreement when she suggested that the Navy might have no Britain left to protect in a war with Russia. But the audience heard out the captain's answer politely – there is perhaps some advantage in *selecting* your audience in collaboration with the Navy's regional officers, and plying them agreeably with sherry on the way in. Overt hostility would be graceless.

The mayor, a Labour man, who had been sitting with his party in the front row, isolated from the rest of the audience by three rows of quite empty seats, asked question number three. Hadn't the spruce captain painted a rather optimistic picture of the Royal Navy today?

The captain's footwork was fully up to this one. 'The Navy didn't come particularly well out of the defence cuts in 1981,' he agreed swiftly. 'We certainly do have problems in the Navy today.' Then he quickly changed gear and went on to the attack: 'Manpower is a problem we *would have* gone through. We *would* have had a tremendous reduction in total naval forces to 65,000. However, along came the Falklands; and because there is a continuing commitment, the ships we were to have lost we are not going to lose so quickly; and the programme of redundancy has been stopped, and we are re-cruiting again. You must remember that the Soviet Navy has half a million people. But our recruiting targets are being met. For every one man we want we get about five or six applying. That is partly a reflection of the unemployment situation outside the Royal Navy.'

There was even a sly answer for anyone in the audience who might have been depressed by the huge size of the Soviet Navy. The Soviet Navy was 80 per cent a conscripted force, serving for three or four years on low pay. 'But they are fairly good,' said the presenter of the presentation generously.

Next question? A man with a mane of white hair and a white beard, who could have been a college lecturer, asked 'whether you are at liberty to disclose' whether the *Conqueror* had had it 'all her own way' when the Argentinian cruiser *General Belgrano* was torpedoed, or whether *Conqueror* had been attacked ineffectually by destroyers accompanying the Argentine ship. Had the Argentine Navy really slunk away and done nothing?

This produced an answer in defence of the decision to sink the *Belgrano* outside the total exclusion zone for ships declared by the British. It was a shrewd move on the captain's part, for the whole tenor of the question, if not the precise words, had suggested that the British Navy had done a bit of bullying and had its nose bloodied for its pains.

'They had been warned on April 25 that any military or civilian ship, aircraft or anything else that was outside the twelve-mile limit would be considered a threat to the military forces of the UK. On that particular occasion the *Belgrano* had two Exocets with her, and it looked very nasty to the task group commander. I don't believe, as a military man, that the implication that the *Belgrano* was heading away at the time is as strong as some people make out. I would not be surprised if the *Belgrano* had been heading south one minute, west the next minute. A ship depends for its safety on weaving and zig-zagging, on confusing the enemy. At that particular time she may have been on a westerly course, but I am sure that minutes before that she had been on another course. The only further point I would make is this. What would the public reaction have been if the *Belgrano* had *not* been sunk, but had returned the next day and sunk the *Hermes* with its Exocets, with the loss of two thousand British sailors?'

A youth in a brown suit, the only *young* person of the few there to ask a question, inquired if, after the Falklands, our whole defence policy should change.

The captain had an immediate answer. 'Perhaps NATO as an alliance should be prepared to operate outside its present area. In a small but significant way we have shown that we have an ability for operating outside our NATO area – not necessarily alone.'

Evidently not all the captain's answers had been absorbed by the audience, because a man in a track-suit resurrected the subject of the aluminium in ships catching fire with a single hit.

'Our ships did *not* catch fire with one shot,' said the patient captain. '*Coventry* was sunk because a large number of arms went off inside her. She sank in seventeen minutes. In *Antelope*, there was a brave attempt to defuse a bomb in the magazine, but it went off and split her asunder. In the case of *Ardent*, a struggle was made to save her when a number of arms went off inside her. She was taking water. Many of the ships survived. *Glasgow* had tremendous fires, but her gas turbines were repaired with pieces of wood so that she could steam.

Sometimes the ship's purser's electric toaster was used to effect repairs.'

The loss of ships must be balanced against the saving of Royal Marines who landed at San Carlos, argued the captain. The Marines had thought the Task Force was absolutely smashing. 'You need air support of three-to-one if you are going to attack in that sort of situation. We had to be ships in the line to give the men ashore a chance. We put 10,000 on the beaches and didn't lose one. We lost a few ships, in doing it – and we expected to lose a damn sight more.'

A man with thick glasses and well-trimmed beard made the mistake of suggesting that all three armed services should be combined into one, in the name of administrative efficiency and cost-cutting. 'Thank you, sir, it is a question I have been asked before,' said the captain ominously.

He was sorry, but he just didn't see the advantages. The North Americans had tried it, had said, 'We will all wear one strange funny green uniform.' But they were now going back to their own uniforms. There was no point in calling a sailor a soldier unless he was *trained* to be a soldier as well as a sailor; and that would cost twice as much, not reduce costs. There was perhaps room for economies being made in common support responsibilities – like chaplains and doctors. The Army already handled all the transport of the Services and the Royal Navy had taken over victualling.

The last question came from a grey-haired man who, although his metal glasses gave the opposite impression, did not appear to be a services buff.

'Why,' he asked, 'have we got this terrific phobia about the tremendous Russian navy when the Americans have also got an enormous navy in the Mediterranean? They must be as repressive as the Russians?'

'It happens,' said the captain, 'that many of our sources of raw materials are still in these parts of the world. I am not sure what the Soviets' interest – in terms of sources of their raw materials – is in West Africa, which is a purely strategic point.

I am not sure what the Soviets' interest is, in terms of their raw materials, in some parts of the Red Sea or Vietnam. They have extended worldwide, and they have an enormous navy. They may not intend to challenge us today with it but they are able to put seriously at risk our ability to use the sea freely, on which we deeply rely as an island nation.'

There was a supplementary question: wasn't a large part of the Russian navy a merchant fleet? Yes, said the Navy team leader, but a merchant navy was an instrument of sea power. The Russians had put enormous effort into undercutting our merchant fleet. They had subsidized their own and increased the size of their merchant fleet enormously, and forced us to reduce ours from 2,700 to 850 ships.

The quick-footed captain had used every question to expand his major theme of the threat to the freedom of the seas. He got hearty applause, and so did the Labour mayor when he said there could be various opinions on nuclear weapons and he had his own (he didn't say what they were). But he certainly regarded the Royal Navy as a peacemaker. He had been in it six years. One of his sons was in the Navy, and had been involved in the Falklands campaign. He presented the captain with a Tower Hamlets crest, with its motto 'From Great Things to Greater'.

It was an affable evening's end for the Royal Navy. The captain had deserved it, steering a very careful course through statistics and policy, not impaling himself on the sort of ideological differences that could have inflamed such a meeting.

But the captain was a perfectionist, as befits a man about to take over an aircraft carrier. He said afterwards that he hadn't liked the fact that there were few younger people there and he hadn't liked the fact that there weren't many middle-class people there. And there was only one coloured man. It was essential to get the points across to people aged twenty-five to forty, because they had no background in what a fighting force was for, having no memory of war.

'I am not here to talk to the converted,' he insisted. 'I always say I am talking to the agnostics and the atheists. I would never turn anyone away, even if they were carrying a great big red banner.'

That this was literally true was proved at a presentation at Gravesend in Kent which I attended to see for myself how typical Bethnal Green had been. There was a much larger crowd, in a much jollier mood (the sherry reception area was distinctly more aesthetically pleasing). Almost everyone was what even the Navy would call respectably dressed, including a group of about six young people wearing CND badges.

From the very first time the captain called for questions, a member of this group put his hand up, together with a lot more members of the audience. The captain selected a middle-aged man who drew attention to the headlines that day – there was a surprise Russian naval exercise in the North Atlantic – and asked how the West would manage to get its own ships into the North Atlantic if the Russians ever made a real attack.

The captain said that in the build-up to a real attack, other things would have to happen first – land and air forces would have to be activated. 'All the indications are that this is just an exercise, confined to the North Atlantic,' said the captain soothingly.

Again up went the hand of the young man in the CND group. But the captain saw the raised hand of another middle-aged man who suggested that not enough was done in peacetime to improve the liaison between the Royal Navy and the Merchant Navy, who each tended to stick to their own ways of doing things.

No, said the captain, even outside the Falklands, the liaison was quite extensive. Some officers went on liaison cruises.

Neither did the CND element grab the third question, which was about the removal of some US battleships from mothballs; nor the fourth, asking whether things would have been different had Britain had an aircraft carrier like the *Ark Royal* near the Falklands (yes, said the captain). Nor even the fifth. This was seized by a man sitting in the dead centre of the audience, well away from the CND group, who identified himself as a member of the European Peace Movement. 'Are you unhappy with our relationship with the USA, which has bases which spring up all over the world?' he asked. 'And where we have no proper interests, but might get involved?'

'I am not a politician, I am a naval officer,' said the captain, to some mutterings from the CND group. 'But we must import our raw materials from overseas, so we need the freedom of the seas. We are a member of NATO. One of the biggest nations in NATO is the USA; one of the biggest maritime contributors. We have lived for a long time under the umbrella that the US is helping to produce. We have to believe in trust, as they have shown their commitment to us on many occasions. I would not like to live in a world totally without that commitment from the USA.' This brought prolonged applause, except from the CND section sitting at the back of the hall.

By the time the captain had reached the *tenth* question, which he said must be the last, the CND group had changed their tactics. It was a different hand in the group that went up, its owner protesting, 'I have been trying to ask a question for the past half hour.'

The captain agreed to take the question. The young man read it out from a sheet of paper. It amounted to: what would be the role of the Navy if a conventional attack by the Warsaw Pact countries was followed by the use of theatre nuclear weapons by the West, leading to a nuclear war?

'Were you reading that question, sir, or is it your own opinion?' said the captain suavely. 'That is the most dangerous scenario you have given, but just because it is the most dangerous, it is the least likely to happen. The Navy's main role would be in the build-up to that situation. Before the Soviets could mount such an operation, military and diplomatic indications would have to be given. The Russians like saturation attack. The Navy would assist in bringing over the troops to be deployed in containing such an attack.'

Thanks to the captain's unruffled footwork, the CND question had been transformed into a preparation for the speech of thanks by the mayor, who said amid applause, 'I admit to being a great patriot, and to that extent I think a deterrent is what we must have.'

It came as no surprise to be told that a considerable amount of man-hours, as well as dexterity, go into the Royal Navy Presentation Teams. (Not much money, however. The Navy has worked it out that its presentations cost only about £1.50 a head, which is considered good value.)

The team was set up in the early 1970s by the Admiralty Board. Its aim is to tour the country, putting the facts to the public about Britain's maritime interests – easily neglected in the era of air travel – and the role and future of the Royal Navy in safeguarding these interests. There are always two teams on the road throughout the autumn and winter. The first team, like the one I watched in action at Bethnal Green and Gravesend, consists of four – a senior captain, a second officer Women's Royal Naval Service (WRNS), plus two ratings – from either the technical branch of the Royal Navy or the Royal Marines. The aim is to see that interested members of the public have a cross-section of naval people to talk to at the sherry reception, and at the coffee-and-biscuits session which follows the audio-visual presentation and the questions and answers. Usually, but not invariably, the presentations are on Tuesdays, Wednesdays or Thursdays, though with travel and visits to industry they take up four days of the week before the usual Friday winding-up day in the office. The team go to civic halls, universities and major industries.

In the meantime, a team of three led by a commander with a Royal Marine officer and a rating visit societies, clubs and smaller industries. Rotarians, Round Table members and professionals are frequent audiences. Their minimum audience is fifty, compared with the one hundred and fifty of the captain's team.

'We try not to send these high-powered teams to talk to

only three people,' said the commander in the teams' Thames-side offices. 'With civic audiences, we have had only a hundred or so before now, but normally there are between two hundred and fifty and four hundred. There certainly were that number in Mansfield – Nottinghamshire – when Torvill and Dean were in the public eye ice dancing. People's environment in the area tends to affect the size of the audience. At Great Yarmouth we were flooded out with people, presumably because it is a port, and the East Coast was widely used by the Royal Navy during the war. Places like Portsmouth tend to say, "To hell with the Navy, the Navy lives here." We never return to the same town for five years once we have appeared there.'

The RAF also submits itself to the verbal front line with its own presentation team, but so far the Army has no comparable mechanism – possibly because the Army tends to be fastidiously determined not to be seen to be interfering in *any* way in civilian affairs.

The team as a whole decides early which places it wants to go for the following season. 'One or two councils,' said a commander, 'haven't been all that helpful. Basildon in Essex, which is very left-wing-controlled, refused to allow us to use its council facilities – a theatre. The chairman of the leisure committee apparently recommended to the council that we should not be allowed to use it, so we didn't push it. We went to an hotel instead, and it was very successful. But of course the unfortunate fact of life, much as we would have liked to talk to the people who opposed our visit, is that people who are not interested don't turn up. It doesn't make for success in what we are doing, but you can't make them come. It doesn't break down on purely political lines. In Sheffield, also left-wing, they were tremendously helpful. We went to the Centre Suite of the Civic Centre. No trouble at all.'

Invitations to hear the captain's team are sent to people from a fixed list which comprises eight separate sections – VIPs such as the Lord-Lieutenants and bishops (ten), local government (one hundred), administration of justice (fifty), industry and public services (two hundred and fifty), education (fifty), media (ten), health (fifty), other professions (one hundred and fifty), associations and clubs (one hundred and twenty), including, says the instruction document in capital letters underlined, 'chairman/secretary of *ALL* political associations', and armed forces (ten).

So sure are the teams of their own ability to cope with all comers that their policy has been that wherever they encounter a CND demonstration outside the hall, they invite them in and answer their questions. 'Provided they are good listeners, we are happy,' said the lieutenant-commander liaison officer at headquarters. 'If they get noisy, it is usually the audience who shout them down – especially was that so during the year of the Falklands. We have never had to cancel a show or call the police.'

Sometimes the questions can unexpectedly provide light relief from the oppressive weight of information about the potential Soviet threat.

Once the team was asked, 'Do Wrens sleep in hammocks?'

This took the team unawares, partly because most of the team could hardly remember what a hammock looked like. The reply they gave off the cuff was, 'Some people prefer to sleep in hammocks, but they are now not generally available and not issued as kit. There would tend to be camp beds rather than hammocks. Generally hammocks are in the past.' End of worries about daughters in the WRNS falling out of hammocks at night.

I asked the lieutenant-commander what struck the teams generally about the public response. 'We are still – and always have been – a maritime nation. The sea *is* in our blood. The Navy has always had a place in people's hearts, though it is not scattered across the country in the same way as the Army and RAF are. This will probably always be so.'

Plainly it will not be the fault of the high-powered presentation teams if he is ever proved wrong.

Nevertheless, from my own experience at Bethnal Green and Gravesend, two qualifications suggested themselves. I asked the Royal Marine member of a team, a twenty-nine-year-old veteran of the Falklands whose loyalty and patriotism were beyond question, what he thought personally of the presentations. I was not unduly surprised when he said, 'I have done this job for nine months and done over a hundred presentations. Personally I think the audience we are getting are probably the wrong audience in one sense – people who have served their National Service, or were in during the war, or are Merchant Seamen, or the Royal Naval Reserve – they have some interest in the Navy and come as an outing for their interests. What we need basically is more of the younger generation. They do tend to stop away.'

It seemed to me that it was shrewd of the Royal Navy to keep its own enthusiasts up-to-the-minute in their knowledge of the Royal Navy, its functions and its problems; but that it would be even more shrewd if it somehow broadened the audiences, almost to the extent of *encouraging* provocative questions. The CND element at Gravesend were, paradoxically, an irritant that helped the Navy's case. And there is always the chance that – perhaps years hence – a remark made by the captain at the lectern, or by individual members of the team in conversation with the public, will suddenly appear to be good sense to a previously unsympathetic young man or woman.

The second qualification I would make is on a simple point of presentation style. Directness of speech is encouraged in the Royal Navy. It is understood and appreciated within naval discipline. It is impressive for a civilian audience to face a successful officer who is rattling off his knowledge and statistics at two hundred or so words a minute. But whether that is necessarily the best way to get civilians feeling involved is a moot point. Diffidence; sometimes the tentative approach; the groping for the right word, the hesitancy – all these things may make Royal Navy men irritated; but they are sometimes the tools of persuasion in civilian life. They are part of the charm increasingly necessary to reach people who would not otherwise be reached in growingly complex and ambivalent times when little is as clear-cut as when Nelson said, 'England expects'. Which, come to think of it, was a rather *humanly* phrased order.

But the Royal Navy's front lines are rarely verbal. The real front lines exist in terms of action – sometimes very testing action indeed, which can include rehearsals for real war.

2

THURSDAY'S WARS

'At these times we have an allowable period to get the submarine we are looking for. If you were actually looking for a submarine in war, you would hope to have it well before then – say half an hour.'

– Principal warfare officer, aboard frigate HMS
Galatea during a mock 'Thursday war'.

'Bumps and near-bumps? I have been here two years, and I think I have seen it all.'

– Commander at Portland Naval base, from which
Thursday wars are held.

The fighter screamed almost directly over the bridge of the Royal Naval frigate HMS *Galatea*, after firing some of its complement of missiles at her. Amid the noise of the attacking aircraft and the shouted instructions on the bridge of *Galatea*, I foolishly wanted to duck and cover my ears. All around me, adrenalin was running high.

The officer who was captaining the ship had something other than the noise on his mind. He wanted to make me understand that in different circumstances, we would not have been the sitting ducks we appeared to be now.

'We had warning,' said the saturnine-featured commander who was driving the *Galatea*. 'In a *different sort* of war, shall we say, we would have put about 180 degrees by now, so we could bring everything to bear on that attacking aircraft. I have got a Bofors gun at the back and would even – ha, ha – attack the plane with small arms. But today I have a difficulty, because if I turned, I would turn right into my own following ships.'

It was war, but war of an unusual sort. The place was just off Portland Bill in Dorset, the day was Thursday and the occasion was a 'Thursday war'. Every Thursday, a variety of Royal Naval ships (some to get practice after a refit, others to carry a variety of naval specialists who are still in training) sail out of Portland naval base – HMS *Osprey* – for a realistic mock war in which they will be strafed by aircraft, engaged by 'enemy' service craft and hunted by submarines. It is a massive and expensive operation, which the Royal Navy believes pays for itself ten times over. First, it earmarks the weaknesses. Second, it polishes the strengths of both men and equipment.

I could clearly see the importance of both points during the gruelling 'war' one Thursday in a foggy, blowy August. It began at 7.30 in the morning on Camber Jetty at HMS *Osprey*, and ended with me – and a lot of others – feeling both queasy and exhilarated.

In the early morning light, an experienced chief petty officer, a comparative veteran with sharp features and piercing light-grey eyes, shepherded a varied assortment of participants in the 'war' into one of Portland's Liberty boats. This boat would take us all out to HMS *Galatea*, berthed far out in the harbour. Squally winds were blowing. There had been patches of rain. The Liberty boat bobbed up and down beside the jetty like a cork as a group of petty officers, leading seamen and seamen sonar operators clambered aboard, plus a group of junior Wrens – a rare sight at sea, normally an exclusively male domain. And there was a party of public schoolboys from Radley, some of them thinking of joining the Navy and all of them wearing neatly polished black shoes and well creased dark grey trousers.

As he collected up his flock, the chief petty officer explained
to me his curious but logical role: it was to see that the 'war'
was *safe*. 'I am duty staff on board – our staff consists of a fleet
chief petty officer, who does the administration, and three
chief petty officers who go to sea from Portland. We look
after the *real* safety of the ship, particularly with regard to
submarines. If the ship decides to do something that is wrong,
I can say, "You aren't allowed to do that, because . . ." I am
also here to assist with the sonar training classes, and to do
liaison between ship and shore.'

I asked him what sort of things could happen that might
endanger the safety of the ship in real terms, even in a mock
war. He gave a slow, wry smile, as if at the memory of uncomfortable moments that might, or might not, be discussable.
Then: 'Oh, they don't say where they are discharging weapons
at us, or they are doing it at an incorrect time. Things like that.
Or, let us say we are going in for a mortar attack on the
submarine and the submarine has incorrectly come up to periscope depth – it is a *real* submarine, remember. A surface ship
could cut into it. I would jump in and say, "Stop firing,
because . . ." And it would be because the submarine's safety
was in danger. Another possibility. We are wired to the
mortars with sonar, and sonar can get slightly out of line. It is
easy to put them *back* in line, it is a ten-second job; but, once
they are out of line, there is a possible danger. So I tend to
spend my time in the war between the bridge, the operations
room and the sonar room.'

Even a comparatively small warship, a 372-feet long, 2,750-
ton frigate like HMS *Galatea*, with a crew of 257 and a
sprightly speed of twenty-eight knots, can look challengingly
big when viewed from a Liberty boat bobbing at water level
against its steel hull. The swaying vertical rope ladder up its
side to its deck was an entirely different proposition from, say,
a domestic step ladder used for painting the living-room
ceiling. Fortunately the party of young Wrens were ahead of
me, graciously accepting assistance to swing themselves off this

swaying ladder up on to the deck. Pride or vanity dictated my brisk ascent of the rungs, followed by an equally brisk and unassisted clamber on to the frigate's deck. Vulnerable civilian morale had been maintained.

The commander who was driving the ship was already on the bridge. He had been there for some time. 'During the course of the day, if you feel we are talking gobbledy-gook, and in the Navy we do tend to use our own terms, will you please say, "Stop it, and speak English",' said the commander disarmingly. Perhaps his varied experience in his twenty-one years in the Royal Navy, including mention in dispatches during the Falklands campaign, had left him with no psychological need to blind civilians with science. His lack of pomposity was a model for naval relations with civilians.

As *Galatea* made her way out of Portland harbour into a channel designated as the only clear one in a defensive mine-field, she was followed by five others – the 'Broadsword' class frigate *Brazen*, the Fleet Replenishment Ship *Fort Austin*, the stretched-type 'Sheffield' class destroyer *Manchester*, the Seawolf-armed 'Leander' class frigate *Jupiter* and finally the Royal Fleet Auxiliary *Gold Rover*. *Gold Rover* was simulating what is called the 'main body' or the high-value unit – the ship that must be guarded at all costs.

Behind them all came HMS *Southampton*, the 'Sheffield' class destroyer, with the admiral aboard. Since it was *Southampton*'s final Thursday war, said the captain of the *Galatea*, it was her show today. She would be directing the campaign. Its aim was to screen the *Gold Rover* 'tanker' from attack by submarines, aircraft and the 'surface threat' – a nice little euphemism for the *Almirante Cochrane*, the former HMS *Antrim*, now sold to the Chilean Navy and on its last war before going on to Portsmouth to be replenished in readiness for Chilean service. This ship was posing as an enemy or (as officers say when their tongues slip) Russian warship out to sink the tanker.

The first consideration, as the ships sailed out to sea through the imaginary minefield, like a gigantic slithering grey sea monster, was the minefield. There was no question of sweeping it, since it was a defensive one, put there by the British to safeguard Portland. The mines would have to be avoided, and the bang and the green flash of a Very pistol on the starboard side signified that a mine had been seen on that side. It meant that *Galatea* and the following ships all had to move over slightly to port.

The captain regretted that it would not be a full action stations war I would be watching; I would have to use a certain degree of imagination. In a war fought fully at action stations, there could be no question of a civilian conversing with anyone engaged in it. Everyone aboard would be in full anti-flash-burn gear – white hoods and gloves. Because there would also be the possibility of chemical warfare, they would also be carrying their anti-gas respirators and their life jackets. Such conditions were called full work-up conditions; everything in the ship would be closed and battened down. And the ship would be in what was called the ultra-quiet state, with the minimum of machinery being operated. All aspects of ventilation, fire protection, hydraulics and power would be sectionalized to minimize the effects of a hit on the ship and maximize its chances of surviving damage. There would be a number of section generators to minimize loss of power if one generator was put out of action.

'There is a requirement for a number of ships to assist in training, or completing the training, of those ratings and officers who are doing various courses ashore,' said the commander. 'There is a terrific amount of work one can do ashore in preparing people for a ship. HMS *Dryad*'s operations training is very valuable, but we have to get their whiskers wet at sea, because being at sea is a bit different. There are a few things to be taken into account, like weather changes. Only this week there was a pea-soup fog. Going into harbour, we had to stop twice. With other ships trying to get into the harbour as well, it was difficult. Two sailing boats came within twenty yards of us before tacking away from us. Yes, we have to get their whiskers wet at sea.'

In a Thursday war at full action stations, men get used to eating in the action stations fashion. They eat a 'pot mess' off a plate with the aid only of a spoon. Disgusting? The commander pointed out that you needed some way of feeding men quickly at action stations. They had to get the necessary sustaining food into their fighting bellies without it taking them away from their 'Action' state for too long. He would hope to feed the entire ship's company in twenty minutes. No weapon system was ever reduced below its functional level. If there was an attack, men would simply put down their spoons. In the forenoon (between eight in the morning and noon) men would tend to have what were called 'action snacks', which would be even more rudimentary. In the operations room itself, they might be Mars bars, which had energy-giving content without interfering with the work of the men.

'If you had crumbly rolls, they would *not* be good for the computer keyboards,' pointed out the commander.

At that moment, as *Galatea* was ploughing further and further into the English Channel, she was doing so in a state known as emission control silence. The sonar and radar systems were not working, so as not to give the ship away to the enemy. Information was being fed to the ship from the *Southampton*, acting in what was called the Radar Guardship Mode. It meant the *Southampton* gave to *Galatea*, and all the other ships steaming out into the English Channel, an adequate picture of what was happening around them.

What was happening at this precise moment was that one of *Southampton*'s two Lynx helicopters had arrived overhead, searching for the enemy ship *Almirante Cochrane*. The Red or 'A' warning went out, and it was immediately pointed out to me that at such a moment in a real war, the Radley schoolboys would *not* be on the bridge, even if the *Galatea*'s flight commander was an old boy of the school. Everyone would be too busy preparing a situation picture for the operations room, even though it might not actually be required. That, said the commander, was the essence of the job: co-operation, making sure that, whatever happened, there was always someone else to take up the baton and run with it.

The man who appeared to be running at that moment, at least mentally, was the navigator, a trim, compact lieutenant who pointed out that the ships were sailing not only through minefields that morning, but also shoals. For exercise purposes the ship always went out on one of two broad routes – one called 'Rat' and the other 'Rabbit'. Today it was Rabbit, to the east of the Shambles. He continued to draw lines on his charts as another mine was sighted: the green Very pistol flare went up, the captain said crisply, 'Come on, alter ship to starboard, get her round!' and there was a babble of other voices: 'Flash, Flash, Flash', 'Eight cables, sir', and 'Charlie Bravo!' Definitely the Navy was doing what comes naturally: talking its own language.

'We have two ways of fixing the position of a ship,' explained the navigator. 'One is visual, and the other is with radar. All I do is report the dials and transfer that position to the chart, and you get the position instantly. You can go for a "fix" once every thirty seconds, which gives you an accurate position of the ship and the ship's track. Once we get to the end of the channel, through this minefield, though, we are in open water, and the threat of mines is not so great.'

The different threat at that moment, following the mine alert, was an attack by an aircraft. *Galatea* had *one* shot at it with her Bofors gun, while the men below went through the procedure of launching one of the Seacat missiles at the attacking Hunter. The officer of the watch, another lieutenant, had reported an aircraft one mile astern; then it was overhead; then it was gone; now it was coming back and attacking from the other direction.

And only one shot fired? In Thursday wars, the expenditure of actual ammunition must be kept to an economic minimum. Hence the single shot. The ship had been given permission to fire only four shots that day. The whole thing, I was told, was a balance between the maximum benefit in training and the minimizing of costs. The whole fleet, for instance, operated under fuel restraint. When it was on exercises, it always had to travel at the most economical speeds. It had to be equally parsimonious with ammunition.

'We would love to blaze away at everything coming in at us. Instead we do all the procedures, but don't really fire,' explained the commander. 'We do sometimes fire at towed targets and launch Seacat at a real target. But not today.'

There was another argument against opening fire. *Galatea*'s job that day was not primarily to protect itself but, with the rest of the ships, to protect the ship which was at the centre of the disposition charts (called 'Zulu Zulu' in Naval parlance) – the Royal Fleet Auxiliary *Gold Rover*, as the 'main body', the supposed tanker. *Galatea*'s role was to avoid risks as much as possible and, in the final analysis, to defend *Gold Rover*, not itself.

On the bridge there was a circular disc about the size of a large dinner plate, in which the areas to be covered were outlined in chalk, with a ship's name inside the chalked off area. In the centre of the circle was *Gold Rover*, with *Southampton* above her to the north – the area thought to present the least threat. The other ships were to the south (the direction of the threat) in a semi-circle. To some extent they were deceived because eventually it was *Southampton*'s Lynx helicopters to the north that spotted the enemy ship and attacked it with missiles, without sinking it.

At this point, *Southampton* decided to send off something that sounds nothing like what it is – a SAG. The initials stand for Surface Action Group, in this case consisting of *Jupiter* and *Manchester*. They broke the protective screen around *Gold Rover* to steam off in pursuit of the enemy, code-named 'Skunk'.

The 'tanker' was without the guard she should have had in this quarter. This posed a tactical problem for *Galatea* and the other ships, which had to steam into new positions, closing up the gaps in the screen created by *Jupiter*'s and *Manchester*'s departure. I was told, in apologetic tones, that all these moves today conveyed only a fraction of the tension they would create in a real war.

Then something happened that was real enough. A fog suddenly gathered around the ships, cutting visibility down to half a mile. This meant there was no further point in having the Seacat missiles at action stations.

'Permission to stand down, sir?' asked a rating.

'All right.'

The commander explained to me that visibility was now so atrocious that there was no point in preparing to attack anything. In real war this decision – taken today for reasons of simple humanity – would probably not be made and everyone would have to remain at action stations, fog or no fog.

The fact that I knew a *real* freighter was somewhere out there (it had been quite close to *Galatea* before the fog set in) made me realize that to produce real tension you do not invariably need a war. This realization, and the fact that the bridge was very warm, started me sweating.

But one officer told me that in a real war, there would be no question of being in one's shirtsleeves.

'One has to be very conscious,' he told me, 'that we are in a very comfortable environment in the bridge, yet the weather out there is very nasty. If there was a problem – like the ship being sunk or badly damaged – and we had to go out there and see to it, we would be improperly dressed in shirtsleeves. In a fighting war we would not be dressed like this at all. I would be wearing full action combat kit, at least two layers – a shirt and a pullover at the very least. We would sacrifice comfort to safety, and try to make the ship as cold as possible to keep what comfort we could. We would all have microphones on, and our faces would be full of rubber. It would not be easy.'

The commander came in on the conversation to emphasize

the relative importance of clear communications to comfort in battle. There were three different states of alert. White was for a non-immediate threat, which was the state at present, since it had been reported that *Jupiter* had been attacked by the enemy ship. Black meant no threat. Red meant danger of immediate attack.

'There is the story,' said the commander, 'of the line of Marines in the Falklands. The man at the head passed the words, "Air warning red" back to the man behind him, for him to whisper it all the way down the line. The men at the front of the line were amazed to see the men at the far end of the line throwing their caps and their rifles into the air with delight. By the time the message got through to them, it was "Galtieri is dead".'

Gold Rover was moved northwards while the ships of the SAG went to sort out the enemy ship. It was possible, it was explained to me, that either *Galatea* or the 'main body', *Gold Rover*, would fire chaff out of their eight-barrelled launchers. Chaff is thin metal strips of different sizes which after being launched would for several minutes hang round the spot at which they were launched, presenting a dummy target which would confuse enemy missiles or radar. It was basically a device for gaining time. Any device was good that gave us information before the enemy had it; or denied information to the enemy; or caused the enemy to think he had information when he hadn't.

Soon the enemy ship was found and crippled, not by *Galatea*, which had taken up a new protective position near *Gold Rover* to protect her, but by the SAG. *Gold Rover* was told to resume its previous course, and moved back into formation. The navigator explained it was now six miles behind us; *Galatea* would go in, exploring every square mile of its own 'box' – a delegated portion of sea three miles in width, and with its length determined by thirty degrees of bearing. It had now been detailed as part of an SAU – Supplementary Action Unit – under the charge of *Brazen*.

Ruling the Waves

I went down to the operations room of *Galatea* to 'see' the next stage of the battle through the ship's nerve centre of electronic devices. It was two decks below, was stiflingly hot, and had no windows or natural light. About twenty people were packed into a space the size of a small living-room, all of them working on radar or other devices.

To a civilian, this operations room looked less like the real centre of the ship than a gaming casino; there were certainly plenty of dim lights, if no sweet music. The fetid air bubbled with signals and voices.

The commander charitably explained one or two things to me, 'before we go further into the room and find things getting rather overpowering'. Ten books of signals were hung by the door; other information was stored in computers. In a real war, I was told, these men would be wearing anti-flash hoods and gloves like the other men in the ship. An able seaman was making and remaking a general operations plot on a chart and didn't answer a question I asked him: principally, I judged, because he simply could not hear it over the hubbub. To a civilian, it was a rather less relaxing fifteen-by-fifteen feet room than a dentist's surgery.

This was even before the commander, who would normally fight the ship in the operations room rather than on the bridge, was told by the scanner operators (two seventeen-year-old seamen) that enemy missiles had just locked on to a target. They did not know *which* target, but they did know that the 'pulse' rate of the missile had changed, denoting that it was now in the locked position.

Watching a screen on which a missile is coming in your general direction, even if it is only a notional one, is quite a revealing experience. The delight when the missile begins to edge away from your own direction and towards another ship is ignoble, even in a game. But so it proved in this case: the Exocet was not headed for us, but for *Jupiter*. The spooky shapes around the radar scanning lines, indicating that the radar was being jammed by the enemy (though partly corrected by our own counter-jammer) did not seem quite so directly threatening.

Meanwhile, one of the two principal warfare officers in the operations room (the men who can fight the ship, if necessary, in the captain's absence) had told the controller of the Seacat missiles aboard *Galatea* to prepare to launch a Seacat at the enemy. This Seacat, the only one operational at that precise moment, was on the starboard side of the ship – the one facing the enemy. To fire the other one, on the port side, the *Galatea* would have had to go about – an operation she would have undertaken if necessary under war conditions, but did not fancy as part of a dummy war, bearing in mind that other ships were in the vicinity.

The gaming-casino atmosphere became more powerful the more one surveyed the operations room of the *Galatea*. Two large horizontal scanners were each sunk into a sort of desk, like two roulette tables. The captain's high stool was beside one of them, positioned so that he could overlook both if necessary, like a master croupier watching the tables. I got onto this high stool, put on the earphones, and tried to make sense of what I heard – which was not much, as each ear was connected to a different circuit and I was also expected to listen to what was said by the men sitting beside me. The fact that the captain, and other men round the tables, were habitually able to bear this without mental disintegration inspired admiration for their dedication. I was, however, not able to benefit greatly from their example, since information, questions and comments came so thick and fast. The United States naval officer who had been occupying the captain's high stool until I arrived showed signs of wanting it back; and the ship was now lurching so violently under the heavy seas that I felt, on the high stool, as if I was doing a high-wire act that could only end in disaster.

I vacated the seat of honour in favour of the US Navy. Instead I watched the principal warfare officer as he reacted to the missiles flying from the enemy towards the main body – the ship that had to be protected at all costs. He watched a round screen called (to complete the gaming-casino analogy) the Tote, a sort of computer that can at any one time hold information about three friendly ships and three submarines being prosecuted (lined up for attack).

'In war,' said the principal warfare officer, 'I would just tell our Ikara missile controller to lock the missile on to the target, he would press the button and that would be that, unless the enemy had the power to decoy the missile away.'

Holding contact with the submarine would be the problem, according to the principal warfare officer; the submarine could go down, to hide behind layers of water at different temperatures. These could bend the sonar beam either over or under the point where the submarine was.

'We have to work out what he *is* doing, not what he *seems* to be doing,' said the principal warfare officer.

They worked six hours on, six hours off if necessary, he added; and the atmosphere of the operations room could sometimes suggest bedlam. 'Concentration is the key,' he assured me.

I was finding my own concentration increasingly difficult. The room was stifling; the noise non-stop; the men hardly recognizable as individuals behind their microphones and earsets; the machinery a bewildering mass of lights, digits and code words; the whole lot swaying about violently all the time as the seas got rougher and rougher – more to the satisfaction of the enemy submarine the chief petty officer (the one concerned with safety and sonar) advised me was there, than to me, I imagined.

The chief petty officer took me into an even smaller, hotter room. He explained that this was the sonar control room. In it sat three young seamen, each facing what looked like a television screen. With its heat and its odours, the room was rather like the changing-room of a Turkish baths.

One of the screens, the chief petty officer told me (as I tried to brace myself to write my notes in the lurching half-light) was in a passive display – it could classify and keep track of ships. The second was set so that it could identify a target and actually attack it. The third was . . .

Here, I have to confess, was a blank in my notes, filled only by the cryptic phrase: 'Sick until 1.40 pm.'

Being seasick in what could be a war is a chastening experience, posing moral as well as physical questions. Supposing one were to be the man with his finger on the button when one felt like *I* had felt as the chief petty officer was talking? So that one had to rush out to the officers' heads (lavatories) at top speed or disgrace oneself? Every sailor, I suspect (it was confirmed by subsequent conversations) is aware of the thought; and every sailor tries to brush it aside. The considerate rating who was assigned to help me in my difficulties, meeting me as I came out of the officers' heads, offered this advice: 'Don't let it get hold of you, sir! You'll be better with something on your stomach, you really will. Shall I bring you some hot soup?' He looked surprised when, hardly out of the heads, I promptly rushed back in again. Another naval man, an officer, advised me that it was a question of mind over matter – that I should keep on working and ignore it. Alas, I had to tell the kindly man that I *had* ignored it for at least an hour and a half, but that those last few shudders in the stifling sonar control room . . . And I had to rush away again, with the officer making sympathetic noises (I hope that's what they were) behind my retreating back.

The commander had previously told me that a sense of humour was vital to a naval man under pressure. One has to work hard to keep one's sense of humour when being all but helplessly sick in a time of (even notional) emergency. Human uselessness can hardly ever take a more ignominious form. The condition must pose a serious challenge to a teenage youth, who is probably finding the Navy demanding in any case. I was selfishly relieved when, groping my way out on to the outside deck to get some fresh air, I found I had joined a number of the young sonar operators who were not part of *Galatea*'s crew but merely joining her for the training during the war. They looked as bad as I felt and unlike me they were not invited into the captain's cabin and allowed to lie on his bunk until the ship reached calmer waters, with occasional excursions into the captain's heads. Neither hyocine nor anti-histamines, the two best anti-seasickness remedies, is completely effective.

One of the young Wrens on board had also been suddenly confined to a cabin where she was heard groaning. But the petty officer of the Women's Royal Naval Service in charge of the party of Wrens pointed out that, since women did not go to sea on duty, it was not a major problem for them: they could pick and choose whether they went to sea on a particular day or not, which serving men could of course not do.

She thought the day's war had been useful for her group. 'Normally we participate in communications between ship and shore,' she said. 'And we are trained to be in a position to train the men themselves. We are basically able to do their job, although we are not allowed to go to sea. It was the first time I have been on a Thursday war, and I got a greater understanding of the conditions the men have to face. It is very easy to feel you are apart from the men, whereas we are really one and the same Navy.'

Once back into harbour – mercifully a couple of hours early because a submarine due to take part in the Thursday war had not been able to turn up – I rejoined active and productive mankind by resuming my interviews on what the day had achieved.

The commander thought the war had been valuable not so much for *Galatea* herself (she had already been given a clean bill of health by the Admiralty) as for the other ships who had taken a more active part in the anti-submarine warfare, and for the young men who had come aboard as part of their studies – the sonar controllers and supervisors, and the helicopter controllers.

'The sonar controllers wanted in-contact time, and they got it,' said the commander. 'We gained tactical benefit for our own operators. It was all most useful. Do you feel better now?'

I asked the boys from Radley what they had thought the Thursday war had achieved for them. One sixteen-year old, already wearing a Navy sweater, said he had learned a lot about the Navy. 'I noticed especially the different life between the officers and the ratings,' he said. 'We lived in the sailors' mess and we had dinner in the wardroom with the officers. The ratings are much more boisterous and jolly, whereas the officers are very much more serious. Generally, I found the whole thing tense and exciting. It was brought out particularly in the operations room, and was most interesting.' He himself, he said, was going into the Fleet Air Arm.

A small fifteen-year old, with a double-barrelled name and a cheerful grin, confessed he wasn't thinking of joining any of the services, but thought he just might be converted by what he had seen. 'I was interested in life among the lads – they were really good and nice, but I was also interested in the general life and atmosphere aboard apart from the lads, who were kind chaps, but quite loud.'

The young man said the Thursday war had taught him a lot about the hard life of the sailor – quite different from the 'luxurious life of other people in England'.

And a bespectacled sixteen-year old said he was going into the Army. 'My eyesight isn't good enough for the Navy. I might have got into the engine room in the Navy, but after seeing the engine rooms today, I think I will stick to the Army.'

Back on shore, after climbing down the swaying rope ladder from *Galatea* and taking the Liberty boat to Camber Jetty, normal non-war naval life was resumed. The chief petty officer who had been so concerned to prevent any submarines accidentally ramming the surface ships had hardly got his feet ashore when a senior officer ticked him off because some of his students hadn't brought their bedding back.

The chief petty officer's light grey eyes narrowed to slits

and he got to work on the culprits. 'Right, you lot. *I'll* fetch your kit, and this will cost you each a pint, is that clear?' Plainly the after-war relaxation was not going to be allowed to get out of hand. It must not be; relaxation can only be part of the sailor's life on board ship.

3

THE SHIPS AS HOME

'I think there is too much automation. The ship loses a bit of character. Obviously they are meant to be improvements. Obviously there are longer ranges to weapons and better protection for the ship, but you do get the feeling that there are just buttons everywhere and flashing lights. An older ship is better than a newish one, it has more character and is more interesting, because more things are manual.'

– Leading seaman on aircraft carrier.

'Are some ships nice and others nasty? I suspect the answer is no. Even if a ship, at the time it is built, is not perfect, it becomes perfect very quickly. A big fleet that doesn't work – and that means one without all its latest equipment – is of no value to anybody.'

– Commander on aircraft carrier.

The Royal Navy – unlike the British Army – has no club-like regiments, in which the sometimes lonely sailor can make his spiritual home. For much of the time his home is the ship. The nature of that ship can affect his mood, his happiness and even, despite his stoic professionalism, his performance as a potential fighting man. The Ship (you can *hear* naval men employing the capital letter) dominates with the aid of its thousands of tons of steel, its history and its futuristic technology.

At sea there is no escape from the Ship. Its influence is all-pervasive. There are differences of opinion about whether it is the hull and the machinery or the men which make the character of the Ship, but no dispute at all about the fact that ships *do* have a character; and that that character, for good or ill, can have an almost hypnotic influence on the individual sailor, however many technical qualifications he may like to think stand between him and raw human vulnerability.

The first element in a ship's character has nothing to do with what happens within her. It is where she goes – a fact which may ultimately be no more dictated by her captain than by the most junior member of the ship's company. 'Of all the ships I have served in,' a twenty-one-year-old marine engineering mechanic told me, 'my favourite was HMS *Sheffield*. That was because of the runs it had. It went to Athens, Mombasa, Abu Dhabi, Mauritius and Gibraltar while I was aboard. It was a good crew, a good bunch of lads.'

The first fact led to the second: an interested crew, stimulated by varying experiences, tends to be 'a good bunch of lads'. Unfortunately the pure sightseeing available is decreasing rather than increasing.

The marine engineering mechanic told me he was probably leaving the Navy. I asked him why. Well, he was thinking of getting married, but that might not have been decisive. 'It is the runs of the ship,' he said finally. 'We seem to go to fewer and fewer places. The runs are decreasing all the time, it seems. The chaps feel this generally. There is not so much to balance the boredom of long periods afloat, when it seems that the only time you get off is for cleaning the ship. We do that in our *off* time. We clean up the passageways or the mess deck. Every three days you do about an hour of that at night, then you go and watch the telly or the videos. That is all there is to do really, unless you further yourself by studying. If you go to interesting places, you tend to forget all that, but not otherwise.'

The need to maintain a presence around the Falklands in the

South Atlantic has been a tangible but incomplete invigorator. Being in the South Atlantic, where there is a specific threat, certainly keeps sailors on their toes. A first visit to the Falklands – a much discussed part of the world the sailor would be highly unlikely to visit except through the Navy – is usually found stimulating and interesting.

One leading seaman working on sonar in the operations room of a destroyer told me, 'The last trip we did, we were away from Portsmouth for only fourteen days, but before that we were away eight months on a Falklands run. We might go to South Georgia to have a check-around. It is a bit of a change for us. In the winter when it was seven feet deep in snow, we had sledging competitions.'

A marine engineering mechanic on a destroyer who had spent seven months around the Falklands in HMS *Sheffield* (the usual time is five months) admitted, 'You get fed up. Perhaps you have a barbecue on the flight deck if it is warm enough. Or you have mess socials, a few games tournaments. But sometimes it can be too cold for anything in the Falklands.'

The Falklands run would be more popular if there were more things to do on the islands themselves. Gradually more amenities are being introduced. This is just as well. The original couple of pubs in Port Stanley were hardly sufficient to cope with the high spirits of men who had been cooped up in a ship for weeks. The sailor has to recognize that he is not in the South Atlantic for the good of his health, but to protect British lives. He usually acquits himself responsibly, getting what light relief he can when he can.

A petty officer engaged on electronic warfare, who said he was on duty virtually twenty-four hours a day when in the Falklands because he had no deputy with his knowledge, told me that he had been down to the Falklands twice. 'I think that last year I had seven hours off the ship in four months. In that seven hours, I just walked around for a bit of fresh air; it was so nice to get off the ship. There is nothing to do in the Falklands.

A couple of hours I spent in South Georgia, just throwing snowballs. I was glad just to stretch my legs on land. But of course the Falklands is an isolated case. We have lots of videos aboard, and watch the box all the time. I watch some of the videos four times. It gets that bad down there in the Falklands, especially on defence watches. When we are on patrol down there, most of the ship seems to be on defence watches seven hours with five hours off; but I haven't got an opposite number, so I am on duty twenty-four hours and sleep when I can. If you are working all night, you are still on duty at eight the following morning. Perhaps you get the afternoon off, but it can be a demanding routine.'

The point about men with technical skills not necessarily being able to double up will be dealt with in more detail later; but a most cursory acquaintance with the fleet and its workings makes it plain that the defence cuts, which seem habitually to fall heavily on the Royal Navy, have a lot to answer for.

But the sort of runs made by a ship is always in the hands of the gods, a fact well accepted by sailors. The Ship itself, irrespective of where it is going, can regulate the lives of its men, from the captain downwards.

Sheer size is an important factor. To the average civilian, all naval ships tend to look rather the same. Their design is similar to the casual eye and it is difficult to infer sheer size from photographs, just as one has to sit in a Jumbo jet before it is apparent that it is a rather different species from a European Airbus. But an aircraft carrier *is* quite a different home from a destroyer, and a destroyer is quite a different home from a minesweeper. Enter a carrier like HMS *Hermes* – over 750 feet long, ninety feet wide, displacing 24,000 tons – through the huge drive-on ramp, and you are in the science fiction world of *Close Encounters of the Third Kind*. A carrier has as many decks as a large hotel has floors; it has as much technology as a dozen factories. It could well have suggested the sorts of device so beloved of space fiction. Aboard a destroyer, like HMS *Newcastle*, one is more unequivocally in something that floats:

the passageways are narrower, the ceilings are more likely to find the top of one's head; and if one is seasick on a really bad day, one will tend to find one is far from alone.

In the slightly smaller frigates, like the 'Broadsword' class (Type 22), 430 feet long and 3,556 tons, things are even livelier. On a minesweeper of the 'Ton' class or 'Hunt' class (360 and 685 tons respectively) one has a distinctly mobile and matey home which bobs around a lot more than a caravan being towed across scrubland. A blowy day may cause gallant officers and men – as it caused Prince Charles during his time in minesweepers – to visit the heads (lavatories) more often than they would ideally wish.

In the time I was able to spend in various ships, especially the anti-submarine-warfare carrier HMS *Invincible* and the 'Sheffield' class destroyer HMS *Newcastle*, I was able to gain a view of the sailor's varying homes, and of his own varying views on them. Though the views sometimes differed, the message was unambiguous – size matters.

It certainly mattered to the captain of *Invincible*, an urbanely courteous son of a peer built on the same scale as his enormous ship (which lags behind HMS *Hermes* only a trifle in sheer size – length 677 feet, displacement 16,000 tons, complement 900 men plus aircrew).

'We are smaller than we would wish,' he told me, 'from the point of view of looking after helicopters and fixed-wing aircraft. When these ships were designed by the naval staff, the intention was to get to sea large numbers of very big helicopters which were then thought to be the best way of finding submarines and destroying them. In the process of building the ship – which really, for a parliamentary reason, was described as a "through-deck cruiser" because carriers weren't politically acceptable – we ended up with a deck which had the semblance of an aircraft carrier. When the Harrier programme was coming to fruition, there was an opportunity to embark a number of these marvellous aircraft to give the ship added capability. The change in emphasis halfway through the building of the ship created its own problems, and one or two things are smaller than we would wish. I mean in terms of aircraft and, to a slight degree, of people as well.'

For a captain of a ship the size of *Invincible*, there must be a special pattern of thought. Such a ship provides a base from which attacking aircraft and missiles can be destroyed while still hundreds of miles away. This means that the captain must think of an enormous area around his ship, not only of the immediate vicinity. There is the further fact that the *Invincible* can embark the flag officer of an anti-submarine-warfare group in a NATO operation in support of the Striking Fleet Atlantic. So it can when the flag officer, an admiral, merely wants to embark to check on how things are going on *Invincible*, or on a whole squadron.

The captain had previously been in the 'Sheffield' class destroyer HMS *Southampton*. I asked him how big a mental adjustment was necessary when he took over a bigger ship. I got the answer: 'It is very different from a small ship, there is no doubt about that. It is different in all sorts of ways. Particularly it is different because it is a dimension removed, not only in physical size, but in capability. These small aircraft carriers really have much more reach. I think in terms of an area a matter of two hundred and fifty miles all around me all the time, and occasionally further. In a frigate you may be thinking of fifty miles, because that is the area over which you have some influence. We frequently have our helicopters at ranges of a hundred miles. Helicopters are fifty to a hundred miles away on a daily basis. We have so much reach now. Not only the captain, but also the operations department in particular, have to think all the while in these terms.'

The captain said he also had to think in terms of a huge number of people – almost 1,000 when the squadron of aircraft was embarked. All the departments were thinking rather differently, had different motivations and aspirations, were turned on or turned off by different thoughts. It was the most fascinating thing, to get all these different men pulling in the same direction; and that was what was expected of him.

In a big ship the captain, while staying aboard, becomes sometimes – in effect – a sort of commuter. This is a direct result of the huge distances between one department and another on the ship.

When I first met the captain of *Invincible* he was in his cabin, a comfortable distance from the bridge. In his dining room, much used when *Invincible* makes her courtesy calls in various parts of the world, were family photographs and two lifesized carved wooden ducks which his wife had given him to commemorate his assuming command of his imposing ship. The captain saw me admiring them and sought to make a point: at sea, and certainly in action, this part of the ship would not be his home at all.

'My job then radiates from the operations room,' he pointed out. 'I would live and work in the operations environment. I have a small cabin directly below the bridge, where the officer of the watch could be keeping his watch. It is convenient for me because I can get to the bridge quickly in an emergency; and I have a private lift to go to the operations room nine decks down.'

This ride down nine floors takes only a matter of seconds. It brings the captain straight into the operations room, where there is a specially high, swivelling armchair ready for him, secured to the floor, and another for any flag officer who happens to be on the *Invincible* at the time, controlling a whole range of ships.

One sight of this operations room made me realize immediately the difference between a carrier and a smaller ship. This operations room was unlike any others I had seen. Normally an ops room is an overheated cavern like that on the *Galatea*, packed almost solid with equipment and people, and leaving very little room to move. On *Invincible* the ops room would not upset even a person given to violent claustrophobia. The roof was higher, the room measured about forty feet by forty feet, and between the various screens, dials and switches there was plenty of space – an almost unheard-of luxury for the average naval man. It was true there were no windows to this ops room. In fact no one on *Invincible* has a window – except the Flag Officer in his scuttle in the stern of the ship and the Weather men, who had to cut a hole themselves so they could see, with their own eyes, what the weather was like outside. But though there were no windows, there was no sense of being enclosed, such was the air space between installations.

'I think it is immensely more complicated than anything I have ever done before, operationally,' said the captain. 'We have game-play tapes. Every day when we are in harbour, we close up the ship for forty-five minutes and run through all the operational equipment. On a pretty regular basis, we get through games tapes. It is not as good as being at sea. We have been spending a week at HMS *Dryad*, the School of Maritime Operations, practising and playing games against other ships. It was very good value indeed. If you can pressurize people by giving them some problems and threats, it is very challenging. It is much cheaper than taking a ship to sea with real aeroplanes and submarines.'

The pressures in a ship the size of the *Invincible* are largely technological. In the Royal Navy, I discovered, technology is looked upon with pride but also with an occasional element of human reserve, rather as those with a modern-built house, with all the latest gadgets, sometimes sigh for a mellow Victorian villa or country cottage. One marine engineer mechanic on HMS *Newcastle* told me that the old *Bulwark* had been likeable 'because on an old ship you have a lot more to do, which makes it a lot more interesting'.

Bulwark was an exception – in general terms, the larger the ship, the more the technology that has to be mastered. A leading seaman working in the Operations Room of HMS *Newcastle* told me: 'Of all the ships I have had, *Bulwark* has the fondest memories, better than on a newish one. This big type of ship is all very much computers, whereas on *Bulwark* everything was manual. Everyone here tends to be a very technological type of person, whereas on *Bulwark* it was a lot more friendly, because there was not so much pressure of equipment and machinery on human beings. On the *Invincible*, the ops room is very much like "Star Trek" – it is amazing. Now I operate in the same way as everyone else. I had to do a course to enable me to join, twelve weeks.'

Sailors are entitled to a little bit of nostalgia, just like anyone else; and any suspicion of the technology on the bigger ships is well compensated for by the steadier ride, the wider communication spaces (that often don't give the impression of being seabound at all) and the fact that you are not necessarily the only man on the ship with your particular type of expertise; you are not necessarily professionally alone.

Sometimes it is the technical men in the middle-sized ships who find their homes the least relaxing. Their home has more complicated technology than a minesweeper, but a lesser pool of expert men to call on in an emergency than in a bigger ship.

In the electronic warfare electronics room in the medium-sized destroyer HMS *Newcastle*, I found a chief petty officer aged thirty-nine who had been in the Royal Navy for twenty years and had learned how to come to grips with the tension. 'I have been on five ships, including two and half years in the *Ark Royal*,' he told me. 'I have been aboard a minesweeper, too. As far as my job on this ship is concerned, the captain quite rightly wants it laid straight on the line *by me* all the time. I have been told, "You can't go ashore unless we are in a relaxed position." It can be a demanding routine. My tendency is to go for a sit-down in the mess when I can, and watch a video to try to forget what it is like outside the mess. If you don't do that sometimes, it is easy for people to go into a psychiatric hospital. A couple of my colleagues turned basically into alcoholic cases because of some of the equipment. The circuitry of one piece of equipment when it was first introduced – it has been corrected now – was such that you could go round and round in circles. I myself remember spending several nights chasing the circuitry when were still working at nine the next morning; and still expected to carry on the next day. So you could be working for forty-eight hours on it, and at the end of that, you were no good to man nor beast. And you had *no one on board you could turn to*, because they didn't know anything about it. You were the only one with any expertise.'

This professional isolation can stimulate as well as depress, and many Naval men said they rather liked the idea of being *the* man in the know. But *professionally* most of the people I talked to preferred life on a bigger ship.

A leading radio operator in HMS *Invincible*, a thin and wispy-bearded man of thirty-three with ten years' experience in the Navy, said he had previously been on a minesweeper: 'I actually put in for a larger ship. On a smaller ship, especially on a minesweeper, there is just myself and one other underneath me. I missed an organization where you can rely on a few people, rather than being on your own all the time. It was my second minesweeper job. I think you have, in any case, got to be on the big ships to keep up your skills; the equipment is more up-to-date. On a minesweeper you are hanging on to a morse key all day – you had a lot of morse. Here it is satellite communications. Instead of teleprinters, you have screens.'

The paperwork in a big ship can be formidable. The leading radio operator said that in a small ship, each radio message received by the ship tended to go only to the department concerned, whereas on *Invincible* there was a 'general broadcast' from which heads of departments noted down what referred to them. On small ships, only three officers read a radio message. On a ship the size of the carrier, many more people were involved.

'It makes it busier,' said the leading radio operator. 'I don't mind it. One thing I have always found is that whenever we are at sea, people never look at their watches to see how much longer their watch duty lasts.' Time went by fast when several hundred signals, incoming and outgoing, had to be dealt with every day. On a minesweeper, perhaps there would be only half a dozen a day.

Dealing with a large volume of work, however, can be much easier in a bigger ship. This is so especially when the winter sets in and the seas around Britain get inhospitably choppy.

The commander who was second-in-command in *Invincible*, a cultured man with greying fair hair, said the bigger ships were more comfortable at sea. In a ship like *Invincible* it very rarely happened that men got seasick, and so the work output was not affected by the weather, as it was in a smaller ship, like the frigate HMS *Lowestoft* which he had previously commanded.

'In a small ship, you may have to stop writing (clerical operations) in bad weather,' he remembered. 'In a ship like this, you continue to work. Bad weather isn't a ship-stopper, but life becomes more difficult and tiring. In a frigate in winter, you can almost guarantee, every other day, to be weather-affected in one way or another. In this ship I have yet to feel the effects of weather personally.'

Even in a middle-sized ship like a destroyer or frigate, choppy seas can cause professional problems. In the tiny catering office off the galley of the destroyer HMS *Newcastle*, I found an eighteen-year-old catering accountant examining some plywood boards a handyman had fitted over the face of the shelves which covered the walls of the six feet by six feet room. There had previously been only comparatively narrow metal bars, he explained. Tins and bottles and packets of sugar, tea, coffee and cocoa had been safe enough in their vertical position, but once they fell over in rough seas they merely rolled off the shelves on to people's heads.

In general, the catering accountant, fair-haired and quietly spoken, was well content with his life aboard his first ship. He was learning about food and the paperwork of catering. But he felt that space was a bit short on the medium-sized ship. Indeed once, when we were both talking in the catering office, and a crew member came in for a pound of sugar, I felt that unless I breathed out, the walls of the office would give way. As the office was directly off the galley, without benefit of a door, the heat was more suited to the Falklands in winter than to United Kingdom waters in summer. I had no difficulty in believing the young catering accountant when he said that, as there were three in his department – a petty officer, a leading hand and himself – things could sometimes seem very crowded indeed.

'It does get cramped,' he said, 'especially when all the chefs come in, because they tend to use this as a rest-room. There are thirteen chefs. They want a quick fag or a cup of tea. They come into here, because you aren't allowed to smoke in the galley itself, and this is the next best thing.'

I asked the eighteen-year old how he reacted personally to life in a fairly confined space.

'It develops your character,' he replied drily. 'You have to get on with people, although sometimes when you are at sea for a few weeks it does get a bit annoying. For me, it isn't so bad. I have a big storeroom that I can go to for a quiet period if needed. I am in charge of it, so I can get down there for a bit of peace and quiet. All the chefs are always in and out for something, so I am down there quite a lot.'

This was sensibly in line, I thought, with the Navy's un-written maxim: use your own initiative. I was not surprised to hear that this young man, on his first major trip, which took him through the violent Bay of Biscay, had managed to make a laugh out of the prevalent seasickness on the medium-sized ship.

'In the galley,' he said, 'especially in very hot climates, it is very, very hot, upwards of eighty degrees. You sweat a lot because there are three ovens, three deep fryers, a shallow fryer and three ranges. But we make a laugh out of bad seas. Every-one rushes out and grabs what they can to stop the food sliding about the surfaces. We try to stop anything the chefs are preparing from falling on the floor. If it *does* fall, we throw it away and do something else. Generally speaking, just as many are eating when it is rough as when it is not. Those who suffer from seasickness are provided with a few ship's biscuits, which are not easy to bring up.'

In smaller ships, men have to be jacks-of-all-trades with good grace. Officers and men told me that on a minesweeper, men had to show the greatest versatility, because there were possibly under thirty men aboard. When I asked a twenty-seven-year-old radio operator in the main communications office of HMS *Newcastle* – a man whose twelve-year experience in the Royal Navy included also frigates and minesweepers – whether this need for versatility made life more interesting, I got a cautious answer.

'Yes and no,' he said. 'When you are younger it is all right. But when you get older, you don't necessarily want to tie up ropes for seamen or do lookouts for someone else. But it is good for you to do that when you are young, because when you do come up the ladder a bit, you know just what to do. And you understand why it can take so long to do it, because you have done it yourself.' This, said the radio operator, made up for the cramped conditions in small ships when you were young. Cramped they can certainly be, as I found out when I went aboard *Bronington*, the oldest ship of her 'Ton' class, a 153-foot long wooden-hulled minesweeper of 360 tons and a complement of around thirty men.

The bridge was the size of a domestic kitchen. There was just enough room for its usual occupants, the officer of the watch and one look-out, to walk round a central cabinet of instruments. Compared to the bridge of a carrier or even a destroyer, it was like a rabbit hutch. Down a short ladder to the deck below was the operations room. Here, two ratings sat on an American cloth bench looking at two radar screens while, behind them, sat the warfare officer and a mine-warfare-trained senior rating. They just about filled the tiny room.

I could just see a row of wood cupboards along one wall. That, I was told, was the ship's office – which, because of shortage of space, had to be included in the operations room. The correspondence officer functions in the room, which also acts as the strong room, since it holds the ship's safe. Money is kept in the safe so that ship's chandlers who supply food, fresh milk or other supplies can be paid in cash if they insist on it. Down on another deck were the ship's heads which, though clean, were so cramped and so obviously made of sheets of inflexible iron, that the commanding officer was quick to tell me that the men got 'hard-time money' for their minesweeper service. On the same deck, inviting collision with elbows, were wall-mounted boxes of small arms. There was also an aluminium-doored radio room hardly bigger than a boot cupboard. This, explained an officer, was always kept locked. 'If a man had ten pints of beer and two bottles of scotch, he might not know what he was doing,' he said. 'He could flick the right switches and broadcast to the world.' The commanding officer's cabin had drawers for the ship's stationery under his bunk and cupboards holding foul-weather gear beside his head.

It was easy to see that, in an emergency, at least the commanding officer would not have far to go to get to the operations room or bridge from his cabin or the wardroom. But fighting the ship with so little elbow room in war conditions would entail a self-discipline worthy of high praise.

The sobering fact is that decisions taken in the cramped conditions of a little minesweeper can affect lives not only aboard it but also lives aboard a whole collection of much larger ships. One officer in *Bronington* explained that once a mine was detected on sonar, it was up to the commanding officer to decide quickly whether to bomb it or send down divers to try to collect it. If the water was too deep for the divers, the decision would probably be to bomb it, but there were exceptions. One of the exceptions would be – as in the case of the mining of the Gulf of Suez in 1984 – when it was necessary to identify a mine to discover who was responsible for laying it. While the decision was being taken, the minesweeper would circle the site of the mine at a range of about 200 yards. If it was necessary to get more ships through a suspected minefield, the minesweeper could lead-in the other ships, sweeping ahead of her as she went; and even if it was not known who had laid the mines, they would probably all be blown up once a single specimen had been recovered.

Such are the types of life-or-death decisions that have to be taken in some of the smallest homes in the whole Navy. 'The advantage is that you can get from A to B very quickly,' said an officer in the *Bronington*. 'In a big ship you can hide away. You can't hide away in one of these little ones. But it is home. If someone shouts, "Fire! Fire!" and you know it is your home, you move.'

But if a sailor anticipates being ill or banging his head against a bulkhead, he should take care to do it aboard one of the larger ships. He will have a larger and more specialized sick-room staff at his beck and call.

The sick-bay of a carrier like *Invincible* gives no visual impression of being afloat at all. The ceilings are high, the passageways between the bunk beds are as broad as they would be in a shore hospital: only the large notice, *Please Remove Your Boots* would look strange in a civilian clinic ashore. There were even black and brown faces in *Invincible*'s sick bay as a reminder that, in a sense, a ship is a cross-section of British society as a whole – even though not many non-white faces are to be seen in other parts of ships. Perhaps not even the most rabid racialist (naval men maintain that a certain amount of 'good-natured ribbing' of blacks and Indians does go on) would wish to take exception to being helped by a black man after falling down a ladder or hitting his head on a protrusion. The Navy has, I guessed, shrewdly counted on this in trying to introduce and encourage black faces. But medical staff do not accept this. One officer told me, 'This gives the impression that the Royal Navy has encouraged non-whites to join the medical branches as an act of policy – not true. We take anyone who meets our entry standards regardless of ethnic origin.'

Be this as it may, I found in *Invincible* sick-bay a twenty-five-year-old leading medical assistant of Indian extraction, the son of a retired engineer. He said that, in a ship the size of HMS *Invincible*, the medical staff had to respond less. 'In the smaller ships like destroyers, you probably have only yourself and a doctor. Doctors take a bit of the routine work off you, but on a destroyer you still do more. With a frigate you do even more; you are there on your own with no doctor – it is very much a learning test. We have two doctors here, and a staff of about ten, which is a lot.'

The leading medical assistant thought there were proportionally *more* injuries on a bigger ship. People tended to forget they *were* on a ship and walked about as if they were in a stationary structure ashore. Cuts and bruises, caused by people knocking themselves against hatches, were often the result. There could also be more colds and tonsillitis cases in a bigger ship. The *Invincible* sick-bay had ten sick-beds, and most of them would be occupied, towards the end of a long period at sea, with colds and tonsillitis patients. When he had been in *Hermes*, there had been thirty beds and almost three quarters of them had been full during long deployments at sea.

Because messes, where the men relax and sleep, can be large on a big ship – up to forty people – illnesses like colds and tonsillitis can spread rapidly to a larger number of people than would be the case on a smaller ship with messes for up to only a dozen people each.

'Say the average age of the ship's company is quite young – and the average age is eighteen to twenty-one,' said the leading medical assistant. 'Say it is their first trip. They tend to get general illnesses like colds, tonsillitis and chicken pox. People on a long deployment tend to get run-down. Some people don't go up on to the top deck for days on end. They aren't getting fresh air; the air is being recirculated. The messes are quite large, and if someone gets something, it won't need to spread from one mess to another to affect a lot of people. The mess I am in myself has beds for twenty-seven. Some messes are smaller, others larger. People with infectious conditions are encouraged to come down to the sick-bay at the earliest possible moment, so they don't infect other people.'

Naturally a few people come to the sick-bay for no other reason than that they are bored, or feel they are in need of a day off after working long hours. In practice, these faces become as well known on a large ship as on a small one: there are not many of them. It is more usual for a man asking for a day off to be running a palpably genuine high temperature, in which case he will be dosed and told to go to his mess for twenty-four hours and try not to breathe over other people.

The sick-bay in a large ship is possibly one of the few departments which would not claim to be habitually undermanned (although in an emergency that optimistic view might change). *Invincible* has one of the most comprehensive medical staffs in the Royal Navy, including an anaesthetist, a doctor, a surgeon and a physiotherapist. They would have been well equipped to deal with the worst injury case the leading medical assistant could remember in the whole of his seven years' experience in the Royal Navy: a Wren who had slipped on some steel stairs and ended up with half her heel hanging off. As it happened, however, this incident occurred not on a swaying ship but a perfectly stationary shore establishment, where the Wren was stitched up. The worst the *Invincible* leading medical assistant had had to do was to put a few stitches into people's heads where they had cracked against pieces of protruding metal, which somehow you didn't anticipate on a stately moving hotel like an aircraft carrier. It wasn't boring when the ship was in port, said the helpful medical functionary, because people still managed to bang their heads when the ship was perfectly stationary.

The sheer paperwork in a big ship has, say naval officers, proliferated in recent years. And when at sea the ship becomes the home of everyone on board, there is no escaping from it, because there are not enough people to deal with it.

The commander who was second-in-command of *Invincible*

said that he lived seventeen miles from Portsmouth; but even when the ship was alongside, he could not get home every night. 'There are nights I have to sleep on board, merely to get through the paperwork. Every single simple thing put down has to be justified – like in so many organizations – in an effort to save money. Actually I think we waste money in this way. Whatever you want to do has a lot of paper attached to it. I am continually being asked whether I can do without this sailor or that officer; you fight it on paper, and it takes time. Every letter that leaves the ship inevitably takes an hour to draft. No bit of paperwork is simple. It becomes extremely time-consuming, and it is beginning to put a strain on some of the middle management officers – I mean lieutenant-commanders and commanders. They will all work hard for a number of reasons; but I don't think it is in the best interests of the service in the long run.'

The commander said he thought that more of his function should be to head off problems *before* they developed, by wandering round the ship and talking to people, rather than waiting for problems to develop and then having to handle all the paperwork necessary to rectify them.

I led the commander off this vexing subject by asking whether a man of his rank was likely to prefer being second-in-command in a big prestigious ship like *Invincible* or in command of a frigate like *Lowestoft*. Since he had done both jobs, he was ideally equipped to say. He thought that being second-in-command of *Invincible* was every bit as demanding – probably more so – than commanding a small ship.

'But command in itself is something you cannot better,' he added. 'In professional career terms, this is more rewarding. But there is no one that I know who would wish to be second-in-command as opposed to command. On a big ship it is professionally more demanding. It is a case of scale. My frigate had 220 people and a role in life. This ship has 1,000 people and three roles. It is a flagship, and it is one of the most important capital ships. It has enormous importance wherever it goes. It attracts public interest in a way a frigate doesn't necessarily attract it. The level demanded of you is higher. People are more critical about bigger ships. You forgive a frigate a mistake, because the people are much more junior – while you *demand* 100 per cent, you can in practice forgive the odd error. In a ship of this size, even the simplest error becomes important because of the impact that can go down the line to other ships.'

The captain of *Invincible* acknowledged that it was difficult for him to get out and about sufficiently in a big ship when she was at sea. Some things happened inevitably more slowly in a big ship, in big and little ways. For instance, the clutches between the engines and the propellers were fluid-filled, not solid discs, which meant that there was a twenty-second delay before they acted. Anyone giving instructions therefore had to think at least twenty seconds ahead. The point was particularly important when moving alongside a jetty. It usually meant he stopped the ship a hundred feet from the jetty itself, and waited for tugs to nudge the ship alongside. In battle conditions, when the crew were working in their flashgear, and having to go in and out of airlocks when moving about the ship, it could take them a long time to get from A to B.

Obviously it is vital in a big ship that men know their way round the whole of it – not just those parts of the ship they use habitually – as soon as possible. On *Invincible*, as soon as new men board the ship, they are told that they must familiarize themselves with the ship in every way possible. A week after arriving, they are handed questionnaires about the ship, and expected to fill them up and return them. They must know where their eight-minute breathing equipment is. They must know not only the way out of their compartment to safety in case of emergency, but also a second and even a third alternative route. The quiz is regularly updated, so no one in the ship can get complacent.

I remarked to the captain that I imagined it was relatively easy to get complacent in a ship like HMS *Invincible*, which is so much like a spacious shore establishment that it hardly conveys the fact that it is floating at all. Well, said the captain, the ship was made safer by the fact that security inspections of equipment were made regularly, as a rotating duty.

'But anything sinks,' said the captain drily, 'and *we* could sink. And that is the biggest possible motivation – to make sure it doesn't sink. We all feel this is *our* ship, so there is no back-sliding in terms of safety measures.'

When one talks about big ships in the Royal Navy today one means, in the absence of the old, obsolete, vast battleships like *Dreadnought*, the aircraft carriers. The aircraft they carry add elements to the tone of life on the big ships which are not observed on the smaller ships – even though some of these may carry helicopters.

What does having Sea Harriers, for instance, mean? It means having the huge hangar of *Invincible*, similar to the set of a James Bond movie climax, with its two enormous hundred-ton lifts to get the ten-ton aircraft up to the flight deck. When the hangar is empty, it is a vast booming place in which people become dwarfs. Full of aircraft, it becomes so packed that the crew have to walk with elaborate care.

On the flight deck itself I found the chief of the flight deck, a small, bearded chief petty officer from Belfast. His job was a peculiarly isolated one, though reinforced by professional and national pride. Both the slanting flight deck of the *Invincible*, and the upward-sloping ramp at the end of it to assist take-off, are British inventions, though now used by several other navies.

The chief of the flight deck had to stand beside the deck with a green flag. When he dropped it, that was the final signal for the pilot of the Sea Harrier to take off. The pilot had already been given a warning via the two coloured 'traffic lights' amidships near the funnel, and swept past the petty officer with a screaming crescendo from his engine.

I was not surprised to find that the petty officer wore very efficient ear protectors. 'There are gaps between the noise, when you can take your ear muffs off. You couldn't wear them for eight hours; you would be mad by the end.'

Some aircraft always have to be at the ready, either alongside the 'island' around the funnel or at the 'range', where they are armed, towards the stern of the ship. The ones that are to take off line up on the flight deck itself, at one of a series of points, measured from the end of the ramp at the end of the runway. A Sea Harrier carrying a full supply of fuel and weapons will be given one of the marks that allow it a greater distance to get airborne. The distance will depend also on the strength of the wind and the direction and speed of the ship.

The aircraft in a modern carrier, it is plain, demand the sort of concentration needed for three-dimensional chess as they are manoeuvred on to the lifts in the hangar, brought up to the flight deck, guided into position, armed, and then given the green flag to take off.

How long would it take from the word go to the actual take-off of the first aircraft? 'If there was any chance of an alert, there would be two aircraft already on deck,' said the flight deck chief. 'There would be more than two on the range, because you can land planes while others are still on the range. This is where we eat and live – on the flight deck. We are either here or sleeping. Sometimes I am working until midnight and things that aren't necessary don't get done. Duty lists won't come out on time. You take everything as it crops up.'

Size is, of course, relative and there are naval men who like a ship like HMS *Invincible* because, to them, it is *small*. They are the ones who have had previous experience on even bigger ships, like the old *Ark Royal*. I found one such, a thirty-nine year-old engineer officer in HMS *Invincible*, the man responsible for all aviation engineering aspects on board in support of the aircraft, from maintenance to weapons.

It was, he said, a question of integration of the flying squadron with the ship, and it was easier on one of the new, smaller carriers than on a bigger ship.

He was showing me the huge hangar of *Invincible* when he said: 'The atmosphere changes radically between when no aircraft are aboard and when they come aboard. It becomes a hive of activity immediately the planes arrive; perhaps there are actually twenty aircraft, filling up every space. The squadrons themselves would take off an engine; we would repair it for them. Any repairs *on* the plane would be done by the squadron's own engineers; anything else would be done by my department. Now I have been on *Hermes* and the old *Ark Royal*, as well as *Invincible*. Though an awful lot of a ship's personality is actually determined by the *people* in it, from the captain downwards, every ship is different. The larger the ship the more difficult it is to get a corporate identity. I would hesitate to call them *factions*, but there are a lot of separate departments going about their business on a big ship; one has to make a conscious effort to draw all these factions together. We bend over backwards at head-of-department level to form a pinnacle of togetherness.'

But, he said, the old *Ark Royal* had a different identity from *Invincible*'s; a bigger crew and a bigger wardroom. 'It is sixty to 120 here. The 120 is a very manageable number and everyone knows everyone else. Because of that, the squadrons themselves and the ship's officers are very closely integrated. In the bigger carriers – and the *Ark Royal* was no exception – there was a certain amount of division between squadrons and the ship. I would not describe the squadrons as being an *imposition*, but one didn't have the unity of these smaller ships.'

However, even relative smallness was not without its problems, according to the engineer officer. Because of things like the centrally controlled engine room, and the general higher level of equipment, the numbers of men had been trimmed: 'Every department is responsible for cleaning its own areas, and simple things like keeping the ship clean become a problem.'

One rating I spoke to on *Invincible* who did *not* regard it as even relatively small put the case for the really small ship forcefully enough to be an indication that though the naval man today may talk much (perhaps too much) about technology, he remains at heart a human being like the rest of us who prefers things small and manageable.

'A small ship is much more *fun*,' he said. 'It is more relaxed. The minesweeper I was in was part of a squadron for fishery protection. You know everyone. The messes weren't up to the standard of *Invincible*, and in a wooden-hulled minesweeper it can be quite bumpy. But everyone mucks in. Even Prince Charles, when he was on minesweepers, mucked in.'

Perhaps the machinery in the Royal Naval floating homes of various sizes has no more deprived sailors of their essential humanity than pocket calculators and computers in civilian homes have transformed their owners into Daleks. In naval *action* at sea the human qualities — including a calm sense of proportion and humour — are essential rather than merely useful.

4

TIMES OF TRIAL

'The system uses what is called a light-pen system. It will allow the operator to use plain language to talk to the computer. That is the revolutionary aspect. Previously we would have had to use a keyboard.'

– Operations officer, HMS *Boxer*, on sea trials.

'Everyone knew that plastic foam mattresses of a certain type gave off oil and black smoke in a fire, but they cost about £8 compared with the £70 of a horsehair mattress. Within a month of the Falklands, plastic mattresses had been taken out and horsehair ones brought in throughout the Navy. We certainly have them, and other safety factors, in case of fire.'

– Commanding officer, HMS *Boxer*, on sea trials.

The operations officer ran on to HMS *Boxer*'s bridge through one door and straight off it through another after two or three words to the captain. I was just quick enough to shout, 'Any snags?' He was just quick enough to shout a cryptic, 'Yes!' – the exclamation mark clearly indicated by his tone of voice – before the door closed on him. The captain steadfastly didn't blink: his public face suggested that nothing at all had happened.

The sea trial of any ship can be rather like that, a tense getting to grips with the half-known, in which a stiff upper lip may be necessary, but in which a moment's complacency, a trifling overestimate of one's own experience and underestimate of the sea's implacable unpredictability, can rob a naval man of his reputation and the taxpayer of hard-earned millions.

So busy and vigilant was the operations officer on that particular day of HMS *Boxer*'s trials that it was not until much later that I was able to discover from him what the trouble had been, on a fairly representative day of what naval men regard as one of the most challenging and stimulating parts of naval life – the sea trials of a brand-new ship.

I had joined HMS *Boxer*, F92, on a warm and blowy late spring day at Portsmouth. There was a faint mist around the lamp standards of the port. The flags flying almost horizontally from the naval base clearly indicated the force three to four wind – not powerful enough to make things really uncomfortable, but strong enough to keep everyone on their toes, and possibly other people's. The 480 feet of the high-sided frigate, its two electronics towers fore and aft of the wide squat funnel, rested high against the quay.

Perhaps she was a more challenging prospect on her trials than many new ships. The ship was not only new in itself. It was *half* new as a type. 'It is a Type 22 frigate with ten metres' extra length let into the centre of the ship,' explained the young lieutenant who met me as I went aboard. 'It has altered the handling characteristics quite a bit. And we have so much new equipment.'

HMS *Boxer*, on her trials, was in fact virtually compiling, for the Navy as a whole, the future handbook on the stretched Type 22 frigate and on the new Ferranti Computer-Assisted Command system. She was the first ship in the Navy to have this equipment, which uses computers to make it easier to get, from the operations room to the captain on the bridge, constant appraisals of the current shipping situation around the ship.

A great deal of time was being spent on this new equipment during the trials in order to minimize the time future ships would have to devote to it. 'We have been on trials for the past nine months,' said the young lieutenant, 'and I don't think we will be operational for another two years.' I was not surprised when, later, senior officers confessed that, yes, they *did* get frustrated and fed up at times, though they knew that the ship was a good one and that what they were doing was important for the whole Navy. Many of them would have moved from the ship before it became operational, and they were therefore setting the ship up for others to use.

But all the modern technology, and all the demands it made, was not going to affect the spit and polish and the general niceties of Royal Naval life that day: a sea trial is as much a test of such matters as of computers and machinery.

The first lieutenant, a huge bearded lieutenant-commander (with an RAF man for a father and nineteen years' experience in the Royal Navy), as he worked a loudhailer beside the bridge, made this immediately plain. He had arrived on board at 7.40 that morning, he told me. What time would he normally expect to finish working during the trials? 'I left yesterday at 14.00 hours because I was playing cricket. Usually it has been between 5.00 pm and 7.30 pm. I get aboard early. I really have two distinct roles in the ship. First, I am the second-in-command; and therefore responsible for discipline and administration, and the sorts of things that second-in-commands normally deal with. I am also head of the operations department, which embraces two groups, the seaman group and the communications group. I am the senior seaman on board. It is my job to unberth the ship – making sure that telephone lines and cables, and so on, are cleared, because you look a bit silly towing a shore telephone line when you are on trials. I do it in slow time – I start half an hour before we sail.'

The first lieutenant excused himself to give his orders about the ceremonial piping of the Commander-in-Chief, Naval Home Command, and the ceremonial responses to other ships at the naval base. These matters of complexity and sensitivity were not explained to me until later in the trials, when they happened to become of pressing and unexpected concern.

The master-at-arms, sporting rather intense tortoiseshell spectacles, and a fine red beard, was going through his regular routine, making sure the ship was properly manned for the trial day, and that every man who should be aboard was aboard.

'I am responsible to the first lieutenant and the captain for discipline,' he pointed out, asking me if the car parked right alongside the ship on the quay, where it was likely to foul one of the hawsers, was mine. (It wasn't, to my intense relief: one does not carelessly cross a master-at-arms.)

'It is my business,' said the master-at-arms, his attitude to me rather more relaxed now that I had established my innocence, 'to ensure that there are no castaways and no stowaways. We are sailing today with ninety-eight per cent of the crew. Because we are coming home again tonight, we can afford to be a little flexible with the rota. If a man was away to attend a wedding or something else bona fide, we wouldn't necessarily bring him back. But if we were going out and not coming back for a week, we expect to sail with a full crew.'

I asked if absenteeism was a problem, especially when trials had been going on for as long as they had already been going on with H M S *Boxer*.

'It is rare for people not to turn up,' said the master-at-arms ominously. 'This week we have had one man away because he was sick. The biggest incidence, from a disciplinary point of view, are people who are half an hour adrift in turning up. I investigate to see if there is a case to answer and the first lieutenant punishes them. If a man has a long record, then he would be passed to the captain. But it is rare.'

I quite believed it. 'I have only been in the Navy for twenty-three years,' said the master-at-arms with heavy irony. 'We take all this as second nature. People outside don't understand. They talk about job satisfaction – well, over the past twenty-three years, I have really enjoyed it.' I believed that, too. A flaming red beard must be a very convenient tool for the imposition of discipline.

To direct *Boxer* out of harbour, the captain, who was shrewd enough after twenty-seven years in the Royal Navy, four of them as a captain, to know that he was on trial as much as the ship itself, stood on the *roof* of the bridge rather than inside it. This enabled him to keep a much closer eye on (1) the side of the ship, (2) the side of the quay – so that he could ensure that they never coincided.

The previous day, HMS *Jupiter* had collided with London Bridge in the course of making what should have been a simple turn, as she left after a week's courtesy visit. The captain of HMS *Boxer* (crest a boxer's glove apaumée, laced and edged on a field of red, motto *'Praemonitus Preamunitus'* – forewarned is forearmed) was taking no chances on this particular day.

'It is very easy to be wise after the event,' said the captain judicially. 'But, almost invariably, these matters are a succession of minor things. Unless one trains to the limit, you don't know what you are capable of when the chips are down.' But he was very careful when backing slowly out from the quay. He did not give me his full attention until all those who should be piped *had* been piped and we were steaming adroitly between the five holiday ferries which had chosen approximately the same time to enter or leave harbour.

For the captain, the son of a medical man who had wanted to be in the Navy since he was thirteen, the trial period had been rather longer than for many others on board. He had stood by with the shipyard – Yarrow Shipbuilders – for seven months before the Royal Navy formally accepted the ship. He had lived up North, miles away from his own pleasant home near Portsmouth, during the fitting-out.

'I had no formal brief,' he said, 'but it gave me a first-class opportunity, as a new man, to get to know the ship, to know the shipbuilder and so on. You probably don't get to form an impression of the personality of the ship – and ships *do* have different personalities – till after the acceptance, during the running tests. Earlier, one is very much an interested spectator. It was a very useful period, great fun and an experience one doesn't often get. Come the great day, the shipbuilder delivered the ship to the Commander Port, Portsmouth. There was a short ceremony in which the ship's builders marched off and the ship's company marched on. One signed on the dotted line. It is probably the only time in one's life that one would sign for £150,000,000, which is what the ship cost.'

Then, he said, the game had *really* started. For a three-week period they had 'built a strong ship', seeing that the organizational factors were right and people knew what was expected of them: action stations, defence stations, emergency stations. Then there had been what was called the 'Fast Cruise'. For this, you disconnected the shore telephone and went for a cruise, getting everyone to do exactly what they would do at sea – except that the ship had stayed lashed to the quay. They had then actually gone to sea for a few days, off Portland Bill, for safety-operational sea training.

'We ran the ship through this test in terms of fire-fighting, man-overboard drills, navigation trials and so on. Once we were assessed as safe, we got on with what we call Part Four of the four trials. And the length of these trials varies.'

They certainly do – as was proved by the fact that, after nine months of trials, HMS *Boxer* was still due for many *more* months of them before becoming operational. But, pointed out the captain, *Boxer*'s trials were long because she was trying out not only a redesigned hull, with a sharper and longer bow, but also a lot of new equipment. Other ships in the 'stretched' Type 22 class would have final trials lasting only three or four months.

I realized the extent to which the new equipment would *not* be allowed to lessen the concentration on basic drills when the first lieutenant set fire to one of the electronic compartments on the operations deck. The fire was declared well and truly out within nine minutes of its being started. The first lieutenant seemed to think that good order and discipline had been satisfied; and the ship forged ahead through a fair swell, past the Isle of Wight and way out into the English Channel. Soon all that was visible on the horizon was sea.

HMS *Boxer* is a Devonport-based ship and was carrying out her trials from Portsmouth because the available trials facilities were there. Also Ferranti, makers of the latest information technology, had a base there.

A great deal of data about the redesigned ship – most of it favourable – had already been compiled. 'We go faster because of the extra length,' reported one ship's officer. 'It is one knot more, which is noticeable and great, considering we are an extra 500 tons displacement. It is a bit like a racing yacht – the relationship of the length to the beam. And we have a greater fuel capacity – a thirty per cent increase – which is proving a great advantage. The wardroom, which is the home for up to twenty officers, is more comfortable, and there has been a certain amount of shuffling round of compartments. We now have a senior ratings dining hall. They used to eat in their respective messes. There is an expansion of the library for junior ratings, plus extra store rooms.'

But it was operational efficiency that was particularly being tested in the sea trials; and one little matter was making me feel rather uneasy about this warship. There were no signs of any guns.

I exaggerate. There were in fact two guns, standard forty-millimetre Bofors guns of Second World War type, both mounted amidships, one starboard and the other to port. A top speed of over thirty knots did not appear, to a civilian eye, to be very useful if there were no guns with which to inflict damage on an enemy or ward off potential damage to HMS *Boxer* herself.

I searched out the weapon engineer officer – a commander, and one of the four 'departmental managers' of the ship, found him on one of the swaying decks, looking over the Bofors guns, and taxed him on the point. I was soon put in my place: a reliance on *guns*, it seems, is now thoroughly old-fashioned.

'Batch One of the Type 22 frigates have been fitted with thirty or twenty-millimetre guns with 1,000 per minute capability,' I was told. 'Ultimately we will get them as well. But the weaponry of this ship is primarily anti-submarine torpedoes, normally launched by Lynx helicopters – two of them when operational. These can be loaded with homing torpedoes: they can go round in decreasing circles under water, looking for a submarine, or they can be launched straight off deck to go out to the approximate site of the submarine and they can then do a zig-zag pattern over the area until they find it.'

The sea trials, said the weapon engineer officer, had proved that the stretched version of the Type 22 could probably operate helicopters more easily in rough weather. The ship could remain in business in the roughest weather, because most of the equipment was well down in the ship and automatic; and, though the equipment would be degraded in bad weather, so would the opposition's. The decks were drier than on 'unstretched' Type 22s.

I went aft and saw what he meant. Behind the ship, which was now making a brisk thirty knots, was a 'water wall', which to my untutored eye looked almost as tall as the ship. It was rather like a huge wave following the ship, overflowing into a fog of spray. This water wall was about 100 feet from the stern. On the previous, unstretched Type 22s, it was only about ten feet away from the stern, and drenched the deck so badly that it became unusable at any speed in bad weather.

Apart from the forty-millimetre guns, the two triple-barrelled anti-submarine torpedo mountings and two Seawolf surface-to-air missile systems amidships, H M S *Boxer* had another formidable reminder that thinking in terms of guns is rather old fashioned: two ribbed, square-sectioned tubes on the port bow, and another two on the starboard bow. They were, I discovered, launchers of Exocet surface-to-surface missiles, the armament that played such a potent role in the Falklands campaign.

This sophisticated equipment was not to be tried out in

action that day: even post-Falklands, the Royal Navy is not allowed to blaze away with equipment costing hundreds of thousands of pounds. The most the weapon engineer officer could test out was the forty-millimetre guns. This perhaps made him a little defensive. 'It was proved in the Falklands that the forty-millimetre gun can deter planes. In one or two cases, we shot planes down,' he said. 'The maximum range is about one mile, so they have to be close before you can put a shot into them. But if you want to stop anybody illegally fishing, for instance, you can't put a Seawolf across her bows, whereas you could put a forty-millimetre shell across her bows, and you could put it into her steering gear, which would effectively stop her.'

The previous day, the breech-block of the guns had been dropped, tolerances were measured, parts were cleaned and greased. Something called a plug-bore gauge – a brass cylinder of a certain size – was dropped down the muzzles. It was dropped down again ten minutes before the firing trials were signalled, just before noon.

In wartime, the guns would be in the charge of a leading seaman and there would be no officer on deck. But when I was aboard *Boxer* there was an officer there, wearing the same sort of white helmet, facemask and long gloves as a precaution against flash burns as the men were wearing. Certainty was being made doubly sure: the officer would see to that.

'We are using live-shoot practice ammunition, with a tracer component so you can see where the shots are going,' he explained. 'It will be a bit noisy. We will fire a parachute luminant flare, and bang away at that.'

The range-finder, in his white protective gear, had already arrived, carrying his gun-sight in a wood box resembling the attaché case of a commuter. Everyone on deck, in their white helmets and orange or yellow ear muffs, looked rather like guests at a fancy dress ball all dressed like Mickey Mouse.

I was prepared for the first bangs from the four-shot clips of ammunition; naively *un*prepared for the deck to thump under

my feet as if a giant down below was ramming his head into it.
It is an old axiom, and a true one, that sea trials are a test of
sailors as well as ships. Being able to think clearly in a numbing
and vibrative din is one of the things being tested.

Accuracy was one of the things *not* being tested, I was
assured. This was just as well. None of the bursts of fire hit the
parachute flares, which fizzled out while tracer streams went
above and below the target. We were firing straight out to sea
in a southerly direction, away from land, and there was no
shipping in the way for at least fifteen degrees on either side of
the firing area. The ship put about, so that the gun on the
other side of the ship could have a go. It was no better. No
hits.

The man was carrying his sight away again, in his commuter's attaché case, when the weapon engineer officer explained why he nevertheless regarded the trials as a success:
'The maximum rate of fire is thirty rounds a minute. I was just
hoping that the guns would have no misfires – that was part of
the reason for the exercise. Otherwise, it is just so the gunners
can get used to the equipment. Aim and accuracy aren't the
objects of the exercise.'

There was some time to go before the man-overboard exercise. It seemed a good opportunity to see how they were
getting on below the main decks, where in HMS *Boxer* the
computerized operations room controls the information
reaching the captain; and the way the sealed-off engines (one
further deck below) operate is controlled from the machinery-
control room.

Access to the main engine room on HMS *Boxer* was – at
least to the civilian eye – as primitive as on much earlier
warships. The air-locking door, sealing off the deck above
from the engine room trapdoor, was sophisticated enough – so
tight that, in chemical or nuclear warfare, there would be an
airlock for men entering or leaving the engine room. But the
two-feet by eighteen-inch hatch, without any nearby rails or
handles on which to get a grip, was difficult to negotiate. The

vertical ladder leading down from it was tucked away to the side of the hatch rather than right underneath it, so that my flailing legs had their work cut out to find it. How even a skilled seaman gets on when dropping down into the engine room in high seas is a picture I prefer not to imagine.

That said – no doubt in compensation for my own initial lack of dexterity – it must also be said that there are very few occasions on which a man *needs* to descend the two vertical metal ladders.

The unmarked pristine white dungarees of the marine engineer officer – a lieutenant-commander and another of the four departmental managers of the ship – at once made it quite clear that the engines were almost fully automatic: masterminded from the control centre above rather than on the spot in the bowels of the ship. The control centre itself was rather unremarkable – like an ordinary clean office with rather more gauges and print-outs than the average factory manager's office.

The officer was enthusiastic about the two Olympus Concorde engines, suitably 'marinized', that give the driving power to HMS *Boxer*. 'Because you need only a small watch, in terms of numbers of human beings, you must ensure that all the controls are checked very carefully. You must ensure they are 100 per cent *all* the time.'

The engine-room staff, alerted by a watch group of only half a dozen (compared with the twenty that would have been needed a few years ago) descend into the immaculate engine room only when something is wrong, or for the occasional regular checks.

The Olympus engines looked like yellow oil drums, each about seven feet in diameter and thirty feet long, one each side of the three-feet wide metal catwalk. They had small doors, almost like the doors of gingerbread houses, through which I was led by an artificer. Once inside the door, I was in a sort of anteroom to the engine itself. Here, in cramped but remarkably clean conditions, an artificer can make all the necessary checks on the marinized Concorde engines. The artificer pulled out a cylindrical grey plug, about half an inch in diameter, and four inches long – about the size of a small pocket torch. This tiny piece of grey plastic is virtually a tell-tale on the health of the whole engine. The tip of the plug which is pushed into the machinery is magnetic and picks up the metal debris created by the movement of the engine, thus preventing it from clogging up the works. The plug is withdrawn at pre-arranged times to measure the amount of debris that is being thrown off by the engine. This, in turn, is an indication of the amount of wear the engine is undergoing. Too much wear in too short a period, and the artificer knows that something is wrong, without even having to get his hands dirty.

The artificer, a twenty-six-year-old petty officer marine engineer artificer, had encountered only one fault so far while I had been aboard. This, he said, was an Olympus trip cable that wasn't working; in the event of fire that could have been serious. In such an emergency, he said, there was a solenoid which automatically 'tripped out' the fuel supply to the engine. But, as a back-up in case this didn't work, there was also a simple physical means of cutting off the fuel supply – a trip wire. The chrome on this wire had come off, which meant the wire had stuck in its casing. He had managed to grease it, which cured the problem.

Faults of that sort, he said, were comparatively rare in the modern Navy. There had certainly been few engine-room faults during the *Boxer*'s sea trials so far.

In the ship's operations room, two decks above, it was rather different. This was where the new Computer Assisted Command System Number One was installed. In this fairly small room, up to twenty-six men can work at any one time, continuously plotting the identity and positions of all shipping and aircraft in the area.

On this particular day there was a rare sight in the operations room, a woman. She was a technical employee of the civilian contractors, Ferranti. And this was not the only surprise: the room itself was less like the normal notion of a ship's control room than a television studio. There was no access to outside light. There were well over a dozen screens around the room. By each screen, there was a pen at the end of a coiled wire.

It was, I was told, the dawn of the light-pen in the British Navy – a development to take the sting out of processing computerized information.

'The system uses what is called a light-pen injection system,' explained the operations officer. 'It will allow the operator to use plain language to talk to the computer. That is the revolutionary aspect. Previously we would have had to use a keyboard, sometimes a QWERTY one, as on an ordinary typewriter, and sometimes alphabetical. This system provides, through the computer, a clear command picture for command appreciation. And by introducing symbology – the use of symbols – it will allow command to identify all tracks – which is friendly, which is an enemy, where we are to rendezvous. It will feed information through from the information computer to the weapons-systems computer, so that the target can be indicated automatically.'

The majority of the ship's company of 250 lived aboard, said the operations officer; but he happened to live locally and so went home at nights. He had been working up to seven days a week, sometimes more than twelve hours a day, on the sea trials.

'This morning it all turned out to work,' he said. 'Usually there are one or two questions, but there weren't this morning.'

They had been doing trials since September of last year. Did it become rather repetitive and frustrating? 'The honest answer is, yes, we do get fed up. There is a sense of frustration. When you see how much of our equipment is involved in the trials, how much is set to work at the moment, you will see that our operational role is limited and that the primary task of this ship is ensuring that we get a sound computer system working at the end of our trials period, a system which can be passed on to other ships of the class. The ships that will use it will be the Batch Two Type 22 – the *Beaver, Brave, London, Sheffield* and *Coventry*.'

The men chosen to work in the control room with the equipment were deliberately *not* selected from the brightest available. They were an average cross-section of the sort of man who would find himself working such machinery. When I expressed surprise, I was told that there had to be a 'natural spread' of intelligence and skill among the twenty-six people using the operations room at any one time, so that if there were any incipient problems in handling, they would come to light. An exceptionally bright group would distort the results and give a misleading impression of the effectiveness of the new system under adverse conditions.

But are there not excessively bright crew members who are listened to when they express their opinions about difficulties? One able seaman was replacing a number of ordinary electric light bulbs, like battery-torch bulbs, in the consoles where various functions are indicated – or should be indicated – in orange illuminated letters. The able seaman said that the bulbs kept burning out – some lasted only about a month. In other words there was some danger that expensive and ingenious equipment would be partly nullified because people with poorer memories might not be able to read the signs. I *hoped* the able seaman had made the point known to his superiors, and that they had listened.

The main problem, it seemed, was with the software for the computer-assisted command system. Other officers admitted there had been considerable teething troubles. One said that, at the time the Navy accepted the ship for trials, it had been estimated that there was still one hundred man *years* of work to be done to get the software perfected; the trials were likely to go on for a very long time, but the Navy was determined to get it right.

But while the arcane workings of the new computer system were getting the attention of Naval men and civilian boffins in the operations rooms, the more basic aspects of the life of the ship were under trial. Just before noon there was a shout of 'Man overboard!'

This drill is regularly carried out. Its purpose is not merely to ensure that any man who goes overboard will be quickly picked up, but to practise feats of seamanship which could be useful in other situations. In this case, the ship made what is called a 'Williamson' turn. The ship was turned to one side through seventy degrees , and then the wheel was turned in the other direction in a way which brought the ship neatly back along her own tracks. 'This is an easy ship to practise that turn,' said one lieutenant on the swaying deck, 'because we have twin screws, and we have controllable pitch propellers that can slide through the water if you feather the blades.'

The 'man' who had gone overboard was in fact a red plastic dummy. A red plastic lifebuoy had been flung out after it, but because of the high seas neither was always visible. All the same, the ship came back to within only a few feet of the drowning 'man', and then slowly edged towards 'him'. One of the dangers of the Williamson turn, I was told, as I watched the exercise from the bridge deck, was that the ship could all too accurately go back along its own tracks and thus cut down the man in the sea: it was necessary to watch wind and water very closely.

On the bridge, the captain, an ex-public schoolboy who entered the Royal Navy at eighteen, was keeping a lively eye on the proceedings as he explained its value to me. 'I like to see these tests involve every member of the watch after a period in harbour, to get them into the routine. Then, when there is a quarter hour to spare, we will do it again, without warning. It is good training for young officers of the watch. They get their ship-handling practice doing this sort of exercise, because they have to judge what the sea and wind are doing, and they get to recognize relative motion and take the speed off the ship so as to bring it alongside the dummy.'

The captain acknowledged that having people overboard in

real life was rare. Refuelling at sea — which the *Boxer* would not often have to do — was a classic case of a period of maximum risk. Large waves could wash a man overboard. Otherwise few men went overboard unless they meant to.

To illustrate the point, the captain pointed to the able seaman who was just about to jump overboard to help save the 'man' in the sea. No, not jump, said the captain on second thoughts — the man had to *walk* straight off the deck into the sea. If he tried to jump he would twist as he entered the sea. If he could steel himself to walk straight off the edge of the deck, he would fall in the right place without hurting himself.

While the able seaman (in wet suit and flippers) was holding the head of the dummy out of the water, the Seaboat was lowered into the sea from aft. The Seaboat was a device of fibre-glass and rubber, much lighter, smaller and quicker than the old-fashioned ship's whaler. The 'man' in the sea was winched aboard in a harness, the able seaman (termed the swimmer of the watch) was pulled aboard the Seaboat, and the whole lot of them were hauled out of the sea, dead level, by the ship's crane.

'Occasionally people are a little doubtful about walking off the side of the ship,' said the first lieutenant. 'If someone said, "No," I would not compel him to go. Once you have trained a man, he is more likely to go in during any sort of conditions. The hurdle isn't really persuading someone that he's not going to get hurt if he steps off the Exocet deck. The difficulty is in the mind of the individual clearing that hurdle. If I expected a man to go in during heavy weather, it would be for real. And when it is for real, people find reserves they didn't know they had. When the *Coventry* went down in the Falklands, there were people jumping into the sea all over the place to pull the survivors out of the water.'

It was important, said the first lieutenant, that people found out as soon as possible the right way to do things. That day's earlier fire-fighting exercise, for instance, had taught the team fighting the fire one great lesson. It was that you didn't get hold of a man in a smoky room if he was near electric wiring, because he was probably live with electricity. You used something like a wooden broom to push, pull or knock him clear of the wiring before you laid hands on him.

The operation of retrieving the Seaboat was fairly smooth, thanks to HMS *Boxer*'s modern crane and tackle. The captain seemed satisfied with the whole manoeuvre. He found the ship itself very manoeuvrable. The controls were on the bridge, and you could get instant response.

Yes, the captain was satisfied *on the whole*; but no self-respecting captain is ever wholly satisfied. After the 'rescue' he told me, 'The engines were slow to build up the speed on one occasion; otherwise it went entirely to plan; my officer of the watch is experienced. It could have been that somebody did not hear the officer of the watch saying, "Wind up speed!" '

The navigator, a lieutenant, requested and got permission to go down to the wardroom for a cup of tea. I decided to slake a healthy thirst at the same time. The new computer system hadn't borne on the navigation system yet, said the navigator. 'This is just another day for me. Most of the navigation equipment is standard, and is fitted to any other ship. The only thing we are having to get used to in the ship is the handling characteristics, this being the first of her class. The turning data is not yet laid down. I have had to obtain data for Batch One ships, and I have had to add a factor to those figures to produce new ones.'

So far, they had discovered that they had to use more wheel to achieve the same rate of turn. Was it possible to do that comfortably for the ship? 'You have to apply seaman's eyes. You may need to turn tighter, sooner. You couldn't just breeze airily into a turn and get on with it; you have to watch the rate of turn. That is what we have established. We have produced turning data, but it is not yet generally available except in complicated form. We want to provide something simpler for convenient use.'

Time for tea was limited. High above the wardroom and its

rattling teacups, the pressures were on. HMS *Boxer* was discovering that not even a warship on sea trials can be oblivious of the general state of the economy in late twentieth-century Britain.

The captain helpfully radioed a message to the harbour: 'If there is no increase in wind speed, I would be happy with just one tug when we come in today.'

Answer from harbour: 'Only one duty tug will in any case be available after 15.30 hours.'

The captain bounced on the balls of his feet, carefully saying nothing. It was several moments before he said to me, ignoring the brutal lesson in the logistics of the 1980s that he had just been given: 'The wind is blowing straight on to the shore. There is a danger that if we stop short, we would drift sideways on to the berth – which is something we like to avoid.'

I saw the point. A captain who ran his ship sideways-on into the quay could hardly plead the economic recession as an excuse. It was perhaps fortunate that a matter of naval protocol interrupted this painful matter. The navigator reported: 'There is a ship to port, sir. It's the *Newcastle*, sir.' He rushed over to the starboard side of the bridge and produced what looked like the fold-up menu of a motorway café, but was in fact a unique and valuable document called a Bridge Card. It listed the dates at which all captains in the Royal Navy were made up to this exalted rank. This was not so the First Sea Lord could send them all an anniversary card. The purpose was a serious one, vital to naval life as it has been lived for centuries.

It was this: when two ships meet, the junior one calls the senior one and asks formally for permission to proceed. One ship is *always* senior to the other; and it depends on which captain was made up to captain first. In this case, it appeared that Captain Blank, OBE, had been a captain since 30 June 1976. 'It makes him four years senior to us,' said the navigator.

Immediately the subordinate message was sent to the other ship by light signal (radio messages can be more easily picked up by people who have no business to hear – like the enemy). The other ship flashed a carry-on signal.

In practice, this meant moving on to the speed trials – certainly one of the most stirring experiences a warship can offer short of real action against an enemy.

I was on the bridge with the captain, the navigator and the rating who actually worked the steering gear (which was like bicycle handlebars shrunk to half size) and the engine throttles (twin bar controls rather like the throttles of a twin-engined airliner).

'We can go from rest to thirty knots in one minute ten seconds,' promised the captain. 'Perhaps one minute thirty seconds if she is a bit scaled up. We would clean her hull before we were operational, of course.'

He turned to the navigator and said, 'Wind them up.'

'Full speed,' ordered the navigator.

The ship's engines didn't sound like a ship's engines at all. They sounded like the Concorde aircraft. They emitted a whine that became a shriek which cut through two decks and seemed as if it were directly in one's own ears. The bow of the ship rose upwards like a car driven forward with the handbrake on; then the ship began to glide forward, pushing everyone in the back as if they were sitting in the seats of an accelerating sports car.

The captain gave a running report. 'Thirty seconds – twelve knots. Forty seconds – eighteen knots. Fifty seconds – twenty knots. Sixty seconds – twenty-six knots.' And so on.

Pride in his ship suffused the Captain. ' "Amazons" – the Type 21 frigates – have a high speed response, too,' he said. 'But their real speed is twenty-eight. You can't run them at maximum capacity because you have to hold it back to preserve the life of the hull.'

The captain then cut the forward power and applied the rear thrust, bringing the speed down to zero in the ship's length which is the minimum stopping distance. Soon HMS *Boxer* was doing a steady six knots in reverse, almost like a sedate car driver looking for a parking space.

Then she went forward again and bore hard to port, everything so smooth and gentle – except that we were now all living in a slanting world, as the ship rolled out of the turn. I saw now what the captain had meant by the necessity of being able to recognize relative motion: at sea it is sometimes difficult to tell with the naked eye whether you are going fast or slow, going straight or turning. All of us on the bridge were bending one knee to compensate for the slope of the bridge, a slope a warship would be unlikely to acquire except in sea trials or war conditions.

Once out of the turn, the ship quickly righted itself. After that it was all anticlimax; obviously nothing had blown up and nothing was going to blow up. HMS *Boxer* steamed back towards Portsmouth. More of the officers went to the ward-room for a well-earned cup of coffee or tea. The captain went to his cabin to reflect on the trials and on his ship.

It was a comfortable cabin. It had hessian-covered walls, gilt wall-bracket lamps, a polished dining table and nicely veneered wall cabinets. The captain saw me looking at the 'cabinets' and opened one to show that what I was looking at was really an aesthetically ingenious cover for the captain's monitoring dials and the captain's safe. One was in the shipbuilder's hands about this sort of refinement, said the captain; and the shipbuilders, in this case, had been imaginative. It was just his good luck. A few bits of veneer had made all the difference.

But the captain didn't want to talk about his cabin, he wanted to talk about the trials. He was pleased with the new Computer Assisted Command System, despite its teething troubles. Because of the simplicity of the light-pen method of injecting information, you had to train a man only for the specific task he was going to perform, not for the whole system. In the past, just to put together a simple picture of ships near you, you had to learn the whole system. 'You can now train a junior sailor to be a surface picture compiler in probably half an hour,' he explained. 'I wouldn't say the trials are taking longer than they should, bearing in mind the new equipment.

We have some sort of operational capability right now; but clearly the powers-that-be would use us only in an emergency. Anything, short of fighting a full-scale war, we could do right now.'

I asked if the ship had benefited in any way from the lessons of the Falklands. Yes, said the captain, they were halfway through the four years it took to build the ship when the Falklands campaign came along. It had been too late to include the improved electric cable coverings that were being fitted on other ships following the Falklands fires, but there had been some changes in design.

'There was virtually nothing new to the Navy in the lessons of the Falklands,' asserted the captain surprisingly. 'What it did was ram home hard a number of issues that were well known but which, for reasons of false economy or complacency, had been ignored in a very long period of non-hostilities. For instance, on the personnel side, departments like to live with one another – stokers with stokers, electricians with electricians and so on. But if you get a bomb on the stokers' mess deck, you end up with no stokers. So we have now split up the various categories, so that electricians will be both forward and aft; some will be with the stokers and caterers. They are dispersed through the ship. That is probably the biggest personnel change.'

Another problem in the Falklands had been the rapid spread of smoke throughout ships when hit. *Boxer*, in common with all other ships, now had smoke curtains breaking up the passageways. Bulkhead penetrations for pipes had been sealed. To make living space more attractive, laminate sheets had been used. But it had been found that, in action, these shattered; the pieces were razor sharp. All laminate in the *Boxer* was backed by thin steel sheeting, so it did not shatter.

And ladders. *Boxer* was using nice wooden ones between decks at the moment, because the ship was involved in a lot of ceremonial visits. Metal ones would later be substituted. And breathing equipment: it now covered the crew *150 per cent*, and was scattered around the ship.

Operationally, too, the ship would be more of a survivor. The engines could be changed in twenty-four hours, and they could be changed at sea. The extra fuel carried gave one freedom from the umbilical cord of the supply ships: 'The Navy feels that our ships, since the war, have been short-legged, and this has been promptly reversed. I could go to the Falklands without looking at a tanker. I can go to America, and back again, without looking at a tanker. That is a bit of extra flexibility available to the Commander-in-Chief.'

As *Boxer* approached harbour, the captain went back to the bridge, satisfied with the trials I had seen and with the trials in general. 'It is an ideal improvement, to provide new technology for a stretched ship of an established type, rather than going for something new every time. We have 250 men compared with our predecessor's 500 – it is a ship very economical on manpower.'

In other words, the modern Navy has at least some of the civilian preoccupations of industry and commerce – a desire to succeed at a time when labour is expensive, sometimes more expensive than the technology.

I found it almost a relief when *Boxer* finally berthed in Portsmouth and the traditionally salty mood of the Royal Navy reasserted itself. Getting the hawsers fixed to the quay, a group of young able seamen who were as much on sea trials as HMS *Boxer* herself, was slightly less than adroit. One of them ignored a coil of steel rope lying on the deck; he stood right in the middle of it.

'Don't stand in the middle of the ——ing rope, man!' bawled the petty officer in charge. 'You need ——ing lessons, you, you, you ——!'

It was not only a reminder that the Royal Navy can still have a rather brisker way with its employees' sensitivities than would be possible in civilian industry. It was also a reminder that even in the technological age, naval men are – and need to be – on sea trials as much as the ships need to be. Only then can they be sure of coping when the trials turn into actual battles. Though naval men feel most alive when they are at sea, it is easy to understand why a shore posting can also be welcome – especially if it is a posting to an exotic part of the world.

5

FIRM AS THE ROCK

'I am in no doubt at all about the strategic value of Gibraltar. And there are some side-effect values, too. Gibraltar is valuable in that it is the only place in the world where a significant number of naval personnel are able to live abroad with their families. But it would be a mistake to take on viceregal airs.'

– Flag Officer, Gibraltar (a rear-admiral).

'We were told by the Ministry of Defence to shut down part of the dockyard because of the defence cuts, and some of it will be taken over by a local private company. We will still be able to support and maintain warships, but if we had to do a refit on any, we could find we had a very full dockyard. What do I think about it? We were just told to get on with it, and we have.'

– Lieutenant-commander posted on Gibraltar.

Under 1,400 feet of solid rock, the lieutenant-commander in the plans room watched the plotting of the enemy ships approaching the Straits of Gibraltar. Half-way up the outside of the vast limestone edifice which is the Rock of Gibraltar, another lieutenant-commander, of roughly the same age, looked out from the windows of his five-bedroomed married-quarters flat to a fine sunlit vista over the harbour: Spain to the right and North Africa to the left, both clearly visible in the shimmering heat-haze.

The two men, so similar in background and age, were engaged at the opposite poles of naval life on Gibraltar, the vital three square miles of rock jutting out from the southern Spanish coast that controls the Straits of Gibraltar – that fifteen-mile-wide bottleneck which could effectively bottle up the Russian Black Sea Fleet in time of war.

Both men, and their varied situations, stayed in the memory long after I had left Gibraltar, just as the highly varied life in Gibraltar (of a piece only in that it is *all* heavy with history) stays in the minds of naval men who have been posted there. Gibraltar is a three-mile-long, one-mile-wide lump of British rock that feels like an island, even if it isn't. But in naval terms it is much more than that.

The lieutenant-commander who was taking part in an exercise battle in the plotting room, situated in a tunnel at the very centre of the huge Rock, and at ground level, was just across a wood-lined rock corridor from the office where General Eisenhower planned the Allied invasion of North Africa in 1942. Photographs of the General on the walls testified to the fact.

The lieutenant-commander who was looking through his large living room window at the millionaire's view (framed by undulating palm trees) of the North African coast, was similarly enveloped in history. In the Battle of Trafalgar, the British casualties were winched up to this high point on the Rock to what was, long before its conversion into quarters, the Naval Hospital. A couple of hundred feet down the sloping rock, in the white, blue-shuttered little house to the north, Admiral Lord Nelson's body lay before being shipped back to England.

In such a little jewel of British history, the Royal Naval man and woman have to be constantly aware of the blunt contemporary fact that the Rock is still vital to a much-changed Britain, and to the whole strategy of NATO. A living history lesson could easily and rapidly turn into a grim defender of the West – using what the top echelon of the

Navy on Gibraltar describes as far more modern, if less visible, means than the old cannons which are still sprinkled liberally round the Rock.

In peacetime naval people have a social life within their service to humanize their jobs, unlike, for instance, the single naval officer who is the Navy's presence on Cyprus, another point of importance to the West. In Cyprus, this officer, assisted by one Royal Marine sergeant, and working in Headquarters British Forces, a collection of colonial-style buildings, has to monitor all ship movements around the Middle East, direct the arrival of all Royal Naval ships and, at the same time, display a diplomatic presence by giving dinner or cocktail parties for people from visiting ships, from the other services or from the local community. In Cyprus, the solitary naval representative has to ask the Army, with 2,600 on the island, or the RAF, with about one thousand, to help achieve his objectives – even if it is the repair of a naval ship. Men who have filled the position say that it is wonderful; that they feel like colts given their head, and that a dinner party for forty-seven, at the detached house which is the married quarter, is nothing to daunt anyone. But Cyprus would not be everyone's cup of tea, being (in naval terms) a solitary billet as distinct from Gibraltar, which is a naval community and a warm remnant of the British Empire.

Gibraltar is indeed one of the very few remnants of Empire which *is* still capable of aiding the Royal Navy's role of protecting British shipping and monitoring the sea-going activities of other countries. As such it is far bigger than its geographical identity as a peninsula of rock at the end of southern Spain.

It remains a stout reminder of imperial values, with its own social atmosphere and standards: you are not likely to find in its narrow bustling streets any copy of *Playboy* or *Men Only*. For the Navy, it means that they can bring their children on the posting without risking their seeing something nasty in the newsagents. Some naval men are often tempted to regard this as a bigger bonus than their overseas salary weighting.

Even the habit of everyone – smart hotels included – of serving condensed milk instead of fresh is a reminder of the rigours of World War Two. English visitors to the Rock, especially out of holiday season, tend to be ex-naval types, a little tottery now, recalling their colourful youth. For them, the condensed milk is a wallow in nostalgia. And where else but the Bristol Hotel, just by the Moorish-designed but Anglican Cathedral of the Holy Trinity, could they still experience the same blend of cultures that developed in the days of Empire: Islamic tiled walls in the corridors, British Art Nouveau fireplace surrounds in the bedrooms? And all within feet of the vigorous and wealthy Indian merchants of Main Street?

'You can "do" the Rock in a fortnight and you are then very much dependent on your own resources to entertain yourself,' said one naval man.

Perhaps. But naval personnel on the 1,400-feet-high defender of the Straits of Gibraltar – the 'choke-point' of the Mediterranean and the Black Sea Russian Fleet – have the satisfaction of a job that means something in real terms.

The number of times in its history Gibraltar has been taken and re-taken indicates all too clearly its importance. It has been called Tarik's Mountain, the northern Pillar of Hercules, the Key to Spain and the Gateway to the Mediterranean. The Romans, the Phoenicians, the Visigoths, the Spanish and the British have all fought for it. Its rocky three square miles have changed little in the midst of this conquest and counter-conquest. The Rock itself has stood firm, reminding all mere humans that they are mortal. At present Spain lays claim to it, but without so far making it clear that she has the means or the will to assume Britain's defence commitment within NATO.

Gibraltar is a popular posting for the five hundred men and women of the Royal Navy and the hundred or so Reserves who, with smaller contingents from the Royal Air Force and the British Army, make up Britain's watchdog of the Straits of Gibraltar. Sometimes its amenities (including big-game fishing, sailing, water sports and gambling at the casino) are financially prohibitive. No matter. A trip to see the Barbary apes is cheap. Folklore has it that the apes – those mischievous occupiers of the ridge halfway up the side of the Rock – are a symbol of British occupation: if they ever leave, the British would leave, too. So far the apes have shown no sign of wishing to discontinue chewing up the camera cases or picking the pockets of unwary visitors.

As soon as he leaves the airport (uncomfortably close to Spanish territory) the sailor steps straight into a miniature museum of British naval history. The *Gibraltar Chronicle* was the first newspaper to carry the news of the victory at Trafalgar; every year on 21 October the Trafalgar Day ceremony takes place at the Trafalgar Cemetery. Every day there is a changing of the guard in front of the old convent which is now the residence of the Governor.

Naval people go on a series of walks called the Siege and Counter-Siege Walks, on which they can see the battlements and the old cannon. At least fifteen sieges are illustrated in the Gibraltar Museum, which includes the old Moorish baths. But the whole southern part of the Rock is really a museum of old buildings: unlike those in the north, which were bombarded to rubble, those in the south were out of range of the Spanish guns which have periodically pounded British occupation. And the most inexperienced naval wife or Wren can take in all these historical pleasures without the fear of being mugged. There are only two hundred bilingual policemen for the Rock's 30,000 population, but violent crime is rare. The social pressures and tensions are not severe and in any case there is nowhere for wrongdoers to run.

The whole history of the Rock perpetually reminds naval personnel of what they are there for. Over recent centuries it has been the Arabs, the Spanish and the British who have vied for the Rock. In 1713 the British were, by treaty, granted Gibraltar 'to be held and enjoyed with all manner of right for ever, without exception or impediment whatsoever'. Despite

this, Great Britain had to fight off Spanish naval attacks in
1727 and 1779. The 1779 siege lasted four years. It was ended
only when the British had set fire, with red-hot cannon balls,
to ten wooden Spanish ships with reinforced hulls on their
fighting side – ships thought by the Spanish to be proof against
fire.

But the five hundred naval men and Wrens on the Rock
now watch a slackening of British influence on some aspects of
the Rock's life, even if there is no slackening of British military
effectiveness.

At the time of my visit, a lieutenant-commander told me:
'In accordance with British government policy, we are disposing of part of the dockyards and turning them over to local
private contractors. If we had to face heavy repairs, or a ship's
complete refit, we would have to call on the private sector.'
From the map, I could see that the Royal Navy was hanging
on only to those dockyards at the 'hub' of the docks' complex,
while those forming the rim of the wheel had been disposed of
to private contractors. Sailors are prevented by their calling
from having an opinion about this political decision; but there
is nothing to stop them praying secretly that the government's
universal confidence in the private sector proves justified.

Even the present Royal Naval Hospital (not to be confused
with the *Old* Royal Naval Hospital which is now turned into
married quarters) is having to trim to meet the needs of the
times. It is a complex of three separate buildings linked by
handsome colonnaded pathways: a fine colonial structure of
the sort that made the Victorians sure that their dignity and
world sway would last for ever.

But when I visited it I was told that changes were being
made to cut costs and make administration easier. The support
manager responsible for the administration, a tall and sardonic
lieutenant-commander who had come up through the ratings'
mess, told me that he had just submitted to Whitehall a plan
for consolidating the hospital in only two of the three buildings.

'We call it Wedgwood Castle,' he said admiringly. 'But it is not a convenient building for its purpose. It is over-large, uneconomical and requires more staff than is really necessary to run it. It was built for two hundred patients and we only require thirty-five beds at the moment.'

The coming contraction seemed sad. But, I was told, the simple fact was that the single most important aspect of the hospital's present-day life was the maternity ward. This would take ten mothers – the most to be expected, by the law of averages, at any one time.

Not that the Navy underestimates the importance of the maternity ward. I found naval people reticent about this point, but there appears to be some feeling that young (perhaps teenage) Royal Naval mothers were sometimes fearful enough at their first confinement, without having to cope with possible language difficulties at the local civilian hospital. Despite the fact that two doctors in the local hospital were Navy-trained, one officer told me, 'If it weren't for the maternity ward of the Royal Naval Hospital, Gibraltar would have to be an unaccompanied posting for naval men. That is the truth of the matter. The standard of medicine practised in the local hospital is faultless, but the language difficulties could be a different matter.'

I must have looked rather puzzled at this explanation. He added, 'There is no more discriminating user of the National Health Service than the expectant mother. She knows what sort of treatment she would expect at St Mary's Hospital, Portsmouth. Here in Gibraltar we have to endeavour to provide that same service.' Between two hundred and three hundred babies are born in Gibraltar every year. This is a high figure for a community of 30,000 people, until it is remembered that a large proportion of that population is of child-bearing age. The previous year, I was told with some pride, five sets of twins had been born – which was ten times the national average per head of population.

But the need to reassure British expectant mothers is not the only justification for the Royal Naval Hospital in Gibraltar. Meningitis and some other conditions are much more widespread, per head of population, than they are in the United Kingdom. The Royal Naval Hospital deals with an average of six cases of meningitis a year, which is very high indeed. Enteric diseases (colloquially known as disorders of the gut) are also more common in this remnant of empire. The hospital deals with an average of ten to twelve a year.

Why so many seriously upset stomachs and bowels? It does not appear to be due to the rigours of naval service. Naval men point out that only frozen meat can be bought on the Rock; some told me they suspected that meat was not always kept permanently frozen, but was allowed to thaw and was then re-frozen – which would not wipe out any bugs picked up during the thaw.

'I suspect,' I was told, 'that most of the meats we get in the supermarkets have been frozen and defrosted several times. When you put it into the fridge, you are left with a dried-out and tough meat.'

But staff of the Royal Naval Hospital said they did not think this, in itself, was necessarily a direct factor in the high number of gut ailments. Such meat would not do harm if it were cooked properly. Certainly no meat or vegetables should be eaten without rinsing them first in a sterilizing agent like Milton; but it would be unfair to Gibraltar to suggest it was alone in this. This precaution applied to all the Mediterranean countries.

The hospital staff boast that, with modern medicines, the average stay is only a few days compared with the four weeks at the time the empire was at its peak. Nowadays, apart from the enteric diseases, the non-maternity wards of the hospital are turned over to the treating of comparatively minor afflictions like tonsillitis, ear problems and women's ailments.

I was beginning to ask myself how the hospital would cope if suddenly faced with heavy casualties due to real naval action

in the Straits of Gibraltar. It has few resident specialists – a
general physician who is also responsible for paediatrics; one
surgeon responsible for general orthopaedic surgery and ob-
stetrics as well as looking after the maternity ward and
women's ailments; and one anaesthetist. True, they are sup-
ported by three general practitioners – one Navy, one Army
and one R A F. And, when facing really seriously ill patients,
there is always the 'aero-medic evacuation facility' for getting
patients speedily back to the United Kingdom. I was assured
that the hospital was certainly capable of doing, say, a bypass
operation for an artery in a leg.

And in case of a real shooting war, which the Falklands had
proved *could* still happen? 'In that case,' said the support
manager, 'we could call on the resources of the local hospital.'
At such times, presumably, the sensitivities such as are experienced by expectant mothers would no longer be a criterion.

It was obvious that the support manager found living on the
cliff edge of possible trouble a challenge rather than a trial.
'We exercise mass casualties regularly – sometimes twenty at a
time, though even four might warrant local help, because we
have very little fat in the way of staff.'

There is a paging system for all the hospital staff. They can
hear the call at all times except when they are off the Rock or
in one of the thirty miles of tunnels inside it, some used for
defence purposes. The four medical officers also carry short-
wave radios, so that they are in touch virtually all the time.
Unless they make covering arrangements with the local hospital, they can never leave the Rock.

It is a Royal Naval medical assistant who at nine every
morning runs the Union Flag up over the hospital quadrangle.
From here it can be widely seen as an emblem of the British
presence which is just as potent as the presence of the sentries
in front of the regimental headquarters of the Army, in the
very centre of the town. I found this naval medical assistant to
be a bearded twenty-nine-year-old veteran who had just
bought a new car (right-hand drive) and was practising driving

it on the right hand side of the road, which is paradoxically Gibraltar's un-English rule of the road.

His day, he said, always started at eight when he read the signal log and abstracted from it all the messages concerning the hospital: admission and discharge signals, general stores' demands and information about patients. Then he did the Defect Books, which every department kept. Sometimes the defect was, 'Another bit of the wall fell off.' (I later asked other naval men if this was true, and they said it was generally believed that the water used to mix the concrete and cement had contained salt, which was breaking down the walls.)

Generally Gibraltar remains a very popular posting. For a couple of pounds or so, naval men and women can make their vertiginous way up to the 'Top of The Rock' bar by Bland Cable Car (properly known as the Gibraltrar Aerial Ropeway) or stop halfway up the 1,400 feet to see the section of mountain road occupied by the Barbary apes. They can drink whisky or gin which is three per cent stronger in alcohol than in the United Kingdom, and half the price, and watch the waves pounding the rock on the sparsely inhabited east coast. Even if those with no liking for the taste of greased plywood may steer clear of the local swordfish steaks, they can enjoy a xenophobic laugh at the fact that the Spanish do not always know how to make a Spanish omelette. And always they can reflect on how lucky they are not to be up in the snows and ice of Norway, or in the comfortable but unpicturesque routines of Portsmouth or Plymouth.

The Rock is a bright hope for many naval men and women, since it offers many more postings than that other remainder of Empire, Hong Kong; and there seems every possibility that it will continue to be British after Hong Kong has been handed over to the Chinese under the agreement which ends in 1997. Gibraltar will certainly continue to be of crucial importance to a Britain with no bases East of Suez.

Its importance can lead to sensitivity even in peacetime. There are frequent exercises. I was in Gibraltar in the middle of one of the two-year NATO exercises, called Wintex. I was to be shown the Signals Centre, which is jointly run with Lloyd's of London on Windmill Hill, to monitor shipping movements in the area, civilian as well as military. There are something like six thousand ship movements a month to be reported on, of which fifteen are probably Russian warships or auxiliaries and three hundred and fifty are Russian merchant ships.

Alas, my trip to the Signals Centre was abortive. Because of the NATO exercise, I was told, the British Army which was guarding it was rather jumpy. They were turning away from it all those people without special passes – as well as, apparently, some of those *with* special passes. 'We will end up in gaol if we try to get in there, I should think,' my guide told me. 'A civilian face will not be welcome.'

Instead, we tried the Maritime Headquarters and Joint Services Communications Centre in the ground-level tunnels at the very centre of the Rock, where I *was* able to get in after I had been spreadeagled against a wall and searched, and my passport taken as security. The sentry had been taken for a ride by innocent-looking callers during exercises before. It was nice to know that NATO's interests were in such safe hands, and I did eventually get my passport back.

The thirty miles of tunnels inside the Rock, at more than one level, have contact with radio masts on top of the Rock. These, I was told, would not be as easy for an enemy to destroy as they might look. The Maritime Headquarters and Joint Services Communications Centre uses only a limited number of tunnels, most of them created in the Second World War. Visitors are whisked through rather breezily, so sensitive is some of the machinery.

Inside the Rock there is certainly a feeling of safety (no high explosive shell or missile could penetrate), if also one of faint claustrophobia. Nevertheless naval men constantly work out how the enemy could get at them, and make their counter-plans accordingly. In peacetime the worst the occupants of this

strange rabbit warren of wood-sided rock tunnels have to
endure are water leakages through the roofs. It means that,
periodically, rooms have to be taken out of commission while
being sealed. A possible widening of geological faults could be
a worse hazard.

In war, the Flag Officer, Gibraltar, whose NATO des-
ignation is Commander Gibraltar Mediterranean, would
move into a camp-bed in one of the offices inside the Rock. In
peacetime his environment is rather more pleasant. His home
is the Mount, a colonnaded colonial-style mansion high on the
Rock, with magnificent views of the sea, a verandah and a fine
ballroom. There are stables in the grounds. Even his office is in
a building near the dockyard, called the Tower, which is full
of handsome Victorian ironwork. The place was built by an
Army engineer colonel in the late nineteenth century. The
good colonel certainly knew what he was about: the Army's
brigadier on Gibraltar and the RAF's air commander live in
rather less grand premises.

It would be almost too easy, despite the presence of the
governor, for the Flag Officer, Gibraltar, to succumb to
viceregal pretensions. The incumbent at the time of my visit, a
seasoned rear-admiral with a public-school background and
wide command experience in the Royal Navy, told me,
'Personally I have no viceregal feelings; there is, after all, a
governor. I think if you wanted to give yourself airs, you
could.'

The rear-admiral pointed out that originally Gibraltar was a
garrison town totally dependent on the services. Indeed, the
Gibraltarians originally came as camp followers serving the
military.

'But,' added the rear-admiral, who was dressed in a working
woolly pullover that was healthily at odds with the hammered-
copper ashtray and 'Arts and Crafts' cigarette box on his coffee
table, 'that was two hundred and fifty years ago, and things
have changed. It would be wrong for the military to behave in
a viceregal or autocratic manner. No one ever briefed me on

it, but that is certainly my view. I don't think it is a particularly clever view – it is just common sense.'

The Flag Officer said there were no problems on the social and diplomatic side of his activities, which were very important. It was in many ways a classless society in Gibraltar: 'So you just dig in and play as full a part in diplomatic and social life as you can. You don't need to bother about who was what and when. You would be unwise, as Flag Officer, to spend every minute of your time in Spain, making lots of friends there. In the same way, it would be fairly ludicrous if you were completely to ignore the people in government and mix socially only with people who were members of the opposition. You just mix as widely as possible, remembering that the leader of the opposition is the leader of the Transport and General Workers Union here. And a very genial man.'

Much of this particular Flag Officer's two-year stint in Gibraltar had been concerned with the winding down of the British presence in Gibraltar in the form of the abandonment of some of the dockyards. They employed some eight hundred Gibraltarians. It was, said the rear-admiral drily, not included in the normal naval officer's training. The men to be made redundant were Gibraltarians and Moroccans; and the atmosphere at the time of the announcement of London's decision was so sensitive that an ill-judged word or act could have caused a flare-up. There was no alternative work. But in the end, the dockyards were successfully transferred to the Gibraltar Ship Repair Company and jobs had been retained.

'By and large,' said the Flag Officer, 'the problems have been sorted out. But there were lots of times of high blood pressure. One could have made the British government's position difficult here by making silly statements.'

I asked the Flag Officer what would have constituted a silly statement. That the British would still be in Gibraltar in twenty years' time – would that have been silly because it could have been provocative? No, said the Flag Officer, that would *not* have been a silly statement. The reverse would have been.

Not that Gibraltar should be regarded by Britain as a jewel in the crown of the magnitude of India. If Spain became fully integrated into NATO, then Gibraltar could be just as valuable, seen as a NATO base, whether she was still British or not. But he did not see any prospect whatever of Gibraltar not being British for a good number of years.

'I am not prepared to say twenty, thirty, forty or two hundred years,' said the Flag Officer. 'It is not going to happen next year, and it is not going to happen in the next five years.'

Extremely careful speaking? Quite. The flag officer in Gibraltar, in his handsome house or in his office with the sea views, must be constantly aware that – whether he likes it or not – he is a big fish in a small pool. Bombast is *out*, despite any of the temptations that his position can provide. The particular rear-admiral I spoke to was obviously used to VIP treatment. We happened to be returning to the UK on the same plane, and found ourselves sitting side by side. The rear-admiral was invited by the pilot on to the flight deck, and was whisked through the Gatwick customs speedily and in solitary state, in order that he might catch a vital connecting flight. He had boarded the plane last, when the rest of us ordinary mortals were already strapped in. Such treatment, coupled with his status on the Rock itself, could be highly dangerous to a man with colonial pretensions.

The rear-admiral showed no signs of falling into this trap: 'It is such a small place, Gibraltar, that in a way your position is an inflated one. You have to accept this, and accept the responsibility of it being an inflated one in local terms. A rear-admiral is not so very important anywhere, really; but if he is important anywhere, he is in Gibraltar, and he has to accept the responsibility of that.'

The rear-admiral was plainly more concerned with his military responsibilities: defending the 'choke point' of the Black Sea.

Fortunately or unfortunately, the casual visitor to Gibraltar cannot see tangible evidence of how this would be done. All the guns on view are from the Battle of Trafalgar or some similar event; not so much as a modern hand-grenade presents itself to the casual view. This, I was told, was deceptive. The Flag Officer himself took up the point. The Straits, he said, were no longer dominated as in the past by big guns.

'We have more modern ways of doing it,' he assured me. 'There is air power, there are missiles which can be fired from here. I am not in any doubt that the Straits could be shut off in an emergency. In peacetime, Russian ships come in and out of here and we have no right to stop them. Even in a period of tension we would have no right – but if it came to war, we would stop them.'

There is a paradox. The Navy, while acting on the assumption that Gibraltar is going to continue to be Britain's and NATO's, is also active in helping the 30,000 local population to outgrow their former total dependence on the armed services. It is represented on the Development and Planning Committee, a part of the Rock's government which meets weekly to consider future projects. It has been specially helpful to the Gibraltar government in advising and assisting on pollution problems.

Such assistance helps to keep the Gibraltarians thinking British. Not that they seem to need much encouragement: a month after the Spanish frontier was re-opened for vehicular traffic as well as pedestrians, the local newspapers were still publishing leading articles warning of the dangers of this crafty 'soft' new move by the Spanish, and claiming it was more dangerous than the former intransigence. I had no doubt such leaders would continue for months or years.

But as far as the Royal Navy was concerned, the opening of the border was the signal for friendly gestures to the Spanish, especially in terms of sport. Spaniards came over to play a Royal Naval football team and there were schools and ladies matches between the Navy and the Spanish, with the Navy sometimes part of a local Gibraltar team.

The Navy's skill at football and at sport generally on

Gibraltar is understandable. A chief physical training instructor at the shore establishment HMS *Rooke*, a small slender man pulsating with bright-eyed energy, told me, 'Before the border was opened, sport was the main recreational outlet here. Now obviously we travel across into southern Spain, so weekend sport has gone down, but during the week we still play as much as we ever did. The guy plays football at least three times a week. He would play for his department and perhaps a social game for his club or pub. Football is the biggest sport out here, the others being road-running and squash.'

At the time of my visit, the Navy was playing grass rugby on a nearby Spanish polo pitch. Before the opening of the border, they had had to play on a hard pitch outside HMS *Rooke*. For this the Navy evolved their own sort of rugby, called 'Tag' rugby. It is unique to Gibraltar, I heard from the chief physical training instructor without surprise. It involves carrying nylon tags in players' pockets, which are pulled out by the opposition in what is more like a game of 'Touch'.

'Tag rugby was the big one before the border re-opened,' said the instructor.

But since the re-opening, the Spaniards had shown they were interested in making sporting and other contacts. Road-running versus the Spanish was especially popular, said the chief instructor: Spanish runners had come across to Gibraltar and naval runners had gone across to southern Spain. He didn't see any danger of whipping up competitive nationalistic tensions by such contests. There was a Gibraltar tradition that, though Gibraltar played the Navy, Navy *and* Gibraltar men were also mixed up in the same team for other matches. It was possible this idea would develop with the Spanish.

Sport is behind one curious fact of Gibraltarian life; it is a community for slimming. Because sport facilities are so near to hand (on tiny Gibraltar, by definition *everything* is close to hand) it is easy to put on running shorts or play football or cricket. Men tend to find no difficulty with the periodic physical fitness tests they are obliged to undergo. Some arrive at

Gibraltar two or three stone overweight, but within a few weeks are back to average. The chief instructor insisted that even if the number of calories taken in were not reduced a bout of football and running would lose the unwanted pounds.

Nevertheless naval men and women are warned on Gibraltar about calories – especially the calories acquired through alcohol. There is a temptation for some people, faced with an inevitably limited environment, to take to the bottle.

The chief instructor agreed. 'Drink is readily available here, and is cheap. We tell them that, out here, they can go one way or the other – you can drink and go down that way, or you can play sport and go up, and still enjoy yourself.'

But though the moral pressure on naval personnel in Gibraltar to take part in sport must be immense, the pressure is unofficial. 'Only in training ships do we have formal PT,' the chief instructor told me. 'Once you get into the Fleet or a shore establishment, everything is voluntary. It is very different from the Army, who have to take a certain amount of physical exercise every week. Sport in the Navy is very low-key in that sense, job-wise. Sport plays a big part, but it is more a recreational activity. We used to have people doing physical training round the deck at 7.30 in the morning, but that has gone now. We instructors are not like physical training instructors used to be, when we had to have muscles growing out of our ears. We have to do lots of other things, like administering a wide range of informal sporting activities.'

The sporting atmosphere of the Rock does not obscure, in the minds of intelligent naval men and women, the reason why they are on the Rock. Even forgetting the commitment to NATO, there is a high awareness that a Spanish government that ran into severe domestic problems might be tempted to distract attention by trying the same thing on Gibraltar as the Argentinians tried on the Falklands.

Sportsmen and women they may be, but naval people on Gibraltar know that the one thing they are *not* doing is shadowboxing. As they eat their swordfish steaks in the Copacabana Bar, or more British fare in the grill-room just a few palm trees up Main Street, they know the price may one day have to be paid in action against a real enemy.

So far, however, they find little evidence that the Barbary apes, and with them the Royal Navy, will be leaving this little kaleidoscope of cultures that is a still colourful leftover of the days of the great British Empire.

But for most naval men, Gibraltar, whether they are posted there or visiting it, can be only an interlude. Much of their lives will be spent at sea in perhaps rather more gruelling circumstances on or below the waves.

6

NUCLEAR AND OTHER SUBMARINERS

'One doesn't actually feel, "We have this terrific fire power." That doesn't impinge on our thoughts. To retain the deterrent has significance, so has being an arm of peace. From some people the great cry is that we are here to kill the world. We are not. We are here to keep the peace, and we do it. The fact that we have those missiles aft is merely the way we keep the peace.'

– Comanding officer, Polaris nuclear-missile-carrying submarine.

'If you contact an enemy submarine at close range, and you are in your pyjamas, you can't very well fight the boat in your pyjamas. It is not the thing. I don't think a commanding officer fighting a submarine in his silk dressing-gown would be the right thing, either. I *never* wear pyjamas.'

– Commanding officer, Fleet hunter-killer submarine.

'There are only two sorts of ships – submarines and targets.'

– Fleet chief petty officer on Fleet hunter-killer submarine.

Just £1 a day. That, said the straight-faced commanding officer

of the Polaris submarine, which had the power to eliminate
sixteen Russian cities or other targets with that many 2,500
mile-range nuclear missiles, was what he got paid extra, on top
of his rate for the rank of commander, for the privilege of
nuclear command.

It was not, I suggested, very much for being the leader of
160 men who have to spend over eighty days continuously
submerged beneath the surface, drinking processed sea-water,
breathing reconstituted air and having their bodies' excreta
shredded into an unrevealing sludge before being dumped into
waters in which an equally lethal enemy could lurk.

The commanding officer was a slight and wiry commander
of forty, who had first volunteered for the Royal Navy's
submarines eighteen years previously. He brushed the question
aside with the briskness of a man who perhaps found civilian
values tainted; who certainly had long ago rationalized every
aspect of his role as a deterrent which would continue to
succeed as long as it continued to be unused.

'It is not a very large sum, certainly,' he said crisply. 'But I
am against pay structures where you get much more pay for
doing a specific job, over which you have no control – and
when I take up command and when I relinquish command is
not under my control. I would not want a system where, on
relinquishing command, I would lose a large proportion of
pay.' Good, convenient thinking.

The commanding officer agreed with me that he was by
temperament an inner-centred person. His answer certainly
struck me as a good example of the cool, careful, calculating
and self-contained reasoning required of the submariner in
general and Polaris nuclear submariners in particular. Submarines are made to lurk unseen. Submariners get their £100
or so extra a month, over and above their surface colleagues'
pay, for their ability to live ungrumblingly in a little closed
world for weeks or months, and to keep their mouths shut
about it once they have stepped back into the larger world.

Prima donnas, their irritated rivals in the surface Navy call them. 'Skimmers!' the submariners are apt to reply, adding provocative comments like, 'Happiness is being four hundred feet *under* water in a full gale.'

Prima donnas they may be on occasion. But it would be rather more true to say, as I discovered on the Polaris submarine, on nuclear-powered attack submarines and on the old type of diesel submarines, that submariners are sailors, only more so. Every sailor has to live a self-contained life in a small universe for much of his time. There is even less room for shallow exhibitionism and dependent behaviour among submariners. Wherever they are among the four submarine squadrons – the First Squadron based at HMS *Dolphin* at Gosport, consisting of diesel submarines; the Second Squadron based at Devonport, with its nuclear-powered hunter-killers; the Third Squadron at Faslane in Scotland, with a mixture of diesel and nuclear-powered boats and the Tenth Squadron (no intervening numbers thanks to some obscure Naval idiosyncrasy) with its four nuclear-powered, nuclear-missile-carrying Polaris submarines – they are trained to be, and *expected* to be, men of singular deliberation.

Men, in short, who can withstand physical and mental pressure and can put a positive construction (like the commanding officer of the Polaris submarine on the subject of his small extra pay) on their lives and work.

I was still outside the gates of the Clyde Submarine Base at Faslane, in Scotland, a mountain-surrounded loch near Glasgow where the four Polaris submarines – *Repulse*, *Renown*, *Resolution* and *Revenge* – are based, when I began to get a clear idea of some of the pressures. A 'peace camp' of caravans, painted with blue and pink murals, overlooked the base from a nearby hill – a constant reproach from those whose morality is based on different assumptions from the submariners', but is as firmly held. The perimeter fencing, with its topping of barbed wire, was often cut by the campers, I was told; but so far no one had penetrated further.

As I went through the security measures standing between

any human being and a Polaris submarine, I could easily see why. The policing, the complicated system of different passes and badges, the fences, the blockhouses and the fact that in certain circumstances one could convert oneself into the equivalent of a target at a rifle range – all these dark necessities remind a visiting civilian of the importance of Polaris in the deterrence of rash aggressive action against Britain.

The submarine itself was another reminder, a 7,500-ton, 425-foot-long black shark largely concealed while at rest, as if basking in comparative tranquillity. Smoke coming from the black fin around the conning tower revealed that the boat (submariners get as angry about having their craft called ships as a surface man would be to have his craft described as a boat) was being got ready for another submerged patrol of eighty days or more. But the exact date of departure was as yet unknown to anyone on board: the world of Polaris is a secret one, resting on the need-to-know principle, and the necessity to remain undetected by foe *or friend* in all, or almost all, circumstances.

I stood on the quay with the boat's executive officer, the lieutenant-commander who was second in command, while he pointed out the chief features of the Polaris submarine. 'We will be on the middle deck, and we will be under water even when she is alongside. Its draught is only twenty-eight feet six inches of water.'

Was this modest draught with or without the missiles aboard?

'I cannot answer that.'

With the first question we were straight into the covert complexities of life on Polaris; and so it went on as I saw more of the boat and of the men. Sometimes it seemed rather like one of those radio-parlour games in which one side tries to get the other to say certain words and the other side tries not to – except that, in this case, the results of the game could conceivably be a matter of life or death.

'All I can say,' said the first lieutenant, 'is that water is used as a ballast when the armaments aren't on. Most of the for'ard of the boat isn't pressurized. At fore and aft, the form is shaped to make it easier to go through the water. The fin around the conning tower is separate from the body – it is just a shell to make progress through the water easier.'

Two enormous flipper-like protrusions were visible, one on each side of the top of the for'ard section. These were the foreplanes which helped control depth. The aft ones, said the first lieutenant, were always invisible under the water. So were the six torpedo tubes, which are Polaris's second armament. The length of the submarine was basically divided into three – for'ard was the operations room and the accommodation; centrally placed were the sixteen vertical tubes holding the nuclear missiles, and aft was the nuclear-reactor compartment which provided the power, and the machinery that transmitted it.

It was certainly a formidable and ominous box of tricks. The resemblance to a great living killer shark was heightened by the black rubber acoustic tiles that had been added during the last of the periodic refits, and which now made up what looked like a scaly, living skin.

Especially in enhanced security states for one reason or another (and they are common in the age of politically inspired direct action and terrorism) the average civilian might well assume Polaris and its precinct to be a cradle for paranoia. In fact Polaris submariners tend always to be coolly matter-of-fact, anxious to establish that their conditions of work are in many respects *better* than in other types of submarine.

I went on to the matt black non-slip upper casing of the Polaris submarine and then down the vertical metal ladders leading to the middle deck. (They *did* seem not quite so pinched and alarming as on smaller submarines.) The first lieutenant showed me his cabin. It was shared with another lieutenant-commander, and doubled up as a weapons engineering office. It was perhaps six feet by six feet. The two bunks, when in position, were practically as close as two pieces of bread making

up a ham sandwich. The wash-basin was underneath a tiny
hinged desk. The wardrobe was the size of a small refrigerator.

The first lieutenant smiled his ruddy-cheeked approval.
'Compared with any other submarine, this is palatial.
Compared with almost anyone else's accommodation on board
this or any other submarine, it is palatial. Some surface ships
are no better – but I am not here to talk about surface ships.
Everyone but the top four officers on the submarine does duty
as watch-keeper, but we don't have anyone in hot bunks –
bunks in which, when one man coming on duty gets out,
another man coming off duty gets in. We do have a few
camp-beds, mostly for juniors or people visiting, like yourself.
Permanent numbers will get a bunk and locker, even though
the rating's locker is perhaps smaller than a railway station
locker.'

I admired the chintz covering of the bunks and the single
chair. Well, said the first lieutenant, if you just happened to be
aboard when the upholsterer came, you could ask for what
you wanted. 'But,' he added, as if I had questioned his submariner's puritanism, 'it will have to last until it is worn out.'
And there was a Tannoy system in the cabin, which operated
at any hour of the day or night.

Against these negative factors was the fact that the cabin led
off a passageway instead of being directly off the wardroom,
as in many smaller submarines. The wardroom itself, walled in
light woods and upholstered in chintz, had various silver
trophies in a glass-fronted cupboard, bronze and chromium
wall lights and a silver plate used at the Battle of Trafalgar,
aboard the namesake of the Polaris submarine I was joining.
There were also four miniature water-colours painted by a
friend of the captain's.

I was not surprised to discover that the officers always
dressed for dinner, with tropical shirt, black trousers and
cummerbund. Possibly there would be a compromise with
normal naval dress protocol – sandals, which kept the feet
fresher, but which are not worn in the operations or mechanics

sections of the submarine, where a steel-tipped boot is needed to protect the toes and a non-slip sole is needed to prevent breakages of limbs against the surrounding metalwork.

Dress aboard such a submarine has very much to do with safety as well as morale. The general lessons of the Falklands campaign have filtered through. White shirts reflect flash burns, and cotton white shirts do not, like nylon, melt on to the skin in fires. Some men were walking about in blue overalls and some in green ones. The material was in the course of being changed to the new (blue) material; but, at that time, there had been a shortage of the new material, and so some men were still wearing the original green.

In many things, the life of Polaris aims at least for an approximation to equality. At one point I found myself having to clamber over an enormous pile of frozen legs of lamb. They had just been brought aboard in preparation for the next two-month patrol. I wondered whether they were for officers, while the rest of the crew had to be content with mince or sausages. Not a bit of it, I was quickly told. The officers ate the same meals as the men – three or four choices, on a menu which was typed out afresh every day.

Food can be the flash-point of resentment in the Navy as a whole; under water it can be an enhanced source of trouble because the world is a confined one dominated (in the aspect of living conditions) by small considerations. In a submarine that must stay below the surface for over eighty days and avoid all contact with other ships, it could be explosive. There is an attempt to normalize the delights of the dining-table, but it is inevitably incomplete. Joints of meat are boned, so there are no bones to dispose of in the potentially cover-blowing waste, and so there is less weight to carry in the first place. Milk is mostly 'Long Life'. Lettuces are 'Icebergs' which, if wrapped in foil, will stay fresh for almost the whole of a patrol. Potatoes come aboard in paper bags which must be turned over periodically so the air can circulate; otherwise the potatoes at the bottom of the pile will rot.

The disposal of the waste can never be what the average civilian would regard as remotely normal. To maintain its ability to discharge its sixteen nuclear missiles at any time, Polaris must remain undetected by *everyone*; and, to make sure of this, the boat has an appointed dustman whose job is both specialized and responsible. He puts an assortment of waste into a hydraulic press, which reduces it to a large solid block. This is ejected through a tube at the bottom of the submarine and sinks to the bottom of the sea, where it will be undetected. He has to be careful to soak cardboard in water and compact it with heavier materials, or the result might float around and give away the presence of Polaris. Solid sewage is chopped up by machine and sent out through the same tube as an anonymous sludge.

Polaris must be highly self-monitoring, and so must its commanding officer and crew. The most normal human wish could, if thoughtlessly indulged, betray the position of the boat and therefore destroy its deterrent value – which is that it could, if Britain came under attack, decimate sixteen enemy targets without putting itself in danger.

I asked the commanding officer whether there was a difference in human strain between life aboard Polaris submarines and others. The commander was candid. 'Yes, there is really. The job of a hunter-killer submarine, for instance, is to detect others – he is in an aggressive posture. We operate in the opposite sense, remaining hidden; and the strain, in so far as our Polaris patrolling is concerned, is to remain undetected. We know that as time goes by, clearly the chances of detection increase with the increased Soviet presence around the world. And nobody wants to be the first one to be detected. That does place a certain strain on the ship's company, particularly those involved in the sonar world, and the officers. It is not something that makes one's life miserable. We *do* retain the advantage, and it is our job to make sure we keep that advantage.'

I found the commander's answer revealing in a way I was to

find answers further down the professional scale revealing. It was the answer of a man to whom *professional* criteria came first: even in the shadow of nuclear power, submariners tend to think first of the job *as* a job rather than as a source of human risk. Careerism can co-exist with sixteen nuclear missiles in the hull, their vertical containers neatly painted white with bright ominous red numbering – rather like magnified launderette spin-driers.

The human mind aboard a Polaris submarine must be more capable than the average of compartmentalization, of shutting out unpalatable thoughts that can have no value in a duty that is seen to be essentially *anti*-war.

I asked the commander what he and the crew thought about being alongside so much firepower. 'I don't think people regard it in that way; it is a professional job they have to do,' he replied. 'Of course we all wish that it will never be used. Indeed most of us – those that think at all about it – understand that that hope is increased by us doing our job. They know that deterrence does work. No one can gainsay that. The fact remains that, because of the nuclear deterrent, we have remained at peace for the last forty years. There is a professional pride in doing it.'

The natural assumption would be that, however necessary, the command of a Polaris submarine would be a very lonely command indeed. It is the commanding officer who keeps the boat's narrative, which is kept in a safe. It is the commanding officer who knows first when the boat is leaving – other people do not know until forty-eight hours before departure, and are not told when they will be back until the boat is already at sea. It is the commanding officer who would have to take the first steps towards firing the nuclear messengers of death in accordance with his secret orders.

But the commanding officer assured me that command was not a lonely business. It was, he said, less lonely than it would be on a surface ship. This was despite the fact that, when Polaris is at sea, she receives radio messages but transmits absolutely nothing in order to remain undetectable, thus preventing the commanding officer from soliciting advice.

'I have many friends who drive surface ships whose commands are much more lonely,' said the commander, whose slight comfortable paunch did not suggest a deeply worried man. 'Basically the shape of the submarine makes it not a lonely place to live, so the loneliness of command does not really become paramount. Plus the fact that we operate with a second-in-command. He and I often share the responsibility of day-to-day decisions, and I may give him the submarine completely, to do with as he wishes.'

In surface ships, the captain almost always eats alone. On the Polaris submarines, the commanding officer eats all meals except breakfast in the wardroom with the other officers, where any incipient resemblances to Captain Bligh of the *Bounty* or Captain Queeg of *The Caine Mutiny* would be readily detectable and perhaps corrected before disaster struck. Captains of Polaris submarines with their fingers on the nuclear button, were not, I was assured, lonely men unless they wanted to be. And the strains of long periods at sea in general were well known by every man aboard.

Other officers and ratings bore this out. They said there was a period ashore when they were bursting to get to sea to do their real job (each Polaris submarine has two crews, one aboard and the other standing down at the Clyde Submarine Base). Then, for the first fortnight on patrol, they were either experiencing a sense of newness or settling down. Then there was a period of flatness after the third week, when it was realized that the newness had worn off, and yet there was still a longer time to go than had already gone. This period was known as 'Patrol Blues' time, when the video films, interdepartmental competitions and professional training or swotting for examinations seemed to pall a little. Then there was the last two or three weeks of the patrol, when spirits rose again and anticipation ran high.

It is strange but true that officers and ratings like life in

Polaris submarines because it is actually more *predictable* in peacetime. Times for leave and times for return from leave are known up to a year in advance, an unheard-of luxury in any armed service. True, the actual date of *sailing* is rigidly kept secret until forty-eight hours beforehand; but men and families know when they are going to say goodbye to their loved ones and roughly when they are going to see them again. Since the Polaris submarines were introduced in the late 1960s, the occasions they have not kept to their timetable have been reputedly few.

While at sea the various moods of the Polaris submariner's life are inevitably agitated by the knowledge that he can in no circumstances send a message home. But they are soothed by a piece of paper which arrives for him every week, containing up to forty words written in printed rectangles. This is the 'Familygram', the radio message which a Polaris submarine can receive, but not acknowledge. It is the psychological lifeline for the human beings inside the submarine. Some decline it, preferring not to be put in the position of having news from home to which they cannot respond. Every man can tell the commanding officer, in advance, whether he wants to be told bad news from home at once, or have it held back until just before the ship returns, when he can conceivably *do* something about the situation.

One rating in his early twenties told me that if Familygrams didn't arrive on time, some people could go into a black mood. 'You just fall out with people for a few days. You get on each other's nerves about silly things – people spilling beer on another person accidentally. But you forgive and forget – you have to.'

Another rating, a twenty-six-year-old leading engineer, said he never put decorations, or pictures of his wife or four-year-old daughter, up by his bunk. He preferred to forget everything ashore. 'I tell my wife that,' he said. 'Her reaction? Nothing, really. She just says she will wait for me. Aboard you work out how far you are through your days away, to get through it. You mustn't think of two months at sea all at once, you must chop it up in your mind. But there are times when you *do* think of ashore, despite trying not to. On birthdays and things like that, you just get a mood. You go and get some beer cans and everyone buys you one. You are allowed three cans a day but you can have more than three on your birthday. If you overstep the mark, they will come down on you.'

This rating said he had never encountered any drunkenness aboard a Polaris submarine. It was a relief for a civilian to hear that. A man's drinking habits, I was told, were clearly visible aboard a submarine and prompt action would be taken if they were excessive. On a different boat, said the rating, he had known one man to get a Familygram revealing that his wife had left him: he had taken to drinking round the clock, until finally his canteen account was closed and the three men who manned the bar were told not to serve him.

Medical problems are a different matter. Vigilance cannot prevent all of them. And the stark fact is that, unless it is to save a life which otherwise could not be saved, the commanding officer of a Polaris will not change course or come to the surface to put the man ashore, thus revealing his position.

Fortunately afflictions are usually minor. 'Like mouth ulcers and spots,' the boat's doctor, a surgeon-lieutenant, told me in his minute sick-bay, with space for only two sick men. 'Constipation is a big problem. People tend to eat less fibre and so get bunged up. We try very hard to encourage a reasonable diet. At the moment, we are trying to encourage an amount of fibre, but it is very difficult. We are probably going to get some additive to put in the bread.'

The medical assistant, a dour Scot, put in: 'The only way at the moment that people can get their roughage is by cereals, and where do you get the extra milk for that?'

Small wonder that regular exercise is urged. It also helps solve another Polaris problem: being overweight. The doctor told me that any officer or rating who went much above the standard ideal weight assessed by life assurance companies would be ordered to get it off, and would be taken out of submarines if he did not manage it. All the same, he would expect about one in ten men to be overweight on any boat at the start of patrol. His medical assistant said that people tended to rush about dieting or to spend all their time eating: it was usually one or other of the two extremes.

Such concerns may help take the medicos' minds off the main fear: major casualties. 'It is just a nightmare, that thought,' said the doctor, 'but my problem in dealing with casualties would be the least of the problems if it came to that.'

Normally problems tend to be small. And they come one by one. The doctor could remember only one case of a man being put ashore from patrol: he had a brain haemorrhage. In wartime he could not have been evacuated, and would have had to take his chance. Most common surgical conditions are regarded as amenable to treatment without an operation. If a man has appendicitis, the normal routine is to administer drugs which will shrink the inflamed appendix down to a scar, which can be removed ashore later. One man had his finger chopped off in a chip-making machine; the severed portion could not be found amongst the raw chips, so the protruding bone was removed and the skin sewn over the tip under local anaesthetic. Another man had a twisted testicle, which was untwisted, also under local anaesthetic. General anaesthetic is not used: the doctor is the only professionally qualified medical man aboard, and when general anaesthetic is used, it is thought necessary to have a trained anaesthetist as well.

'But here you do at least have a sick-bay, which you don't on a hunter-killer type of submarine,' said the doctor. 'I was sleeping in the torpedo compartments of my last non–Polaris submarine. It was standard procedure, because they were so short of accommodation.'

I asked the doctor if he ever took stock, as a medical man, of the possible effect of Polaris on an enemy. He said it did not worry him at all, and turned the conversation on to the positive side in the usual way of all Polaris submariners by adding, 'It is *safe* aboard for all of us. There is less radiation in the boat, dived, than there is on the surface on a sunny day. And if it does go bang, there is no point in worrying about it.'

What about at the psychiatric level? Very few problems really, said the doctor promptly.

'People just get fed up,' he said. 'There is a stage that people go through – they find incredible things wrong with their bodies, little lumps that have been there twenty years. They pick round and feel. But I am not aware of any major psychiatric problems. If there is trouble, it is usually through the non-arrival of the Familygrams. I have seen people reduced to tears by that.'

The medical assistant chipped in again: 'Young lads, when they first join, do think about the nuclear weapons, but once they realize the improbability of shooting one off, though it is *possible*, they feel better about it. People tend to realize that, if we had to shoot one off, we might as well head for Australia, if we could. Some people do dwell on it a little bit, but most of them accept it. Very, very rarely do people say, "Take me off it." I *have* seen it happen – once last Christmas while we were ashore. The doctor just gave the man a sedative and let him go home, and after a few days he was fine.'

It is not usually the grinding of teeth that is the welfare problem, but the filling of teeth. The medical assistant told me he had had precisely three days on a dentistry course 'and the rest is experience over the past five years'. Men were given local anaesthetic for the extraction of teeth. They were given no anaesthetic at all for fillings, because all he did was 'clean it up a bit and put in a temporary filling, which lasts three or four days at a time or until we get alongside. You aren't actually drilling any further into the teeth.' All the same, I was not surprised to hear that having teeth filled was not a popular pastime; or that Polaris submarines had now adopted the system of putting a dental surgeon and an assistant aboard the day before the submarine was due back in port, so that escape was impossible.

On Polaris, mundane routines familiar or at least comprehensible to a civilian alternate with the need for absolute alertness which few civilians can imagine. I had not expected the usual Royal Navy practice, of leaving the first examination of the sonar screens at any given moment to the most junior of seamen – those perhaps aged no more than seventeen and a half – would apply to Polaris.

But it did. In the sonar room of the submarine I was aboard, I asked a twenty-four-year-old petty officer who had been seven years on Polaris whether being the first visual contact with approaching ships or other objects had made him nervous in his younger days.

'A bit nervous at first,' he confessed. 'You sit at a set and have the ability to recognize when a target comes up. Behind the background noise, it is difficult at first. Then you start to realize what you are looking for actually looks like, and you get a bit more confidence in yourself as the patrol goes on. Then you have to guard against over-confidence. One day you are asking the opinion of someone else when it isn't necessary and the next day you might just sit there and disregard something which turns out to be an attack.'

Paradoxically it is only when young Polaris sonar operators are relatively experienced that it really occurs to them that their careers may be on the line, depending on what they see or don't see on the sonar screen. Until then, the petty officer or officer above them tends to check and double-check on them. It is only later that their judgement is relied upon without being checked, and it occurs to them that their judgement could make or mar their careers.

I asked the petty officer of the sonar room whether spotting a specifically Russian ship increased the tension. 'Yes, you increase your awareness of what is on the trace. You look more intensely at it. You look into everything when it could be a contact; otherwise you look at it and say something to your mate and then look back again. Once you feel you have got something, you concentrate more on the job you are doing.'

In such a case the Polaris boat turns *away* from the Russian, to escape detection – just as it would do if the ship above were a French or even a British one. The prime priority is to remain undetected at all times, and no gung-ho desire to get a closer look at Ruskie will be allowed to compromise this absolute necessity. A particular Polaris submarine *could* be the only one on deterrent patrol with the capacity for horrific retaliation (there is *always* at least one operational on patrol) and the credibility of the deterrent would be compromised if it were detectable and detected.

In a sense Polaris enjoys an ability unique in battle: the ability to turn and run *honourably*. This, and the higher pay, makes it more attractive than surface ships to many ratings, some of whom have volunteered for submarines and some of whom have been drafted in despite any lingering reservations about the possibility of firing off nuclear missiles.

One rating told me that he arrived on Polaris by natural progression: 'I have always loved the sea and always loved messing about in boats. The Navy was a natural progression from that. Then I thought – submarines! Get under water, less sea-sickness and out of the way! You can hide better under water than you can on the surface, and if you can't be found, you can't be attacked. It was secure, I reckoned. The fact that we are trained to get out of the way makes it feel more safe.'

A strange sort of life, indeed – feeling safe and secure within a few feet of sixteen tubes containing enough destructive power to wipe out a decisive slice of a nation or nations. Maintaining a sense of the realities must be difficult among the small cares of daily life; a life which becomes so circumscribed that, on coming home, every crew member has to wait forty-eight hours before driving a car because his sense of long vision has gone; and, if he is diplomatic, the same time before trying to discuss serious domestic matters with his wife and children, because his adjustment to them (or to any other sort of outside person) has become eroded.

The Royal Navy knows this, and keeps crew members of

Polaris submarines busy with periods at watch, drills, exercises and off-duty entertainments. But the commanding officer does not do watch duties. He has deliberately been freed of much day-to-day work, unlike his American counterparts two lochs up from Faslane, who concern themselves with more detail.

The effect on commanding officers is curious. They might have too much time for private thoughts and perhaps private fears and doubts, if boredom was ever allowed to set in. They are aware of this fact themselves, as is the Navy. The commanding officer of the Polaris submarine I was on told me over lunch in the wardroom (more chintz upholstery) that in his spare time he was writing his first novel, which would be about naval life. And when I came ashore and spoke to the commanding officer of the alternative crew, it turned out that he was a student at the Open University: 'I have one degree already, and I am now doing a science course. You can arrange to get ahead with some work, and then catch up when you get back. Most commanding officers have other interests. Perhaps it is model-making, painting or serious reading, but they have *something.*'

This commanding officer of the stand-down crew, a commander who looked as if he were made of thin steel, admitted it was quite a shock, after two months of spare-time study in monastic separation from the cares of the ordinary world, to come ashore to everyday realities: 'Having to think about money again, for instance. For two months or so, you don't think about money at all. No need to. And the car. If it breaks down, either your wife fixes it, or she is without a car for two months. Ashore, you focus your mind on all these things again.'

Such a compartmentalized life might be thought to carry with it the prospect of schizophrenia. Such is the durability of the trained human organism in the face of understood pressures that it almost never happens. The Clyde Submarine Base does not apologize for its main purpose. It has an illuminated white and black painted Polaris missile on a plinth within its wire fences, visible to the 'peace campers' in their quaintly painted caravans high on the adjoining hill. Whether the conspicuous public display of an instrument (necessary or not) that can take millions of lives is a sensitive or politic act must be a matter of opinion. The opinion of officers and men aboard Polaris who I spoke to about the peace camp and its philosophy was represented succinctly by a senior officer I met ashore.

I had asked him what his personal feelings were on the subject. I got this answer: 'I am quite happy that in our society people who don't agree with something can state their objections, though I have difficulty with the way some of them go about it, disrupting my sailors' lives when the sailors themselves have no opportunity to respond. They cut the perimeter fence and that sort of thing. As for ratings themselves, I have heard of one or two who don't approve of Polaris and have moved out. We are not a completely voluntary force, and I believe that, if someone has a strong view against nuclear weapons, he should not be in the Navy at all.'

Such fringe nuclear compunctions need not concern the Royal Navy's second sort of submarine: the rather smaller hunter-killers that are nuclear *powered* but do not carry the enormous destructive power of Polaris. Only a rating committed to the Greenpeace philosophy of turning a hopeful back on nuclear power as a whole could be worried by life aboard one of these so-called Fleet submarines.

There are fifteen, all about 4,200 tons, 272 feet in length, with a complement of around one hundred and twenty, and an armament of homing torpedoes that can be used to attack other submarines or surface craft. These Fleet type submarines are divided into the 'Valiant', 'Churchill', 'Swiftsure' and 'Trafalgar' classes. Life aboard them resembles that on the Polaris submarines in some respects: the long contact with a closed world beneath the sea, the difficulty of finding sufficient occupations to fill the few free hours, the uncertainty about what is happening to relatives ashore, the absolute need for compartmentalizing the mind so that thoughts about discontinued human relationships do not invade and sap professional morale.

To all these factors must be added another which does not apply to the Polaris submarines: unpredictability about how long the boat will be at sea. I went aboard one of the older, 'Churchill' class boats – the *Churchill* itself – and spoke to the commanding officer in his six feet by six feet cabin. The picture of the Queen proclaimed patriotic sentiment; the sharply curving ceiling proclaimed that I was on a rather more confined boat than Polaris.

The idea, said the commander, was that after their time in base, the hunter-killer submarines would go on patrol and assume the posture they would do in war, which would be principally to hunt down enemy submarines. Usually it was a question of two or three weeks at sea. But this had never been certain and was even less so after the Falklands crisis.

'We were away ninety days when we went to the South Atlantic, including one stand-off in San Carlos Water,' said the commander. 'But that was split up; otherwise, on ninety days of patrol, it is difficult to maintain morale and achieve effectiveness. We were submerged all the way – 8,000 miles – which was faster and more comfortable and we were at the most economical speed most of the way. There is a speed at which you start burning up the nuclear reactor if you go above it.'

The position of the hunter-killer submarines is not automatically kept secret from crew members, as it may be in Polaris. People looked at the compass and guessed anyway, said the commander. There were six-hour watches. Normally, at the end of his watch, the officer of the watch would give a six-sentence speech to the new watch on where the boat was, what it was doing at the moment and what it would be doing during the next six hours. The boat was freer to broadcast than Polaris submarines, but tried not to.

I asked the commander if his orders allowed him to divert in case of sickness in the crew, a thing which Polaris submarines will not do, even in peacetime.

'I would have to divert,' said the commander. 'We don't carry a doctor, only a chief petty officer with some medical training, so what we have really is a complicated first-aid ability. A broken wrist would get an elastic covering and pain-killers. For anything serious I would have to divert. It would be nasty if it happened at the Equator on the way to the Falklands, but the decision would depend upon the degree of urgency.'

Perhaps human equability aboard Fleet submarines is greatly helped by the habit of splitting up long periods away from home into smaller sections if possible. This is done on most operations, whether winding-up after refits or going down to the Falklands and back. On the ninety-day Falklands round trip, it is usually found possible to arrange a short time ashore on the Falklands. This effectively breaks the patrol up into two forty-five day sections. Sometimes these sections are sub-divided into smaller sections, when the crew are given specific objectives, whether mock firings of torpedoes or crossing-the-line ceremonies when going across the Equator.

'The highlight of our last trip,' said the commander, 'was visiting San Carlos. We visited a soldier in a foxhole with water up to his waist, and shared a cup of tea with him.'

No doubt such contacts are salutary in their effect on the Fleet submarine crews: someone is always worse off than one-self. This is a fact that has to be borne always in mind. Even the level-headed commanding officer admitted that, after ninety days at sea, during which he had bumped against the solitary chair in his cabin every time he wanted to look for something, he had 'frankly come to *hate* that chair'. And even the thought that in a smaller conventional diesel submarine your head at night had to rest in a recess in the cabin wall sometimes did not seem sufficient solace.

Perhaps a sense of humour was the saving grace? Possibly, thought the commander. 'When you are long at sea, the more simple, the more childish your sense of humour becomes. And one flares up more easily. You find yourself laughing much longer than you would normally have done at a simple joke.'

He had also noticed that, on the occasional long trips, one's horizons became more limited. This could be beneficial in some ways. Inhibitions about public opinion, which could hold one back ashore, tended to recede. He himself read a lot, but one of his officers had taken to knitting on long trips. The officer didn't acknowledge that other people were there, just carried on knitting: 'I thought him very brave, knitting in front of the troops, so to speak.'

Most civilians compelled to share the hot-bunking routine of Fleet submarines, slipping into a warm bunk just vacated by someone else leaving to do his watch duty, would probably take to behaviour much worse than knitting. 'Iniquitous system!' said the commander. It was mostly junior ranks who had to do it, but not totally. Any officer additional to the boat's complement, who had to come aboard for special reasons, had to sleep with the ship's company in the for'ard compartments – the 'Fore-end Hilton', as it was sometimes called.

The commanding officer, and some of the crew, had found that getting through one's duties could be easier if one's sleep was split in sections, like the periods aboard. The theory was that three meals a day was too much, so that at lunchtime you didn't eat; you retired to your bunk and had a sleep. That enabled you to stay up all night on duty if necessary. The commanding officer himself said he didn't get into his pyjamas for these brief siestas, because the first and last time he had tried it, a crisis developed.

'If you contact an enemy submarine at close range,' explained the commander, 'and you are in your pyjamas you can't very well fight the boat in your pyjamas. I probably get down to my underpants. If something is going to happen, it is going to happen fast. Sometimes I will simply take off my sandals and flop down, and that's it.'

At seven in the evening, said the commander, he often

popped into the wardroom for a chat, but usually didn't eat. Then he would watch a movie, continue his rounds of the ship, probably spending some time in the control room before turning in at perhaps one in the morning. He survived, he said, on only six hours of sleep a day, with a longer period every fourth or fifth day. It was a regime that prevented putting on weight.

I said I believed him.

But the energy of the men aboard the hunter-killer submarines has to be contained within a capacity for stillness and silence. When stalking an 'enemy' submarine or surface craft – which in reality may be a friendly freighter – silence is vital. No hammering, no laughter, no unnecessary movement; all speech to be in hushed voices. Dumping of 'gash' – the boat's rubbish – has to be postponed, although it normally takes place every twenty-four hours. Showers are put out of operation by lessening the pressure, which also affects the taps. Getting rid of the sewage can be a major difficulty, which is why the operation is included in exercises. The submarine has to head away from the 'action', dump the sewage and then get out of that area and back to the action *fast* – it is possible, otherwise, to foul one's own periscope and make visibility difficult.

Such are the facts of life to the men of the hunter-killers, who can detect fishing grounds one hundred miles away and merchant ships at over a hundred miles distant.

The commanding officer said it was 'up to my bosses to tell me what to hit', but he had his own firm theories about the way to approach a target. You always had to get in close to have a look at it, first to identify it and then to hit it. You could fiddle around using three quarters of the range of the weapons. But that way, by the time you had seen and assessed the target, the Sub-Harpoon long-range anti-ship missile would land to one side of the target rather than on it.

'Too clever by half,' rapped the commander dismissively. 'Go straight in! That's the thing. Get in close and make sure of it.'

Unlike on the more passive Polaris, the hunter-killer crews have to be 'psyched up' to their tasks. Perhaps this helps take their minds off the more restricted life aboard: the officers' eight-berth sleeping area leads straight out into the wardroom instead of on to a passageway as it does on Polaris. One deck down to the senior ratings' mess, I found an even greater awareness of the relative confinement.

'It is far better on Polaris,' said a bearded fleet chief petty officer, 'as far as living conditions are concerned. You have got somewhere else to go, other than the mess. The only other place we have to go to here is our bunks, and when you draw the curtains that is the only privacy you have. At meal times, you can't smoke. You have to go outside and smoke on a different deck.'

But, he added, rather to my surprise, he would *rather* be on a hunter-killer than Polaris. Oh, it was much *easier* on Polaris, because routines were more regular, whereas on the hunter-killers you tended to work from day to day.

'That makes it more interesting,' he said. 'My job on here is harder than on Polaris, because you are dealing with the unpredictable. It is crisis management.'

Another reason crews tend to like life aboard the hunter-killers is that they do not have to share a boat with an alternative crew; it is always 'theirs'. 'You are giving the Polaris away to somebody every time you get a new crew,' said the fleet chief petty officer.

New equipment is the sore point. The men on the hunter-killers reckon that if there is any new technology going, Polaris will automatically get it first, and they will follow. When I was aboard, the hunter-killer men were doing the professional splits between the old-fashioned method of putting things down on paper and feeding them into the computers. They were doing both, and grumbling about duplication of effort, an experience which may strike a sympathetic chord among many civilian office workers.

Some of the men hoped that the computer would be

thoroughly established as quickly as possible, while others sighed for their past days in the older diesel submarines, when administration was a matter of a few simple forms.

A chief petty officer, a comparative veteran in his thirties, told me: 'The whole Navy has changed completely. Now there is so much emphasis on the paperwork, the administrative side and the computers that you end up in the situation that I have recently left – where the paperwork was complete but nothing had been mended. According to the computer the work had been done, but actually nothing had been mended. You get bogged down.'

But it is not usually large professional matters, but small personal ones, that cause the most irritations to the hunter-killer men. These can get under the skin more insidiously.

'Like movies,' said one rating. 'Everyone outside the Navy thinks that if you have a hundred and twenty people together for two months, you are going to have fights and claustrophobia. It is nothing like that. What is for dinner? What's the video? What's tonight's movie? These little things that break up the day are important.'

Even when on the Falklands run, an attempt is made to keep the supplies of movies and video tapes of television programmes fresh. Old ones from the journey out are left in the Falklands and new ones picked up for the trip home.

'You must remember,' said a rating, 'that you can't do just *any* hobby to pass the time. If your hobby is reading, fine. If you want correspondence courses, fine. But you couldn't do model-making, you could pollute the atmosphere. You are very limited as to what you can do hobby-wise. You just haven't the space to store stuff.'

The officers of *Churchill* had found a way to make the point that their lives weren't exactly open and carefree, either. They had christened their confined eight-berth sleeping quarters after a sign they had spotted in Charleston, South Carolina, on a visit to the USA. It read: 'Slaves' Quarters'. Only, they felt, for them it was no mere historical relic.

But even they were glad to concede that *usually*, in peace-time, their lives tended to be more placid and less unexpectedly demanding than those in their mirror-image part of the Navy – the part that would fight well *above* the sea.

7

THE FLYING ÉLITE

'The most critical factor in the Falklands war had nothing to do with machinery, it was to do with men. We had thirty-eight trained Sea Harrier pilots. We could not have produced any more at that time (it is different now). If we had lost every Sea Harrier pilot, we would have lost the war.'

– Commander in Royal Naval Air Command.

'Women can't be pilots. Every pilot has to go to sea. You can't send a WRNS person to sea. It is a fundamental thing, which is accepted by the women. If you look at the situation of a dog, it doesn't want to be a cow, because it doesn't know how to be a cow. So it hasn't raised its head. It is rather like God saying, "You can *see* people fly, but you can't fly yourself." Icarus. Just that.'

– Senior officer, Fleet Air Arm.

'Pilots are aged between twenty-one and thirty-eight, by which time the brain cells are deteriorating.'

– Officer in Fleet Air Arm.

Ask any of the 7,500 men of the Fleet Air Arm whether their

organization is the same as the Royal Air Force, and you will probably get your ear burned by the reply.

All right, they will tell you, perhaps the RAF pilots *are* equal in skill and courage. And, yes, the skill of the ground staff of the RAF may not be inferior to that of the Fleet Air Arm. But there is one big difference: the RAF flyer is tied up in rules, regulations and red tape while the Fleet Air Arm pilot is expected to use his own initiative, and is backed if he does his best for the service, even if things go wrong.

This tenet of belief provides for the strong feeling of *esprit de corps* within the Fleet Air Arm, that highly individualistic branch of the Navy that is the guard and eyes of the surface fleet. A frigate can 'see' thirty-two miles using radar, and two hundred miles through a Lynx helicopter. And a carrier equipped with vertical take-off Sea Harriers is a formidable combination in any corner of the world.

A pilot in one of the Fleet Air Arm's twenty squadrons, which together control nearly three hundred aircraft, told me, in tones which suggested he was surprised I hadn't already heard: 'In general terms, there is no difference between a Fleet Air Arm and an RAF pilot. The same mechanical skills apply all the way. The environment for a junior helicopter or a Sea Harrier pilot in the Fleet Air Arm is probably more demanding than for an RAF pilot, because he won't have the supervision that a new member of the RAF will have. But as far as *mental attitude* is concerned, it is entirely different from the RAF. The naval attitude is, and always has been, that responsibility rests with the man on the spot, the man doing the flying. He makes his decision based on what is sensible, and what he knows about the guidelines. The RAF are exactly the opposite. Their rule book says that unless it is specifically permitted, you can't do it.'

Surely such views were just part of that service tradition that your own outfit is always superior to everyone else's? The pilot stuck to his jaunty cigar and his guns.

'No,' he said, 'the RAF have rules to cover any eventuality, and the man on the spot loses a certain amount of flexibility. I have always just tried to operate in a sensible manner, bearing in mind the guidelines and rules laid down by Command. I don't think the Navy would try to slaughter you if you were trying to do your best job for the Navy, within what is sensible, whereas the RAF wouldn't thank you for it. It happens quite frequently that if someone is trying to do their best for the Navy, they won't get shot, but in the RAF you are going to take a hit if you break the rule.'

The pilot recalled the occasion when one of the Fleet Air Arm pilots had got lost and landed on a Spanish freighter. He said the Fleet Air Arm had given the man some latitude because of the circumstances, whereas the RAF would have court-martialled him, and made him a card-indexer. The Fleet Air Arm pilot was flying again the following Monday.

Such stories, as I was to discover, are part of the potent folklore of the Fleet Air Arm, whether the men who hold to it are operating the helicopters (Sea Kings, Lynxes, Wessexes and Gazelles) or the twenty-plus Sea Harriers. It almost makes up for a general feeling of being under-financed and under-resourced, a feeling no less marked in the Fleet Air Arm than in the general service: possibly *more* marked in view of the fact that comparison with the RAF can be invoked.

With the exception of Portland's HMS *Osprey*, all the Fleet Air Arm's air stations were wartime air stations, updated in the postwar years. Search-and-rescue is carried out from HMS *Seahawk* at Culdrose in Cornwall, HMS *Daedalus* at Lee on Solent and HMS *Gannet* at Prestwick in the North. The Flag Officer Naval Air Command is at the headquarters in Yeovilton in the West Country, alongside HMS *Heron*; an operational and training station of some magnitude, though Culdrose is the largest *helicopter* station in Europe.

Yeovilton, as headquarters of the Royal Naval Air Command, is responsible for all *dis*embarked aircraft and their personnel: the rules change when the planes take their operational place at sea in ships. The Command has to provide trained men, air crews and serviceable machines for the front line, which is at sea. For that reason the life of the shore establishments varies from hour to hour, minute to minute, as with the ebb and flow of a vast and noisy man-made tide.

My first impression on the Yeovilton airfield was that the ratio of aircraft on the ground to those in the air varied sharply from minute to minute. Experienced hands told me that this ebb and flow was mild. The most extreme high peak of aircraft on the ground had been at the time the Falklands Task Force was being mustered; the most extreme trough had occurred once the Task Force had set off, because all the assets had departed, and would not be coming back for a long time. On that occasion, the Fleet Air Arm stations resembled ghost towns as much as they are ever likely to do, short of a world war.

In more normal times, the peaks and troughs are created by aircraft coming back from sea to be refurbished and the crews to be refreshed and retrained; and by a steady increase in the number of take-offs and landings for short flights undertaken by pilots in training. All the stations, with the exception of the purely operational HMS *Gannet* at Prestwick, are training establishments as well as the 'sharp end', ready for operations.

All but two squadrons could embark quickly in an emergency. Front-line squadrons could embark in a matter of hours. The second-line squadrons, whose predominant task is training aircrews and maintenance men for those front-line squadrons, would take slightly longer to embark. And the squadrons that do fundamental training, like 750 Squadron, which trains observers using Jetstream aircraft, would not embark at all.

The Fleet Air Arm's assets at Yeovilton boil down to two broad categories – the vertical-take-off Sea Harriers with their deadly missiles and the helicopters that would carry the Royal Marines into battle – the Sea King Mark Four and the Wessex Mark Five. Both are administered from Yeovilton, where a group of stone aggregate buildings near the airfield has replaced the group of wooden huts in the village of Yeovilton itself that served as headquarters during the Second World War. The move, in the late 1970s, was followed by the arrival there of more esoteric branches like the cost accountants, while the wardroom block, rather nearer the air-strip than the head-quarters building itself, has increasingly taken on the appear-ance of a rather large yacht club. In the rather incongruous reproduction-beamed bar, built on the end, can be found the nearest thing to late-night drinking practicable in a force that rises early. Often in this smoky bar there is a sprinkling of 'bum-freezer' dress jackets amidst the sports jackets and flan-nels. Here the integrity of the Fleet Air Arm will be defended valiantly, sometimes touchily. This is especially so when an outsider mentions an unpalatable fact such as the disappearance of the huge old aircraft carrier *Ark Royal* in the late 1970s; and the implications of that on the Navy's future as a possessor of fixed-wing aircraft.

'We have *never*, since 1912, been without a recognized air role,' one officer told me. 'It has continued. However, news-papers seem to think that unless there is a fixed-wing presence in aviation, there is *no* aviation. But every frigate has its own helicopter. About six years ago, we had more observers in the Fleet Air Arm of the Royal Navy than in the Second World War. Every single helicopter has to have one. The observer will fight the aircraft while the pilot flies it.'

And, of course, comparisons with the Royal Air Force will be invoked to prove that the naval flyer is in a class by himself.

'RAF training is completely different from ours,' one officer told me. 'The way they fly machines is different from ours. The Navy says, "We will do it now, and worry about the paperwork afterwards." The RAF says, "We will look at the paperwork to see if it is possible to do it, and if it is, we will do it." It is a slightly different method of looking at life.'

Several anecdotes have been honed and polished in late-night conversations in the wardroom to prove the point. When the Royal Marines aboard one ship had to be flown out to one trouble spot, they had a number of two-inch mortars among their equipment, each with a very necessary and very heavy baseplate. The RAF had taken the mortar tubes, the mortar bombs, but no baseplates; instead they had taken beds for their own airmen, who were going to have to spend a long time in the area.

I asked if the Fleet Air Arm would have done a similar thing to help its own men. 'We would NOT have done the same thing,' I was told with no lack of emphasis. 'The job is, if necessary, to fight the enemy. A bed doesn't help to fight anyone. This plate was vital. It was the only supporting weapon they had, and it was important they had it. Sailors would worry about *beds* five years after they had tried camping. When Navy men go ashore in similar circumstances, they bring everything else except their food, they bring bullets and everything necessary to fight the enemy – the most important thing is to do the job.'

What did I suppose that the expression, 'Send a gunboat!' *really* meant? It no longer literally meant, 'Send a gunboat.' No, it meant, 'Leave it to the *Navy*, because the Navy will do it, whatever it is.' The term had first been coined in the Boxer Rebellion, but now it meant, 'Send the Royal Navy, because if you do, whatever you want done is going to be done.'

Perhaps it is just as well that the Fleet Air Arm is so sure of itself. If there was a war, the Royal Navy's role would be to safeguard the Eastern Atlantic shipping routes so that food could get into the country, and to put Royal Marine Commandos into Norway to stop a Russian advance down towards Denmark. For the Fleet Air Arm, it would be a time of re-thinking and of urgent action. Front-line aircraft would immediately embark, leaving behind a training headquarters and the second-line squadrons (which would immediately be made up into front-line squadrons) and go off to sea as soon as ships were there to take them. The second-line squadrons would go off in civilian ships taken over for the job. Some aircraft would have to be kept back to train more aircrews. The Fleet Air Arm would physically take possession of stores from the manufacturers – helicopters would be of obvious use here – even if the *matériel* might have to be taken to the fighting men by merchant ships or – yes – the R AF.

It was becoming obvious that the Fleet Air Arm, perhaps more than the Royal Navy as a whole, required a certain sort of hair-trigger personality. I asked one officer at Yeovilton, a commander, if there was any difference not only between the Fleet Air Arm man and the R AF man, but also between the Fleet Air Arm man and the man in general service in the Royal Navy.

He thought there might be: 'I will answer your question in a roundabout way. It is much easier to create *esprit de corps* when you have an exciting image and a positive end-product to everything you do. We are fortunate in that we have an exciting image, which appeals to the youngsters, and we have always got an end-product. It is not a nine-to-five job, at this air station, for the rest of your life. You train and then you go to sea or to another air station. At sea you have to integrate with the ship's company. Having done that, we might think, "You are just the right sort of chap to go on to a different aircraft." So it is relatively easy to get the right sort of person that you require because of the image, and the employment you are going to give him. He would not necessarily be brighter or more adaptable than the general-service man would be, but he can *see* the effects of what he is doing. The set-up happens to be one that would be ideal as a demonstration on management courses: it is a more *visible* job, and we can get the best sort of recruit.'

Pilots and aircrew who have to go to sea are all male (anyone who cannot go to sea cannot be in a Fleet Air Arm crew, and women cannot go to sea). But not all the Fleet Air Arm's bright recruits are men. Indeed, it uses women in some roles that would please the most rabid feminist.

I met one such at Yeovilton, a twenty-one-year-old air engineer mechanic attached to the Naval Aircraft Support Unit. She had soft brown eyes, neat gold earrings and a patient, yet outright, manner. One would have guessed her to be, had she not been working at a bench with the aid of a thirty-pound tool kit, an office or shop worker.

That, she told me, was precisely what she had *never* been interested in. She had always preferred doing things with her hands, and moving about, rather than sitting down all day in one location. And she was very keen that I understood from the start that the work she did was much more than fetching and carrying for the men.

'I have been doing this for twenty-two months,' she said. 'It is the servicing of aircraft, but at a deeper level than the squadron can do for itself. We do major repairs. We start work at eight in the morning, by the aircraft in the hangar. It suits me. Before I joined the Navy I worked in a garage to find some form of mechanical work, and I enjoyed doing it. I worked on the servicing of cars – changing clutches and engines, any sort of work on cars. My father is a plumber, and this was something I did off my own bat.'

Was it a job that required a lot of physical strength? 'Not really,' she said casually. 'The most that you lift is your toolbox, which we have to carry from the tool controller to the aircraft we are working on. Everything else is too big for you to lift – man or woman.'

The majority of the men around her at the work-bench accepted working with a woman quite readily, she said. Only a minority obviously didn't like you being there in what they obviously thought of as a man's domain. They usually didn't show their resentment, but there were the occasional remarks: 'Oh, she can't do *that* – she's only a Wren.' And so on. But the majority of the men accepted you once you had proved to them that you could do *their* job as well as they could themselves.

She was unmarried and living in Fleet Air Arm quarters, which at least had the advantage of being near the job; some of the other women had their own houses or flats, usually within a radius of ten miles, and had to cycle or motor in. At the moment she didn't have a car, but when she fixed up a flat for herself, she would get an old banger to drive to work, and service it herself.

Evidently she was a young lady who knew what she wanted, and seemed to have found it in the Fleet Air Arm. I asked her if she would want to cross the great divide and become a WRNS officer.

'No,' she said at once, 'because I enjoy the sort of job I do, actually working on aircraft, and you can get to warrant officer WRNS in time. To get to leading hand will take me five years, to petty officer another five years, and to warrant officer another five years. I like what I am doing.'

The picture of her satisfaction was almost *too* cosy. I asked her if the job had its frustrations. Yes, said the gentle-mannered young woman slowly. It was possible to 'get a bit of a down' on the general naval atmosphere sometimes. Just general moans about the food you were given, and the fact that if you were on board (by which she meant in any naval establishment, albeit on land) you had to have your meals at set times. But these were the sort of things that could be solved if you lived out; and she would live out as soon as she found a place to live.

Often for women and men, the Fleet Air Arm is not their first choice: they go into general naval service and then move sideways, often with psychological and financial advantages. One twenty-nine-year-old male petty officer running a small section within the Naval Air Support Unit, working on Wessex helicopter radio systems, said that he had joined the Navy ten years ago on a whim. He had had a good job in civilian life as a metallurgist, but realized he could be stuck in a factory for years. He happened to bump into a naval friend of his 'at a time I was fed up with the weather'; and it had gone on from there. He was nineteen, he had never been abroad, and he suddenly realized he could be stuck in the steelworks for the next twenty years. He joined as an artificer, made a voluntary branch change to electrical mechanical engineering, as it was then called, and found himself earning £24 a month more.

Why the move to the Fleet Air Arm? 'When I applied for my branch change, I had some difficulties. The Fleet Air Arm was one of the options I could transfer to. Having got married, I looked at the draft situation and thought that the Fleet Air Arm was probably the easier of the possible options. I can do as many front-liners as in general service, but there are fewer places that you can be drafted to,' he said. 'You feel more central to things.'

His domain, when I met him, was two hangars at Yeovilton, with fifteen aircraft in one of them and five in the other. Of the available one hundred and fifty aircraft, eighteen were in the hangars having some sort of attention, including some Lynx helicopters from the Portland station. But his time was now spread between the hangars and the office, where there was a new word-processing computer which took two days a week of his time, feeding into it reserve aircraft progress reports, details of man-hours expended, and completion dates.

In modern conditions, the computer sometimes receives unwelcome tidings. Sometimes there are delays in getting black-box spare parts for the older Wessexes, sometimes there is a lack of equipment to carry out prescribed modifications. At the time I met him, the electrical mechanical engineer had just found that he had ten aircraft on which to make a certain modification, but only eight kits to do it with.

'It takes quite a lot of chasing sometimes,' he admitted. 'It is liaison between us and the stores system. Sometimes it is quicker to talk direct ourselves. I will sometimes bypass the head of stores – and he is quite happy about it – and go to the man he would have gone to anyway. I would go to the head of station supply, or the head of the modifications department. I have had occasions, during modifications, when we have dealt direct with manufacturers of certain items of kit. Long hours normally occur when an aircraft is near completion, and about to be released for service. Eighty per cent of the time, it is an eight-to-five working day. I go home at night to my own house in Yeovil by car – 70 per cent of senior ratings have a car.'

And pleased to use them for the homeward journey after the more frustrating days, I imagined. Such days tend to increase as the financial pressures on the Navy increase.

The point was underlined by another man with the Naval Aircraft Support Unit, a bald and red-bearded fleet chief petty officer, a senior artificer in his early forties. Plainly he was no congenital grumbler. I asked him if he now, after twenty-four years in the Navy, would prefer to work in his craft in civilian life – say with British Aerospace. He said it would have to be a very good employment offer to persuade him to leave the Navy. He was very well paid – after deductions something like £850 went into his bank account at the end of the month. He might be able to get that sort of money in civilian employment, but there would be the 'embuggerance factors' in Civvy Street, by which he meant trade union activities. He had always felt a responsibility for what he did in his job, but it seemed that an awful lot of people in civilian life didn't take responsibility for what they did and didn't want to. He would find it difficult, he said, to change to that form of working life.

Having said that, however, he acknowledged that the Aircraft Support Unit's vital work was under constraints of manpower, money and spares which sometimes caused problems.

I asked for examples. 'Spare parts have always bedevilled certain aircraft. We had an aircraft in production, due to be built by May, but it was set back for a month because of four bolts. The manufacturers couldn't supply them for a month, which meant finding another job for that crew of men, because they couldn't practise any flying without those four bolts. It has been like that for some years now.'

Was that the only case he could think of? 'No, we are doing some major modification to a helicopter, and it is the first of that type of helicopter to have that modification done. There is a leaflet telling us how to do it. We have got a third of the way through the job and are finding that the leaflet is hopelessly inaccurate. We have got to go back to the appropriate auth-

ority and say, "This doesn't work." A meeting will be re-
convened in the Ministry of Defence next week, and we are
still waiting for the results of the air engineer officer's visit.
That represents, in terms of delay, at least two weeks, and I
suspect it will be a great deal longer because the modification
leaflet will have to be re-written. A lot of sheet-metal work
and rivetting is involved and the leaflet is hopeless.'

Such frustrations, however, had not spoiled the Navy for
him. Coming into the Fleet Air Arm with two 'O' Levels and
an interest in engineering, he had gained his qualifications in
the service, served in HMS *Invincible*, the large carrier, and
later came to Yeovilton to go into the two great hangars of the
Naval Aircraft Support Unit, with one hundred and fifty
people swarming all over a variety of aircraft like diligent ants.

Normally, he said, he worked only in the daytime, but
during the Falklands campaign everyone had worked round
the clock, two shifts of twelve hours each. It was a time of
high adrenalin. Generally he liked the 'settled' nature of the
job: work could usually be planned. Very rarely was an aircraft
taken out of action unexpectedly because it was thought to be
unsafe. Aircraft were inspected every eighteen months by an
independent inspection organization within the Navy. But
since he had been in the job, he had never had to provide an
aircraft at short notice except for the Falklands; in war, of
course, it would always be different.

Perhaps part of his relative contentment was caused by the
fact that, though his job mostly concerned dealing with
machinery, which he liked, it was leavened by work dealing
with people. This, the divisional side of his work, was one of
the great satisfactions of naval life.

'The divisional side of the Navy is so different from civilian
life,' he said. 'It means looking after the interests of the people
under you. Divisional work takes quite a lot of my time. But I
find that work very rewarding – the routine administration of
twenty-five sets of personal documents for people who work
in the same area as you do. The satisfaction in seeing people

progress through the Navy and further their careers, encouraging them to take advantage of what we can offer in the way of promotion, and gaining educational qualifications. Every division has a person with a family death problem, or someone whose marriage is breaking up. Dealing with this definitely comes under the title of job satisfaction. There is a higher incidence of marriages breaking up in the services than in the country as a whole.'

'But,' chimed in an officer, 'interestingly enough, the Navy has the lowest rate.'

'Well,' said the senior artificer, 'the Navy has a higher proportion of people living in their own homes – though that leads to people being more separated than if they were living together in a married quarter. It may be a reflection on the divisional system, the break-up of marriages; I don't know. I have been married seventeen years, and we have one son. I have seen the strain in my wife at times, and been very grateful for the way she has coped.'

But I parted from him on a positive note. When he had just become thirty, and the time had come for him to sign on again for the Navy or leave, he had been married six years. He and his wife had spent a lot of time talking over whether he should re-engage, part of the doubt being that he was now married.

'Eventually,' he said, 'we decided – and it *was* a joint decision – that I would stay in the Fleet Air Arm. Why? The fact that I *enjoyed* it! My wife said she would rather have me in the Navy, and coming home reasonably happy, than coming home extremely miserable as a civilian.'

For such a comparatively small segment of the Royal Navy as the Fleet Air Arm, there is a great diversity of jobs. That almost certainly contributes to the sense of perpetual interest that its men and women display.

Some of the skills have developed to a point of sophistication which probably exceeds that of the comparable areas in civilian life. Fire-fighting is an obvious case. The possibility of a Sea Harrier crashing, perhaps into an air-station building, is one that calls for a high readiness to practise the most advanced methods of fire-fighting.

At Yeovilton's fire station, a building not very different from a civilian establishment, I found a leading airman handler – the sort of man who only a few years ago would have spent most of his time flagging down aircraft at air stations or on the flight-decks of carriers.

Now his job was distinctly a two-role one, with the fire-fighting aspect no longer a secondary one. He had spent two years with a front-line squadron attached to HMS *Hermes*, and after that expected a minimum of three years at a shore establishment, based in the fire station.

'The branch is a small one and uncertain of its future, with the air-traffic world changing so rapidly,' he said. 'And the technique of the fire-fighting side has increased to an intensity where the aircraft handler has got to be a different man entirely. Years ago he was strictly an aircraft handler for ships, with fire fighting as the secondary role. Whereas today an aircraft handler is trained very well in the field of fire-fighting and can handle incidents at sea or at buildings ashore. The job is entirely different. We work on the maintenance of fire extinguishers on a monthly basis, we check all the fire alarms, and carry out a fire-practice survey of the place in hand. It is much better for people to be involved with aircraft in this way, rather than just marshalling them. It is necessary for the fire-fighter to know all about ejector seats and such things.'

Were emergencies frequent? A few weeks ago, he said, a Sea Harrier with two personnel on board had crashed on the A37 road. His colleagues were called in to form the back-up at the scene; he himself, on that occasion, went to man one of the fire engines at the fire station, maintaining back-up cover for the flying still going on.

Plainly a stout stoicism amidst unpalatable facts can be a feature of Fleet Air Arm life on some grim occasions. It is never certain whether an emergency will end up as a mere incident or a human tragedy.

The naval airman handler said that in 1972 he had got there first at a crash of a Whirlwind (an early type of helicopter). The aircraft had engine failure when approaching the airfield, and literally fell out of the sky on to its side with a great crash, at the bottom of the runway. He had thought that everyone aboard must be dead. In fact nobody was hurt. There had been a little fire on the aircraft, and when he arrived the aircrew were getting out of the emergency exits, safe and sound only a few seconds after sending their 'Possible fuel starvation' message and falling out of the sky.

On the other side of the coin, a Sea King helicopter with five men on board struck the top of a cliff less than ten miles away from its base, Culdrose, and disintegrated in a field, mercifully missing houses but killing all five inside the aircraft. A search-and-rescue helicopter was landed nearby in the same field, with fire extinguishers on board. It was night, and in any case there was nothing that could be done to save the personnel on board.

It was a job, the naval airman handler told me, in which you could never know too much. The people in it were deep specialists (like many of their colleagues in the Navy as a whole) and the equipment provided by the Navy was first class.

'We possibly have the best back-up facilities for accidents in the country,' he said. 'Probably the best in the world. I have been to America. I have been to the Far East and the Middle East. But as far as I am concerned, we are far superior in that field.'

Only one thing disturbed this experienced specialist – the fact that in his opinion the younger men sometimes did not have enough interest in the job, or the adaptability to carry it out zealously. As far as he was concerned, 'we are one of the branches in the Navy where discipline is of the utmost. We can't afford to have people who answer back under orders. But the young men of today have a completely different outlook on life, and treat the leading hand, the petty officer, in some cases even the chief petty officer, with disrespect – which I find intolerable. It expresses itself in that the man doesn't want to work, or is not interested. He feels that he is only there for an emergency, and that for the rest of the duration of his watch, he can be more lackadaisical than he should be. The casual approach of young men is not good enough on a fire station.'

This comparative veteran thought that the system might be wrong as well. When he was doing his first training at H M S *Raleigh*, discipline had been instilled into him and he would never have dreamed of answering back to a superior.

'Today the situation of *Raleigh* must be questionable,' he added. 'I don't know whether they are being treated too much with kid gloves. Discipline, at this point in their careers, *does* have a bearing on what men will do in an emergency. We weren't told twice to do the job in hand. I have got half a dozen lads in my mess and it is the devil of a job to get them to get the Hoover out of the cupboard and Hoover the carpet. If you can't instil discipline in the mess decks, then you certainly can't expect them to carry out their duties in the field, where it matters. We have got to get men *out* of the environment of being civilians.'

There seemed to be an underlying feeling among aircrew of the Fleet Air Arm that R A F *training* was miles ahead of their own in the sophistication of its methods, if not necessarily in its results. One of the aircrew I spoke to told me: 'That aspect needs improvement. The R A F have training to a "T". The R A F have got the lot. I have been trying to get a tape recorder that I can plug into a communications system. You go to the R A F training centres and they have recorders, they have video film of every aspect of their training from the students' point of view. It is absolutely wonderful because, unlike us who have to make do with a blackboard, they are able to make a presentation which says, "This is what it is like in real life." Here there is no chance of getting fibre tips and rulers. I sit at home and make up my own graphs now. We have had a camera demand in since I don't know when. The RAF have given us stuff just because we have a good liaison. It is not often you have a chance to talk about these things, to be honest.'

Such, it would appear, are the sort of constraints imposed on a primary defender of Britain and NATO by financial squeezes. It must be counted as a tribute to the Navy that in these circumstances, the sheer rigour of important training transcends the limitations in physical facilities.

Just how rigorous the training can be I was told by members of the branch dealing with safety and survival, which is a vital part of all pilots' and aircrewmen's training. Things are made as safe as possible *for* these active participants. Most of their equipment is checked on a fifteen-week cycle by experts: their flying helmets, their flying overalls, their Mae Wests, their parachutes, their jump-seats, their life-rafts.

But if all this is done for them, the aircrew have to do more demanding parts of survival training for themselves. They have 'dry' briefings, but later they get wet when they are dumped in a swimming pool and winched out, as if from the sea. Later they are blindfolded, driven fifty or sixty miles and left there for three or four days, to simulate having crashed in the middle of nowhere. They carry their survival equipment and get out of the situation in the best way they can. They are watched by their taskmasters, unseen, from a distance, just in case things go badly wrong. They have radio equipment within their safety kit, which emits signals that can be picked up by the rescue services bearing in on them. They do all this at least twice a year, sometimes three times.

Experienced pilots sometimes say that the rigour of the training is *not* matched by the rigour with which the introduction of safety equipment is handled – again, lack of resources rather than lack of will being the cause. 'A bit more financial help would be an improvement,' one pilot said. 'Within the Navy, we appear to be poor relations.'

Training is rigorous. Pilots and aircrew, at a later stage of their training, have to drop helicopters out of the sky from two hundred and fifty feet in a way they would actually have to do it if their engines cut out – except that they do it with an instructor sitting beside them, and with the use of the engine again fifty feet from the ground (helicopters are *not* expendable in training). In every other respect it is as realistic as if the engine failure were real, and deft handling of the controls could make all the difference between a written-off aircraft and crew and a merely damaged aircraft with a surviving crew.

The men themselves obviously have within them that element of gung-ho without which a man is less than a man (though they will tell you that 'cowboys' are ruthlessly weeded out as a danger to the service); but such spirit cannot wash away completely the disadvantages of some underfunding. I asked one twenty-five-year-old observer, with experience flying in Sea Kings from Culdrose, what he would like to see changed or improved.

His answer was thoughtful and not disagreeable to his superiors. 'I think, sometimes, it is a bit frustrating being in the front line. It appears that what you are doing is not understood by people up on high, particularly on equipment and things like that. You feel there is a problem with something, and it doesn't appear you are getting full support. It takes such a long time to get equipment that it appears that nothing is being done.'

A superior officer interjected at this point: 'It is quite a fair comment, and I don't think it will ever change. You come across things where it would take a fiver to get it changed, but you just can't get it altered. It has to go through channels, companies, et cetera, and that is very frustrating.'

Emboldened by this, the observer opened up even further. 'You can possibly see a piece of equipment and you think that would be excellent, far better than we have at present, so why can't we have it? If we feel there is something wrong with a piece of equipment, we must report it and make recommendations that we think would overcome the difficulty. That gets sent all the way up the line to the people who decide on these sorts of things. A current case in point is the active sonar on the Sea King helicopter, which is very old. There are better bits of kit on the market, which I feel we could do with. Modifications have been carried out on these pieces of equipment many times and I feel that, rather than be modified any more, the powers-that-be would do far better to go for something new. But it all comes down to money. There are other priorities elsewhere for allocating money.'

I asked him if that was a big frustration, or just an occasional twinge.

'It can be badly frustrating,' he said, 'when you are actually on an exercise looking for a submarine which you know is there, but you just can't find it. It is very, *very* frustrating.'

In war conditions, would that put him seriously at a disadvantage? 'I don't think we would be at a disadvantage, no. The equipment we have is good and the operators are trained to a fairly high standard, so they do get good results out of the equipment – but the results could be better.'

This optimism sounded genuine, though it did not wholly accord with his own previous remarks. Of one thing I had no doubt: his misgivings were real, not bred out of personal grievance. As an observer, he had to process new information coming at him at a rate of more than one item per second, and pass on the results to the pilot who, in the opinion of many experienced Fleet Air Arm hands, is becoming more of a bus driver to the observer's brains. His basic attitude to his job was enthusiastically positive: 'I think it is an excellent job, very enjoyable and rewarding. One of the most rewarding things you can get in it is to find a submarine and carry out an attack on it.'

Those on the ground share this underlying excitement of the job, an excitement which could hardly be duplicated in civilian flying and its ground back-up. The air traffic controllers at Fleet Air Arm stations are a breed used to working fairly constantly with the unexpected, and taking it with calmness.

The hours are more elastic than they might be in civilian life. Traffic controllers normally work in the control tower – very much like that for an ordinary airport – on five-hour watches. It could be noon to five in the winter; while in the summer men could work in the morning, have the afternoon off and come back for the evening flying, some of them staying until two o'clock in the morning. The day is usually split into day-flying and night-flying sessions, with some rest in between for meals.

But the strange hours are not the biggest challenge. One air traffic controller told me that flights were more 'organized' in civilian life. 'At Heathrow, there is no way in which, within the space of a few minutes, you will get a sudden increase in aircraft movements. But at Portland Fleet Air Arm station, for instance, you can suddenly have two or three aircraft without any warning whatever; you can get an extra load of three hundred per cent of the normal; you can't define the pattern of unexpected things that may happen.'

Another in this stoic traffic controller sphere told me that the Fleet Air Arm air traffic control workload was also probably more affected by weather. It was, he said, because the aircraft relied more on the air traffic controller than civilian aircraft did. Civil aircraft, he said, did a great deal of their own positioning and recoveries of their true courses, whereas it was all done by the controllers in the Navy.

Another controller said that fuel shortages were probably more common with naval aircraft than civilian ones. 'You get occasional engine failures, which in a single-engined aircraft are critical. That gives you more control problems. An aircraft might be working on an endurance of fifty minutes – that is how much fuel he has got. If he is going to do a forty-minute search, the worst situation you could have at Yeovilton is the weather deteriorating around here and the diversion airfield at Boscombe Down going out at the same time. You then have to make sure you recover your aircraft in the shortest possible time. Time becomes absolutely critical. You would have to take one aircraft out of the way to let someone else, with less fuel, come in.'

Did that often happen? A number of controllers racked their memories and then one of them came out with an example of the sort of three-dimensional chess game that can be played with planes and their fuel.

'There was a formation of fixed-wing aircraft at Culdrose – nine in the formation, and not all of them with much more fuel than was necessary to do their displays. The weather went out. We had to recover the aircraft *not* in the order of their formation, but taking the ones with the least fuel first. The degree of control necessary to take control of nine aircraft, and feed them in at three-mile intervals, in an order other than their formation, is quite considerable. Fortunately you really don't have enough time to get into any emotional states, when getting back aircraft which are running out of fuel. In the case of this nine, we recovered them all. Yes, it *is* different from working at Heathrow.'

It is perhaps a quantitative measure of that difference that a civilian airport like Heathrow would control aircraft only within the last thirty miles of their approach, whereas the Fleet Air Arm, at any one of its stations, would control them for up to one hundred and fifty miles.

All the same, the degree of responsibility resting on the pilot at the controls of the aircraft and the observer advising him from his instruments is very considerable indeed. I put the point about the suitability of 'cowboys' to one experienced trainer of pilots.

'About twenty per cent of pilots fall out as unsuitable,' he said. I asked if that wasn't rather an expensive drop-out rate, bearing in mind that training a Fleet Air Arm pilot can cost anything up to £2 million; but came up against that constant sobering fact about the Navy: the imbalance of machinery to men.

'Bearing in mind,' said the trainer, 'that the cost of an aircraft can be £9 million, losing a wrong pilot halfway through his training can be cheap at the price.'

The flying élite definitely play a vital game with very high stakes. Taxpayers may hope the stakes do not increase, but the Falklands crisis proved that they can never be sure. The flying élite could well be involved in another shooting interlude, though it is unlikely that their personal privations would be as great as those that could be suffered by certain other sections of the Navy.

8

LAND-AND-SEA BUDDY-BUDDIES

'You fight the elements first, then you can fight the enemy . . . The warmest accommodation, the quietest, and the safest from the point of view of not showing a light, is a snow hole.'

– Sergeant-major, Royal Marines, on exercises around the Arctic Circle.

'The Parachute Regiment have played the "enemy" in exercises in Norway for the last two years, but they didn't like it – it was too cold for *them*. I was told that three hundred of them put in their chits to leave.'

– Corporal, Royal Marines, member of training team at Commando Training Centre, Lympstone, Devon.

'Don't leave things around. They can even tell by your shit. Don't laugh. If you have got diarrhoea, your morale is probably low. They can examine your urine and tell what condition you are in. It is getting to be an exact science. So don't foul it up. Is that clear?'

– Royal Marines lieutenant talking to recruits.

This sort of cold can numb the mind. I had been in or near the Arctic Circle in varying states of mind and discomfort for almost a week, when I came across the philosophical West

HMS *Boxer* during her trials. Guns are a minor part of the fire power of a modern warship, but they are fired for practice, as they were on HMS *Boxer*. Complete flash gear would be worn at Action Stations.

(*Facing Page*) Britannia Royal Naval College, Dartmouth, where officers are trained, is architecturally more historic than the premises available to ratings in training but can present just as tough demands, as cadets find as they use ropes to scale a wall. The passing out parade can be ample compensation and provides the young officers with a chance to see the Inspecting Officer, the First Sea Lord.

For ratings, the first sight of naval training is at the New Entry Training Establishment, HMS *Raleigh*, at Torpoint in Cornwall, where these recruits are receiving classroom instruction in rigging a chain stopper, as part of basic seamanship techniques.

A Third Officer ATC at Culdrose became the first WRNS ATC to qualify there for 15 years, though others had come from other Naval Air stations.

Training for Royal Marines is remarkably tough and demanding. At the Commando Training Centre, Royal Marines, Lympstone, Devon, recruits run with poles or cross over water on monkey bars.

Arctic exercises in Norway can be demandingly realistic for the Royal Marines. A Sea King helicopter of 846 Squadron is seen (*Top*) about to pick up members of 42 Commando. Engines of almost all vehicles have to be kept running during the most intense cold, which can reach more than 40 degrees celsius below freezing. Snow-holes are vital, but even trenches give some protection against both "the enemy" and the winds that exaggerate the biting cold. These Royal Marines are in an anti-tank defensive position, using an 84mm anti-tank weapon.

(*Above*) A Royal Marine points out the stark Arctic terrain to the author during one of the regular winter exercises in and around the Arctic Circle where in the deepest cold, metal objects will weld themselves to human skin and survival rests on constant vigilance.

(*Below*) Marines train with one of the articulated snow tractors which are the only vehicles capable of handling virtually all conditions.

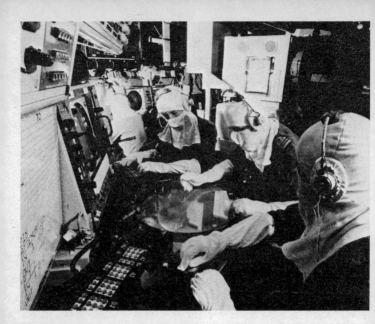

Sailors become used both to sunny naval visits and to working under pressure in tight conditions
(*Below*) HMS *Invincible* leaves Gibraltar after a visit, and (*Above*) the operations room staff of a ship wear flash gear at Action Stations.

Indian Royal Marine rifleman. He was holed up in a snow-choked Norwegian village in the middle of pure white nowhere, notionally helping to fight off a Russian attack.

The biting cold during the Royal Marine exercise had never been far from my mind nor, I imagined, the minds of the Royal Marines taking part in their regular Arctic defence preparations. The nineteen-year-old West Indian Marine admitted that some of the men thought that black Marines couldn't possibly cope well with the Arctic climate. 'Sometimes I have heard that buzz going around,' he told me nonchalantly. 'Personally, I think what happens up here is strictly down to the individual.'

Too true; it was a valuable shaft of insight. Human temperament can make the difference between survival and death when the temperature is minus forty degrees Celsius, sometimes lower. On exercises in or near the section of the Arctic Circle that covers part of Norway, the clinically deep cold can dominate and condition every thought, every action. And it is vital to think clearly at all times.

'It is only when it is minus thirty that it starts getting you down a bit,' insisted the Marine. 'Anything above that is all right; anything below that you may have to work to adjust yourself to.'

He was being modest. Certainly at twenty degrees below freezing, carelessness can be uncomfortable and potentially dangerous. At forty degrees below, in the sort of conditions out of which the adventure story writer Alistair Maclean fashioned his literary reputation, the cold can corrupt one's body into becoming one's own implacable enemy, an unpredictable dispenser of discomfort or – if one forgets the drill or fails to keep moving – a dispenser of injury through frost-bite or death through hypothermia. Two Royal Marines on exercises in Norway went on a simple three-mile skiing trip when a blizzard suddenly sprang up, bringing visibility down to one foot; both died of hypothermia only a few yards from base.

The cold monopolizes the attention of some young Royal

Marines who go up the snow-strewn valleys of North and South Norway for their first annual exercises in Arctic conditions. It is not easily forgotten by the more experienced members of the Royal Navy's toughest and most directly combative element.

'Even the toughest Royal Marine would not venture out without his thermal long johns,' they are told from the outset.

They make their cautious way across the snow and ice in thermal socks, two-layer thermal boots with non-slip soles, thermal trousers, two or three pullovers, thermal long johns, thermal jackets, caps with earpieces and chocolate Rolos to suck for energy. Mars bars, though otherwise ideal providers of quick calories against the biting cold, are apt, in this sort of climate, to become so hard that they crack the teeth rather than vice versa.

'You have got to have the cold at the back of your mind all the time,' said a hardened veteran, in one of the Norwegian valleys north of Oslo where the temperature was about minus ten – warm by Norwegian winter standards. 'Taking your gloves or mitts off can be completely out of the question; you would get frost-bite in the really cold temperatures. You must remember not to touch any metal equipment with your bare hands, because the skin will stick fast to it.' The actual conditions, I found, were a great incentive to one's memory.

Every year from January to March about 3,000 of the 7,500 members of the Royal Marines go to Norway and into Arctic conditions for what is far more than a merely theoretical exercise. Their task in war would be to stop 'an enemy' (a euphemism for the Russians) invading Norway and thereby coming within striking distance of Denmark – a circumstance that would enable the Russians to free that part of their fleet now penned up in the Baltic, and also to dominate the Barents Sea and much of the North Sea. The theory is that the Russians would come over the top of the country, in the Arctic Circle, and drive the defenders steadily south by a series of hooked amphibious landings which would be made progressively down the west coast of Norway. Or they would ignore the neutrality of Finland and Sweden by sweeping straight through them to Norway. A third option would be for the Russians to try to 'muscle' their way across the very top of Northern Norway, well into the Arctic Circle, and drive down it with their land forces.

In war, the function of the Royal Marines would be to help ensure that none of these moves succeeded. And the general view in the Royal Marines is that, with the help of other NATO forces, they would have a good chance of doing so.

One Marine with twenty years' experience said that he thought the Royal Marines were better trained than the Russian equivalent. 'At least we are better trained in what we have to do, which is in defence. We are far better masters-of-all-trades, whereas the Russian equivalent, the Naval Infantry soldier, has just one job, to get ashore and establish a beachhead. The Russians are trained in offence. The theory is that you can invade with a three-to-one advantage, but it doesn't always work like that. The Argentinians had two to one against us in Operation *Corporate* in the Falklands and should have been able to hold us off easily, but they didn't. And the Russians aren't really totally different to the Argentinians. They are both conscripts. The Russians have some sophisticated kit, but a lot of the outcome is to do with handling and morale, the terrain and the leadership.'

The confidence of the Royal Marines is based on a varied and honourable history. They were first formed in 1664 to fight the Dutch. Since then they have taken part in many tough campaigns. Those fought in the Falklands are the most recent and easily remembered, but Royal Marines have fought in India and Burma, captured terrorists in Malaya and even gone to the New Hebrides in the South Pacific to quell a rebellion by tribesmen who had declared unilateral independence on the Island of Espiritu.

Their amphibious skills have been an effective deterrent in policing actions. 42 (spoken as 'Four-two', *not* 'Forty-two')

Commando – the one with whom I spent some time in the Arctic conditions of Norway – was effective in helping to stem the flood of illegal immigrants from China into Hong Kong in the late 1970s. A few years later it fought in the Falklands for Mount Kent and Mount Harriet. Parts of it were also involved in the re-taking of South Georgia and South Thule.

The Royal Marines have therefore had an authentic opportunity to learn something about morale, terrain and leadership, the three factors which are said to be dominant in their calling on land and sea.

On their annual Arctic exercises in Norway, they regularly have the chance to learn even more about all four factors, plus the chance to perfect a remarkable stoicism. They can have practice even *before* they get there. Marines flying out from RAF Lyneham near Swindon are called at 4.20 in the morning for the 6.20 flight in the cold, noisy troop-carrier Hercules to Gardermoen in the (usually colder) South of Norway or to Evenes in the North.

On the Monday I joined a group of Royal Marines for the trip from an icy England to a much icier Norway, we were all in the Hercules with our inelegant but effective safety belts fastened when the voice over the speaker system announced: 'Weather conditions over there are still too bad for us to get in, so the flight has been put back twenty-four hours.' All the suitcases and other kit, which had been piled up in the centre of the Hercules and tied down with webbing, were disgorged amid groans and ironic cheers. When you are winding yourself up to sleep in snow holes while the blizzards blow about you, it is difficult to wind yourself down again.

Even the Royal Marine Commando Band, forty sturdy lads who are normally the most equable of company, growled rebelliously. The band were going to be disbanded in a few months because of defence cuts. They were on their way to play in the Arctic Circle, for the first time, to remind the world what it would be missing. To enable the band to meet a commitment in Narvik, the delayed flight (this time requiring a 2.00 am call) had to go up to northern Norway first, taking with them all the passengers who wanted to go no further than the south. More delay. At least it was practice in the buddy-buddy system of the Royal Marines, in which men work in pairs, each helping the other – even if the help on this occasion could only be watching luggage while the buddy fetched hot cups of tea.

Even minor help is not to be sneezed at when encountering the weather conditions of the training areas for the first time. When the plane arrived at its northern stop to deliver the bandsmen, it turned out that fog and snow made landing at the southern military airfield of Gardermoen impossible. It needed a landing on an almost snowed-up civil airfield, a coach trip to Gardermoen, an overnight stay in the officers' mess at Gardermoen and a three-hour train journey before I finally made contact with 42 Commando, the people I had come to see. Already I had taken the point that in Arctic conditions everything, but everything, is unpredictable.

Hardships promote a healthy desire for the maximum comfort *possible*. In the officers' mess at Gardermoen, I commented to my neighbour at table about the excellence of the tasty sausages.

He happened to be the quartermaster. 'I arranged them, actually. Normally in Norway you can get only the local spiced sausages, which the men don't much like for breakfast. I got hold of a local meat merchant through someone's brother-in-law, and asked him to make sausages especially for us. We got a recipe from England and they experimented. It took a year of correspondence to produce these sausages, and even now they haven't got the skins quite right.'

Such finesse is laudable, given the Spartan and icy conditions outside the messes. I was warned about the conditions in my trek to get to the workface of 42 Commando. An experienced Royal Marine told me: 'You must think everything out deliberately in advance. You can get frost-bite from any number of things. For instance, if you don't wipe the snow off your hands after you have fallen over. Or you can go skiing for a long period, and forget what the wind can do to your face: it can drop the temperature another twenty degrees. The field rations are such' – I was to discover this for myself – 'that they supply between 3,000 and 5,000 calories a day, and in a way that means you can go for three days without a crap. Everything is dehydrated and needs nine pints of water. You can boil up a block of porridge, put dehydrated apple chips in it, put some sugar on the whole lot and eat it. When you want a pee, you usually go to the central point to do it. There is a saying when people boil up snow to get water: "Don't drink the yellow bits." But it is not only because of hygiene that we use a central point; it is to help us cover our tracks.'

Another veteran added this advice: 'You must keep mental track of what you propose to do and think it through before you do it. If you want to do your boot laces up, you do not put your gloves down on the snow or ice, you put them in your pockets. If you want some water, it means you have to make it. This means you have to dig a hole, put a tent round it, and use the heater inside it to heat the snow. This takes a bit of doing. If you want a pee, you just go ahead and do it, but evacuating the bowels can be difficult – you are probably dealing with nine layers of clothing. You dig a hole, and if you touch the surrounding snow, you will know all about it.'

Strangely enough, said the veteran, dehydration could be a worse problem in cold climates than hot ones. Men were working hard and perspiring in a large number of clothing layers. It was easy to forget how much liquid one was losing, especially in the run-up to the final co-ordinated exercise in early March.

'You fight the elements first, then you can fight the enemy,' said the sergeant-major who greeted me on my arrival at 42 Commando, twenty-two years in the Royal Marines after leaving home at seventeen, moustache neatly trimmed, thinning hair neatly in place under his green beret.

I was now well away from civilization, except for a few roads snowed up for the winter and a few chalet-type holiday hotels; some closed, some taken over by the Marines for the winter. The first lesson Marines must learn, said the sergeant-major, was how to survive; only then could the subsequent aspect – tactics – make any sense.

I saw what he meant. We were in a valley running north-south. It was to the west of the main central north-south valley in Norway, and was a simulation of it. The Russians would have to come down the main valley; by using the similar valley, the Marines could gain some knowledge of what they would be up against, and how to respond.

Fields for miles around were covered in unbroken snow, merging into other 'fields' of snow which were in fact lakes or rivers frozen over and covered so deep that one could not know for certain what they were. The sight of boats in the middle of what appeared to be fields was at first startling. There were road signs warning of elk, but there was not an elk in sight. Nor could I see any cattle; they were all in heated wooden sheds for the winter. Sometimes the snow had piled up into drifts ten feet or more deep; very occasionally running water could be seen through cracks in the ice as it came down from mountain streams. There were almost no civilian motor cars in sight, and those few had chains on the wheels. The sergeant-major's Land Rover had an Arctic heating system, consisting of hot air tubes directed at the windscreen and a massive steel box between driver and passenger; and it had metal-studded tyres for better grip. But there were plenty of places used by the exercising Marines that could be reached only by the articulated, tracked vehicles used by the Marines. These can bump you about like a pea in a whistle, but can reach almost anywhere – even across a lake if the ice is two or more feet thick.

The first rule of survival is that you must get yourself, as soon as possible, out of the snow and wind. The Royal Marine can build one of three types of home: a snow hole, a tented trench or a smaller tent for ten men which is big enough to have a cooking stove, two petrol lanterns and a sharp and lethal machete for cutting your way out if the whole lot catches fire. In the snow holes or the smaller tented holes, illumination is by candle only.

I spent some time in each form of shelter as the exercise progressed. They vary in practicality and comfort. The snow holes can take over three hours to create. They always consist of an *upward* entry into the snow. This can be achieved by using a high drift or, in flat snow, by digging a preliminary three-foot-square hole and then digging horizontally from the bottom of that hole and on a slightly upwards incline. The object of the upward entry passage is to ensure that cold air (which falls) will always empty itself from the snow hole. A foot-wide trench may also be cut into the floor of the main chamber of the snow hole, so that cold air falls into it.

With the aid of your elbows and feet, you slide via the narrow tunnel into the seven-by-seven-foot cavern, put down plastic insulation mats on the ice (*not* on the earth which is colder) and put your sleeping bag on that. Four men will sleep in such a snow hole, with the inevitable candle always burning. The candle keeps the temperature up to a tolerable level. It also does something even more vital: if it remains alight, it tells the man on watch (and there is *always* a man on watch) that there is still enough oxygen to support fire and, therefore, breathing. Using the candle, it can be rather alarming to wake up in the morning and find the glistening snow ceiling has sunk during the night almost to the level of your nose. But without the candle, you might not wake up at all.

A ventilation hole is vital in roofs of snow holes. It is made ingeniously. You push a ski stick, handle first, through the roof, from the outside. Every half hour, the man on watch inside waggles the stick around to keep the hole around the stick sufficiently open.

The snow hole is most effective above the tree line of mountains, where the snow is really deep. It is the most secure and comfortable of all the forms of Arctic home, say the experienced Marines, but it can take up to five hours to make.

Rather more popular, because it saves time (and is usually in practice built further away from the enemy lines) is the tented hole. It has room to take four men, their sleeping bags and their military rucksacks which can hold between sixty and eighty pounds of kit.

I visited one of these. It had been built by Marines who were dug in near a bridge that was notionally about to be blown up. They had to guard it while it was there, and see it was blown up if it had to be.

'It took us one and a half hours to get this one up,' said the oldest (aged twenty-six) Marine in it. 'We can normally get one up in an hour, but it was complicated by the weather. It was very hard work.'

The youngest, aged seventeen, said from his sleeping-bag, peering through the dim light of two candles placed in recesses cut into the snow wall, at the bottom of the tent, that he was tired. 'I haven't had more than four hours' sleep at a time for a fortnight,' he said.

I asked him if the group would try to get some sleep now, but one of the more experienced Marines chipped in first. 'We are not going to *try*,' he said. 'We are going to *succeed*.'

I wished them luck, though reflecting that I would find sleep easier in the ten-man tent. This is a structure which, comparatively, feels very luxurious indeed. It is normally built, as in the case of the one I visited, near the headquarters and re-supply base and therefore even further from the enemy.

The structure was on the same principle as the more modest tented hole. But because it had more space, it also had more amenities. The structure resembled a medium-sized suburban bedroom, with a low sloping roof. Straw was spread over the snow floor. Plastic insulation mats, resembling green imitation lawn, were put over this. Sleeping-bags were placed on top. The tent above the two-foot-deep hole had an inner insulation skin to keep in the heat provided by the cooking stove and the lanterns.

It was no surprise to learn that those two hardy survivors, the sergeant-major and the quartermaster-sergeant, were based in this tent, with the two drivers, two storemen and the company clerk.

This tent was at the village of Maurvangen, in the grounds of a chalet holiday hotel complex deserted by the owners for the winter. The Marine whose turn it was to act as cook poured me a cup of tea. Both of us were almost totally unaware of the snow swirling outside, thickening the layer already over the chalets.

'We had a Chinese meal last night,' he said with casual pride. 'I put it in the pressure cooker. Strips of meat, bamboo shoots, water chestnuts, noodles, mixed herbs, Swiss dressing and a bit of water. We would have steak chasseur if we got the chance.'

'We *will* have steak chasseur,' promptly corrected the sergeant-major.

In these sort of exercises in Arctic conditions, the only better shelter in the field than a ten-man tent is a 'Penthouse' tent. This is taken off the back of a four-ton lorry and added to it like an outsize holiday caravan. It is the domain of engineers who do running repairs on a fairly sophisticated level during the exercises. In one of these, I discovered the roof was high enough to allow men actually to walk upright as they attended to the repair of machinery: a bonus almost unknown in Arctic conditions. The Penthouse tent had its own generator and even a portable stereo player.

'Just a perk, really,' said the corporal in the workshop.

'There is no mystique about staying alive and happy in the Arctic, it is just common sense,' said the sergeant-major.

Accustoming oneself to the conditions, however, has its complications. One Marine showed me the kit he had to carry at all times. I had to brace myself to lift it up, let alone carry it on my back. Another Marine showed me what he always carried in his windproof jacket. It included six different types of ski wax for all types of weather; a combined ski polisher and scraper; and an eyeshield against the sun's ultra-violet rays, which can damage Marines' eyes as the snow and ice can damage their feet.

This kit may have to be carried while bracing oneself against a high wind. A modest breeze can bring the temperature down a further twenty degrees; in severe blizzards temperatures can come down to minus one hundred. Any prospect of actual fighting will have disappeared long before this: Marines and enemy alike will have got their heads down and kept them there. Even in much easier conditions, engines of vehicles will have been kept running all the time, or may have to be re-started with the aid of blow lamps.

Special tactics have to be devised when men are under maximum strain, facing punishing conditions. When I was with the exercises, 'our' forces were withdrawing down the valley as if under a Russian attack. There were three main locations, one behind the other, all of them having to be put into retreat as the enemy advanced, and preferably without the loss of any of 'our' Marines or equipment.

K Company 42 Commando were notionally blowing up the bridge near Hindsoetri, which spanned a frozen, boulder-strewn river. The Marines were under pressure from the weather and from the brigade commander, an eagle-faced brigadier who descended by helicopter on an ice-covered road, his pilot nonchalantly holding up a drooping rotor arm so that civilian motorists could pass underneath it.

'The river is still frozen and, if the bridge were blown, would be a major obstacle,' said the young lieutenant who was second-in-command. 'You could not get a tank across, and you could not get troops across. You would have to replace the bridge. We are also guarding the bridge from the enemy during the period we are deciding whether or not to blow it, thereby keeping the commanding officer's options open. You have to sign two NATO forms which lay down the circumstances in which you blow up bridges.'

I found the commanding officer himself, a gentlemanly man

with a face suggesting the ultimate in calm, in his office. Office? His office was the back of a Land Rover. A small desk was placed longitudinally. He was busy with the bridge-blowing form which the demolition guard commander and the engineer commander each had to sign.

'It is *not* an exercise in bureaucracy,' he insisted. 'It is clarification of the situation for the guard commander, and it is very necessary.'

The Marines were dug in, mostly in camouflaged tents, around the bridge. Notionally they were ready to pound everything in sight. But the lieutenant admitted that the air threat (a potent factor in an actual enemy advance) could not be simulated in this exercise. All the same, at least one difficulty of war – finding out what, more or less, is going on – was realistic enough. The commanding officer himself was trying to reach units on the other side of a high mountain, with a high-frequency radio which would 'hug' the surface of the mountain, whereas the usual frequencies would be blocked by it.

In such circumstances, around a crucial point such as a bridge, almost everybody has to take his hand at sentry duty. I found a medical assistant on one-hour sentry duty overlooking a valley from which enemy fire might come. He was also ready to cope with any injuries that might occur. He nearly had one to cope with as I, climbing the slope to talk to him with the aid of two ski sticks, missed my grip on one of them and fell into two feet of snow, my bare hand suffering a trace of frost-nip because I did not wipe the snow off my skin immediately. Frost-nip is minor and corrects itself with the application of warmth; it is only frost-*bite* in which the tissues are attacked and permanently damaged.

The medical assistant wore glasses but said that, fortunately, he was long-sighted and could therefore see the enemy if they showed up. The machine gun he was manning could fire between six hundred and a thousand rounds a minute. It was just as well his eyesight presented no real problem. In a real war, medical assistants would indeed have to go beyond the skills they more usually employ.

This particular medical assistant told me about his more usual concerns. 'Normally I deal with sprained ankles, injuries to knees and people burning themselves with their cookers,' he said. 'I deal with frost-nip, where the surface layer of the skin goes white, and with frost-bite, when the whole tissue is damaged. It often happens. Two cases so far have been sent back to the United Kingdom. One will not come back; he will be rated "Arctic unsuitable". Such men stay in the Marines. But if they came to the Arctic again, the cold would first attack the affected tissues. The Marines accept that such men are no longer suitable for Arctic service. It doesn't prevent a man being a good Marine.'

Later in the day I had a good chance to experience the sort of conditions that can easily produce frost-bite. Supply lorries were sent out to a rendezvous point to meet a unit which needed re-supplying. I went with them. The sun had been so bright that during the day the temperature in its direct rays had barely been at freezing point. But now night was coming on; the sun had disappeared and the temperature started to drop dramatically. I pulled the ear flaps on my Marines' hat down, grateful for my standard-issue mittens and my double-layer moon boots. Moon boots consist of a loose, quilted underboot and a big loose overboot, also thermally proofed; these are fused to a non-slip sole about twice the length of ordinary shoes.

The sun eventually disappeared altogether; the dark became deeper despite the reflected light from the snow; the men on the re-supply convoy grumbled and growled. But still the unit to be re-supplied did not turn up. The air began to be painful to breathe. If we had stopped there much longer it might have begun to 'burn' the lungs and freeze stiff the hairs in the nose, both of which can make breathing more difficult and painful. After an hour the re-supply convoy moved out, as it would do in a real war to avoid being pin-pointed by the enemy.

Another rendezvous with the unit wanting fresh supplies would have to be arranged later. I was unworthily grateful for the reprieve from the biting cold.

'Training in the conditions of actual war!' said the sergeant-major dismissively. 'They will have to try a different place and time, that's all. These things happen in war.'

The Norwegian public (those few who venture outdoors: sentimental feelings about snow are more common in the British, who don't see so much of it so much of the time) take the Marines' mock battles with good grace. The Marines go out of their way to make sure that this continues. They even package up their excrement and take it away with them rather than leave it to be revealed by the Spring thaw.

Such precautions have their just reward. Friendly waves are common from the local population. The sergeant-major thought he knew why: 'The Norwegian is used to conscription and to being in the Reserves. He puts on his uniform, takes his rifle from under the bed and goes and fights, or at least exercises. In England you would not get that, because Britain hasn't been invaded since 1066. Norway was invaded by the Germans in the last war, and doesn't want to be invaded again.'

Such tensions as exist between local population and exercising Royal Marine Commandos are minor. Again, the Marines struggle hard to ensure that this is so.

'These lads work hard and they would like to play hard,' said the sergeant-major. 'There is some heavy drinking at the weekends; but there is always that restraint, that tension – they know they must not go too far. In Britain a few fights in home towns, scattered up and down the country, might not be noticed. But they would be noticed here. The Norwegian is a very orderly person. So our lads, on top of all the other strains they have to face, have to watch themselves when they are enjoying themselves.'

After a week of these conditions, I felt a great admiration for their restraint.

★

No human mind and body could meet the needs of Arctic exercises without thorough prior training well before there is a flurry of snow in sight. The Royal Marines, as I earlier saw for myself, are given a taste of things to come almost from the time they first put on the uniform of the Royal Marines (minus the green beret until they pass out successfully).

Any casual stroller on Woodbury Common in Devon who strayed too far from the footpath might have refused to believe his eyes. From behind a hessian screen, and through holes cut in it at the requisite heights, he would have seen a corporal of the armed forces pushing out first his head, then his arms, then his private parts, fore and aft.

The casual stroller would have heard the appreciative laughter of forty-two combat-kitted young men, aged between sixteen-and-a-half and seventeen-and-a-half; but might not have guessed that he had been present at an important, indeed vital, part of their education.

The unconventional tableau was composed of Royal Marines being innovatory in their methods of training, deliberately providing a laugh for the youngest recruits in their first two weeks (called the 'Induction Fortnight') to fix in their incredulous minds the vital necessity of personal hygiene at all times – even in the field, even in the frost and rain.

The twenty-one-year-old lieutenant in charge of the troop of forty-two, which had been marched over from the nearby Royal Marines Commando Training Centre, four miles from Exmouth, faced the young men with such confidence and buoyant poise that I found it difficult to believe that he himself was scarcely four years older than the inexperienced troop he faced. I had already had one small but significant indicator that this tall lieutenant had moral as well as physical courage. When I had asked him what his father's job was, he hesitated fractionally and then said, obviously rejecting the temptation of important-sounding euphemisms, 'A clerk.'

Obviously he was well-suited to tackling life head-on, which is a prime quality in the Royal Marines, whether in coping with one's personal background, with gunfire or with hygiene.

'It is *all* hygiene in the field,' the lieutenant told the junior recruits, who were receiving the same basic thirty weeks' training as the (aged eighteen to twenty-six) adults, but slanted in its presentation to suit younger and perhaps more tense minds.

'You have been learning about hygiene and personal administration back in the camp,' said the lieutenant. 'We are now going to teach you in the field. You can be in the field for a long time. If you can't look after yourself, then you can't fight. Clean yourself and you feel better. And if you feel better, you fight better. You have to look after yourselves from your head to your toes. If you don't clean yourself, you aren't worth the rifle to fight with. First of all your hair . . .'

Out came the corporal's head through the hole in the screen. The sergeant who was team leader, a tough Scot in his late twenties who looked as if he might gargle with razor blades, stepped forward and smartly attacked the corporal's hair with a sodden face flannel.

'Your hair gets horrible,' warned the lieutenant. 'You have got to comb it. That gets the nits and fleas out. Then you have really got to *clean* it. Plenty of soap and water. Next the face. Camouflage cream is the best producer of zits. At the end of ten days your face would look like Mount Vesuvius. And nasties in your ears! You can be tempted to leave it, but you must get right in there and get them out.'

The sergeant obliged with a vigorous wiping of the corporal's face.

'Next, teeth. If you come down with toothache it is agonizing. You can't be a good soldier and have bad teeth. Nothing better at five in the morning than cleaning your teeth. It wakes you up a bit. Smoker's toothpaste is best; it comes in a tin and doesn't burst in the field.'

The corporal had his teeth cleaned in a foaming display, courtesy the sergeant.

'Then shave. It makes you look smart and it makes you feel better. And when you use gas masks, if you have grown two days' beard, it breaks the seal of the mask. Bonded razor blades are no good. You get issued with standard pressure-razor blades in the field and that is all.'

One of the more daring recruits piped up at this point: 'Can the sergeant wash our faces as well?'

The joke fell flatter than flat. 'No,' said the lieutenant. 'Next, hands. Under the finger nails as well. That is where all the crap goes. After two days of exercises, your hands will get very hard. I recommend a small pot of vaseline – not perfumed lotion. Next, down to your parts.'

The corporal was allowed to attend to his own parts without the help of the sergeant.

'Seriously,' the lieutenant told the laughing recruits, 'you have got to keep your parts clean, or you will go down with dhobi-itch or crabs. That can be very nasty. Powder them up when you have washed and dried them. Now feet! You have got to look after your feet. Probably the most important bit. You have got to dry your feet and powder them up. If you don't put powder on, when your feet get wet, you are going to get blisters. We are talking *big*; they will stop you walking. They will burst, and you will get blisters *on* your blisters. No joke.'

The sergeant resumed his help to demonstrate the cleaning of the feet.

'Armpits. Wherever you are, there is no reason why you should not strip down to the waist. Wherever there is hair, it attracts lice and dirt. The arse . . .'

Having disposed of that, the lieutenant added some general principles of hygiene in the field as distinct from civilian life: 'You don't want to smell of roses. If you are in the jungle, you can smell deodorant miles away, and the same with cream soaps. Just a basic soap, so it doesn't pong. Plain talcum powder. One person here had Brut. You can smell it miles away. Also, you are going past civilians and they are going to think the Marines are a bunch of whatsits, aren't they? Questions?'

There were three or four, almost all dealing with matters which had already been covered. I was told that a survey had shown that six months into their training, junior Marines had remembered only 15 per cent of what they had been taught, though refresher training quickly raised this total.

The sergeant wound up the session: 'Always make sure you clean your equipment afterwards. If you cut yourself, and your razor is dirty, you will get some nasty infections. Go back to your ranks.'

To the stray civilian eye, it might have seemed an idiosyncratic method of training. But the lieutenant immediately and succinctly justified it when he turned to me and said, 'This is the point; if they know we have a sense of humour among all the shouting we have to do, then they will know that training can be fun and learn quickly.'

But it was made plain to the young men that, despite the jokes, the point being made was vital – especially in relation to hygiene. Inter-service rivalry is exploited to get the point across. The sergeant team leader took up a typical attitude when he told me that hygiene was one of the Royal Marines' biggest prides.

'It is not the thing in the *Army* to wash the camouflage cream off their faces when they go to dinner in the evening,' he said. 'But it is absolutely taboo with us to leave it on. You get the camouflage cream off, you eat, you put the cream on again! I would be kicked out by the chef, or the other members of the galley, if I tried to eat with camouflage cream on.'

The instructors prefer to get the point across by jokes rather than by shouting; but shouting there undoubtedly is in the junior Marine's first weeks of training. It is shouting to create an atmosphere of urgency rather than to wound the recruits' pride. But its effect must be memorable in sixteen-year olds who are almost always — the training teams say — still schoolboys at heart.

Its justification, say veterans, is that it takes eight weeks to change a civilian into a serviceman who can live in the field, look after himself and fire his rifle; and another twenty-two weeks to turn a serviceman into a Royal Marine Commando. Thirty weeks to change a complete life style; so there is no room for tentative methods. The Royal Marine Commandos have to be kept up to their establishment strength of about 7,500, and though there is now less wastage because of high unemployment in civilian life, the demand for new men must be met with the greatest possible speed and with the least cost to the taxpayer. A sense of urgency is a vital necessity; if that means a few short sharp shocks to the recruits, so be it.

Though they are naval men, the Royal Marines are an individual breed and quite unlike the average *matelot*, as Marines refer to sailors. The average Royal Navy man does not expect to meet an enemy face to face; and his *own* face can reflect that basic fact. By and large, it is the face of an intelligent manager or technician rather than that of a physical combatant. The Royal Marine, like men of the Parachute Regiment and the SAS, tends to have a bearing and face that suggests that its possessor could be picked up and used as a battering ram. Battering rams are precisely what they may have to be; and their faces reflect it. If a sergeant has a scar on his nose, it is considered bad form to ask about it: it may have been a military or private fight, and if it was the result of a mere civilian accident like walking into the edge of a door, the possessor is not likely to want this fact revealed.

Unlike the Navy, and like the Army, only moustaches may be worn, and they are well-trimmed and macho. Beards denote skin afflictions, not individuality: they are generally taboo. Eyes are alert and ready for anything. Tattoos are liberal but usually out of sight. Hairstyles make the average short-back-and-sides look like unkempt decadence.

The training reflects the type of human being who is sought, and the Commando Training Centre itself reflects the training.

It is not an institution that is afraid to wear its heart, head and rules on its sleeve. Just behind the entrance on the main Exeter–Exmouth road is the circular guardroom of rugged stone blocks. On its *exterior* is a glass case full of trophies, including the Golden Tiller won by the Provost Staff in 1984 in the Inter Departmental Regatta and the RSPCA award 'for services rendered', a model horse in bronze. It may seem risky allowing such trophies, some solid silver, to be on the outside of the guardhouse, until one realizes that Royal Marines are very, *very* rarely mugged or robbed – it would require a lot of courage.

Inside the guardroom, and directly beside the reception desk, so that no one can miss it, is a photograph of a Royal Marine with his hair cut in such a way that the effect is of a thin metal plate moulded to the shape of the head. Under it is the caption: 'Hair shown in this photograph is the expected standard for Commando Training Centre, Royal Marines. Signed, Regimental Sergeant Major.'

Any recruit too dense to deduce from this that he has entered a macho world is then confronted with a notice-board on which are advertised the judo club, some sporting events and a stag night with 'Melissa Blondie and Exotic Dancers'.

If this is the Marine's university, it is plainly the university of life, and a rugged sort of life at that. The young men who face the haircut photograph and the notice board for the first time have had some preparation for what will transpire, but not much. At the recruiting office they have been given simple tests like the Royal Navy mainstream. If they are reasonably articulate, conform to the nationality regulations, pass the medical tests, and are of good character, they are passed on to the potential recruits' course at the Commando Training Centre.

The service pays their fares to the camp and back home, but there is no suggestion at this stage that the young men are necessarily joining the Corps; they spend three days at the Centre, and are then reported on by the training team, which usually consists of a lieutenant, a sergeant and four corporals. About one thousand new Marines are needed every year. The brightest hopefuls are told to go back home and expect a letter inviting them to join in five or six months' time. Less bright youths are told to go away, get more training and come back in six months' time for reassessment. The remainder are told, 'Sorry, we don't think you've got what it takes – I shouldn't bother to try again.' These constitute 43 per cent of those applying.

Those who are invited to join are told to report on a given Monday, and are sworn into the Royal Marine Commando Corps the same night. Then they start their Induction Fortnight. It is not unusual for quite a number of youths to say, during this fortnight, that they would be happier in some other career. Normally the sergeant and perhaps the lieutenant tries to encourage them to give it a longer try; but while I was at the Commando Training Centre one youth confirmed that he wanted a discharge, another was being discharged with a dislocated finger, one man was put into a remedial troop until he was fitter, and two complained of being homesick but were talked out of leaving.

The sergeant in charge of the troop I watched took me into the grounds of the Centre to show me the activities of men towards the *end* of their course, so I could compare them with the young recruits I would be seeing later. The experienced men had been twelve weeks in training, and warmed up with press-ups for ten minutes so they didn't damage muscles when going over the assault course.

'You can cause injury to muscles if they are cold,' explained the sergeant. 'They have to do as many press-ups as they can in a minute. We are looking for forty in a minute. *Quality* ones, not just dips. One day they will do a mile-and-a-half sprint, then they have to put a pack on their back and run twelve miles. Recruits don't have time to go out at night, but trained

Marines are crappers, they are out of their brain with drink. They will drink heavily on Saturday and Sunday nights, but be all right to fight on the Monday morning.'

Veteran Marines say that young men joining today are fitter than the ones joining in the 1960s. They *need* to be. Men were carrying telegraph poles, swinging from an iron frame twelve feet above a pool of water, storming a brick wall, leaping a pond, and carrying their comrades, fireman-style, for a two-hundred-metre run which had to be completed in ninety seconds. The thirty-foot-rope climb with full kit (36 pounds) was regarded as one of the simplest things these twelve-week trained recruits were faced with. It was useful, I was told, if a helicopter couldn't land but could lower a rope to be climbed.

To maintain a competitive spirit, which helps men to fling themselves about risking life and limb, there was a notice-board in the field on which were listed the records set for the assault course, which had to be completed in five minutes or less. The all-time record was two minutes thirty-seven seconds, the term and year's record each being two minutes fifty seconds.

For the junior recruits I was with, such achievements were a long way distant. They assembled on Woodbury Common, parts of which were covered in dense woodland, at nine on a Saturday morning – halfway through their Induction Fortnight – for their very first taste of life in the field. The lieutenant, the sergeant and the four corporals took over an old brick-built wartime decontamination centre as their field headquarters. They got the recruits to make up the camp beds, install the camping-gas cooker, the paraffin lanterns for illumination, and the trestle tables (with green baize table-cloths) on which maps would be consulted and food consumed.

The ultimate aim, said the lieutenant, was for the men to be able to do a six-mile run with full kit, broken by obstacles, in seventy-five minutes. If any youth thought he couldn't manage it, it was pointed out to him that officers were expected to do it in seventy minutes, carrying full kit and rifle.

'To a certain extent,' he said, 'the sergeant and I stand back, and leave it to the corporals. If a proper bollocking is needed, they send the recruit to the team leader and he may, or may not, decide to send the offender to me. If they send him to me, it is like being struck by a thunderbolt, it is divine retribution. I have to appear as this aloof character, which is a little annoying.'

In the field, the recruit's home is a nylon bivouac and his philosophy is what is called the buddy-buddy system. The buddy-buddy system is indeed the cornerstone of life in the Marines. It is based on the theory that two heads are better than one, and that a man in difficulties should always have a man by his side to help him.

The buddy-buddy system, which helps to get bivouacs (bivvies) put up in less time and ensures that the cooking is done by the better cook of the two men, depends on the ability to mix and be unselfish. Some sixteen- or seventeen-year olds find this a new and daunting concept at first.

'They have to be tougher than the average naval man,' the sergeant told me. 'They have to face a lifestyle which is in the field, and demands greater physical and mental activity. They have to cope with fear, the elements, the prospect of capture, the unknown. They must have a tough mental attitude and be physically tough as well; they must have a well directed aggression. But with all this, the recruit has got to be able to live with the forty or so members of his troop. He has got to have a good mixing capability. He has got to look after his buddy or oppo, and his buddy or oppo has got to look after him. They will basically eat, sleep and so on together.'

The point was soon demonstrated when the youths in unaccustomed combat clothes were lined up, parade fashion, on a patch of grass enclosed by the trees of the common. They were split into four rows or sections, and allowed to pick their buddies. Some chose people they had met on the train down; others simply settled for the man who happened to be standing beside them.

Tolerance, it was explained, was a necessity. I was told that in a previous troop one man was a member of the National Front and, in the same section, there was a black youth. 'So of course, we put the two of them together,' I was told. 'That is the Marines' sense of humour, and they became firm friends in the end. You must teach them tolerance – religious, spiritual, political and racial tolerance.'

The buddy-buddy system is not designed to form cliques but a troop spirit – 'we don't want little ghettoes growing up between them'.

Co-operation is encouraged at all levels, as well as the buddy-buddy level. More than one young recruit got sworn at for just standing there instead of helping a man near him who was in difficulties. Gradually – usually very gradually – men get used to helping the next man in such tasks as making really watertight the plastic bags in which spare dry shirts, denims, socks and training shoes must be kept at all times, so that a Marine is never in the position of having two sets of clothes wet at any one time. Recruits are also expected to help one another, especially buddies, when doing the cooking or putting up the bivvy in which they will both live.

On his first days in the field, the recruit seems to spend his time putting up his bivouac, taking it down and then putting it up again – all so that an operation which at first can take half an hour can be brought down to only a couple of minutes.

The corporals hammer the right points home, first showing the recruits what a bivvy consists of – two nylon sheets, an upper and a lower, the lower spread out on the ground and the upper about two feet above it, tied to two trees about eight feet apart.

'This is going to keep you out of the wet and the wind,' said the corporal to the half of the troop who were having a bivvy lesson while the others were having cooking lessons. 'You can get your head down in a bivvy nice and easy. It is two pieces of nylon, but it is going to be your home.'

The two sheets of nylon, called ponchos, have a hood in the

centre, because their original use was to provide a waterproof smock and hood in which marching or resting troops could protect themselves from the rain.

'You must tie off the hood, otherwise you are going to get wet,' barked the corporal. 'Tie it off with a draw cord. You never actually wear these as waterproofs, that went out in the First World War' – an exaggeration; they are still occasionally used for their original purpose – 'but you still get your ponchos with holes in. Tie the bivvy itself up with a quick-release knot, so if you have to leave in a hurry, you don't leave pieces of string to be found by the enemy, so that he knows you have been there, and how many of you there are. Only one twist round the trunk of the tree. You have to *buy* green string, none of this gardening rubbish, because that breaks too easily. A ball of green string will last you most of the way through training.'

The corporal turned to camouflage, describing it as a skilled and individual art. With a big knife he started hacking at the undergrowth in the woods. 'Lay long ferns on the top, with smaller ones on top of those, right? So it looks natural. Don't put bits of pine tree on the ground, because it doesn't look natural – pine trees don't have foliage until well above the ground. Don't have the inside of leaves pointing outwards. Stick some pieces of undergrowth into the soil, as if they were growing there. Don't have anything too regular; make it look natural. There! That's how to do it. Now how long do you think it will take you to take down this demonstration bivvy and be out of here?'

One recruit piped up: 'Half an hour, sir.'

'We put this bivvy up in three minutes,' riposted the corporal crushingly, 'and we were slow because we weren't actual bivvy partners. We should have been able to put a bivvy up in about a minute, and do the camouflage in another five minutes. When you put a bivvy up, *you put it up*, you don't fart around. You say to your oppo, "You take the top poncho and I have got the bottom one," and you get on with it.'

I was to find out a lot more about bivvies and the buddy-buddy system before I left the scene of the training. But now I went to search out the cookery part of the field instruction while the other half of the troop practised with their bivvies.

A corporal was attacking a number of cardboard cubes with a jack-knife. They were twenty-four hour ration packs, probably the only source of food to a Marine in the field unless he can catch some animal and skin it. My last contact with such packs had been with the Army, some five years previously, and I discovered that the available range of packs had been narrowed. At that time it was a choice of A, B, C, D, E or G, whereas it is now down to A, B, C or D. The contents of individual boxes, however, were more wide-ranging; and all the food still had the really essential property – it could be eaten cold or heated up.

Don't be lazy, a corporal was telling this half of the troop. 'Don't say, "I can't be bothered to cook it" and eat it cold.' That did not give as much calorific benefit as heated food, which was especially important in fighting.

The corporal barked out some tips about how to deploy the contents of the packets and tins in the ration packs while in the field.

'You are better off in the field taking the sugar, whether you like it or not. It is all calories. If you don't like soup, throw it in with the main meal. If you are so inclined, you can put the dried apple flakes in with the main meal as well, or have them as a sweet. Use the packets of salt. Sweat will lose salt out of the body, and if you don't take salt you start going down with cramp. Right? Packets of chewing gum – useful, it helps you clean your teeth afterwards. Right?'

The corporal opened one of the tins of processed meat and threw it, jagged lid upright, at a recruit, who managed to catch it without cutting himself – a useful accomplishment in the field.

'Next, toilet paper. Don't forget that. If you want to go for a crap, it is better than grass. The snack – it is beef spread.

Biscuits. They are quite tasteless. However, if you dip them in that beef spread, it's quite tasty. People tend to ditch these biscuits when they get them because they don't taste at all.'

The corporal threw one at the recruits. 'Manhole covers! Watch your heads, they do hurt! However, on exercises, when the helicopter doesn't arrive to collect you and you have to spend another night on the ground, you will find these biscuits very useful. Guys on the Falklands lived on these for a month. No problem. Don't try to cook individually, share it with your buddy. One does the cooking while the other is cleaning the weapons. Mix all the food in one tin and share out of that tin. Don't ditch the tins that held the food. Take the bottom out as well as the top, and squash the tin flat, with the top and bottom flat inside it. Save plastic bags, and put your scrap or gash in them. If you start leaving it around, the enemy finds how many of you there are. Twenty minutes is enough to cook a meal, understand?'

'Yes, corporal!'

'Good. There are roughly 5,750 calories in that pack. You have your cooker with solid fuel pellets. The proper way to put it out is to blow it out or put your boot on it. You have the best ration pack in the world – the Americans' are too sweet, they have a tin of three hamburgers and the bottom two are deep in fat, so if you eat them cold, they are rubbish. Right?'

'Right, corporal.'

For a moment the whole troop, reunited after their bivvy and cooking lessons, were apparently deserted by the training team. I, clad in combat clothes (but with a civilian shirt and an unbuttoned combat jacket to make it clear to people who might want to talk to me that I was not part of the hierarchy) was the sole mature adult on the scene. Three recruits immediately produced cigarette packets and lit up; one recruit in the first row threw a packet of cigarettes to a chum in the third row, and a murmuring of grass-roots opinion on the trainers became progressively louder.

The corporals reappeared abruptly. 'No smoking in the jungle!' roared one.

'You get people in the jungle called trackers,' roared another. 'And they can smell you three miles away – and that is when you haven't washed. The native can smell you in the wind, and he can smell your food. There are head-hunters who help train the British Army forces in jungle warfare. In South Africa, scouts never used to wash for a week, because the native used to smell him for some reason – the wearing of after shave and things like that. In the field you *don't* smoke, you don't shout, you keep your talking down to the minimum, you don't have a smoke with your buddy and tell him what a good night you had last night. Understood?'

Wouldn't it be better, I asked the corporals, if adults were mixed in with junior recruits? Yes, they said, that could be done, but there were reasons against it.

'There is a great difference between sixteen-year olds and eighteen-year olds and over,' said one corporal. 'The older man has probably been on the dole, he has a girlfriend, he knows more about life. Most of *these* guys haven't had a drink in their lives. Probably they have just bought their first packet of fags. When they arrived, they were all wearing T-shirts; we said, "Get *them* off for a start." For them, this was an extension of school. But if you put adults and juniors together half-and-half, then the adults would see the juniors were getting away with lower standards and drop their own standards. You mix in a *few* younger people and it might work. Junior troops are a pain. They need a lot more nursing to get them up to standard.'

At one time, said the corporal, the juniors had an extra ten weeks, but that had been changed: it was now a common syllabus. So even when the juniors got into a unit, it might be eighteen months before they had settled down and ceased to be kids. They would be in trouble if they didn't settle down. 'In a unit the sergeant-major doesn't nanny people, he says, "When you are told to be there at a certain time, you are there or you are in trouble." It will take a lot of time to get some of these to that stage.'

By the middle of this particular day in the field, one recruit had slashed the tip of his finger on his jackknife and had been promised a sticking plaster the next day if his finger was starting to fall off; one had asked if he could smoke on parade and been told he couldn't; and the bivvies which had been set up by the recruits in the wood had been pronounced 'horrendous' by the sergeant. He maintained, in a tone of voice that would have cut through steel, that the troop hadn't 'got the message' about the buddy-buddy system.

'Don't stand there just looking at him trying to get that bivvy up. F——ing *help* him!'

One of the corporals explained to me, 'At the moment they are like schoolkids. To some of them, it is just a cowboys and Indians game. Quite a few of us instructors feel that the recruits should not come in quite so young. But the government says we have to do it, so we do it.'

I felt bound to point out that I had tried to put up a bivouac myself, and had found the whole thing rather primitive and fiddly. The sergeant said a new bivvy bag would be coming in shortly: they had 2,000 already in the Naval stores, but when they would be *issued* was a different matter. They might be kept for war conditions, in case there was another Falklands.

At this point the quietest of the four corporals turned to me and prophesied that, if there was another Falklands, a lot of the stuff being taught on the course would go out of the window. 'I was in the Falklands,' he said. 'I brought back a lot of photographs, one of an Argentinian with no head, and it is strange coming back to *this* sort of thing. After the Falklands, a lot of this stuff we don't need to know. It was a question of digging two feet down and getting into the hole as fast as we could. A lot of stuff you learn in training would be worth a ball of chalk down there. We used elastic, not string, for our bivvies; but if a recruit now showed up with elastic we would nip it in the bud, because others would say, "If he is using elastic, we want to." Recruits must learn the basics first, even if they adapt the knowledge to the conditions of the real field.'

In a free society, such training must obviously tread a subtle line between the Foreign Legion and the polytechnic. The young lieutenant, whose style of leadership I saw then and later to be very much one of leading-from-the-front, insisted that juniors were *not* treated like the Foreign Legion. That would only destroy their confidence. The Marines didn't want supermen, they wanted men with the will to learn, and to be built up. If the recruit needed self-confidence, the trainers tried to instil that in him; if he was too cocky, they tried to curb that aspect of his character.

'I have never met a sergeant-major who was a sadist,' said the lieutenant. 'You can forget Windsor Davies – that's an out-of-date stereotype.'

But the strain of training to be a Royal Marine is great enough without sadism. As buddy-buddy pairs of recruits prepared their main meal in their mess tins, I asked three pairs what they had found most difficult so far, and how satisfactory they found the – sometimes arbitrary – buddy system. Most said they found the washing and ironing of kit the least attractive job. Most got on with their oppos well enough – those who had met previously rather better than those who had no personal knowledge of the other at all. Two who had selected each other as oppos told me they hadn't known the other was a Catholic until both told me.

One pair's answers struck me as more revealing than some of the others. I shall give them the fictitious names of Harris and Jackson. Both were sixteen. They were trying to follow the cooking instructions on their steak and kidney pudding (to 'boil' it) by putting it, dry, into their mess tins and trying to heat it up. Both were possibly flustered. Jackson found the basic ironing and the cleaning of lockers difficult to take, but regarded the field 'as a bit of adventure'. Harris said he didn't like being told what to do about washing and ironing; he presumed he should *know* what to do. His mother had been pleased that he was joining the Royal Marines, but didn't really want him to leave home. His most pleasant experience in his first few days in the Marines was in meeting a chaplain: 'He was really nice. Everyone else is so strict.'

I lost sight of the quietly spoken Harris as the troop were lined up to have their cooking criticized. They were then, as a safety valve, allowed to stand individually in the front of the group and tell a funny story. Three did; and the joke about the Marine who slid his shiny boot under a woman's skirt was the cleanest. Two demonstrations were set up by the training team, one showing a buddy-buddy pair entering a wood to get their heads down in all the *wrong* ways, talking loudly, arguing about who was supposed to be carrying what and (said the sergeant) very likely ending up dead; the other pair doing it in all the right ways, almost completely silent, keeping watch for twenty minutes before putting their bivvies up, making sure they were facing towards any possible intruder, and never *both* separated from their kit at any one time, not even when defecating.

'You see?' the sergeant asked the assembled troop. 'When they are told to get packed and get out, the two good ones are off almost immediately. These other two men will probably end up dead, and other men will have to get their bodies out or try to save them – to the danger of other people in the section's lives. Do you *now* understand what we mean by the buddy-buddy system? But it is every man's responsibility to know his personal kit and where it is. You can't expect someone else under gunfire to take your kit. There is no way I would risk my life because some idiot keeps spewing his kit all round the area. We are talking about dying here. You are going to be in a combat situation at some time in your career. You would not waste your time on anyone who hasn't taken the lessons he has been taught. You won't help anyone who has flagrantly disregarded the rules of fieldcraft . . . Fifty press-ups for that man who talked! Sixty for you, too! You ask any questions, you talk to me, right?'

While still trying to sort out, in their own minds, the difference between a buddy for whom one would lay down one's life and an idiot who deserves to be dumped, the troop were lined up elsewhere for a water drill. All topped up their bottles and were lectured on the necessity for guarding water, not spilling it, and pooling it between buddies for cooking and shaving.

Then they had to pack up their bivouacs and put them up somewhere else. Events tumbled over one another like waves on a sea shore till even I, who had to follow it only intellectually and not physically, began to see the day as a blur. Dirty mess tins were hurled into bushes by the corporals and the recruits had to crawl on their knees to recover them.

The sergeant: 'I want you to bring back your bivvies to where you had them first. In an hour I want to see you standing by your bivvies. One hour. Disappear!'

More criticisms of the bivvies resulted. The troop was sent off for a run of five miles or so, in the deepening dark of the evening. I was sitting in the brick blockhouse with some of the training team, trying to work on my notes in the light of a paraffin lamp when Recruit Harris suddenly appeared.

When I had talked to him a few hours previously, he had been pale. He was now as chalky white as Hamlet's father's ghost. Though he had only just finished the run, he was not sweating. He was swaying between two other recruits, who were trying to hold him up. His eyes were staring sightlessly ahead. Whistles were blown. The lieutenant and the sergeant appeared.

'Dehydrated,' said the lieutenant. 'Apparently he has had only coffee all day, and that empties liquid from the system, anyway. Tea is much better. Sit him down.'

Harris collapsed limply on to a chair, still staring straight ahead, not saying anything.

'Donald, eat this,' said the sergeant, thrusting a tasteless biscuit at his mouth.

No reaction.

'Bite it! Chew!'

No reaction.

The sergeant was handed a hot sweet cup of tea. 'Donald, drink this. Hot sweet tea. Take little sips – yes?'

No. Harris only moved his mouth slightly.

'Donald, how many fingers am I holding up?'

Still no reaction.

'Come on, Harris!' said the sergeant, trying a more pressing approach. 'You have *got* to drink that tea.'

But Harris was past the point at which either kindness or barked orders could reach him. To everyone's relief, a truck arrived to take him back to the Commando Training Centre. His combat jacket was thrown over his shoulders and a blanket thrown over that, and he was helped into the vehicle.

Harris at least escaped the final putting up of bivvies that day. If putting a bivouac up can be demanding, sleeping in one can be even more so – certainly to a civilian unaccustomed to such pursuits. Though I had been invited to a camp bed in the training team's watertight blockhouse, I had said that I would prefer to experience a bivouac in the field, so that I could see for myself what it was like. When Harris fell out through heat exhaustion, instead of having a bivouac to myself I experienced field conditions even more exactly by sharing one with Harris's buddy Jackson.

Living in the field requires a quick adjustment of standards and expectations; to very young inexperienced men this may be difficult. In real field conditions it would be not merely a matter of comfort but of safety too. This I discovered when trying to wriggle and slide into the bivouac (the highest point of the 'roof' only about eighteen inches off the ground) without knocking the camouflage off the top of it. I did not succeed. The camouflage was replaced and a new start made.

While the recruits wore training shoes or nothing on their feet in their sleeping bags, I admit I cheated slightly. It had taken me so long to get my unbroken Marine boots on that I was fearful that if I took them off I would never be able to get them on again – certainly not in time for any feigned 'emergency' that might be organized during the night. I kept my boots on, which made wriggling into the sleeping bag, and then wriggling the sleeping bag forward so that it was as deep as possible into the bivouac, even more difficult. It left my head near the open end of the bivouac – a space that would normally be filled by the recruit's full kit bag.

As instructed, I rolled up my combat jacket and put it under my head as a pillow. Result: a cricked neck. There was a further complication. No one had warned me or anyone else that Jackson had entered for the 'Loudest Snorer of the Year Award', with every chance of winning it. To misquote the Duke of Wellington, it may not have disturbed the enemy, but by God, it disturbed me. Finally, unable to sleep because of this, and because of the light of a full moon, I solved both problems by taking the kit bag from under my head, unfolding it, and spreading it *over* my head. This cut out the light and some of the noise. I had been told that it was by individual improvisation that men survived in the field; I began to see what was meant by that.

The major discomfort in a sleeping bag is not what one would most expect: being cold. The sleeping bags themselves are reasonably warm; indeed they keep the recruit probably warmer than he would be in an ordinary bed at home. But once the underside of the bag has been pressed flat by the sleeper's weight, the ground underneath it can be clearly felt – undergrowth, stones and all – and, by the early hours of a frosty morning, the cold from this source does increase. Privacy, however, is no real problem. Though two men are sleeping side by side in a space tapering down from eighteen inches, and no more than three feet wide, the sleeping bags make the whole thing quite impersonal. In general, conditions in the field make such a big mental adjustment necessary that things which would cause social embarrassment in civilian life come to be taken as a matter of course. Necessity is the mother of acceptance as well as of invention.

But there are penalties for not thinking ahead. At about three in the morning, with the ground beginning to get frosty, I realized I would have to make a call of nature: I had been drinking tea with the sergeant and corporals while the recruits were having to manage on their water bottles filled with rationed water. The process was far from easy, entailing wriggling the sleeping bag backwards out of the bivouac, wriggling out of the sleeping bag and staggering off to find a suitable spot which was *real* bracken and not camouflage. The rule that there must be no lights around bivouacs, even when they are being put up and taken down, is good for the preservation of night vision. This was just as well, as the moon was now covered with threatening rain clouds. The sergeant had told me he *hoped* it would rain heavily in the night to get the recruits used to damp kit; it looked as if his prayers would be answered. They *were* answered as I left the bivouac. By the time I got back again, and had managed to crawl into the bag and the bivouac, there was a steady downpour, splattering on to the nylon sheet and pressing its coldness down against the side of my face.

This made sleep doubly difficult. I assumed from the lack of snoring from Jackson's direction that he too was finding it difficult to sleep. I *did* manage to get some sleep, even in what for me were unaccustomed circumstances. But it seemed a long time to 6.30 in the morning – the time the troop had been told to be up and making themselves a 'wet' in their mess tins, to wash, shave and clean up, so as to be ready on parade near the blockhouse within an hour.

At this early hour of the morning, kit was inspected yet again and retribution inflicted for offences. Offenders were sent off to form a row on the right flank of the troop, with pithy comments from the sergeant or the corporals on their inadequacy in cleaning their kit.

'Call that razor clean? You can go down with toxaemia and all because you are too bloody lazy to clean your razor. Don't tell me you have cleaned it, because you haven't.' Another addition to the row on the flank.

'You are going in for the "Shittiest Mess Tin of The Year Award", are you? There are enough bugs in there to put you down with gastro-enteritis. Then your men will be carrying your kit and doing your job, and there will be four other people off sick!' In addition to the offender being sent to the growing row of offenders, his mess tin was thrown by a corporal, with a gesture of contempt, into some nearby bushes.

'You've got enough muck at the bottom of that mess tin to dig out with a spade. Don't tell me that tin's clean, because it isn't. You calling me a liar?' Another recruit was sent to join the line, another mess tin was flung derisively, this time over a corporal's shoulder.

A corporal told the men in the line of miscreants to start doing benders – an especially tiring form of press-ups in which a position has to be held in which the arms are bent halfway. In case I should be feeling sympathy for them in their plight, he told me, 'They are not working together, and they have no get up and go, no motivation.'

'They said they hadn't enough time to get their kit clean,' put in the sergeant. 'If they had got up bloody early, they *would* have had enough time!'

The recruits whose mess tins had been flung all over the place retrieved them by crawling on their hands and knees all the way. It was good practice, as it happened, for their penultimate trial of this particular training session – the endurance course. As preparation, they were told (without explanation) to leave all personal possessions beside their kit on the ground and to take off and also leave on the ground any watches that were not waterproofed.

These precautions were by no means redundant. The recruits discovered this for themselves when they reached Peter's Pool, a pond with a rope along its centre. They had to wade through the pool, clutching the rope and being led by the young lieutenant, who shouted, 'Come on, keep it moving! Follow me, men!'

The lieutenant had water up to his neck – and he was a good head taller than some of the recruits, who had to half swim and half drag themselves through the pond, sometimes under the surface, before wading out on the other side, drenched, to find a long hill ahead for them to climb. From there they ran down into a water tunnel through which they had to swim under water, their lungs nearly bursting. Then another hill, a clamber over two long structures rather like concrete sheds, and into the real teaser of the endurance course – what the corporals termed the 'Smartie Tube'. This was a tricky tunnel with an uneven top and bottom. Sometimes it was hardly big enough to get through with full kit, and sometimes it was full of deep water. By the time they staggered out of this tunnel, several recruits had blood flowing from grazed hands and arms, and had to be pointed in the right direction by the corporals, who encouraged others still in the tortuous tunnel with shouts of, 'Come out of there, or I'm in there and get you out!'

At the end of this the recruits, without much pause, ran back the four miles to the Commando Training Centre. And before they left their training, said the corporals, they would do it all with full kit, and in seventy-five minutes.

Some of the recruits were already showing signs of impressive stamina. Two of the smaller ones came out of the Smartie Tube breathing almost normally, while larger men puffed and blew like beached whales; and at least one was as capable of a joke as one of the corporals as he entered the Smartie Tube.

'Watch out for the adders in there,' said the corporal.

Replied the recruit, who was obviously already on his way to becoming one of the tough and practised Royal Marines I met in the Arctic conditions of Norway, 'I used to piss adders as a hobby.'

It could easily be the unofficial motto of the Royal Marines, who remain part of the Navy, though they operate on sea and land – perhaps making amphibious landings, perhaps being held offshore in enormous troop carriers like the old HMS *Bulwark* as a deterrent, perhaps being flown to trouble spots by air.

From time to time there is talk of detaching the Royal Marines from the Royal Navy and making it a separate force, or even attaching it to the British Army. Seasoned Marines grumble that the Royal Navy would much rather spend its funds on a shiny new frigate than on the Royal Marines, though it is pleased to claim the Marines as its own when they do something creditable.

They say they are much more highly trained and specialized than the British Army, and much more direct and combative than the rest of the Royal Navy. And they also say that they effectively keep their independence by telling the Navy they are soldiers while explaining to the Army that they are naval men.

A change in the honoured status quo of the 7,500 men of the Royal Marines is therefore not likely to crop up just yet, if ever. The buddy-buddies will go on in what is, effectively, a form of tough independence within the Royal Navy. They are a highly disciplined force, but even they only have to work within the Royal Navy's present tough discipline, not the even tougher discipline of the past.

9

GOOD ORDER AND DISCIPLINE

'Many a man, in those days, got a month of it [sacrifice
of privileges], without ever knowing what his offence
had been; and if he was not content to take it without
inquiry, he might perhaps have found it doubled.
Flogging was the only punishment that was limited, but
the limit left quite large enough to make it most formidable. Under that system the ships were generally in a
first-rate state of discipline . . .'

– Lieutenant, writing in the 1860s.

'People today can't afford to lose their rate status or be
fined. It is bad for their career. So behaviour is better in
the Navy, without a lot of heavy-handed discipline. I
think discipline now is very fair, not severe. For the
people who do actually get into trouble, whatever they
have done, they deserve what they get.'

– Leading seaman aboard destroyer, 1980s.

In the middle of the last century one highly individualistic
captain ordered his crew to adopt red serge frocks with red
woollen comforters as standard uniform, and to parade before him in that colourful attire. Another, the captain of the
Harlequin, dressed his crew up as harlequins.

'It does not appear yet to be thoroughly understood,' wrote

a contemporary critic of the Navy, 'that a ship does not belong to her captain and crew, but to the service.'

It was, to continue the understatement, perhaps a time for strict discipline at the bottom rather than at the top. Even at the time of the First World War, naval boys could still be caned for drunkenness. Ratings could be given twelve lashes with the cat-o'-nine-tails at the captain's discretion for mutiny – though they could no longer be ordered to wear a wooden collar for swearing, as they were in the eighteenth century. And the maximum permitted corporal punishment was down to only forty-eight lashes.

It is only in very recent times that the Royal Navy has lived down its tradition of summary severity. In 1860 a young captain wrote to his influential father-in-law at the Admiralty, claiming that discipline was slack because the captain's despotic authority had been watered down. He reported that men demonstrated against their officers by throwing their mess tins or pieces of shot around on the lower decks or jeering. Punishments were so trivial that the men laughed at them and were incited to go further. Solitary confinement was a farce, because the fore cockpit used was so stuffy that the door was always left open, so that the prisoner in 'solitary' could in fact laugh and joke with his mates.

'Flogging has been condemned very generally, I believe, out of the service, but certainly not in it,' he wrote to his well-connected father-in-law. 'I believe you will not find an officer in the service who would be glad to dispense with it, and hardly one who will say that he thinks it could safely be abolished.'

In the days when the average sailor was thought to be interested only in 'rum, bum and baccy' (alcohol, sodomy and tobacco), the direct and unsubtle methods of Captain Bligh of the *Bounty* might have been excused as the only available path to good order and discipline.

Captain Bligh and his school are no longer there. It is no longer necessary that they should be. They would be greatly out of place in a Royal Navy in which the sailor is more likely to receive his pay straight into his bank in the form of a draft than into his palm in jingling coin; in which old hands are apt to say, 'It's a married man's Navy now'; in which the 'musical suitcase' (stereo radio-cassette-player) is a more prized possession than a hangover, and in which, one leading seaman on a destroyer assured me, 'We are allowed three cans of lager a day, but on our last period at sea, when we had been at sea so long, people actually gave up drinking. They often didn't even bother to draw their beer because it was too much of a routine.'

The leading seaman who told me this, a recently married twenty-five-year old, said – as if I didn't believe him – that this last point was really true: 'There were twelve guys living in my particular mess, and after a while there were only three of them drinking. They were fed up with this cans-of-beer routine. There is one chap in the mess who looks after the beer, and he comes around with a piece of paper with everyone's name typed on it. You sign next to your name. They give a signal that the beer is ready and the one chap collects it for the whole of the mess. Routine! Of course when the men got ashore it was a bit different.'

Different, but even then not as different as it might have been in the past, when there was little for the sailor to do in a foreign port except drink and hope that the drink would not rule out his second business, fornication. Nowadays there are still bars and nightclubs and ladies of the town; but there are also shops selling cameras, quartz wristwatches, pocket calculators, radios, micro TVs and other desirable status symbols. The fleecing barmen and the district tarts are up against something even more powerful than morality: consumer technology.

It is true that when they finish up ashore on the Falklands after demanding months at sea, the Navy can still be – as one Falkland Islands barman put it – 'a little active'. But for every one who goes ashore after finishing off his ship beer ration of three cans, determined to have a skinful and a woman in the first half hour, there are half a dozen or more of a different mind. They will have spent their time aboard preparing for examinations – perhaps an 'O' Level in Geography and Maths – prior to going ashore, when they will have a couple of beers and a look around the local sights and shops.

'We go to fewer places now, and we know when we arrive that we may not be coming back,' said my leading seaman informant. 'People want to have more of a look at the sights and not get themselves badly fuddled with drink. *That* was for the days when there was nothing else to do, and sailors weren't expected to be interested in the topography of the places they visited, or in their history.'

This leading seaman had had eight years in the Navy and had been swotting to get qualifications that would stand him in good stead when he left it. He acknowledged that tensions could grow to explosion point during prolonged periods at sea. It was silly things that did it, he said. Someone might simply knock a cup of tea over and a swearing match might develop. It rarely came to blows, because if two people were upset with each other, there were many more people present who kept a cool head and would say to both, 'Oh, come on! Have some sense, both of you!' That usually worked. When men went ashore at a foreign port – and many spent three evenings ashore during a five-day visit – more and more didn't want or didn't need to get drunk to release the tension.

Political, national and local rivalries can still produce explosions among naval men, aboard and on shore. There is a city in which one football team is regarded as Protestant and the other as Catholic, and a too-decisive win on either side can cause name-calling in the mess while at sea, even after the consumption of no more than the regulation three cans of lager. I was told that fights sometimes broke out when things became a 'political rally', but the participants were usually told to shut up and, if incapable of arranging it themselves, put to bed. Then someone would keep an eye on them all night if necessary.

In all the messes I visited to put questions, the theme of self-management of potential disciplinary offences emerged strongly. Officers, of course, are simply *expected* to conduct themselves with decorum at all times, though I saw one or two reddened faces, and heard some animated conversation over glasses which could have contained an honest whisky or rum. Ratings, senior and junior, are expected to keep their behaviour within bounds manageable by the mess; it is only if they hawk their offences to a wider audience that serious trouble may be expected. If they come back aboard late at night the worse for wear, and enliven the mess with full and frank opinions on matters sporting or racial, it may be tolerated. If they start broadening their audience by staggering down passageways with their conversation stuck in the same groove, the honour of the mess will have been impugned. They may well end up before the first lieutenant and be given a fine or extra work at night. Neither is a very terrifying penalty when the sailor knows that shortly he will be at sea again with nothing to spend his money on, and will possibly be working till late at night in any case.

The master-at-arms on a ship – especially a small one – is not only the senior rating responsible for regulation (discipline) on the ship: he has also to handle matters like mail, travel arrangements, and drafting. He is not well pleased, and neither are his staff, when the paperwork is interrupted by the misdoings of a sailor who may well have also irritated the local police. This is especially so when the local police happen to be foreign, and the honour of Britain is at stake. The public-relations importance of the Navy in foreign ports is hammered into both officers and men.

The leading regulator of one of the smaller ships (a rating with the same sort of function as a regulating petty officer) told me that on a small ship the regulation was probably done by only two people. He did not seem to feel that this was too few; indeed he gave the impression that most cases were run-of-the-mill and to be played down if possible, even at the time.

There was, for instance, the case of the Antwerp bicycle. While his ship had been in Antwerp, a sailor was seen coming back on board with a push-bike. It was late at night. As sailors do not normally take their push bikes with them on their travels, it did not require a Sherlock Holmes to infer that the bicycle was not his own. And even a Dr Watson would speedily have jumped to the same conclusion when the sailor, once up the gangway, turned and threw the bicycle into the water.

The gangway on such visits is invariably manned. The sailor, no cunning Professor Moriarty, had disposed of the evidence under the very eyes of the men assigned to man the gangway. The Belgian police were contacted. Has anyone reported losing a bicycle? Time passed. Eventually the Belgian police reported that no one had reported the theft of a bicycle.

The offender escaped with a warning about his conduct. Despite the apparent risibility of such circumstances, the actual theft of property – especially the property of friendly or un-friendly foreign nationals – is *not* regarded as merely risible.

If someone *had* reported the theft of the bicycle, the leading regulator told me, the man would have been charged with theft. Some police forces might have left the ship to deal with it; other police forces might have wanted the man to come back and face a civil action. Basically it would have come out the same way in the end, with the affronted bicycle owner compensated and the offender left in no doubt that he had better keep his hands off other people's bikes in future – or at any rate not throw them overboard.

According to the leading regulator, the first two nights after landing were the time for the 'run-of-the-mill drunks'. After that, it died down.

On those two nights, they *prayed* for no drunks, but usually got one or two. 'They are not normally fighting drunk, you understand. They are just incapable-of-walking-properly drunk. Provided that the officer of the watch was there and the gangway staff could control the man, he would have to be examined to see that his condition was not due to a fall on the head. Normally he would then be written down in the log and turned over to the sick-bay if necessary, and a watch kept on him for the night by his own mess mates to make sure he didn't choke on his own vomit. The watch kept would be just by his mess mates, if he was not violently drunk. I would not deal with it personally. In the morning, our chief would get the report from the gangway staff and the man would be brought here, to the regulating office. And I would find the relevant charge and type out a charge sheet. After that I would arrange the officer of the day's table (the list of defaulters) and I would do the prosecution.'

First, said the leading regulator (and I began to see why a busy leading regulator always prays that sailors can handle their drink and messes can handle their drunks) the charge would be read out to the man. Then he would state the facts to the officer of the day and the man would have the chance to question anything he had said. It was all very proper and judicial; and, at this stage, a purely investigatory charge, to see if there was a charge to be answered. If the officer of the day thought there was, the man would be told he would go before the first lieutenant. In that case the master-at-arms himself would take over and arrange the first lieutenant's table. The man would then go before the first lieutenant or, if he had done something particularly grave, the captain.

I asked the leading regulator what had been the worst case he had encountered in the two years he had been in the job. It was not drunkenness as such, he said.

'You get some very nasty assaults around in Portsmouth,' he said, adding quickly. 'It is about 70 per cent civilians assaulting our men, and 30 per cent our naval men attacking others. Most of it we call "Rate Bashing". They wait until they get a *matelot* on his own, and then have a go at him. Those younger lads ashore! Whether it is because the *matelots* have got money to spend while a lot of them ashore are unemployed and skint, I don't know. A lot of the trouble revolves around women.'

It was to be expected that other men on other ships would bear this out. One gnarled petty officer on one of the aircraft carriers, his legs curled up under him on a table like some experienced alley cat, assured me: 'The *matelot* in the Navy is better off with money than the man in the Army because he is in port for a short period of time. And they out-stud the R A F and the Army. They have better skill at it.'

I relayed this view to the fleet master-at-arms on the *Invincible*, a highly composed and quietly spoken man with the benevolent smile of a good family doctor, and a pair of chromium-plated handcuffs visible in a glass-fronted cupboard by his side in his office.

'I would not have said the Navy are better womanizers,' he said mildly, 'though every sailor likes to think he is. Every sailor wearing his blue suit likes to think, in his heart, that he can drink fifteen pints of beer, too. In my experience I wouldn't say so. The average man's beer consumption is four pints.'

Masters-at-arms, plainly, have a job which gives them a realistic rather than a romantic view of mankind. This one, when I saw him, had been master-at-arms on three ships, the previous ones having been HMS *Herald*, a 2,500-ton survey ship with a complement of 115 men, and HMS *Birmingham*, a Type 42 3,500-ton, 280-complement, destroyer. He had enjoyed, in short, a very wide and varied experience of ships and men to call upon in the performance of his disciplinary job.

I asked him in which sort of ship his job was easiest. 'It is a difficult question to answer, because usually on smaller units you have a wider spread of jobs. In HMS *Birmingham*, as well as being master-at-arms, I was flight deck officer, controlling helicopters on and off the ship, as well as doing other coordination work. It could be that the purely disciplinary functions are more demanding in a ship the size of *Invincible*. It depends on the mix of the ship's company. That is very important. You can never really say in advance, "This ship will react in this way." But if someone sticks on you twenty or thirty really bad lads at once, they can give you a lot of work. I would say, at the moment, there were ten or twelve I could point out and say, "I will be seeing a lot more of them than of anyone else."'

But most of the disciplinary offences, pointed out the mild fleet master-at-arms, not anxious to blackguard the ship's company, related to things that would not be offences at all if done by civilians. They were offences only within the context of a disciplined service. The main thing was absence – people not coming back on duty on time. Usually it was a matter of hours rather than days. The people who went off for longer than that were in a tiny minority; usually it was one hour or two.

What, I asked, was the explanation? 'The usual problem is sailor's things in a foreign port,' he said.

Such as? He looked almost uncomfortable. 'Oh, you know, taking some lady home and leaving early the next morning and wondering, "Where am I?" It was nice when he was flushed with beer, but in the morning, it is a different story.'

'Tell him about Australia,' prompted someone in the office with fewer prim sensibilities than the fleet master-at-arms.

'Er, yes,' said the fleet master-at-arms. 'We had a young man . . . well, a young lady tied him to the bed and left. This was in Australia, you see. They are fairly liberal sorts of people, the Australians. He met this young lady ashore. They spent the night. He obviously upset her in some way; all right, he was so drunk he couldn't perform, so she tied him up and went off in the morning and left him. He only just caught the ship. Her brother turned up and released him; took pity on his cries for help. That was an exception. But there will usually be one fairly amusing one.'

On a big ship, said the fleet master-at-arms, he had to deal with cases which, in a smaller ship, where everybody tended to know everyone, would be simply 'headed off'. This applied to all sorts of offences, including wilful disobedience. On a big ship, you sometimes felt you were sitting there waiting for the problems to come through the pipeline, instead of having a quiet word in advance of the trouble.

But the ship did get a pep-talk *before* it got to a foreign port about the sort of places to see and the sort of places to avoid; it was done in the form of a ship's broadcast based on information supplied by the British consulate and the local police. It was delivered the night before the ship berthed.

The fleet master-at-arms obviously knew off by heart all the sailor's problems and his Achilles' heels. 'It went like this,' he said. 'If we have been at sea three weeks, he has got a fortnight or three weeks' money in his pocket. He may be there for four days, with another three weeks at sea to come. The sailor has always got money in his pocket for that four days, whereas your soldier in Belize is there all the time for a year, so he has got to pace his money. The sailor has got his money and he knows it has only got to last him four days. He can spend £75 a day.'

In one respect, at least, the falling relative value of the British pound has been helpful to naval discipline.

There were no longer, pointed out the master-at-arms, 'cheap places to go' for the sailor. 'Singapore used to be considered a cheap place to go. If he went to Singapore ten years ago, the sailor had eight or nine dollars to the pound; now there are only two-and-a-half or less dollars to the pound. He is kept short of money to spend on *anything*, and because in general the Navy doesn't go very far any more, there is more novelty in going to places. So sailors spend their money looking round much more, or they spend it on cameras to take photographs, because they might never have a chance to go back. They do this rather than drinking themselves senseless and creating problems.'

The fleet master-at-arms thought the Navy was now attracting a more intelligent and aware type of person. This had its implications on the discipline side. The eighteen-year old or nineteen-year old the Navy was now dealing with was of a higher level than the eighteen-year olds who had joined with the master-at-arms. 'We ask him to do a lot more. You don't want a sailor who can just ram bullets into one end of a gun and out the other. Yes, in the first few weeks everything is done for you and thought for you. But as it goes on, more is left to the individual's feeling of responsibility. We expect him to *know* when he should be getting his hair cut and keeping himself clean. As he gets more rank, we expect him to behave. It is a quite different atmosphere.'

It *has* to be totally different in the case of men who work in the operations rooms. I had this made clear to me while I was in the operations department routine office of HMS *Invincible*, where I found a thirty-six-year-old chief petty officer, who looked understandably older and graver than his years, in his tiny kingdom. He had converted it himself from a store. The room was no more than six feet by six feet, and its occupier warned me not to put my feet on a certain spot on the carpet on the deck, domed at that point, or it would give off a booming sound which would carry through a large part of the ship. Tucking my feet carefully under my chair, and thankful that the ship was not throwing me about, I asked him what the routine officer of the operations room was expected to do. Well, he said, he was the co-ordinator of the six sub-branches of the operations branch of the ship. He tried to get everyone in the right place in the ops room at the right time, detailing the duty watch party, getting people away at the right time for special professional courses, like damage repair and fire fighting.

I gathered that getting *enough* people into the ops room at the right time was not always easy. It was in fact jolly hard, said the chief petty officer, because they were undermanned: it was deliberate policy to keep the numbers of men down; only so many beds had been put into the ship, and that was that.

If he wanted to make sure people *would* be where they ought to be, and do what they ought to do, he knew the best way to do it. He tried to see and tell them all personally and individually. Then they would turn up: 'You feel *you* have failed somewhere along the line if they don't turn up. That is the way to look at it.'

In perhaps only one respect has the greater sophistication of naval men worked against discipline. The chief petty officer put his finger on it when he said with obviously ambivalent feelings: 'Lads are cleverer than they used to be ten or fifteen years ago. They are clever enough to work a flanker if they don't want to do something. We have to tell them to stop hedging. A perfect example: "Navy Days", when ships and men are on show to the public. Generally speaking, outside the leave period, it is popular. We would normally get volunteers. But this year it will be happening during our leave period, when about 65 per cent of the ship's company are on leave. We have to cover it with 35 per cent of the ship's company. These guys have to work that much harder. There are people who otherwise wouldn't be on duty, but may still find themselves on duty because they have to cover it. It is unfortunate when people try to drop out, but it happens.'

The policy is to fill the sailor's spare time with enough activity – be it cleaning the ship or sport – to absorb energy that might otherwise be dissipated into anti-social behaviour.

Sport is a much-loved outlet. A leading seaman aboard HMS *Torquay* (which was the Navy's only navigational training ship when I went aboard, and was due to be scrapped the following year) told me with enthusiasm about a trip the ship had made to the West Indies, with a crew that included a descendant of Sir Winston Churchill.

'The first port of call was at St Vincent after thirteen days at sea,' said the red-bearded sailor, who had served seven years in the Royal Navy. 'There was no class between us and the local people. We were glad to get there after a fortnight at sea. We were there five days and, as you know, it's hot. But I personally took part in a lot of sporting things, cricket and soccer. We played against the West Indians, and they are very good. Most of the nights we went out drinking, but I don't mean getting drunk. When we got time off, we spent it on the beach, having a bit of sport.'

Their trip must have been something like that of HMS *Bristol*, the Type 82 County Class destroyer, which, in transit from Bermuda to Wilmington, North Carolina, and in temperatures hitting the high eighties, set her men to break their own relay running race record. The men managed it by twenty-six minutes.

Yes, they did something like that on the *Torquay* in her days in the West Indies, remembered the leading seaman aboard the navigational training ship. Part of the time they had been quite tired, and even when sailors went ashore to taste the attractions of the West Indies, they were advised to stick together as members of a mess.

In this way, the Navy hopes to promote safety and discipline while sailors are ashore. The leading seaman said that the crew had received a printed sheet of advice about which areas to go to and which areas to avoid. But it was *advice* and not instructions.

'And I don't always take notice of it, frankly,' admitted the leading seaman with a knowing grin. 'They advise us to go to a certain bar, and more often than not, when you have been at sea for a few days, you are looking for something different, so . . .'

It was a mistake, said the leading seaman, to underestimate the sheer cussedness of the average sailor, even today: 'The *matelots* would rather go in the bars they are told *not* to go in. It is not just because you can pick up girls there; it is just the way the *matelot* has always been. Cussed. Most people would go straight to the Black Tarantula bar, or whatever, if they were told to keep out of it.'

But today, he said, it was mostly down to self-discipline; and the self-discipline of the average sailor had changed, though there were exceptions sometimes in the case of very young men out on their first ship. They were away from the UK for the first time, feeling their feet, and they hadn't really thought out the implications of the fact that they were going to have to live peaceably together with the other lads for perhaps two or three months.

He saw it like this: 'They seem, once they have got into the routine, to start to get at each other's throats. Yes, they are a bit homesick, maybe. It doesn't get out of hand, because if they do step out of line, someone has a word with them, or they are put right before it can go any further.'

Sometimes, perhaps especially in an older ship, where equipment is apt to be relatively primitive, the strains faced by a homesick and restless young man can be formidable. The leading seaman recalled thinking, during the West Indian trip, that a more modern vessel than the old HMS *Torquay* might have been a better bearer of the flag. There was always something going wrong with the old *Torquay*, ending up with the machine in the engine-room called the evaporator, whose vital role was to convert salt sea water into pure drinkable water. Not only had the evaporator gone out of action, but some of the ports the ships had visited did not have purified water suitable for taking aboard as drinking water. So the crew had had to live with a water rationing system rather like that which civilians ashore had suffered in the 1976 drought, when water was turned off for certain periods of the day.

In a ship with severely rigid discipline, such deprivations might have sparked off a modern version of the mutiny on the *Bounty*. The fact that it all passed off peaceably could have been due to the sensible approach to discipline taken in HMS *Torquay*.

A twenty-year-old midshipman, due to become a sub-lieutenant the following week, told me that rules of behaviour on the ship were of a sort that made sense. For instance, no smoking in the operations room or in the refrigeration department because of the gases there. And flexible interpretation of the standing orders on drink: it depended on who was in the bar; if there was need for a social drink, perhaps among senior officers, the bar was kept open.

I asked the twenty-year old, whose sensible manner belied his extremely youthful appearance, whether the discipline aboard had been different for him at the start of his time as a midshipman – a young officer in training.

'Not on this ship,' was the prompt answer. 'On certain ships, you can find it is completely different; officers in training get their bar bills restricted to a certain amount. It depends on the first lieutenant really; on the *individual* responsible for discipline, rather than on the ship. I have heard stories about officers in training being overworked, and people in the wardroom treating them as if they were separate beings. One officer I know said he was very badly treated when he was in training; no one talked to him. It was as if he was out of another world. That stemmed mainly from the first lieutenant's attitude, which a lot of other officers in that ship adopted. They follow the first lieutenant. That sort of thing is very, very rare now.'

In a small ship, discipline is every bit as important as discipline in a destroyer or carrier. Men are living elbow-to-elbow, and a hiccough in the wrong place can throw the whole system out of gear. Experienced sailors say that discipline aboard a minesweeper or other small ship is not different but is simply 'scaled down'.

It must be, in fact, discipline with a human face. While aboard HMS *Bronington*, the old wooden-hulled, wooden-decked minesweeper which Prince Charles commanded when he was in the Royal Navy, it was immediately easy to see why. Men live at close quarters with officers; a starchy, ultra-formal discipline could easily inflame deep and dangerous resentments.

In the wardroom where the Prince lived, conditions were pleasant enough, with built-in chintz sofas. There was a signed photograph of the former commanding officer's well-known parents, a cartoon presented to Prince Charles when he returned to the vessel for its re-dedication, and a commemorative print presented to Prince Charles of Mary Port Pier in the Channel Islands. But even in this wardroom, there was a tight use of space which would make calm tempers of the utmost importance in an emergency. The folding dining-table, used by up to five officers, was designed to serve also as an operating table for surgery. A string of hooks from a slender girder across the centre of the ceiling, an officer explained to me, was for the operating lights. The freezer for food was not in the wardroom but outside it in the passageway, though it bore a crest which included the Prince of Wales's feathers.

Some ships, said the commanding officer, a lieutenant, had a non-smoking mess and a smoking mess. But it was difficult to arrange that on a ship this size. There were two quarters for ratings, one with the forward magazine for the ship's gun in the bulkhead, the other with the sonar boom which would be lowered to help detect mines. This was disguised, in its off-duty moments, as an upholstered circular sofa. Ten bunks were compressed into the larger quarters. Though an officer was quick to point out, 'We give our lads more space than the United States Navy', it was easy to see that a bad atmosphere on board, caused by faulty discipline, could be very dangerous indeed.

The commanding officer said that it was important to be able to tell friendly moans from more serious ones, and to be able to tell early.

'You can get fillet steak, and they say they are fed up with fillet steak,' he said. 'Some people always like a friendly moan; they want to get something off their chests. You don't pay too much attention to that. You must make sure the ship is kept clean, but not in a niggling way. During their morning watch, the men clean the bridge and the next watch will clean a certain area of the ship. Every man has a single part of the ship to keep clean, which would take him ten to twenty minutes – unless there was a captain around, when he might spend half an hour on it. But if he is thorough one day he could almost miss it the next day. The routine is that floors should be *clean*, rather than that they should be vacuum-cleaned *every* day. A man vacuum-cleans my cabin every other day. There has to be some sort of rule, because I have, in effect, forty housewives on my ship – the number of the crew – and you get a situation on some ships where one of them is keen and he will end up doing everything, and that is not fair. You have to say to someone else, "Look, your quarters aren't as clean as Joe's; do something about it." All this is laid down in the captain's standing orders, but you have to remember that the main thing is simply that everything has to be clean every day. It is said that a small ship's routine is more relaxed, but you have full Navy discipline backing you up if you need it.'

So the ratings, in fact, stand to attention every evening as the commanding officer of the ship makes his rounds, just as they would do in a grander ship, and the ratings' possessions are expected to be laid out tidily. Once a month, when the captain of the squadron makes his inspection, everything is expected to be stowed away. Nothing is expected to be standing carelessly in the messes or the passageways.

One might expect the sense of confinement on a 170-foot minesweeper to be even greater than would be imagined from the ship's physical size. All men live and work in that part of the ship above the waterline, so that they have a chance to get out if the ship hits a mine or is otherwise attacked. But though the men share this very small space, the sense of being hemmed in is paradoxically said to be less than on some bigger ships. One rating said that, in a minesweeper, you could quickly get out to some fresh air on the deck, if you felt like it and duty permitted; whereas in a carrier, though the cabins and passageways were larger, you found that when the aircraft were flying, you had to stay below deck all the time and sometimes breathed no outside air for days.

Although they cannot escape very far from one another the men can get some fresh air on deck, and this is an asset to good order and discipline, albeit of an accidental kind. A more deliberate asset is the system of pre-empting trouble by having frequent welfare meetings, chaired by the commanding officer, who is president of the mess. The meeting, never held more rarely than once a month, consists of the chief navigator, a senior rating, a leading hand and one representative from each of the ship's messes.

The subjects for discussion are many and varied. Should

there be a ship's dance? One of the able seamen has said he is a hairdresser and, if provided with scissors, will cut hair for £1 a time – 50p for mess funds and 50p for himself. Would this be acceptable? The video – was it worth the hire charge? That cricket match ashore – how much was required to cover the matter of refreshment?

All such matters are thrashed out in as democratic a discussion as can be managed in a disciplined service, at a meeting with all ranks present. The answers to those particular questions came out as follows. Yes, there should be a ship's dance. Yes, the hairdresser had a deal, 50p per haircut to go to him, the other 50p to the ship's dance. No, the video was not worth the money, since few people were watching it (at sea the routines and the limited space available are not conducive to video-watching; while, alongside the jetty at Rosyth, the sailors like to spend as much time as possible ashore). For the cricket match a box of sandwiches and two cases of beer would be sufficient, possibly funded out of the savings created by discontinuing the hired video.

Any steam not let off at the welfare meeting tends to be let off on the wooden deck of the minesweeper, which is a little marvel of intensively used space. As well as a one-man decompression chamber for the divers, it boasts also the sweep wires, the floats and the misleadingly called 'kites' for the sweep wires – and an open air gymnasium which includes one of those machines where aggressive (or for that matter genial) spirits can be discharged through the lifting of a simulated weight.

In such improvisational ways aboard the baby vessels of the Royal Navy are energies channelled and good order and discipline maintained. It must go some way towards ameliorating being fed from a galley smaller than the boxroom of a Victorian villa, and having to put up with the other inevitably primitive conditions aboard such sprightly little ships.

There are many other oblique but simple factors behind the greater sense of responsibility generally shown by sailors today, a sense which means that more discipline can be internal rather than external. To a civilian it may seem strange to bracket food with discipline. But naval men are sure that there is a direct connection; that the fact the Fleet today is, on the whole, well-fed has an important bearing on the relative docility of the average naval man.

In the huge carrier *Invincible* I found the supply commander secretariat, the commander responsible for provisions, drinking copious coffee and complaining of a slight headache – it had been a 'Ladies' Night' aboard the previous night, he explained (apologetically rather than boastfully). It did not seem to affect his grip on his job, which was to deal with six thousand catalogued items – each of which might be a thousand cups and saucers or one engine, and the total value of which might be around £12 million.

In the seven months' deployment to the Far East which *Invincible* had just finished, they had taken from stores to the ship 100 tons of naval stores and 300 tons of food.

'We are really running an hotel for 1,000 people who have no other alternative sources of food,' he said. 'We have a captive audience. Unlike an hotel, where the guest stays for a week or fortnight, our guests are here the whole time. That is the way you have to look at it. Therefore you have to produce a menu which is not repetitive – many varieties the whole time, and tasty – because food becomes very emotive, especially when you have people kept in a tin box with nothing else to do.'

The commander pointed out that, unlike the Army and RAF, whose men had the alternative of feeding in town, the Navy had no such alternative for much of the time. *Invincible* had spent between 55 and 60 per cent of its time at sea. And, of time spent ashore, very little had been spent in the base port, which meant that sailors couldn't go home to eat or at least go to dine in a reliable and familiar restaurant.

'Meal times become a social event, when we are at sea,' reported the commander. 'If there is a morale problem, they will always start bitching about food. It is a barometer, really, of how things are going.'

To nudge things in the right direction, the ship's company had a wide choice of self-service menus – at least five main courses at lunch and about twelve vegetables, including five different sorts of potato. The ship got through about thirty fifty-six pound bags of potatoes a day. Generally in the evening there would be a choice of four or five main dishes.

All this had to be done on a budget of £1.20 a day per head and – a tangible factor in morale and discipline – if the officers wanted more, they had to agree, as a mess, on what they wanted extra and had to pay for it. It might only be a wider range of marmalades for breakfast, but they would be expected to pay for them. The mess committee at that time, I gathered, had fixed a figure of 35p per day for extras.

'You have to be seen to be playing the game,' the commander told me. 'Sailors will always think, "The officers are seeing us off," if you are not careful. You have got to educate them, pointing out that officers are paying for everything above £1.20 per day. They have to *know* it is coming out of the officers' own pockets. It is my responsibility to make sure officers are not being fed at the expense of the ship's company. I think that could have happened in the past.'

I did discover one little piece of social distinction out of which an inspired agitator might make something. The officers' food and the ship's company's food was cooked in two separate galleys, though with the same entrance. And there was more space around the equipment in the wardroom's (officers') galley than in the ratings'. Why this should be so when, I was assured, the wardroom had only two alternatives for lunch and dinner compared with the ship's company's four or five, I was never able to discover. It certainly made life easier for the chefs operating in the wardroom galley, but I was told these men rotated between the different galleys, so that an above average cook who, on one trip, made a good job of the officers' roast beef, could on another occasion improve the standard of the ratings' food, be it roast beef or mince.

At any rate, the two galleys certainly had the advantage that, if one was taken out by enemy action, the other could cook for the whole ship. This would be so, I was told, even if the one knocked out was the ratings' galley, which cooked for eight hundred, compared with the wardroom galley's normal clientele of 130. I was shown over the galleys to prove the point. One of the chefs, complete with white hat, told me that when they were at sea, they baked seventy-five large loaves of bread a day, plus about six hundred rolls of all shapes and sizes, plus buns and cold sweets. For a 'Families Day' while the ship was in harbour, he remembered making an additional 3,000 buns, and 1,000 mousses or trifles.

The Navy is anxious today not merely to feed its men more than adequately but to be *seen* to be doing so by everyone concerned. Officers are extremely sensitive about the slightest suggestion that they are favoured at those two social events of the day, lunch and dinner. When I observed that ratings' chairs in the dining room were of plastic, while the wardroom's were upholstered, I got the swift retort from an officer: 'Ours aren't as comfortable and are more difficult to repair!' The information was offered in the tone of a boast rather than a complaint: officers know their authority is more readily exercised on a well-fed and comfortable ship's company which does not feel its officers are unfairly favoured.

The technique appears to work. Such disciplinary problems as reluctance to appear at 'Navy Days' if it is leave time, or shouting in the ship's passageways after a night out, are mild indeed when measured against those of the navy of Captain Bligh or even of the latter half of the nineteenth century, when ratings were not expected to get restive merely because they had to eat ship's biscuits riddled with weevils and sleep on the deck; or because rats chewed the calluses off the bottoms of their bare feet. The days of the lash had their reasons and, thank heaven, so have the days of the individually responsible sailor.

Naval legal luminaries now look back on the old severities with dry humour. This I discovered when I discussed naval discipline with the assistant to the Navy's top legal authority. The last of the hangings from the yardarm, said the assistant to the chief naval judge advocate encouragingly, were around the late 1850s, the last being of a Royal Marine aboard HMS *Leven* during July 1860 in the River Yangtse. Encouraged, I asked him what appeals procedure against summary justice by captains had been introduced into the 1884 Naval Act, which was supposed to reform the system.

'The answer to that is very simple,' said the legal functionary. 'There wasn't any.'

The Navy claims that, today, its disciplinary procedures are more or less in line with civilian practice. If so, the road to reform was certainly a long one, starting at a point where pressed ruffians had to be kept in some sort of order by the exercise of unsubtle but arguably inevitable terror.

For many years – in fact until 1957 – the Naval Discipline Act of 1884 was the cornerstone of naval discipline. For misconduct in action, the penalty was death. For communicating with the enemy, the penalty was death. Mutiny was rewarded with death, as was failure to suppress a mutiny, or incitement to mutiny. Striking a superior officer, or attempting to strike one with a weapon, was punishable by death. After this list, there are no prizes for guessing the penalty for desertion to the enemy, failure to protect convoys, arson in dockyards and murder. Death in each case. And the death penalty for misconduct in action, a rather broad term, was *mandatory*, not within the discretion of the court martial.

Any non-capital offence could be tried by the captain summarily. 'Knowing the Navy, it surprised me, when I read it, to discover that the maximum power of the captain under the 1884 Act, section 56 (2), was to impose a maximum of three months' imprisonment,' said the assistant to the chief naval judge advocate, a lieutenant-commander of thirty-two, a qualified barrister whose previous appointment in the Navy had been supply officer aboard a frigate.

The legal hub of the whole of the Navy is a fairly modest suite of three offices in the Royal Naval College at Greenwich, occupied by the chief naval judge advocate and his staff. The chief naval judge advocate, at the time of my conversation, was a captain in his early forties, also legally qualified as a barrister. A man in his position is expected to have had a broad range of experience, both inside and outside the Navy, which he can bring to bear on complex legal problems. He is always a senior supply officer – in other words one who could conceivably command a shore establishment but not a ship. Generally he will have worked as supply officer on a ship. He will probably also have worked in the Ministry of Defence and been secretary to a high naval officer of some distinction. To broaden his general legal expertise he also sits as an assistant recorder in the Crown Court, trying civilian criminal cases.

There is also a functionary called the judge advocate of the Fleet. He is a civilian, a QC with chambers in the Temple. His job is to review all contested courts-martial transcripts and to write to the Admiralty Board if he thinks there has been a material fault in a trial, recommending the Admiralty Board to quash the conviction.

'The rest of us are straight supply officers, with the additional qualification of being barristers,' said the assistant to the chief naval judge advocate. 'There we differ from the Army and the RAF.'

I asked him if he found that he was prone to think like a civilian rather than like a naval man. 'Well, my legal training has been mostly civilian,' he said. 'Before I was on the frigate, I was doing my bar examinations and pupillage, in civilian chambers. If you think of the criminal law, there is no difference between a serviceman and a civilian. But obviously, having been in the Navy thirteen years, you tend to appreciate the problems more when you are presented with the facts. You can see how they have arisen. You apply both your civilian and naval experience to the problems.'

Naval justice, especially at sea, can still be summary. But checks and balances have at last been built into the system, notably those allowing for appeal by petition against conviction or sentence or both, whether the original hearing was summarily in front of a captain or by court-martial.

'Basically,' said the assistant to the chief naval judge advocate, 'it runs very much along the same lines as civilian practice. For instance, at a court-martial, if you plead not guilty and are found guilty, and if you say you are not happy with the evidence or the way it was presented, there is appeal by petition to the Admiralty Board, and further to the Court Martial Appeal Court, against both conviction and sentence. If I were to summarize the difference between the old system and the present system of discipline in the Navy, I would say that obviously the Navy has moved with the changing social climate, and moved away from the corporal-punishment stage. Our discipline would reflect what would be the socially accepted standards in civilian life today.'

The list of offences for which something nasty can happen to a Navy man is still formidable to the casual civilian observer, though at the time of my conversations with the Royal Navy's legal mandarins there was speculation that, in the 1986 quinquennial review of services' legislation, the death penalty would disappear.

But even today, some naval men are occasionally defensive about naval discipline, admitting that it is still summary in its nature, but claiming that the man in the street does not understand why, or realize that there are checks and balances built into the system.

'Yes, our system of punishment is something that tends to get criticized by outsiders because of its summary nature,' the captain of a frigate told me. 'But it is inevitable, because of the nature of the service, that the captain of the ship or submarine has wide-ranging powers of punishment, and needs them. With approval, and dependent on his rank, he can send a man to detention quarters in port. A young steward deserted in the

United States, and was sentenced on the way home to forty days' detention. On arrival at Devonport, he was locked up in Portsmouth. A wrongdoer could get extra work, he could be fined, or the captain could de-rate him – reduce his rank.'

But, said the captain of the frigate, though the Navy did have this system of summary justice, it was basically a very fair system. The man accused always had recourse to a court-martial if the alleged offence was one that could get the man deprived of his freedom.

'If the offence would get you locked up, then you have the right to insist on a court-martial,' he pointed out. 'You are given time to think about it and then brought up before the captain who says, "What's your decision?" We don't have many courts-martial because people prefer to take the captain's punishment, and get on with it. A captain's powers are less than a court-martial's.'

I asked this particular captain whether he thought the system really was fair by modern standards. His reply was prompt: 'We would not want it any other way. I don't think Jack would particularly want lawyers, and the full panoply of the law. You are being tried by someone who understands your problems, not a strange magistrate who doesn't. The understanding may tell for you or against you, but at least he understands. A divisional officer (or friend) normally represents Jack before the captain. The first investigation would be carried out by the officer of the day, who decides whether there is a *prima facie* case; he can dismiss it, but not punish. It is passed to the commander by the second-in-command. If *he* has the powers to punish, he will do so. If it is too serious, it is passed to the captain, who will investigate and come to a decision; and then either punish directly or submit an application to the flag officer to inflict a particular punishment. With all these checks and balances, I think it is a fair disciplinary system today and I think Jack gets a fair deal. But the summary nature of naval discipline simply *has* to be.'

And alongside this newly thought-out discipline is the fact

that the Royal Navy, despite its professional objectivity, and its immersion in modern technology, still has some of the idiosyncrasies that give it a human face.

10

HUMAN FACTORS

'The only time I have ever had to go to the sick-bay was when I had to have stitches in my head. I forgot myself when coming aboard and didn't lean far enough forward when going up a ladder. I caught my head on the metal floor above. I was a bit encumbered at the time, since I was carrying my golf clubs.'

– Lieutenant-commander aboard a destroyer.

'The second-in-command in a big ship is called the commander. I am *not* the executive officer. That is an American term. I am not anti-American, but I just don't like it. We have perfectly good titles we have used for hundreds of years, and I don't see any reason to change them.'

– Commander, second-in-command of aircraft carrier HMS *Invincible*.

It is an irony that one of the Navy's most humanly endearing traits is also one that helps to isolate it from the general public. Its loyal use of naval terminology in everyday conversation – so that a naval guest will ask his baffled hostess not for the lavatory but the 'heads' – is at one level an assertion of brotherhood. Unfortunately at another level – that of making the Navy's values and value known to the average civilian – it is a negative factor of some magnitude. Some of the obscure naval terms are hotly disputed within the Navy itself.

The man in the street could be excused for thinking that the Navy has dragged him into Alice's Wonderland when a sailor standing in a shore establishment says he is 'going ashore', when in fact he means that he is leaving the shore base for the village, town or other expression of outside life.

Nor are other dinner-party guests likely to feel included in what is going on if an argument breaks out between two naval men about how many miles it is from London to Guzz. Of course the explanation is crystal clear to the naval men themselves: GUZZ was the call sign for the Port Admiral, Devonport, in the last century, and so Plymouth became called Guzz. Civilians may be pardoned for not knowing this fact – as, indeed, they may be pardoned for not knowing many things about a Navy which often does not go out of its way to make itself easily understood.

There is also likely to be confusion over the camel. It would not be assumed, certainly not in inland towns, that a camel could ever be part of a ship's equipment; but it is – in the form of a tank secured to a ship to provide it with extra buoyancy. This contingency hardly ever occurs today, but the term remains. 'Pass me that dead marine, old man' – confusion again. The civilian would say, 'Pass me that empty bottle.' And he would be quite baffled if asked to open the Fanny – the name given to any cylindrical tin. He might think he knew what 'Show a leg' meant – 'Get out of bed' – but he would be partly wrong: the term dates back to the time when women as well as men went on naval ships; it was by displaying a leg outside the bed that the ladies were able to convince those in authority that they were entitled to stay in bed when the men had to get up.

Then 'ticklers'. Even some naval men themselves might be baffled by this term, while others would know that it meant tobacco issued by the supply officer in days gone by – tobacco which was free of duty to serving men in the Navy. Civilians could be mightily irritated by its use, as they would be by the use of the word *rabbit* for a supply of tobacco generally. 'Very well,' the civilians might say after the explanation, 'so tobacco used to be carried or smuggled by gutting a rabbit and storing the tobacco in that; but can't you use simple civilian terms?'

The answer, as in so many cases, is *no*. Some naval men don't see why they should abandon their own jargon just to ingratiate themselves with civilians. It would make them feel gauche if they tried – as they might feel gauche in using baby talk for the benefit of a young child. And naval men *do* sometimes talk to the rest of us as if we were uninitiated children, and they were members of a higher order. A harmless, very human fad; but it does not, in practice, help human relations between naval men and the civilians who do, after all, elect governments and pay taxes.

The Navy is perhaps aware of the need to show itself in a human as well as a sometimes baffling professional and technological light. The awareness is reflected in actions and arrangements at the unofficial and official levels.

One of the human links between the Royal Navy, which is chiefly at sea, and British civilians, who are almost always out of sight ashore, is the linking of ships to specific cities and towns, rather on the pattern of 'twinning' towns in Britain and the Continent.

Before its scrapping (which was due in 1985) the old HMS *Torquay* had close links with the South Coast holiday resort of that name. During one summer visit to the town, the ship raised over £2,000 from various sporting and athletic events like sponsored walks and a one-hundred-mile relay race in the town. Local sporting charities benefited. The ship sponsored a children's ward in a local hospital and gave help to a hospice in the course of being rebuilt.

One leading seaman aboard *Torquay* told me that in the fourteen months he had been aboard, the ship had made more than one courtesy visit to Torquay. 'It is the ship's home and we always get a good reception there. We march through the town, and there is a reception afterwards with the mayor and all the civic dignataries, and there is a "Ship's Company

Dance" arranged by the town. If anything, this year's reception was better than the last, perhaps because people thought it would be the last time they could look over the ship.'

Some visits to 'home' ports are more successful than others, a fact well known to all worldly sailors.

I asked one leading seaman aboard the 'Rothesay' Class frigate HMS *Lowestoft* what contact he had had with the East Coast town. I got a rather disappointed answer: 'Last month we stayed at Lowestoft for four days. There is nothing much to do in Lowestoft; there is really nothing. You can see the recession has got the place; so for holidaymakers you have to go to Great Yarmouth, ten miles up the road. There were some dances, but you had to find your own amusement. There wasn't really much integration of the ship with the town, not in my experience. We didn't feel wanted at all there. When you are on most ship's visits, people are pleased to see you, they welcome you with open arms, but in Lowestoft it was terribly difficult. Say you go into a bar, in certain ports people will look after you and buy you beers and say, "It's nice to see you." In Lowestoft, that never happened. You had to make your own entertainment. Yet the trip was well publicized. I think they must be very withdrawn in Lowestoft.'

East Anglians do indeed tend to be withdrawn people, waiting to see if people are to be trusted before they extend the hand of friendship. That, I said, might have something to do with it – that and the fact that the recession had badly hit a never-too-prosperous town, making people disinclined to spend beer money on themselves, let alone others.

'Yes,' said the lieutenant aboard HMS *Lowestoft* who had overheard the conversation, 'but in fairness, at the official level, the hospitality was good, showing that Lowestoft is pleased to have a ship that it can call its own. We were actually at anchor one mile off shore, so we were not too visible; and in any case there had been other ships in there in previous weeks.'

Another leading seaman backed this point up. 'Wherever the ship has been, if there have *not* been many ships there already, you are made more welcome. The major ports are getting a little bit fed up with seeing ships all the time. I have been to Lowestoft twice in HMS *Lowestoft*, and it was really good. There was a big dance put on in one of the dance halls on the pier. There was everything laid on – food, drink, receptions, football matches.'

The leading seaman said he had once been in HMS *Glamorgan*, which was tied to Wales. 'When you go down to Wales on that ship, you get looked after; you really do. They have official receptions for you, with three or four lord mayors all slanging one another in the after-dinner speeches. The people of Cardiff organized a lot of things for us.'

Perhaps the recession has taken the edge off naval visits to adopted home ports, as it has taken the edge off much else. When the adopted port is overseas, especially the wealthy USA, the hospitality has tended to be more spectacular in a civic sense and perhaps more friendly in a personal sense.

HMS *Bristol*, the Type 82 'County' Class destroyer completed in 1972, a relatively new ship, has adopted the city of Wilmington, North Carolina, and vice versa. She has paid five visits to Wilmington in about the same number of years. As she sailed up the Cape Fear River to berth in her adopted city, a volunteer band performed on the flight deck, with a piper on the fo'c'sle. There was a ship's party and banquet in a local park. British sailors went over the huge Second World War battleship *North Carolina*, now converted into a floating museum.

A lieutenant in HMS *Bristol* told me, 'The people of Wilmington can't do enough for us, either at a personal level, or for the wardroom. Officers get invited out to lunch. Junior ratings get invited to go swimming. Everybody extends invitations. If you have just gone ashore, they stop their cars and ask, "Are you from the ship?" And then they say, "Can we offer you a lift into town?" or "Can we show you around?" I was with a friend having a quick lunch at a hamburger sort of place. When people heard we were English they said, "Can we take you anywhere or show you the sights?" We invited them back on board for a guided tour of the ship.'

The lieutenant remembered when he had been in HMS *Bacchante*, the 'Leander' Class frigate, it had gone to Fort Lauderdale in Florida. 'We invited the Mayor and a good cross-section of local citizens aboard. But it was not quite so good as with HMS *Bristol* at Wilmington. In Fort Lauderdale, there had been several ships before us, and people can take only so much of the novelty.'

The irony is that in seeking to establish human contact with people ashore, both in home waters and abroad, the very friendliness that is being strived for can put landlubbers off. Perhaps this fact had encouraged the Navy to keep itself to itself, not really expecting civilians to be interested in its life and problems, nor especially sympathetic in its reaction to them. This diffidence could have reinforced the stereotype of the naval life which has come down through the centuries and which has perhaps not been sufficiently modified in the light of new circumstances. The exaggerated stereotype, of course, is one of monasticism relieved by splurges of drink and sex. Perhaps it would be a productive move if the Navy could find some way of putting its *people*, its *humanity*, more on view – though it would not be too easy to say exactly how that could be done, since the Navy is now so closely tied to such formidable (and perhaps, to civilians, offputting) machinery and electronics.

Plainly the Royal Navy does try. HMS *Intrepid*, the 11,582-ton assault ship, is rather ferocious-looking, as befits its role in amphibious warfare. Its lines, with most of the superstructure well forward, as if thrusting to get at the enemy, make the ship look anything but warmly human. But on overseas trips in peacetime, even *Intrepid* does her best to show a warm and human face. A young sub-lieutenant aboard her told me, 'When we went to the Mediterranean, everyone was most interested in the ship. We had a lot of parties for underprivileged children. Through the local council, we would invite twenty or thirty such children aboard. The sailors would get dressed up as pirates, and do bits and pieces of entertainment for the children. No matter what the size and character of the ship, we do try to give children's parties like this.'

But the Navy does not always have to go to the people. Sometimes the people are invited to it. Once a year the Royal Navy puts itself and its humanity on display through a public show which becomes, in effect, a piece of nautical theatre. Strengths are certainly emphasized, weaknesses smoothed over and grumbles silenced; but the so-called 'Navy Days' are the only certain ones in which any member of the public, without necessarily being on any civic list used by the Navy for its cocktail parties, can come face to face with the human beings of the Navy as well as with some of its ships.

The Navy Days are usually held on the three days of the Summer Bank Holiday, at Portsmouth, Portland, Plymouth, and Rosyth in Scotland. During this time, all available ships fit to be looked over by the casual public (some other ships will be in need of a refit, some will be operational and some out of bounds for security reasons) have open gangways. The public can go aboard and talk to the staff aboard, who may well be giving up some of their leave for the privilege of, in effect, telling taxpayers all about what they are getting for their money.

The vastness of the event, the concentration of the grey warships and of the more highly coloured souvenir stalls ashore, the hordes of people on the jetties, all may make the event to some extent more of an occasion for rehearsed explanations rather than for informal conversation between sailor and civilian. This may be a pity, though inevitable. The average sailor, as he often proves when in overseas ports, is perfectly capable of being an ambassador for his service, but he may find it difficult to converse in depth on Navy Days. Usually the briefest of answers to the briefest of questions have to suffice.

But for all their inevitable limitations, the Navy Days do make the present-day Navy a reality rather than an abstraction for all the civilians able to get there. When I went to one at Portsmouth, late in the Summer Bank Holiday, the approach roads were solidly filled with traffic. I had to leave the car at a multi-storey car park on the outskirts of the city and walk down to Victory Gate of the Naval base, by Portsmouth's Hard. When I reached the gate that Sunday afternoon I was told that within only sixty minutes of the gates opening, there had already been as many people in the base as had come during the whole of the previous day.

The police office just inside the gate was already busy with minor incidents. An eight-year-old had become separated from his parents and was still on the flight deck of HMS *Illustrious*, which was now crowded with sightseers. Could an announcement be made? And someone had stolen some bottles of beer. '*How* old?' inquired the incredulous gate policeman who took the telephone call. '*Eleven?*'

Especially in the blazing sun, Navy Days can demand almost naval toughness from their willing visitors. People queued by North Corner Jetty at Portsmouth for over half an hour to get aboard the carrier HMS *Invincible*. When aboard, they had practically to fight to get to the souvenir stalls set up in the cavernous hangar – empty of aircraft since the Air Squadron had disembarked. Visitors were impressed by the general vastness of it all, rather than by any specific details – indeed, more serious visitors commented that crew members were so scattered on the big ship and so concerned with keeping the crowd in some sort of order that the answering of questions was virtually impossible.

The British passion for queuing, however, was fully satisfied. Visitors were told that they would probably have to queue two hours to get aboard HMS *Sealion* – the 'Porpoise' Class patrol submarine which is one of the Navy's oldest, having been around since the beginning of the 1960s.

'You can't do anything without queuing,' said one cheerful overseas lady who had driven down from London, 'and people are obviously enjoying that. I thought I was queuing for a submarine, and found I was queuing for an ice cream. I got into a different queue, and found that was for trips round the harbour. Some people didn't seem to care *what* they were queuing for, as long as they were in a queue. That's the British for you.'

It was also a day for naval families to come together in a rather less constrained atmosphere than that of a 'Families Day' aboard a ship. Dozens of proud parents were wandering around the jetties with their naval offspring, some of the children looking rather sheepish at this family intervention in their professional lives, others trying not to look too proud as they showed relatives round *their* Navy.

'Not a bag of chips, *please*, Dad!' scolded one junior Wren who was in a bad humour already. She had previously been telling her Wren chums in the Arena, during an air display, that she'd done something amiss and been told to do cleaning-up duty on some heads. Only she called them 'baths', in deference to the visitors.

From the Navy's own point of view, it is a substantial benefit that it can, in controlled conditions, show off its high standards of neatness to a Britain that has moved strongly towards informality and an equivocal attitude to any form of discipline. The captain of a minesweeper told me, 'We would polish these floors every day anyway. My lads were complaining a bit about extra work, but at the end of it they feel a bit of pride in the result. It is useful, from the public's point of view, to see what they are getting as taxpayers, and it is good for us and them to show them how we keep things neat and tidy.'

Some twenty-four naval ships were on display at Portsmouth on the Navy Days, though the largest carrier, HMS *Hermes*, was out of bounds, together with a number of smaller vessels. The organization for managing such an 'informal' event is formidable. I was not surprised when the Navy Days' secretary, a commander, told me that preparation for the *next* year's was already under way well before this one opened.

The Portsmouth Navy Days' secretary, who also handles some of the preparations for the Navy Days at Portland, Plymouth and Rosyth, works from an office in HMS *Nelson*, the shore establishment just up Queen Street, with the historic HMS *Nelson* figurehead proudly displayed at the black and gilt gates.

'It is an enormous task,' said the commander, a bearded Glaswegian with a high forehead, a rather scholastic air, and a naval flying background. 'Some people are already asking about next year's Navy Days. The English Tourist Board wants information for its magazine and publications, and so on.'

He'd started planning this year's show in September of the previous year. By early January, he was given the first indication of what ships would be available to attend the Navy Days. The ships are allocated by the Commander-in-Chief Fleet. In practice they are bound to change – perhaps drastically – between January and August. The previous year, the commander had been allocated a nuclear submarine and planned to feature it prominently in advertising; but ten days before the event the ship was withdrawn.

To make sure that the public never succumb to that very human condition on hot days – enervated boredom – the main Victory Arena always has displays every half hour. It may be a drill, a sporting competition, a gym display or an air display. Integrating all these events takes some organization; and the Navy Days' secretary also collaborates closely with the display director, a pilot lieutenant-commander from HMS *Invincible*, to make sure that as many types of aircraft as possible are shown off to the public.

'All this is very important in terms of public relations,' said the Navy Days' secretary. 'Our aim initially is recruiting, so it has to be a massive public-relations exercise; and then we raise money for charities. Three years ago we raised about £10,000. Two years ago it was £20,000. Last year we raised £60,000.'

Generally rising attendance figures testify to the technological and human appeal of the Navy Days. In 1980, the attendance was 84,192, in 1981 it was 81,025; in 1982 the ships were not open because of the recent Falklands campaign; in 1983 there was an all-time record attendance, possibly helped by Falklands memories; and in 1984, 89,213 people turned up.

The Navy is quick to point out that, in showing its technological and human face at the Navy Days, it is *not* costing the taxpayer more money. 'The cost of the ships is something you don't have to worry about,' the commander told me. 'Ships have got to have their duty watches on board anyway. For each of the ships which is in the harbour for Navy Days, there is a specific reason why it *should* be in harbour – maintenance, taking on fuel or stores, or because it is a leave period. It is all part of the annual running cost of the ship. It could be regarded as a way of getting *further* value out of the ship.'

In the day-to-day life of the Navy, the amount of ordinary human contact between officers and ratings varies according to the circumstances. On big ships, it is inevitably limited while on the tiny minesweepers informal human contacts are more usual. But at least once a year, naval discipline and good order will be breached and the nearest possible approach to equality between officers and ratings established. This is in the pantomime season around Christmas. It is a firm and extraordinary naval tradition. Naval people will insist on having their own pantos. In the hectic excitement of the theatre, protocol will be relaxed (slightly!). Even the most status-conscious officer becomes rather fond of sporting his red shirt, yellow cravat or Pierre Cardin pullover, though almost certainly it will be roughly the same attire as the junior ratings are wearing.

I was swept into the rehearsals of two examples at either end of the country – Faslane in Scotland and Plymouth in Devon. The identically easy atmosphere of both convinced me that what I was seeing was indeed a tradition and a norm, not an isolated exception.

'This is none of the usual sod's opera while aboard,' I was told at Clyde Submarine Base, where, in the Sportsdrome 150-

seater theatre an engineer lieutenant-commander was trying to knock his twenty-five-strong cast into shape without the usual naval thunderbolts of authority. 'This is definitely a co-operative effort, half naval people, half wives of civilians on the base,' he told me. 'The naval people are mostly officers, I think – after all, one of the reasons people select you as an officer is that you are outgoing.'

The commander was dressed in a red polo-necked sweater under a camel cashmere V-neck sweater. He wore beige slacks. He was supposed to be playing a quavering old man – 'three-score years old' as he would have it; he frequently fluffed his lines and called on the prompter, or argued with the director (who happened to be of inferior rank).

'Three score years *and twenty*,' insisted the prompter.

The lieutenant-commander director sighed and tactfully sought to distract my attention. 'We've worked in a few naval references,' he told me. 'For instance, one of the characters, instead of saying, "fifteen revs a minute", says "going round and round at four hundred and twenty", which would mean something to a naval man.'

It certainly did not mean much to me. Looking suitably distracted, however, I took a seat in the stalls.

'Three score years *and twenty*,' quavered the commander. 'That woman will never be able to do anything important and worth thinking about!'

Again the prompter intervened. 'That *boy*. That *boy*!'

'It's coming,' said the director placatingly to his superior officer. 'It's coming.'

I decided I must be going. It was only when I got outside that I realized I never had found out what the pantomime was called, let alone what it was about. I am sure that during the performances everyone had a wonderful time – even the audience. It would certainly have been an example of the human face of the Navy.

The other pantomime rehearsal I witnessed was in a rather more advanced state of preparation. I was able immediately to grasp the fact that it was Jack and the Beanstalk. The staff of the Royal Naval Hospital, Plymouth, with helpers, were giving a dress rehearsal for men and women from local old people's homes. A lieutenant-commander (the hospital administrator) was front-of-house manager; the only man there in a dinner jacket. He helped to show the more able elderly to their seats and to wheel the disabled to advantageous positions at the side of the hall. At many and various times during the evening, he helped old ladies and gentlemen to the venue where they might attend to calls of nature.

A surgeon-commander, the most senior naval officer present, was on the stage playing the part of the Baron. The overblown lady to whom he is eventually to be spliced was played by a petty officer in the regulatory (disciplinary) branch. She certainly took the belligerent attitude to him that the script required. The only concession to the Baron's naval seniority was in a modified version of the old pantomime piece of business when the overblown lady (Jack's mother) pushes the Baron back across the stage with great nudges of her enormous bosom, the two protagonists staring at one another face-to-face. In *this* pantomime, Jack's petty officer mother rammed the (captain) Baron only in the side or the back, never doing it to his face. *That* might have been a little too much, even at Christmas.

It was arguable that some measure of equality had been achieved, because the captain was following a script written by a lieutenant in the medical services and was under the direction of a lieutenant (in a red shirt and cravat, naturally). No doubt there were sound theatrical rather than naval hierarchical reasons why a sub-lieutenant should play the Good Fairy, while the least senior person in the production, a weapons electrical mechanic, played the back end of the cow.

Naval jokes were few and far between. They fell flat with a dull thud at the feet of the aged audience. The old folk responded with wildly enthusiastic cacklings only to the bawdiest humour, concerning knickers and udders.

The pensioners from the old people's homes joined in the singing of old favourites with a will and showed every sign of enjoying their free evening. On succeeding nights, the audience of naval people and their friends paid £1 for their tickets. The producer said he hoped the show would break even: 'We started these pantos with £20 from the hospital welfare fund, and we haven't cost them much. It's a way of letting our hair down, really.'

It is also, I imagine, a way in which the Royal Navy can soften its inevitable technological image in a highly technological age, and show that it is composed of human beings like the rest of us. If more widespread, such evidence of humanity might be worth more than thousands of pounds spent on formal publicity and recruiting drives. The charm of human foibles should never be underestimated, even in a disciplined service.

The Royal Navy may have largely outlived its predilection for a tot of rum (the rum ration was done away with years ago); it is no more dedicated to 'baccy' than any other section of the community. But it still has one age-old human foible that continues colourfully despite lack of encouragement from the top: tattooing.

Yes, there are occasional cases of the tattoo going wrong because of a dirty needle. Yes, there are occasions when the 'Mabel', in large letters on the manly chest, can cause problems once that chest is in the marital bed with Janice. Yes, there are occasions when a young rating will celebrate his entry into a tough man's world by having a big-busted beauty tattooed on to his biceps, only to cringe abjectly when his mother sees it. Yes, a few beers may suggest exotic designs that sobriety may regret.

Despite all this, tattooing remains a socially acceptable practice in the Navy. Chiefly it is ratings who succumb, junior or senior, though it is not unknown for officers to take to tattooing in a way probably not seen in the other two armed services.

Sometimes, in some messes, I have realized that only my own rolled up sleeves have revealed totally bare arms. Often, on the way to naval bases, I have passed tattooists' shops, a sight not common outside the naval towns. At Portsmouth, strategically placed between HMS *Nelson* and the main Victory Gate of the naval base, I saw a shop window with a mermaid-like girl painted on it in swirls of colour almost resembling an Art Nouveau style. Above the window was a board proclaiming 'Taffy's Tattoo Studio'. On the opposite side of Queen Street was the 'Brew House' public house; Portsmouth's historic Hard was only a few hundred yards down the street, which is littered with black painted ships' anchors and chains.

Inside the studio, which I had no reason to suppose was untypical, were a number of young men. None of them, I would have thought, was over twenty. Their neat hairstyles announced their naval identity without need of words. In the back room, beside one lad in a worn American-cloth swivel chair, sat the tattooist Taffy, otherwise Mr Douglas Bull, former miner and steel-worker. He was a man with a heavy moustache, a heavy gilt identity chain on his wrist, a heavy gold wristwatch, heavy gold rings on three or four fingers, and a walking advertisement for his trade all over his arms and his chest.

Certainly, he said, he would talk to me about the intricacies of his art and trade when the last of his customers had departed. I sat down on one of the black American-cloth benches and studied the decor. The walls were covered practically from floor to ceiling with paper cutouts of dragons, sorceresses, snakes and other exotic shapes. There was a notice reading: 'You Must Be 18 to Enter In.' Another read: 'We Buy Gold. Spot Cash or Tattooes Arranged for Gold.'

On the benches were numerous albums of coffee-table size, containing pages of examples of possible tattoos. I did not realize that a human skull could suggest pain until I saw the design for 'Born to Die'. There was another skull, with a cigarette between its teeth and the inscription 'Smoke It'. There were figures of girls in frilly knickers, and of Donald Duck with a leek in his hands and the inscription 'Wales Rules'. There were graceful old sailing ships, and girls with exaggerated nipples. There were children as angels and wolves' heads. There were nubile blondes with forked tails, and nine poses of Jesus. There were family messages, and there were skulls with snakes coming out of the eye-sockets.

In short, forty-eight pages of reverence, aggression, sex and sentimentality, all laid out neatly for the clients. I observed two other notices: 'You Must Be 18 and Able To Prove It' and 'Ladies Tattooed in Private If So Desired'.

'Something or other sparked it off when I was a small boy, I suppose,' said Mr Bull after the bright blue light on his tattooing machine had jumped and flickered for his last customer that day. 'I was always keen as a young lad. When I was sixteen I had my first one, and the interest grew from there.'

He had been in Portsmouth seven years, after being a miner for five years and a steel-worker for seven. I asked him if naval people made up most of his clientele. 'No, 40 per cent are. And petty officers, I would say, are 40 per cent *of* that 40 per cent. There are occasionally officers, but they are few.'

In the course of any one day, it was impossible to predict how many tattoos he would do. Sometimes there were hardly any; sometimes he would do a dozen. It would probably average out at six to ten a day at between £5 and £20.

I asked the tattooist if he could tell, whatever they asked for, if the men were naval or not. 'Yes, I can, mostly. Even in their civilian clothes you can generally spot them. They stand out in a crowd because they are a bit smarter. I mean the haircut and the way they walk.'

Did the Navy approve of their men being tattooed? 'What the hierarchy thinks, I don't know. But I think they have to accept the fact that tattooing practically goes hand-in-hand with the Navy.'

Some naval men went in for very large pictures, or had the

whole body covered, he said. If they wanted something large and detailed, they were asked to think about it and let him know later. Then he would draw something for them, and ask whether they liked it. Only then would he do the actual tattooing. But having the whole body covered was a rarity. 'And that is not the sort of thing you make money on, because you put so much work into it and get so little money out of it. I would charge about £200 over a period of time – probably about ten or twelve sittings. You probably only get two or three of those a year.'

Mostly, the naval men wanted a pattern that was sentimental. Often it included a girl's name, and often that girl's name became out-of-date in the sailor's life. 'Name cover-ups are *very* common,' said the worldly tattooist. 'Mostly it is to get rid of a girl's name. We can cover it up with something else – say a few small flowers.' I said I was glad to hear it – especially after seeing a further notice in the studio, which read: 'All Tattoos Guaranteed 99 Years.'

When I talked to him, the Portsmouth tattooist was worried about the effects of the economic recession on his business, like a lot of other people in Civvy Street. Compared with last year, business would be down about 25 per cent. 'It is exceptional for trade to go down by that amount,' he said gloomily. He was grateful to the Navy, because it gave him a wider selection of people to meet in the course of his job.

I asked him if anything else had struck him about his Navy customers. He immediately said, 'They are generally a well-mannered bunch. Through the Navy you meet people from all over the country, and they are generally very well-behaved. Yes, we do occasionally get one who has had too much to drink, and we don't usually tattoo those. We get them out of the shop. When they drink, they might get something they might regret in years to come. We don't get many with regrets.'

He had never had any trouble because naval men had been aggressive, he said with some pride. Then he added slowly, as

I got up from his swivel chair in which I had been talking to him (but not getting tattooed), 'You know, the closest I have got to trouble was when a man in my chair bent towards me to ask a question, went to sleep halfway down, and fell on me.'

Plainly the tradition of tattooing, one very much from a rougher age, is compatible with a more thoughtful and more self-controlled sailor, whatever the aesthetic and hygienic doubts that may persist in some official quarters. It may be absurd but the Navy, like any other human organization, would be oppressive without its little human absurdities. The human factor can make the difference between a man feeling at home and a man wanting a change as soon as possible. In this respect, at least, much the same applies to the Royal Navy's women.

11

THE FEMININE ROLES

'You don't find snobbery so much between ratings and officers as between officers' wives and ratings' wives.'

– Lieutenant-commander, previously a rating.

'Wives all band together to support one another when their husbands are away. You get more closeness than in civilian life.'

– Wife of submarine commanding officer.

'I always say women are more logical than men. There are certain jobs women do better than men.'

– Commandant, Women's Royal Naval Service.

The answer is almost always the same. Ask any Women's Royal Naval Service officer or rating how women get on in the Navy in an age of more civilian sexual equality, and back it will come: 'Very well, *considering* . . .'

On the other hand, ask wives of naval men how satisfied they are with their involvement with the Navy, and the answer will be wildly unpredictable. One will reply, 'Varied and stimulating.' Another will say, 'If I see another married quarter, I will scream.' And yet another will say, 'I wish my husband had a job that didn't separate us for months at a time.'

The Navy regards its relationship with its own personnel as

more important than that with their spouses. This may be true; though the influence wives exert on men should not be underestimated at a time when Defence cuts are expected to have the effect of keeping men at sea for longer periods of time. And the great majority of Wrens (an expression used *only* of ratings) or WRNS (an expression that can be used to cover both officers and ratings) believe *that* relationship to be a good one – considering . . .

'Considering *what*?' you ask. Considering, you are told, that there is one great hurdle, one matter about which women have less 'equality' now than they did in the days before Nelson. In that immeasurably far-off era, some ships carried *more* women than men. Today women in the Royal Navy – unlike some other navies – do not go to sea like the men, though they go to sea for limited periods on special jobs. And since they do not go to sea for long periods – even as the floating camp-followers of the pre-Nelson navy – they cannot acquire the combat experience necessary for promotion to the highest ranks of the service.

'It's a "Catch-22" situation,' I was told by a first officer WRNS who, in the personnel-selection department of the training establishment for ratings, HMS *Raleigh*, near Devonport, was doing one of those jobs that could have been done, equally suitably, by a man or a woman. 'I think there is some scope still for development of the role of women in the Navy, but I don't think we can go too far, because of the environment. If we were sending people to airfields like the RAF or to camps like the Army, it might be different. But going to sea is different. It is difficult to see the Navy overcoming this, because of the strange environment of a ship at sea.'

What about the command of shore establishments? 'Well,' said the first officer, a petite figure with a roundly humorous, unresentful face, 'there have been female first lieutenants and COs of shore establishments. But because we are not the seagoing side, we do find it difficult to amass sufficient experience to do some jobs. That is why it is a Catch-22 situation. I served with the US Navy at a NATO base. Even their rampant feminists can see how finite is the progress they are going to make; and the US has made concessions we have not yet made. Pregnant ratings can stay in the service; and when they are ready they can go back again after the birth. That is something we haven't done. I think the Americans have got some good service out of the people they have allowed to stay. On the other hand, the US women officers I have known have been very, very competitive, because they were fighting for a position, which we are not doing in the same way.'

Like Britain itself, the Royal Navy is becoming a property-owning democracy. Or, at least, a democracy in that it is increasingly property-owning. Many men own their own houses and chop and change them according to the requirements of their job, like any civilian. Some women in the Navy have houses or naval quarters in their own names, sometimes living with husbands who share the costs.

These contemporary facts help to condition the roles, lives and attitudes of the Navy's women, both serving members of the Women's Royal Naval Service and civilian wives of serving men. It gives them greater independence and security, while perhaps throwing into relief the negative fact that the modern Royal Navy does have its 'haves' (those with their own property) and its 'have nots' (those who have to live a nomadic life between one married quarter and another).

At least in this domestic aspect the split is not on sexual lines. But professionally the Royal Navy does limit the role of its own women while allowing for great variety within those limits.

This fact appears to be accepted without resentment, given that the alternative might be gruelling service at sea. Even women in the Royal Navy who are unmarried career officers and who, at least from that point of view, would appreciate more scope, are half glad that they haven't in fact got it. The first officer at Dartmouth said that a friend of hers in the US

Navy had been made a captain two years ago, and was now competing on mercilessly equal terms with one hundred and fifty men and four women.

'That sort of pressure on a woman makes it difficult for her simply to do her job,' said the first officer. 'She is always looking at the people who are looking at *her* and who can affect her future. We women in the WRNS can compete with *one another*, but we don't need to compete with our male counterparts, as well. I know one US commander who is *married* to a commander. While he was away, she had a taxing job and two children at home. They were earning enough to pay for help to look after the children, but I think the children must have felt they were thrust into the background. The parents were both dominant people, immersed in their careers. How the children will grow up I don't know, because they are still only children.'

This was certainly not the face-saving rationalization of an essentially dependent personality. The background of the first officer plainly indicated a person who could survive on her own in strange territory. After getting her university degree, she left home to work in personnel for a department-store chain. She joined the Royal Naval Reserve because she had relatives in the Navy, and because it was a way of getting to know people while off her home ground. The Reserve unit had been only half a mile away, and that had been *one* of the things she had joined. It had enabled her to make friends, and had then led to what had been her career for the past ten years – the career she had wanted.

If women are unlikely to be included in the front-runners in the Royal Navy, they are compensated by not having to undergo quite as gruelling a preparation for the job as the men. The first officer at HMS *Raleigh*, who had left it for eight years and then returned for another spell of duty there, estimated that she had been on the parade ground only twice in the intervening eight years.

Perhaps that consideration does reconcile women to the fact

that, when there was a second officer WRNS serving in a Royal Fleet Auxiliary off the Falklands as meteorological officer, it was counted as somewhat of a blow for the cause of women.

The role of women in the Royal Navy has been a slowly expanding one, with its peaks and its troughs. The WRNS were first formed in 1917, were disbanded in 1919 after the end of the First World War, were re-formed on the outbreak of the Second World War in 1939, and made a permanent part of the Navy in 1949. There are now three ways of entering: a rating entry for those aged seventeen to twenty-eight; cadet entry from eighteen-and-a-half to twenty-four in the case of those wishing to become officers; and by direct entry for those who are graduates or who have certain professional qualifications of primary importance to the Navy, and who wish to become officers.

The personality difference between officers and ratings does not seem to be as great in the WRNS as it does among the men of the Royal Navy: many, or even most, of the women could pass socially as either officers or ratings. There are mild differences in etiquette, such as that rule that *Wrens* are ratings, and officers always WRNS officers. But such little differences do not cause much resentment.

Perhaps the fact that things are physically easier for them in training and in service is of some comfort. At HMS *Raleigh*, they point out that girls are recommended to run two miles three times a week as preparation for the course, but that while girls have to do a lot of parade-ground drill in their early weeks, they then tend to settle down into a career slot quicker; boys of the same age will have to do their sea training as well as their training ashore. Girls, they will tell you, are put under the same sorts of pressure at *Raleigh*; but in fact it is not *quite* such a high pressure. The girls go out on Dartmoor for compass training, but have only one overnight stop. Young men may have far more. Girls are given instruction in self-defence, but do not have to use it against young men who are undergoing the same lessons. Like the men, the young women have to undergo a swimming test. Unlike the men, they do not have to *pass* it.

There is also the maturity factor. The would-be members of the WRNS tend to be slightly older than the men – between seventeen and twenty-eight years old. The average age is eighteen, and their average academic standard is higher than that of the young men. If the traditional belief that young girls are more mature for their age than young men is true, the demands put on them in their training must be objectively and subjectively less than those put on the boys. But officers told me that the first few weeks could be a time when young women used up a lot of paper handkerchiefs on tear-stained eyes. About 14 per cent leave.

Accommodation for Wrens is usually better than for male ratings of corresponding seniority, a fact which first becomes apparent at *Raleigh*. Dauntless block for Wrens offers its young women – 175 at any one time – accommodation which officers describe as 'slightly superior' to the environment the young men are enjoying a few blocks away.

This was certainly so. The same applied at the training establishment for WRNS officers, Britannia Royal Naval College at Dartmouth. Here young officer trainees had single rooms, no worse than the average reasonably stylish civilian bed-sitter, in what was referred to as the Talbot Hilton (Talbot being the block in which the young women are housed). There were heating radiators, double wardrobes, and chests of drawers in rooms painted a delicate magnolia. Here young WRNS officer cadets spend their first fourteen weeks. The bathrooms are communal, but have individual cubicles. The laundry rooms are a mass of gleaming stainless steel. The whole effect conveys the impression that WRNS are not expected to tolerate circumstances which are aesthetically inferior to the ones they might have at home. Men, be they ratings or officers, are not quite so lucky. As one WRNS officer put it to me: 'This was surplus accommodation before we came here from Greenwich, where they used to be trained. The director of

WRNS drew up her requirements and said, "*This* is the minimum standard for us." And we managed to get everything we asked for.'

WRNS officers in training enjoy a jocularity which is not so noticeable among their male counterparts. It is not only a question of the teddy bears that adorn beds; it is the Talbot Duck. He is a plastic duck with a plaque. He is given to the WRNS officer in training who makes the biggest mistake of the week – putting last year's date on a memo, or allowing her natural diffidence to trap her into saluting a petty officer. The Oscar is awarded to the girl who does something particularly noteworthy – like passing her swimming test at the third attempt, after being a backward swimmer. And on Talbot's notice board there is always a notice giving what is called the 'word of the day', which has to be somehow worked into the duty log. One day the word was 'abnegate', and others were no easier to incorporate into a naval log. It all sounded rather like carefree fun compared with the atmosphere of the young men's training.

The first officer WRNS at Dartmouth assured me, however, that young WRNS officers did a microcosm of everything a male officer did, with the exception of the physically too-demanding. 'They do supply, administration and management studies, and they get to understand the various types of ship, aircraft and weapons so they know some of the terminology the men use. They do a substantial amount of time on naval history and strategic studies, and the remainder is on operations and warfare-type matters. That reflects the emphasis given to all students while they are here.'

This particular officer pointed out that WRNS officers were in a small field – there were only 270 at present – so the number of WRNS officers in really important jobs would be measured in 'penny numbers'. But there had recently been a superintendent WRNS (equivalent to a captain) who had held a tri-service job in NATO Headquarters at Brussels, which could have been held by any male captain in the Navy,

group captain in the Royal Air Force or colonel in the Army.
And a woman had recently taken up a job as an assistant
director in one of the directorates of the Ministry of Defence.
This, I was told, was definitely a 'first', and attempts were now
being made to introduce a better career structure for women.

With the prospect of better career prospects ahead, female
officers under training subdue their irritation at some of the
petty restrictions, as do their sisters serving as ratings. I asked
one very poised brunette – who was training to be an officer
after serving as a rating for two years following a failure at her
original Admiralty Interview Board – whether she felt the
Navy was in any sense repressive towards women.

She answered, 'I had no opposition at all. Through the
training, I have had all the help I could have had. I haven't felt
constrained as a female in the Navy. Some people think we are
lectured on what to wear off-duty. We don't have any lectures
on dress as such, but we are given a few midshipman's lectures
on how people should dress, and we are told beforehand what
is expected of us. Skirts, blouses, dresses, smart co-ordinates.
Slacks? Only for appropriate occasions; we would not be able
to come down here in the evening in trousers. I should think
the only appropriate occasion might be Bonfire Night on
November 5. There aren't many occasions when trousers are
permitted. Anything extreme in fashion is out. I don't know
what the *exact* position is, because none of us have tried to
challenge it. Any of us coming here accept quite readily the
sort of standard which is expected. One accepts there are to be
restrictions. As with anything else, some of them seem quite
petty at the time; but they are probably there for a good
reason.'

Even the restrictions on the amount of time recruits could
be out in the evening were easily accepted, insisted this naval
officer's daughter, who did not let her father know she was
joining the WRNS as a rating until just before she left home.
Yes, they might have to be in by one in the morning during
the week. But that was not really inconvenient. And they

could stay out till two in the morning at weekends (though, in fact, there was only one weekend during the term – in the middle of it – when the concession could actually be used). Guests could stay in the division's ante-room until 10.30 at night, which she hadn't found an inconvenience, either. People were often glad to get to bed by 10.30.

'You have to wear your hat in the corridors, though not in the rooms,' she said. 'But we accept these little oddities.'

A WRNS officer quickly backed the point up by explaining the Dartmouth cap rules for young WRNS. The staff didn't wear their caps; but, because they were 'jetting around the place', the officers under training *did*. Caps had to be worn at all times outdoors; it was therefore easier for the would-be officers to take their caps with them in the corridors by *wearing* them than by carrying them. In fact, suggested the WRNS officer, the rule put women on the same footing as men, because their male counterparts had to have with them all the kit they were going to need.

There is certainly a rigid insistence, among WRNS officers at Dartmouth, on correct saluting. If an officer under training passes a staff officer inside the college, and the staff officer is wearing his or her cap, then the officer under training must salute the staff officer *even indoors* – which would not apply to the rest of the Navy. If the officer is *without* his or her cap, then he or she is not saluted. Even if the staff officer is in a car, if he or she *has* a cap on, he or she is saluted.

Wasn't it rather difficult, I asked, to ascertain from looking at a moving car whether: (1) there was an officer in it; and (2) whether he or she had a cap on?

'We try to encourage the individual to be observant,' was the tart reply.

It is difficult to resist the conclusion that WRNS officers and ratings, rather more than their male counterparts, are from the outset given more coaching about their personal behaviour. Experienced officers say that if this is so, it is because the women are always in a minority throughout their service, just as they are at Dartmouth, where there are about ten WRNS officers to five hundred men training at any one time.

'So whatever the girls say or do in the bar is more conspicuous, because there are so few of them,' said one officer. 'Everything is more obvious.'

One officer under training agreed. 'It is rather nice going into the bar, where we do get quite a lot of attention. We are always treated very well by the midshipmen. They might make a pass at you, but you have to remember that conditions probably do put things slightly out of perspective here. There is quite a lot of pressure on a lot of people. You are seeing people morning, noon and night, which is not normal in other circumstances. Some of us like to be seen with the officer cadets and others say, "Stand back – we are not going to have anything to do with them." It is passed down to us from course to course, though nothing is in writing: never get involved with midshipmen. Staff certainly warn us not to get involved with staff officers. It is quite sensible, because it would not be good for you to get into an involvement which couldn't go on.'

Certainly the women of the Navy are conditioned from the first to realize that, just like the men, their treatment will depend greatly on professional standing. If would-be WRNS officers at Dartmouth have their single rooms, the girls at the ratings' training establishment at Torpoint in Cornwall have to make do with dormitories for five in Dauntless block – one of the identical brick and plastic-fronted cubes that make up almost the whole complex housing the young men and women. Having passed the portrait of Princess Anne (who opened the block in 1982) the girls at this social level will live in a mess with standard fitted bookshelves, standard fitted wardrobes, and cupboards on the top of the wardrobes which are too high for all except six-foot Amazons to reach.

'Well, it teaches them the value of cooperation,' said the quick-witted third officer who showed me round.

Young women I spoke to there seemed to have less difference in intelligence between them and their officer contemporaries than the difference between their male counterparts; but they are still virtually in quarantine for the five weeks of their training. Officers say this is because there *is* only five weeks to put in a lot of activity and learning; that the girls can use the mini-Naafi Club to make their purchases and the (no men allowed) bar and disco for their entertainment. They are told to stand up for their seniors, and to smile and call them 'Ma'am' or 'Sir'. They are not allowed to smoke in their rooms, only in the recreation room, and they are not allowed to have food in the messes. Staff even watch the recruits' alarm clocks. This, I was told, was not to make sure they would be on time in the morning, but to make sure the clocks had not been set too *early*. Sometimes, officers explained, girls were so nervous about the possibility of being late in the morning that they would allow an hour and a half to get washed and dressed. In such cases, they had to be gently told to put their alarm clocks forward. Between five in the morning and half past five is thought to be virtuous; four-thirty is thought to be an unnecessary restriction on necessary sleep.

When I said I doubted that such tender concern would be shown to the girls' male counterparts in the Navy, WRNS officers tended to agree with me.

'Yes,' said a first officer at HMS *Raleigh* training establishment, 'there *is* a difference in the disciplinary problems between males and females. Our philosophy of training is different from that of men, because we are dealing with a very different sort of person. Males doing their Part One (initial) training here are sixteen to seventeen, whereas the girls are eighteen-plus. So on the whole – there are exceptions – they are more mature and educationally better qualified. So perhaps they are treated better.'

But was there any difference in the philosophy of training just because one group of people were male and the others female? No, said the officer; at least in the sense that since 1977 WRNS personnel as well as the Navy's men had been subject to the Naval Discipline Act. But *yes*, in the sense that there was a difference because women tended to respond to a different sort of motivation than the young men.

No doubt this view would not appeal to more militant feminists, but the Royal Navy says its approach is based on simple human observation. As this particular officer put it, 'Lots of the time you have to shout at boys. But girls don't respond to being shouted at. They respond far more to a quiet talking-to. They also tend, in some ways, to have a greater sense of individual pride in how they look. Normal female vanity takes over, so it is not so difficult for women to reach a good standard of kit. For males, the big bogey is the kit; not so with girls.'

Was the male defect of untidiness balanced by the female defect of bitchiness?

'There can be a little bit of cliquey-ness,' admitted the WRNS officer. 'We work very hard at stopping that. The petty officer Wren has her finger close to the pulse, and can usually detect when that is going on. When there is a girl who is, well, a bit *silly*, the other girls aren't very patient at letting her down gently. In the first week, they are very different individuals, fighting for survival. At the end of the first week, heads start gently to appear above the surface, and they start looking round in a more human way. The worst case of bitchiness in my experience concerned a girl who was younger, less mature and smaller than the rest, and who was being harassed. Constant niggling. We watch. If, after a couple of weeks, a class is leaving a weaker one out, someone might sit down with the class and say, "Look, this isn't good enough." But because five weeks is a short space of time, they have to learn fast. We do get dependent characters here; some of them survive, some don't. Those who believe that the Navy is going to solve all their problems and that the Navy is here as a welfare organization – those are the ones who don't survive. We have to teach them to be self-reliant. The Navy is a good manager of people, but there is a limit. We are not a charitable organization.'

But in one sense women ratings *do* get a better training than the men in the art of understanding the problems of others – whether they are caused by being too far behind one's colleagues or too far ahead.

Male ratings under training at HMS *Raleigh* select a class leader at the outset and stay with him. Female ratings change their leader every day. The advantage of the female system is that the strong and confident get an idea of what it is like to be an underling, while the less strong get to understand how difficult it is to lead a group when some people are not pulling their weight. Experienced officers say that, in a class of between twenty and twenty-five, all the girls get to be class leader at least once. And they respond much better to leadership when they are back in the bulk of the class.

Girls I spoke to at HMS *Raleigh* were certainly irritated at not being allowed to watch television; but most believed that their first experience of the Navy was better than that of the young men. The more ambitious are irritated by the fact that WRNS officers and ratings do not go to sea as part of their training for more than the odd day, from which they are expected to gather more understanding of what their male colleagues do.

One eighteen-year-old Wren writer I met at a remote naval base said she had always been keen on joining a disciplined service (she had once wanted to be a policewoman); she accepted the fact that it was difficult to meet people except those on the base itself; she was prepared to accept also that she would miss her family. But she did think that many Wrens felt too distanced from the sea itself.

'I do think we should be able to go to sea once in a while so that we can *really* get an idea of what life is like aboard a ship,' she said. 'I have been on three ships for a day, and a submarine just for one evening. It would be helpful if we could see them in a real working situation.'

No doubt the traditionalists in the Royal Navy would suspect this idea of being the thin end of what could be, later, a very thick wedge: having women afloat as a normal way of life. But even WRNS officers who are more than content with the naval life, in general terms, feel that one of the major bonuses – travel abroad – is largely denied them. One officer told me she had in effect been penalized because she (then a rating) had gone through the officer-selection procedure at about the time she could have expected a foreign posting as a rating.

'Jobs for WRNS officers abroad are few and far between,' she told me. 'There are two in Hong Kong, two in Gibraltar, four in Naples, one in Norway, two in Nato Headquarters and three in Washington. The majority of jobs for officers in the WRNS are nearer home – like Brussels. Most of us can expect one foreign job if we are in the right place at the right time.'

But even this disadvantage can sometimes become an *advantage* to some women, as it was to this particular one. Feminists might be irritated by her reasoning, though it seemed sane enough to her: 'It is *not* a negative factor, because in any case once I get married, there is no way I would take a foreign job, and spend two years away from my husband.'

The truth seems to be that the 'old-fashioned' notion of female dependence has been largely unaffected by naval experience. So perhaps has female logic. One vivacious WRNS rating under training at HMS *Raleigh*, a charming girl with blonde ringlets, assured me, 'We get a better deal than the boys; we are not run around and made to stand to attention all the time. But we get the same rotten food – what they served up last night was *disgusting*, hard potatoes and everything with soya in it. But we did get big portions.'

Men in the Navy have a heavier weighting factor in their pay – the 'X' factor – which, in practice, means that they are better paid than their female counterparts in rank. It takes note of the fact that the men go to sea and the women do not. But the X factor is not one that occasions many WRNS officers and ratings any significant irritation, because employment in the WRNS has two great advantages over civilian life. One is passive, the other positive.

Both advantages were succinctly expressed when I spoke to one first officer WRNS in an influential position in the Navy. 'I think that what attracted me at first was that I come from a very happy and secure family background; and I was aware that my family would not be agreeable to me branching out in pastures new away from home, unless there was some form of structure and security to what I was doing,' she said. 'That was the first reason. And then in my home area there was no sort of job except being in an office, which didn't strike me as a rewarding or progressive career. The Navy did offer me an opportunity of leading my own life, but on a basis that my parents could support me in and understand.'

This particular first officer was obviously energetic and aspiring, if not ambitious in the more self-serving sense. I asked her if she ever suffered frustration because she knew she could never ever reach the highest positions of power in the Navy simply because, as a woman, she could never have experience of service at sea. Her reply was immediate. 'This probably sounds strange to you as a civilian, but I believe I am a professional woman and that whatever job I am given to do I would do it professionally. I don't think of myself as a woman in a man's world, but as a professional person who has been asked to do a job. I expect to be totally acceptable on the strength of my professional ability, and I think I have been. When I think of the responsibility which I have had vested in me, I find it very difficult to think of a position I could have been in, in civilian life, which could equate with it and give me the same satisfaction.'

Would she be prepared to attain complete equality with men by going to sea and perhaps bearing arms? 'I have never personally felt that I wanted to go to sea. I have no great desire personally to serve at sea. That doesn't mean I don't think I am *capable* of serving at sea, and if there was a requirement to do it, then – fine! As far as women bearing arms is concerned, I feel personally that there is no need. We are not employed at sea in a combat role, and I just don't believe that the requirement exists at this time for us to have training in the use of arms. If someone is about to bump me on the head personally, that is a different kettle of fish. The new entry training syllabus does include self-defence, but at the moment circumstances suggest that I am not in need of firearms training.'

Though WRNS come under the Naval Discipline Act, this WRNS first officer insisted that women *as women* were much freer in the Navy now than they had been twenty years ago. Prior to the Act applying to the WRNS, any girl who 'deserted' could not be brought back, and – at least theoretically – that no longer applied (though in practice the Navy is sceptical about the usefulness of trying to hang on to anyone who really wants to break free). But the old etiquette, under which women always served under women and men under men no longer applied, said the first officer. She personally had a fleet chief petty officer working under her, and this was now common. A male divisional officer could be the understanding brother-figure to whom a Wren would be expected to bring her problems, and vice versa. Twenty years ago it was still thought that 'only ladies can understand ladies' problems'; now that was no longer the supposition. As for any further progress that women could achieve in the Royal Navy; 'It is an evaluation based on the Navy's *requirements* at any particular time, as I see it.'

All in all, one can usually predict the sort of women who will find the Navy rewarding. They are forceful, cheerful, resourceful extroverts who, by and large, rejoice in the power their job and uniform gives them. Those with reservations tend to be women with more thoughtful and reticent characters, the sort of characters that may perhaps be more prone than others to regard themselves as taken advantage of, or put upon.

Of those I met, two stand out in the memory as being examples of the opposite poles of job satisfaction. I came to think of them as the 'Rigorous Regulator' and the 'Sombre Steward'. Both were obviously intelligent and conscientious.

Both were serving in Gibraltar when I met them. But one seemed to luxuriate in her job while the other did it diligently despite inner reservations.

The leading regulator Wren was twenty-four, with a shock of thick hair, a bright smile and a collar and tie that both had virginal cleanliness. Her skin looked vibrantly clean, as if she had just scrubbed it in a bath.

The disciplinary side of her job as a regulator was something that brought a twinkle to her eye. 'On watch, we deal with ships arriving. When the men go ashore and have too much to drink, it is a bit of a job to arrest them and take them back to their ship or, if necessary, put them into cells. It tends to happen during exercises. You can count on two instances with each ship. We get the odd guy who gives you an awful time, but nothing on a regular basis. Unlike the women's police force, there is always someone accompanying us; either the civil police or, more usually, a male regulator. We work in twos. When we arrive at an incident and feel it necessary to have some back-up we use the radio to call up assistance. We take a course in self-defence – a bit of judo and a bit of ju-jitsu. It is mostly to do with defending yourself and, if necessary, to make an attack – but that is highly unlikely.'

The Rigorous Regulator thought that her seven months in Gibraltar had given her more practical experience than the previous seven years. There had been times on exercises, over a weekend period, when they had as many as thirty-three incidents of various types to attend, which was as many as you would get in one year in an ordinary unit. Gibraltar, said the regulator, was a place where sailors let off steam, though they were cautioned before they came ashore not to go too far.

Plainly the demands of the work had not deprived her of her sense of humour. 'We had an Omani ship in here recently. I was told to pick up a man who was the worse for wear. I couldn't make out what he was saying at all and I was just about to push him up the gangplank of the Omani ship when he managed to tell me he was with the Irish Guards.'

Possibly the background of the Rigorous Regulator made her a natural for the WRNS. She had always wanted to join the police force but when her cousin – a Wren – came home on leave and discussed her life in the Navy, it became a toss-up between the police force and the WRNS. Then she had thought it might be possible to combine the advantages of both by doing policing work in the Navy. But it hadn't been possible to go directly into the Navy as a regulator, so she had become a steward, serving in officers' messes. But she always knew her vocation was to become a regulator; her grandfather was in the Navy, her father was in the Army and both her male cousins were in the Navy.

She had been happy in her choice, she said. She had been lucky to become a regulator and to get a draft to a place like Gibraltar: a foreign drafting was every WRNS officer or rating's ambition. 'It is definitely a place where you have to make the most of it. To be happy here, you have got to get involved. I am glad I came, it has been a definite experience, especially jobwise.'

The Rigorous Regulator had only two irritations. It would be nice, she said, if the women regulators could be treated like policewomen in the sense of having their own rooms; but some had to share. At home, 75 per cent of the WRNS officers and ratings would be renting their own flats, whereas in places abroad with high rents like Gibraltar, only 5 to 10 per cent were renting their own flats.

The other irritation was more rooted in her own specific circumstances. She felt that she needed more money. This, though not an uncommon affliction, was heightened in her own case by the fact that she had previously been posted to London. In London, she got a £300 a month lodging allowance which virtually doubled her pay. She missed it when she no longer received it.

'Still,' she said, characteristically putting a positive gloss on a trying situation, 'there is no scope for social life here, so I don't spend much money.'

The Sombre Steward, like the Rigorous Regulator, had become a steward in her early days, but unlike the other, she had *remained* a steward, looking after officers in the wardroom. She had joined when she was twenty, and had had jobs at a wide variety of shore bases. She was now twenty-seven, a tall sharp-featured girl with a quiet voice and large brown watchful eyes.

'It is quite fun,' she said. 'You make lots of friends and an awful lot of acquaintances.'

She found the job varied – cleaning kitchens, bar work, waiting at table, booking accommodation. I asked her if she liked it. A moment of silence. Then the answer: 'I do, up to a certain point. I have done eight years this year, and you do get nasty jobs to do; quite a lot of the steward's job is mundane. I shall do my nine years, and then leave. I would not say I object to being a steward, because I was working in the catering world before I joined the Navy. I have given the Navy all I have had to give for nine years and I don't feel the Navy can offer me a lot else now. At thirty, I shall be the right age to do something else.'

I explored her thinking a bit further. She told me the issue was really one of respect. As a steward she had to call men 'Sir': 'And there are some people around that you respect whereas with others, you say it because you *have* to.'

How many, I asked, in the latter category? – 'There are a few. Their attitude towards us! For example, they can take advantage of your good nature sometimes. I do enjoy my job, and over the years I have had a lot of pleasure, but some of them treat you more like a servant or a slave – whereas I *don't* see that as my job.'

An example? – 'Sometimes there are a lot of officers who come in late for meals, and they are not well-mannered towards us, and generally give us a lot of aggravation, when it is not really necessary.'

I was trying to build up a picture of the sort of behaviour she resented; I asked her to elaborate. 'For instance we had a

course in here on a Sunday night, and they were very ready to
lord it over everyone. They came in late, nine of them
altogether. I said, "Can I have your mess numbers?" and took
their orders for dinner. They said, "How about a smile from
you first?" That didn't go down well. They said, "Are you
married?" I said, "I don't see that is any of your business." I
mentioned it to a lieutenant-commander, and he said they
were winding down after a hard week. I said, "They have
been winding down *all week*." But I have to say that Royal
Naval Reserve officers are very pleasant; they are more in
touch with the rest of the world.'

Dexterity in coping with nine young naval officers, who
may have sniffed a wine cork, could be a matter of temperament: humour and a steely tolerance would seem to be
highly desirable, if not absolutely necessary. The Sombre
Steward acknowledged that when she first joined the
WRNS, one of the first things said about her was that she
was very intolerant of people who didn't do what she
wanted them to do.

I asked her whether, if she had not been in the specific job of
steward, she would *still* have wanted to leave the Navy. 'I
honestly don't know. I was glad I joined it, but I think the
WRNS is changing.'

It is an oddity of the trend towards sexual equality that some
of the ways the Navy is changing in this regard fail to appeal
to members of the WRNS like the Sombre Steward. She
explained it in her cautious, thorough way: 'We are being
amalgamated with the men in some respects. In Portsmouth,
we used to have inspections in the evenings; it is something
that always happened among the men but had never been
heard of amongst the WRNS. We were told that it was part
of the plan to bring WRNS more in line with the men. I feel
I am not prepared to have someone coming in and out of my
room.'

She acknowledged that this was a state of mind originating
in her own temperament. Even more reasonably and fairly,

she also acknowledged that having been in the Navy would stand her in good stead when she looked for civilian employment. It had taught her a lot about people in general, and about tolerance and respect.

Whatever the occasional grumblings, and even departures, the top hierarchy of the WRNS has a confidence, which would be remarkable in any organization, that they have got the role of women in the Royal Navy exactly right. So much so that it can even regard as healthy the discontent of Wrens who want to leave the service.

I put the point to the very top WRNS officer, the commandant, in her pleasant and airy, but not excessively ornate, office just off the Mall. A pleasantly spoken lady with a cream dress, black court shoes, three rings and a youthful mane of now-greying hair, she had the aura of a governess rather than the head of a sector of an armed force. On top of her bookcase stood photographs of visits to classes and courses: the professional and personal memorabilia of an unmarried woman whose personal and professional lives had been closely intertwined.

I said that, among WRNS, I had noticed extremes of enthusiasm: women seemed to be either like cats with saucers of cream – confident they had fallen into their life's work and enjoyment – or disenchanted; little in between.

Was that healthy? 'Yes, that *is* healthy,' said the commandant. 'It happens in any job. It is interesting that, at the moment, the average life of a WRNS rating in the Navy is eight years and that of a WRNS officer nine years. That is quite a long time. Of course you do get people who want to leave. Take my personal staff officer. She is leaving the WRNS at her five-year break point, when she has the choice to leave, because she is getting married. You can get other people who want to do their full eight years' service, but then want to do something else quite different. It happens in civilian jobs. You can never have a perfect system where everyone is happy with their lot, because at times people have to go where they don't want to go because of the needs of the service.'

Where discontent existed, said the commandant, it was usually because of a package of circumstances rather than disenchantment with the WRNS as such. Someone's favourite grandmother was ill at home in the North of Scotland while the WRNS officer or rating was in the South of England, or something of that kind. Even in such cases, it was quite possible to advertise for a swapping of jobs through the Royal Navy's newspaper, *Navy News*. Provided the respective captains agreed, it was possible to exchange drafts in the case of women as well as men – a service unique to the Royal Navy.

The commandant herself came from an exceptional enough background to make her judgements highly individual ones. Her grandfather was an admiral. Her father was a naval officer. Her mother was a WRNS officer during the Second World War. She admitted that this background was her motivation, and that having a communal life at boarding school had helped to prepare her for many of the demands of the WRNS. When asked what she had not enjoyed in her time in the WRNS she admitted drily, 'I am a very poor person to interview, because I haven't *not* enjoyed one single part of my life in the WRNS.'

She did not agree that her boarding-school background might have been the thing that fitted her for the WRNS. 'I don't think boarding school has had an important effect on me in that sense,' she told me. 'What I *do* think is that you can't be a loner. I am the sort of person who likes people, and likes living in a community; and there are a lot of extramural activities that go on in the Navy. For example, I used to do skiing, walking, sailing and playing tennis. You have got to enjoy the community life. I can believe that community life is not for everybody, but if you are a young rating there is little opportunity to be by yourself. You have got to get on with other people, and enjoy the communal way of life. Boarding school helped me personally, but there are not so many girls that come from boarding schools today.'

Would it be easy to be a professionally devoted WRNS officer or rating and be married?

'A quarter of the WRNS are precisely that,' said the commandant. 'I would not expect it to be more. It used to be far less, when it was not the thing in the country for women to go out to work. Now everyone goes out to work, and you sometimes get women going out to work and men staying at home. The whole life of the country as a whole has changed, and in the Navy both husband and wife sometimes want their career.'

There was no objection to marriage, said the commandant. The insistence was on somebody who was a good person, who was efficient at their job and who was prepared to be mobile. A marriage with one partner *not* in the Navy could be difficult, and that was why WRNS sometimes left the service. She had recently met a WRNS officer in an establishment in the West Country, married to a civilian with a job in London. Eventually the couple had found it was just not working.

'She was very, very sad that she was going to leave,' said the commandant. 'But she was going to join the WRNS Reserves, so she can still share a bit of the life.'

There were cases, said the commandant, where the husband of a WRNS officer or rating had a trade which enabled him fairly easily to follow his wife up and down the country in various jobs. Sometimes it worked, sometimes it didn't. A WRNS officer or rating needn't necessarily be an extrovert by temperament, but she had to be a person who didn't want to go on staying in one routine job. She had to be flexible, she had to be prepared to accept more discipline than she would in civilian life and she had to be prepared, if the need arose, to put the needs of the service before her own: 'There may be some occasion when you are required to stay late, and you have to cancel everything you had planned to do, even if you have the most wonderful theatre tickets.'

Were such paragons becoming more rare? 'No!' said the commandant forcefully. 'We actually could get three times

the number we have now. We have masses of people wanting
to join the service – we always have done. It is difficult to
define why. Perhaps it is the lure of the sea. I just don't know.
But we can recruit easily and I can't see any reason why we
should change in that respect. Often recruits say they have
wanted to join from the age of eleven.'

But what about that barrier to women's progress to the
very top of the Royal Navy – the fact that women are not
allowed to go to sea in warships? The question was being
asked in several quarters at the time I put the question to the
commandant. The Americans, the Dutch and the Danes were
doing experiments by having women on *stores* ships. Other
NATO countries were thinking on similar lines.

But the WRNS had no plans for allowing women to sea in
warships. This did not displease the commandant, who plainly
had a relaxed attitude in acknowledging women's limitations
as part of an armed service.

'There are jobs that women can't do because they don't
have the physical strength to do it,' she said. 'Air mechanics –
including some of the men – can't lift some of the heavy
engines they are working on. I don't think there is room for
rethinking women's role and extending it. The role we play
now is the role the Navy needs us to play, and we cannot
extend it.'

Women in the WRNS were able to get a broader band of
experience than women in the RAF or Army and there were
a large number of jobs in the Royal Navy that could be held
by either a man or a woman. In the Women's Royal Army
Corps, the assistant adjutant to the Royal Artillery was *always*
a woman. But the flag lieutenant to a naval flag officer could
be either a man or a woman. In shore establishments, the
captain's secretary could be either a man or a woman.

'This is thoroughly healthy,' said the commandant. '*Very*. It
is healthy for the Navy, and for the people concerned. It gives
a greater choice; and I think that sometimes women do things
a different way from men, and so you get a job looked at in a

different way. We are good at the intelligence world, we are good at the computer side, we have the patience to do weapons analysis – it appeals to a woman's mind. We are naturally quite good at welfare.'

But the 'no women in the combat role' rule remains. Was the commandant, and were the majority of women in the Navy, really happy about that?

It was a question of space on a modern warship, according to the commandant. Weaponry had to be tight-packed in the ship. Creating additional accommodation for women would take up the space that should be available for this weaponry. Women could not simply share the existing cabins with men.

There *may* be women in the WRNS who would like to go to sea in a combat role. If so, I personally didn't find any. The commandant thought there might be one or two here and there who would like to see women in warships, and therefore able to take up the highest positions in the Navy.

'I say that, if the government ever decided that WRNS should serve in a combat role, we would actually be recruiting a different sort of person,' said the commandant.

An imitation man? The commandant wouldn't say. All she *would* say was that it would require complete dedication to the ship. Men, with their 'little hobbies' aboard, were happy to give that dedication: 'But a woman likes to do various other activities, like going to discos and other things she could not do aboard a warship. You would be looking for a different individual, totally dedicated to their job.'

And they would have to be, ideally, as strong as men. The commandant recalled that classic case of a woman afloat in modern times, the WRNS officer who went out to the Falklands on a Royal Fleet Auxiliary as meteorological officer.

'She was good at her job,' said the commandant,'but didn't have the physical strength to open the bulkhead door en route for her briefing, so someone else had to interrupt their job in order to open the door for her.'

Even in war – perhaps *especially* in war – women on warships
would be of questionable benefit. At present, their war role
would be to free as many men from shore jobs as possible, so
that they could get off to sea. The flexibility of the WRNS
jobs arrangements would help this process: they would be
serving, behind the lines, the men who would be doing the
actual combat tasks. The Falklands conflict was a good example. Because the Navy was not allowed to call up the
reserves, the women had to fill many jobs previously held by
men – always short of going to sea in a warship. They did
almost everything else, from joining planning sections in the
Ministry of Defence to standing guard as security women at
the gates of shore establishments.

Generally, in peacetime, the women of the WRNS appear
happy to be in some areas better educated than their male
counterparts (Wren ratings often have five 'O' levels and a
couple of 'A' levels as well) but yet delegated to playing a
subordinate role. The commandant, who herself served as a
rating for three years, ending up as a leading Wren in the
communications field, said that one of the values of the
WRNS was that their very *presence* made Royal Naval men
work and behave better. At Dartmouth, where both men and
women officers are trained, there had once been one term
without a WRNS course. The men under training had not
taken so much care about their manners and appearance as
they usually did with women present. A blend of men and
women was good for the morale of each.

The statement was one that only the most rabid feminist
would find surprising or deplorable; but plainly the Navy
could be an uncomfortable place for anyone who saw the basic
role of women differently.

*

In forging their way towards the highly potent if sometimes
vague ideal of sexual equality, some naval *wives* appear to be
luckier than some of the women who have chosen to make the

Navy their calling. At least in their accommodation arrangements.

The Navy's general 'sort-it-out-for-yourself' philosophy, sometimes felt by the Navy's internal critics to be *laissez faire*, has its benefits for those women who marry naval men. They are left to their own devices far more than they would be in a service with a more paternalistic approach. The strong trend in the Navy for buying one's house, like any civilian, is an expression of this and pleases many wives who would rather buy and sell houses than spend all their lives in a series of standard married quarters.

'The Navy believes in letting you do things for yourself,' said the wife of a lieutenant-commander on an overseas posting. 'When you are going back to the United Kingdom, they are quite content to let you do your own packing, just as they will let you choose your own married quarters' decor within reason. And I have no doubt that if you could swim home on top of the packing cases, they would be even more pleased.'

Some wives see this as a benefit rather than a disadvantage. It enables them to breathe. It is possibly more true of officers' wives than those of ratings. In a rather free system, they appear to know how best to use the system to get what they want.

One officer's wife I visited in Gibraltar was living in a handsome five-bedroomed flat in a converted old hospital. It commanded magnificent views but, like other flats in the block, had an eccentric layout because of the building's previous use. The living-room was vast. So was the dining-room which, as the wife pointed out, was *full* of chairs. The Navy had an obsession with chairs, she said; they were determined you should have enough; she had twelve, plus two carvers.

But getting the flat into a condition that was acceptable had been a long process. 'I had to choose new curtains and paints throughout this flat,' said the cheerful and competent naval wife. 'People either like these flats or dislike them – some find them too old, too dark and too unmanageable. This one was in a bad state, aesthetically. There is an incredible division of labour. If you need a curtain rail put in, you go to the Property Services Agency. If you want curtains, you have to go somewhere else, and if you want your vacuum cleaner fixed, you go somewhere else again. If you want your flat redecorated, you have to keep on nagging and nagging. These curtains took a phone call a week for two months. Perhaps I exaggerate a little, but not much. Of course you have to keep in mind that the curtains will cost a fortune, which some people tend to forget. It took a fair amount of reminding to get the curtains. You mustn't lose your temper. You should realize that if you ring repeatedly, they will get fed up with it in the end and do it. I tried to work on the principle with all the redecoration that, as I was occupying the place for only two years, I should find paints and curtains that other people who came after me would not find offensive. That is the technique really – to choose something that later occupants won't object to. Provided you do that, you will probably get things done.'

The principle of self-help, on which the Navy is often content to rely, does not indicate a lack of concern for the domestic matters which are on wives' minds. On the contrary, in recent years, such matters have been thrashed out in consultation, re-thought and re-re-thought in a way that would make the ruffians of Nelson's Navy laugh their rotting teeth loose.

At one stage, Taste Committees were set up at the Ministry of Defence to consider how the best aesthetic effects in decor could be obtained within the inevitable standardization of a disciplined service. Reports on how successful these committees were vary. Some think they did indeed make a contribution to the paints and curtains in naval quarters, others that all they proved was that what Mrs Bloggs regards as heavenly taste Mrs Bates could well regard as social and aesthetic death. Six colours were sought which, it was calculated, could be used in the same room without the effect being positively hideous. Not everyone would agree that the committees were successful.

The married quarters of ratings are frankly and intentionally not so good as those of men who have earned a higher place in the Navy. This is asserted by wives of ratings, and admitted by wives of officers.

I visited a group of ratings' wives in Edinburgh House, Gibraltar, a series of green-painted tall blocks of flats built in the 1940s and 1950s. In the opinion of one of the wives with enough experience to know, Edinburgh House was easily the least desirable accommodation she had lived in since she had married.

The flat in which we spoke was occupied by a chief writer and his wife. It had three bedrooms, a bathroom and lavatory and a tiny lounge in which incompatible colours struggled for supremacy. The carpet was a green-brown mixture – standard issue. The chairs and sofa were covered in flame-red covers – a standard issue. The curtains had a sunflower design in browns, creams and oranges – standard issue.

'You don't have a choice; they don't match and they won't do anything about that,' said the chief writer's wife, whom I will fictitiously (as in the case of all the names that follow) call Mrs Myers. 'I could move out to a better married quarter, a house outside the town, but I prefer to be central and near the town. In any case the colours would be no different out there.'

She had been in the flat eighteen months and said she believed that when redecoration was due, you had the choice of three colours for the walls: blue, yellow and stone.

Did that grate on her? 'It doesn't matter to me personally. I look upon this as not being my home. Women do complain about these quarters, but it doesn't worry me. The quarters are clean, and that's what matters to me. The colours are all perfectly good ones, but they don't match, and that's that. Unless your chairs are falling to pieces, you can't get them changed.'

'You don't get them changed even then!' put in Mrs Soames, wife of a chief petty officer artificer. 'It can take you years to get things changed. My chair covers are all in holes, but they haven't lasted five years, so I can't have new ones.'

But there are considerations more central to naval ratings'

wives than such irritations about decor; and they are not all *dis*advantages. In such naval quarters, there can be a sense of community, an ease in making friends, that would elude women living in their own homes in civilian localities.

'It is certainly easier to make friends in these quarters,' said the wife of the chief writer. Mrs Peel, wife of a chief petty officer, put in: 'My three children are always out playing with others. They are going to miss it when we go back home to a private estate.'

'You certainly make friends more easily than you would in England,' said Mrs Yeovil, wife of a chief petty officer medical assistant. 'I lived in England at a naval establishment for five years, and never knew a soul. You socialize a lot more here. There are mother and toddler groups and wives' clubs, which are good for introducing people to other people. You don't get them in England.'

The advantage can turn to a disadvantage in terms of loss of privacy. 'There is *no* privacy,' said the wife of the chief petty officer medical assistant. 'You aren't private in your own house.' The wife of the chief petty officer artificer agreed: 'I lived in my own house for five years. Here everyone knows what everyone else is doing. If you have an argument with your husband, someone will hear it, and tell someone else, who will tell someone else, so everybody hears about it.'

But such disadvantages were obviously containable, if not trivial, to this group of ratings' wives. Even the fact that they had been brought within the jurisdiction of the Naval Discipline Act, which meant that they were almost as accountable to the Navy as their husbands were, was not a great point of complaint. 'The Naval Discipline Act doesn't have a great deal of effect on us in practice,' said Mrs Forbes, wife of a petty officer weaponry electrical mechanic, and one of the most forthright and analytical members of the group.

What mattered to these wives far more, it was immediately obvious, was something else. They felt that they were too often treated, in official transactions, as if they were mere appendages to their husbands rather than people in their own right. It seemed as if the inevitable demands of bureaucracy rubbed up against the wives's sense of individual identity.

Mrs Myers, the wife of the chief writer, put it like this: 'As a naval wife you are sort of regulated. If you go into the naval library for a book, the first thing you are asked is the rank of your husband. You aren't treated as an individual.'

This struck an immediate chord in the other ratings' wives. 'You go to any administrative establishment and you are asked not who you are, but who you are the wife of. You are not a person in yourself. I wouldn't say they didn't treat you as a human being, but they treat you as a man's wife, not as yourself. It doesn't happen outside in the civilian community, so why should it happen with the Navy?'

'Yes,' said Mrs Myers, 'it can happen in the library or the hospital. It is bad when the library asks if you are a senior or a junior rank. What difference can it make? I don't like the idea.'

Mrs Yeovil, a more experienced naval wife, said placatingly, 'Why they ask your husband's rank in the library is because, if the books don't come back, it is quicker for them to find out the husband and say, "Can you tell your wife to bring the books back?" than looking through the files or telephone directories for the wife.'

Mrs Myers was not appeased. 'I still don't like it. Why can't you be a person in your own right?'

'Because,' put in Mrs Forbes, 'you are only here because your husband is here. If it is only for administrative reasons they want to know your husband's name, it is fair enough.'

Mrs Peel, the wife of the chief petty officer, said that most women accepted the system. But she knew of one woman who had a grievance about the Post Office. On Gibraltar, as it happened, this was run by the Army. If you cashed a postal order at this Post Office, you had to give your husband's name, rank and telephone number.

'I opened up a savings account at the Post Office,' said Mrs Yeovil, 'and I had to write my husband's name down.'

'I think that's disgraceful,' said Mrs Forbes. 'A Post Office is a Post Office, and should behave like any other.'

I was not too surprised to hear of these (containable) resentments, having come across much the same thing among wives of men in the British Army. But I was left wondering if, with a little hard thought, the Royal Navy might perhaps devise a scheme for identification which was watertight without subjecting wives to these sorts of niggling irritations. Could perhaps wives get by on their own names, plus a sexless serial number which could be quoted, and used as a way to get fuller information only if really necessary? Some way of making everyday transactions less irritating to naval wives would certainly be welcome.

In the case of Mrs Yeovil, the fact that she had her own job helped. She herself was quite sure of this.

'I am on night-sister's duties at an old people's home,' she told me. 'I work from 8 pm to 8 am. I do only two days a week. But I wanted to get back into nursing. I had been out of it for ten years, and I thought this was a good opportunity to get back. I think it makes me feel more of an individual human being in my own right.'

But jobs are not always easily accessible to naval wives, especially if they have young children or if their husbands are located at inaccessible points. In some cases, frustrations can escalate – though the naval wives on Gibraltar said that in the last two years there had been only one wife taken before the captain for being drunk and shouting.

Most wives, of course, would not dream of getting drunk or shouting, even if disillusioned with their lot as naval wives. What they are far more likely to do is direct their resentment at their husbands, which cannot be good for the Navy, or even put pressure on their husbands to leave it as soon as possible, which again cannot be good for the Navy.

I asked the group of naval wives I found in Gibraltar whether in fact they would advise their husbands to stay in the Navy at the end of their present contracts.

Mrs Soames: 'Officers won't ever admit they are wrong. That rankles with my husband as much as anything else. When everyone knows the officer is wrong, it must have a worse effect on discipline than hearing him say, "I was wrong." But my husband has just signed on for another ten years.'

Mrs Yeovil: 'My husband has been offered early retirement. A lot of senior rates were offered it. I think he is tempted because, trying to get civilian employment, he would stand a better chance with twenty-five years to offer a new employer than twenty years. He is considering the police force or prison work. I definitely advised him to sign on when we were younger, because it was security for the family. But after twenty-two years I would advise him to get out.'

Mrs Peel: 'I just leave the decision to my husband. He is the one who has to do the job. It is no good me saying "Come out" if he couldn't find an alternative job.'

Mrs Forbes: 'I would not want my husband to stay in longer. We have had a good life for the last few years. But he has been away a lot, and he is forty, and I feel he has given the Navy enough time and energy. He notices that he gets older and the officers get younger. The officers from university are the ones that cause a problem in a lot of cases, because they think they know it all. The ones that come up through the ranks are a lot better. The others are not trained to *listen*.'

Mrs Myers: 'If I were to advise him, I would advise him to come out after twenty-two years and look for a civilian life. But the prospect of going out frightens him, though the longer he leaves it, the worse it will be.'

Analysing discontent where it exists can always be a risky business. The stated reasons are not always the true ones, even though the people who advance them may sincerely believe they are. These and other naval wives I met said they let their husbands worry about their own professional worries and focused more on the domestic details of their own lives. But there was usually the feeling behind the statement that their husbands were now being asked to do more work to make up for decreased numbers, were under increasing pressure because of this, and were, in consequence, more often resentful of officers who did not appear to understand the reality of their problems.

It was perhaps significant that this thread seemed to appear most often in the conversation of the wives of senior ratings rather than either officers' wives or those of junior ratings. There was a feeling that it was *their* husbands who – as a wife *not* on Gibraltar put it – '*really* run the Navy'; and that, as working pressures increased, this fact was often forgotten. Right or wrong, serious or trivial, this *feeling* often existed, and it cannot be helpful to the Navy. But the impression given was that it might be cured by fine tuning in the attitudes between officers and ratings, and it was not an issue to send anyone to the barricades.

Yet, trivial as they may be, it is possible for grievances to be long repressed, possibly dangerously so. Unlike the British Army, the Royal Navy does not employ families officers. There is no direct equivalent of the friendly major to help sort out family problems when husbands are away – as they can sometimes be for periods of months rather than weeks or days. For the naval husband separated from his family, there is the support of the divisional officer; in the Navy, a man's immediate departmental superior is expected to give advice and help on personal problems if required. For the wife, there is a welfare system, but it is external to the fabric of the Navy, not built closely into its formal structure.

In these circumstances, wives of naval men find that they must – and do – dig deeply into their personal resources to meet the challenge of what men and wives both claim without hesitation to be the worst feature of naval life. This is human separation. They have to be able to switch from one sort of life (with a husband) to another sort (without one) without breaking down from loneliness when alone, or exploding with anger when suddenly faced with a second decision-maker in the house, after being the only fount of authority for children, the milkman and the garage man.

'Wives get strength from the group,' I was told. 'It helps when a wife lives on an estate with other naval wives. It is the ones who do not have this support who experience the most trouble.'

But it was a *man* – a comparatively well-paid commander – who told me this. Wanting to check it direct with wives, I raised the point with all the wives of Navy men I was able to meet. The consensus was that the wives who were the most fortunate were those in specific smaller sub-sections of the Navy which had their own identity and 'clubbability' – like the Royal Marines or the submariners. And this despite the fact that, in these parts of the Navy, wives could often face very long periods of separation.

It can be a double-edged sword. The clubbability of some sections of the Navy can at first make wives feel excluded rather than included. Near the Clyde Submarine Base at Faslane in Scotland, I spoke to the wife of the commanding officer of a hunter-killer submarine, who was often away for periods of two months or more. She was a bright, attractive woman of thirty-three, who *looked* younger than her years but *talked* older. She had been married at eighteen and now had four children. The oldest one was a boy of thirteen. He was moving into the usual adolescent problems of rebellion, which usually focus on the father rather than the mother – *if* father is there. The house, full of books, records and pictures, was a double-fronted cottage overlooking a loch: it underlined the impression of a woman with a distinct personality, many interests and some internal resources; a woman very much in charge of herself and of her active environment.

But she confessed that, as a young wife, she had found the rival demands on her husband's attention made by the Navy rather difficult to accept. 'I have been married fifteen years, and I am used to it now,' she said. 'With a young wife who has just got married, it is difficult to adjust. I can remember, when we first got married, thinking that the Navy was dividing up my time with my husband, and wasn't just a normal job. Most submariners are exceptionally close to their submarines. For a young wife to understand that is very difficult. Submarines are black tubes, perhaps, to the wife. But the men live and work in them until they become part of them.'

The wives, in short, are challenged by male loyalty to a private club. They respond to this by turning that mental attitude to their own advantage when their husbands are away. It is then *their* turn to form what amounts to an informal club of wives, all of whom share the same problems, and will share them for exactly the same length of time, until their husbands come home again.

'We try to arrange something for every weekend when the husbands are away,' said the commander's wife. 'We have organized a party for fourteen children. We have organized a skittle alley. A party of us with children aged between two and thirteen went to the Edinburgh Tattoo. If the younger girls are feeling a bit down, you can usually get them to see a different side to it. Some of them haven't heard from their husbands. All right, we tell them, it is going to be another three weeks before you hear, but there is nothing to worry about; they go out and they come home. They *will* be home.'

Such friendly support stops well short of the patronage that a commanding officer's wife was once expected to exercise over the wives of those lower down the naval social scale.

'You are no longer required to be the equivalent of the colonel's lady,' said the commander's wife. 'Some of the other officers' wives are older than me. You make a point of getting on, and enjoying one another's company, but you are expected now to be the Lady Bountiful only to a certain extent. At the ship's dance, perhaps, because you will tend to be looked at as the commanding officer's wife. I personally go out of my way *not* to push myself as "the captain's wife", because I would far rather people should talk to you easily rather than say, "Oh God, it's the captain's wife!" and shy away. We are in the same basic situation as anyone else. But you must be very careful not to say the wrong thing – I mean about what his boat is doing or not doing. And you have to be very careful not to give a bad impression of the Navy or of submarines.'

On formal occasions, said the commander's wife, it would be indicated who were the people who would want to talk to her. But it would be up to her to decide what she was going to say to them. She always liked to be told in advance who people were and what the husbands did.

'Yes, you do put on a different face to a certain extent for formal occasions,' she said. 'Generally I am called by my Christian name. Senior ratings and lads call me by my Christian name if I go down to the pub for a lunch-time drink. All the wives, regardless of who they are, call me by my first name normally. But with a formal do on board during the working day, to me it is always "Ma'am" or "Mrs So-and-So".'

The clubbability of the submariners' wives tends to resemble a protective alliance rather than a lifelong loyalty. As the commander's wife put it, 'I enjoy very much the close-knit community, which is very much there with the wives and families while the boat is away. But it doesn't hover once the boat is home. You don't see very much of the other wives when the boat is at home.'

The problems of re-integration once the husband is home are often almost as severe as the problems of coping with loneliness. I could easily imagine a woman with a strong personality like the commander's wife causing her returned husband to say occasionally, 'Look, *I* live here, too.' She admitted this did happen.

But the wife of another commander at Faslane, a very quiet person, who could not so easily be visualized in a personality clash with her husband or anyone else, said that she too found it difficult to re-adapt to the presence of a husband: 'For the first few days, it is quite difficult, because I have been used to just the two of us in the house, me and my two-year-old daughter. I think it takes between three and four days to adjust. Perhaps the naval wives' life helps them to be a bit more independent.

You develop a few more skills and resources than someone with a husband always coming home. I take an interest in the car and the house a little more. We make an effort to go out more than most people do.'

But such wives make an effort *not* to be seen as great ladies taking the problems of the ratings very much to heart and offering advice whether it is sought or not. Ratings' wives made it equally clear to me that they did not expect condescension or patronage from officers' wives.

On the Churchill Estate near Glasgow – a virtual suburb for submariners' wives – I met the wife of a leading radio operator who put the contemporary attitude of such women in a nutshell. She had two children, had been married for six years to a husband who had been in the Navy nearly ten years, and had a healthy mistrust of rank as the only bridge to friendship.

'Yes,' she said, 'I would mix with wives of broadly the same rank as my husband, because they are usually on the same estate. If you are of higher rank, you go to a different place. In practice you mix with your own kind. But as a matter of fact, some of the officers' wives are much more friendly than the ordinary people on this estate are. Some of the *other* wives can be snobs. I knew one when we were living at Portsmouth who didn't want anything to do with us because her husband was in the surface Navy and didn't get as much money as my husband, who was in submarines. It didn't worry me, but it worried her. We got more money than *her* husband did. That will get up some people's noses.'

Such snobbery must be a great life-waster when women are facing a common loneliness. The hierarchical system of the Navy generally cannot totally be blamed for it. To a great extent, it is self-imposed; fortunately, it is said to be comparatively rare.

But it can exist, and sometimes the results can rankle for years. The point came up in a revealing conversation I had with a group of officers who had once been ratings but had broken through that professional and social barrier by their own efforts. I asked one of them whether officers like himself encountered social snobbery in the wardroom or even at work. His answer was immediate: 'Most ratings and officers get on quite well, because they are professionals doing a similar sort of job. Quite often when you are socializing and your wives are together, that is where you get the snobbery. I remember a particular instance. There was a girl I knew quite well, who started going to coffee mornings. She had been to about three of them when they realized she was a rating's wife and she was asked not to come any more. She was told, "This is not a ratings' coffee morning."'

The comment loosened the tongues of the rest of the group. 'I have an example of that,' said another ex-rating officer. 'I remember that, when my wife used to go to the wives' get-togethers at Culdrose, there was a much stronger class system between wives than between husbands. She said herself that people were graded in accordance with their husbands' rank. They would say to her, "Are you an officer's wife?" rather than simply, "What is your name?" I don't think it particularly bothered her – nothing particularly bothers her, not even me – but she was aware of it. As far as I was concerned, if she didn't like the atmosphere of any group, then she didn't have to go; and she didn't. That was a problem quite easily dealt with. It is not just the Navy, this sort of snobbery. It is a reflection of what exists in civilian life.'

A man may forget an affront to himself, but never one to his wife or children: the ignoring of this elementary maxim, of growing importance in the Navy with a large number of ex-rating officers, may have created ill will and even affected the careers of Dartmouth-trained officers. I was to discover that husbands of wives who had been slighted in this way tended to remember the exact details of the circumstances, even when they were protesting that it had left no ill-will.

But it must be added that not every ex-rating officer I spoke to took a gloomy view of naval wives. Some maintained that social differences were breaking down in accordance with what was happening in civilian life.

'In these days a lot of ratings have studied with the Open University,' said one ex-rating officer. 'A lot of senior ratings are far more qualified than the officers are. A chief artificer can earn a lot more money than a lieutenant in some cases, and that puts him higher on the social scale.'

I questioned this. Surely social barriers were not based exclusively on cash, since many shopkeepers earned more than university professors? 'I take your point,' said the officer. 'But if the chief petty officer lives in a posh house at the top of the hill, and the officer is living in married quarters, it must *tend* to break barriers. I do think barriers are being broken.'

Another officer who had crossed the same professional fence said his wife had never experienced any social difficulty as the wife of a rating. 'When my wife has socialized, there has never been any question of what she was, or where she came from. She has been in circles with senior officers' wives – coffee mornings, keep-fit things and so on – and there has never been any question as to what her background was.'

Perhaps, I suggested, it was a question not of background as much as personality: could his wife pass, socially, for an officer's wife even before he had become an officer?

'Well, she is not a northerner, like me,' said her husband. 'She would pass as an officer's wife. But there were other wives around at that time who weren't officers' wives, and who did not particularly seem like what you would expect an officer's wife to be, and *they* weren't discriminated against, either. It depends on the particular community a wife finds herself in, rather than her own personality.'

In short, how a naval wife fares – as with so much else about the Navy – varies according to the nature of the attitudes she happens to find around her. And that can vary greatly, often depending on the most senior figures in any particular professional and social landscape.

PART II

WAYS OF GETTING IN AND GETTING ON

12

DON'T KNOWS AND KNOWS

'I don't know whether I would be terribly happy in the Army, fighting on a man-to-man basis. We are looking for a different type of person. The Army person is all action – go, GO! Whereas men in the Royal Navy can be sitting on a mess deck for six months on patrol – same old days, same old weather, same old letter to send home. This is the sort of thing you have to be able to cope with.'

– Careers information officer (lieutenant) at Royal Navy Careers Office.

'Why did I volunteer to be a school prefect? Because I thought the school was falling apart.'

– Would-be artificer at Royal Navy Careers Office.

The sixteen-year-old lad with the shiny black shoes and the unhappy pimpled face didn't know. The Royal Navy careers adviser gave him every *chance* to know, but still he didn't. He didn't know why he liked English best as a school subject. He didn't know why his stepfather no longer gave him any pocket money. He didn't know who his real father was. He didn't know the type of ship in which he would most like to serve if the Royal Navy accepted him as a rating.

'What did you achieve in the Scouts?' asked the careers adviser gently.

'How do you mean?' was the reply.

'You say you like cricket. What is your particular prowess at cricket?'

'Pardon?'

In another room a taller, better dressed, better spoken young man, aged twenty, was giving an entirely different performance in *his* first face-to-face interview with the officer recruiting staff for the South-East Region in their headquarters in High Holborn. He was being screened before his application was considered for forwarding to the Admiralty Interview Board, which makes the assessment and final recommendation on officer entries.

He, too, was a comprehensive school boy. He came from the Midlands. But he spoke standard B B C English, sprinkled with self-deprecating smiles, as he faced his interviewer across a small table – a female, second officer W R N S. He plainly either *knew* or knew how to *ask*. He also had family problems, but he had obviously formed clear opinions about them. Unfortunately his mother had died and though he was able to get on with his stepmother, his sister couldn't; and an argument had rather spoilt his own birthday. His parents thought the Navy would be a good idea.

All this was said in the light but positive tones of a man reporting scientific facts rather than being submerged in emotional confusion.

Why hadn't he done as well in his 'A' Levels as his 'O' Levels? 'Because, I suppose, I had had one success and I thought I could automatically have another,' he said with his charming smile.

'He used his charm – didn't he just!' said the W R N S interviewer privately to me afterwards. She had valiantly battled to keep her professional detachment during the actual interview.

Thus, in one day at one of the Navy's Careers Information Offices, did two elements of late twentieth-century Britain – the intellectual rather than social *haves* and *have-nots* – direct themselves towards their hopes of a place in the sun. And with a *woman* as the would-be young officer's first contact with the Senior Service! Nelson, always the innovator, might have approved, but many of his contemporaries would have been speechless.

The Navy, in fact, probes just as deeply into the selectors as the selectors themselves will later have to probe those presenting themselves at any one of the Royal Navy Careers Information Offices.

That point was rammed well home to me, before I had the chance to see candidates themselves, by the commander who was one of the Navy's five regional careers staff officers – the others being at Bristol (for the South-West), Derby (the East), Birmingham (the West) and Glasgow (Scotland and Northern Ireland). He was a tall, alert man with magnifying spectacles which gave him the air of an oil or plastics executive rather than a military stereotype.

He made it unambiguously and proudly clear that, though the Army and the Royal Air Force might do things one way, the Royal Navy did it another when it came to selecting its future officers and men, because that way was 'right for us'.

'We in the Navy actually recruit our own people, as compared with the other two services who do only the initial recruiting. We actually select our own ratings; in the other services their final selection is done by a central authority. That, at least, is true for ratings selection, not true for officers, who we refer to the Admiralty Interview Board for assessment and the Ministry of Defence for final selection. In order to do this we have a permanent careers service which covers all Naval Services, the W R N S and so on, with the exception of medical and dental officers, and the Queen Alexandra's Royal Navy Nursing Service, where we handle the initial process, but where the final selection is done by the naval medical authorities.'

This on-the-spot ability to choose ratings, and to powerfully advise on officers and others, gives status, power and responsibility to the men and women of the Careers Service. And they are left in no doubt that they had better employ it well. All are people who have done their full service in the Navy or Royal Marines. All of them have completed their twenty-two or twenty-seven-year contracts with the Navy. This means, in the case of the warrant officers and chief petty officers who make up the bulk of the careers staff, that they are still in their forties.

The quality of the people going into the Careers Service was now very high, said the commander. The Navy now took only the best. He happened to be standing chairman of the recruitment board for the recruiters, and he knew. They recruited only to fill gaps in the service. There were now about three hundred in the permanent Careers Service. Some fifty were officers, acting as careers officers, and the rest were careers advisers, who kept their ranks as warrant officers, fleet chief petty officers or chief petty officers. Only about one in five of the hopefuls who go before the recruitment board are appointed.

'We are looking for ability to communicate with the young – especially the young; to be tactful and diplomatic with the public and to be able to represent the service in its widest sense,' said the commander.

Such are the ambitious aims. I asked if I could see how some of the professionally trained careers officers and careers advisers coped, after their six to eight initial months, with the young people walking through the double swing doors in High Holborn in the hope of a naval career. To an outsider, it seemed possible that the pressures and the training of the careers information officers and careers advisers could make them too self-consciously aware of their own correct states of mind and too little aware of the young people they were dealing with.

'No, no,' said the commander. 'What we have to remember all the time is that we are dealing with people's lives. We are very, very conscious of that.'

And the lieutenant who was the careers information officer

Fleet hunter-killer submarines, nuclear-powered but not nuclear armed, can also remain submerged for long periods. This one, HMS *Warspite*, is submerging after a visit to Gibraltar.

The Polaris submarine HMS *Renown* with some of her crew of 143 in the Gare Loch, Scotland (*Right*).

(*Above*) In the torpedo storage compartment aboard the nuclear submarine HMS *Resolution*, the crew are with 16 Polaris missiles with more fire power than all the bombs dropped by both sides during the Second World War. They take it very matter-of-factly.

(*Below*) Health of the crew is a vital concern aboard any submarine, but more especially in the nuclear-powered Polaris type, which stay submerged for the whole of a trip that may take two months. Here, in HMS *Resolution*'s health physics laboratory, a medical technician measures the acid content of a water sample.

Diesel submarines, though perhaps less glamorous for their crew than nuclear submarines, still patrol the seas or stand ready at HMS *Dolphin*.

Rescue work of helicopters can be for Royal Navy vessels or civilians. (*Above*) A Sea King Mark 2 of 819 Naval Air Squadron, based at HMS *Gannet*, Prestwick Airport, Ayrshire, Scotland, winches a casualty from the deck of a patrol submarine. (*Below*) Another helicopter makes a rescue from the Motor Vessel *Craigantlet*, breaking up on rocks in heavy seas.

Above) Foul weather can be overcome by aircraft aboard carriers – with proper procedures. Sea Harriers of 800 Naval Air Squadron aboard HMS *Hermes* in the Atlantic during winter are lashed down until immediately before take off.

Below) Sea King helicopters of 820 Naval Air Squadron prepare for lift-off in rather easier conditions from HMS *Invincible*.

(*Above*) Minesweepers are among the smallest and, say officers and men, the most informal of all warships, though they do not necessarily endear themselves to the many sailors who are prone to seasickness. But the seas are quiet as the new minesweeper HMS *Waveney* leaves Portsmouth Harbour for South Wales Division Reserve.

(*Below*) The fifth ship to bear the name Ark Royal is the third aircraft carrier of the Invincible class, the others being HMS *Illustrious* and HMS *Invincible*. *Ark Royal* is here being fitted out in the River Tyne before being commissioned.

The British and Russian Navies watch one another vigilantly and ceaselessly. (*Above*) The Russian Krivak 1, *Razyashchy*, looks at HMS *Invincible* whilst operating in the Gulf of Aden and the Sverolov cruiser *Zhdanov*, flying the flag of the Commander Soviet Mediterranean Squadron, is watched (*Below*) by the crew of a Sea King helicopter from HMS *Invincible*.

Women do not play only stereotyped roles in the Royal Navy. They can, for instance, form WRNS Air Operations Teams as at Royal Naval Air Station Culdrose in Cornwall (*Above*) or be staff officers of helicopter squadrons delivering important signals to aircrew (*Below*).

in charge of the London area and who was detailed to explain to me the process of recruitment at the sharp end assured me: 'The most important person is that young man who walks in through the front door. We always keep that in mind.'

In some cases, the young man or woman will not be a complete stranger. Every careers adviser has an allotted number of schools in his area and aims to pay each of these two visits a year – the first to get to know the school and the second to give a presentation for fourth- or fifth-year pupils. Perhaps the presentation will consist of a film and a talk, or an audience-participation programme on Britain and N A T O, or a visit to a Royal Naval Training Establishment or, very occasionally, a trip out to sea.

'We hope that some of it rubs off. We don't go there to hard-recruit,' the lieutenant told me. 'It is all very low key. Later, perhaps, the lad contacts the nearest careers office, or sees a coupon in a newspaper. We give him the literature he has asked for, plus a prepaid postcard to send back to us. Then we give him an appointment to take part in the selection procedure.'

Five would-be ratings had been asked to come in on the day I visited the office. Only two turned up.

Nothing unusual about that, I was told ruefully. Not at this time of year. There was a *bit* more employment about for youngsters. It was a beautiful summer morning and some might say, 'I'll go to Margate instead.' Schools were in the middle of their examinations. The majority of people who intended to leave had mostly been seen by the selectors already; and those who came at the last moment were possibly not those the Navy really wanted.

By the time I saw them, both the candidates had talked at the front desk and been told about the Rehabilitation of Offenders Act. Under this, candidates do not have to reveal certain convictions against them after a period of five years, though the Navy expects all others to be declared. Failure to do so is regarded as a serious matter.

'The only thing that would instantly debar a man is if he has not yet completed at least fifty per cent of any court order for supervision,' explained the lieutenant. 'The Navy, I believe, has always prided itself on the fact that we have had a good system for allowing people who have been in trouble to come into the service – whatever they may have done before being regarded as being behind them.'

The test room was like a small classroom with a dozen plastic desks. Each desk was bare except for a couple of documents, at which the candidates were instructed not to look. The first of these forms was simply a questionnaire about personal background, which candidates are expected to fill in line-by-line, on the instructions of the careers adviser. He was a chief petty officer who stood at a small lectern and tried to put the two young men at their ease with a consideration that might seem to some to be overdone rather than underdone.

'We do everything in pencil, and you are not allowed a rubber. Don't rush ahead and don't worry that you will be left behind, because you will be given time to go back later,' he instructed.

The two candidates had chosen to sit at desks against a wall at the very opposite side of the room from the lectern, a fact which may have been psychologically revealing. Neither gave a clear-cut personal impression. The one in the front row was the one with the polished shoes and the neat school blazer. The one sitting behind him, four years older at twenty, was dressed in scuffed running shoes, faded jeans, a soiled blue and white leather blouson; he had inconclusive evidence of a moustache and his hair, though clean, was untidy. He was left-handed and wrote with the paper sideways-on, as if he thought that I, sitting next to him, might otherwise crib his answers.

Both young men scribbled patiently line by line through personal details varying from brothers' and sisters' occupations, spouses' occupations ('If no spouse, leave blank'); subjects liked best at school, subjects they did not take at school; activities they did in their spare time (by ticking off items on a provided list); whether they had been a school monitor or prefect; further education if any; any exams taken; shorthand and typing speeds if applicable; occupations past and present; jobs they would have *wanted* to do; whether in Scouts or Cadets; what connections with armed forces; what job was wanted in the Royal Navy.

End of form. The two candidates, after being allowed a short time to tidy up their personal form, were then referred to the second document on their desks. This was the form which would take the answers to the coming academic test.

I asked if I could take the test as well to get some idea of its nature and relevance. It lasted forty-four minutes and was divided into four parts, each of thirty questions. It would be invidious to reveal the actual questions, but I can give an idea of their character.

The first section related to reasoning capacity, and consisted of seeing logical patterns in shapes: if first you see a circle, then you see the left-hand half of the circle, what do you see next? (The right-hand half of the circle.) And so on. I found I had time to answer only twenty-two questions out of the thirty in this section, four of them wrongly. The second set of thirty questions was on literacy (fitting correct words into sentences); I got all thirty right. The third section concerned numeracy. I answered all thirty questions. Seven answers were marked wrong.

Using myself as a humblingly vulnerable yardstick, I came to the conclusion that the questions so far were a fairly valid measure of my capabilities. With one qualification. My marks for reasoning would surely have been higher if the actual material of the tests had been matters with which I was habitually dealing, rather than abstract shapes that had not featured in my life since my schooldays. For the two candidates, one aged sixteen and the other twenty, the academic test so far seemed to be a valid test.

The fourth part of the test, and my first flicker of doubt, concerned mechanical understanding and aptitude. I did not finish all the questions – only twenty-one out of the thirty –

and was marked correct for only fourteen. Again, the actual candidates, being fresh from the classroom and its habit of dealing in set answers, may have been more accurately judged by the questions: I possibly thought too hard and too realistically about questions which had a classroom answer.

The booklet of questions handed out at the last moment to the two candidates and myself looked decidedly on the well-worn side in spite of the careers adviser's urgent instruction: 'You must not write on, or mark, or lean on your questions sheet.' Yes, perhaps there is a case for reviewing such question sheets more often, but also, I suppose, it is a reflection of the heavy usage of this book. In any case, the need to validate each changed question on real recruits makes change a lengthy process.

That is not to say the questions are not a rough and ready guide to the candidates – especially as, in practice, the effective pass mark is on the low side and a single contretemps over a specific question would be unlikely to debar any candidate.

'You will never hear the phrase "pass mark" used here,' said the lieutenant. 'If you use that term, people may go out of the door feeling a complete failure, whereas they might meet someone else's requirements. We avoid that. In any case, I had one high-up from the Inner London Education Authority Careers Service in earlier this week and he didn't finish the test. The point is that it is only an indication that the person can be trained in the time available. If the candidate does not reach the required standard for his branch of choice, but gets even the minimum marks for another branch of the Navy, he is asked if he wishes to be considered for entry into that branch rather than the branch he has originally asked for.'

We were talking in the lieutenant's office while the results of the tests were being worked out by the careers adviser who had supervised the academic test. Compared with the current minimum score for the least demanding branches of fifty-two, I got eighty-five. The candidate in the neat blazer got over ninety; the older man in faded jeans got seventy-three.

Both were therefore well within the academic requirements, and went on to their next test. The blazered boy, who wanted to be an artificer, took what is called the Vincent Mechanical Diagram Test – solving complex diagrammed mechanical problems. He would subsequently also do another advanced mathematics test. The young man in jeans went to do his personal interview with the petty officer who was his careers adviser.

The interview took place in an even more cell-like room than the test room. It was without a window. It measured no more than a domestic box-room and it had a distracting air-extractor fan going full blast. The only picture on the walls was a naval one showing a ship and a helicopter. Such rooms were kept deliberately spartan, I was told, to help concentrate everyone's attention, especially the youth being interviewed, on the job in hand.

The room's success in this respect seemed slightly to unnerve the candidate. The first question was: how old was he?

'Nineteen years, twenty-three days.'

'What?'

'I mean twenty years and twenty-three days.'

'Where born?' – 'North London.'

'Any brothers and sisters?' – 'One brother, father retired early.'

'Interests in common with him?' – 'Nothing really special.'

'What does your mum do for a living?' – 'Operator in factory.'

'How long for?' – 'Six years.'

'How do you get on with Mum?' – 'Fine.'

'Interests in common?' – 'Gardening.'

'Your younger brother – what does he do for a living?' – 'He is unemployed at the moment. He used to be a painter and decorator.'

'How do you get on together?' – 'We mostly share the same sort of interests, in sports and the like.'

'What sort of house do you live in?' – 'I share a bedroom with my brother.'

'What do you dislike about sharing?' – 'Nothing.'

'What do you do to help in the home?' – 'Nothing specifically, but if I am asked to do a job I do it – putting a plug on or washing dishes.'

'How much do you pay for your keep?' – '£15 a week.'

'What highlights can you remember of your early days at school?' – 'Nothing in particular.'

'Where did you come in the class in your senior school?' – 'I was about average. They tried to keep the class together as much as possible. When I started, I was above average.'

'What subject did you like best?' – 'English. I liked reading. My English teacher wasn't my favourite.'

'Who was your favourite teacher?' – 'The physical education teacher. He took a liking to me, and I was good at school sports.'

'How many teachers did you dislike?' – 'I didn't dislike any of them intensely; I got on with most of them.'

'What happened to the GCEs?' – 'They thought it would be better to enter for the CSEs.'

'What did you feel about your examination results?' – 'I was a bit disappointed. I thought I would do better than that. I just concentrated on a few subjects, design technology and English. I thought they would stand me in better stead when I left school.'

'What was your ambition at that time?' – 'I didn't have any ambition as such. I tried to plan ahead, taking everything into consideration; but I didn't think of a specific job at that time.'

'Why didn't you stop at school to improve your grades?' – 'I thought I didn't need to. I thought it would be better to gain experience and money outside.'

It must have been obvious to the careers adviser (and possibly to the candidate himself) by now that a rather negative picture was emerging. But the careers adviser did not reveal this by his manner, which remained neutrally inquiring and helpful. He asked what responsibilities the candidate had had at school, and was told there was no prefect system. He had tried at all sports, and swam for his London borough. He tried for football as a career after school, including Tottenham Hotspur, but saw there would be no future in it for him.

The careers adviser allowed a more challenging tone to creep into his voice. 'Truancy: how often?' – 'Never.'

'Why not? I thought everyone had a go at truancy to find out what it was all about?' – 'No, things were tight at that school.'

'Pocket money at school?' – '£1 a week, given to me by my dad.'

'What did you do with it?' – 'The usual thing, sweets and so on.'

'How did you supplement your pocket money?' – 'I tried a paper round, but I didn't get up. I did it for about a week, I think. I tried working in a shop, but it was too much like hard work.'

The candidate then listed a number of other jobs he had done, with wages varying from £27 to £75 a week. A colleague he had worked with had then set up in his own business and he had gone to join him in that. Only it folded up after four months. He was now self-employed in electrical work at about £150 a week.

'Why not join a firm?' – 'They are not taking on twenty-year-old apprentices.'

'What do you do with your £150 a week?' – 'Not much, I don't know where it goes. I have to buy a lot of tools.'

The next section of questions dealt with the candidate's spare-time activities: he had been in the Sea Cadets, he had restored an old motor car, and he was interested in driving.

The careers adviser asked him what was the basic principle of the car engine and was told that petrol was ignited by a spark which drove the pistons, which then turned the wheels.

Then came a question which was to be a crucial one in the careers adviser's recommendation on the candidate: 'Did he have a girlfriend?' He did; had been out with her for fourteen months and saw her four or five nights a week – 'We go to the pub for a drink, that sort of thing.'

The careers adviser left that subject.

'Looking at life today, what is the proudest thing that has ever happened to you?' – (After a very long pause) 'I can't think I have been outstanding in any way. Anything sporting, I suppose.'

'The least proud thing?' – 'I can't think of anything.'

'Why the Navy now?' – 'Because it can offer me more than civilian life can.'

'What is the Navy's main commitment?' – 'To protect this country.'

'Yes, that is one thing, what is the other? What are we part of?' – 'NATO.'

'For what reason?' – 'Protection of allied countries.'

'Is there anything you have been dying to tell me, but I haven't asked you?' – 'No.'

'Anything you would like to ask me?' – 'No.'

On this note, I left the room while the careers adviser raised with the candidate the subject of past offences and the Rehabilitation of Offenders Act. He would not afterwards discuss this part of the interview with me – 'It is always done in confidence between two people' – but he was able to let me know his general findings.

He was *not* going to accept the applicant for the Navy at this particular time. Why? 'His record at work is unstable and he is not progressing in any aspect at all. His motivation is very, very weak. But I think in twelve months' time he could make the Navy, if he does as he is told. I have advised him to go to the Royal Naval Reserve. Physically there are no problems at all.'

And then came the explanation for the significance of the questions about the candidate's girlfriend: 'Settling down in the Navy would be a risk. He spends four, five nights a week with his bird. When anything gets tough, he would probably miss her and want to go back home.'

The difficulties about getting up in the morning had been another danger sign. He had left jobs because they were mundane and he was going to have to do a lot of mundane jobs in the Navy. 'He didn't come motivated towards the Navy, I thought.'

While the written report on the candidate was being prepared, the lieutenant careers information officer told me that a negative approach was a fairly usual one in some candidates. 'They have tried all other jobs; nothing has come right for them and so they say, "Right, I will join the Navy." A lot of them look at you quite blankly when you put the question they must have been expecting: Why did they want to join the Navy? "I thought it was a good idea," they say. You ask them why we need the sort of ships we have got, and their response is, "Why should I know that? *You* are going to tell *me*, aren't you?" They wouldn't do that with industry, but the number of people who try to do this with the Navy is incredible. It seems to be their divine right, when all fails, to go into the Navy. There was a time, even, when judges sentenced people to go to prison or join the Navy. That doesn't happen any more.'

The question I had expected to hear, one that almost invariably would be asked in the Army, was not asked. What would the candidate's attitude be to being ordered to shoot someone, or to being fired upon?

'It would be one of the questions we would ask a Marine,' said the lieutenant. 'One of the reasons people ask to go in the Navy is that they would not be asked, in a face-to-face confrontation, to shoot someone. We need a different sort of person, one who can stand long periods at sea. You can't walk off a ship. In the Army you can go for a walk. There is no other kind of life which can be put on an equal with a man's life at sea. It is for a different sort of man.'

The candidate whose interview had just been finished was told immediately that he had not been accepted. No references were asked for: they are only called for *after* an acceptance, to back up that decision. The papers of successful candidates are sent with a recommendation to the Ministry of Defence, which makes the final decision. Sometimes the procedure takes three weeks, sometimes six weeks, sometimes with difficult cases two months. In the case of candidates approaching the deadline for applying – the thirty-third birthday – the procedures can be hurried so as to get a successful candidate into the Navy. Candidates who do not get through are usually advised to wait a full twelve months before applying again.

The man who was asked to come back need not have felt uniquely cast-down. 'We have been going through a period where we find that perhaps one in fifteen have been successful,' said the lieutenant. 'I can remember a period when, if they came in through the front door, we would practically lock it in case they walked out!'

It is an irony that, at a time of high unemployment, more and more people are trying to stay on in the Navy at the end of their twenty-two years' service – often to join the careers service – and that fact means that fewer young candidates can be offered jobs. The Navy is therefore able to pick and choose even more stringently.

Every weekday brings an average of twenty would-be sailors into the Greater London careers office. If, at the end of the week, five out of the hundred are accepted into the Navy, it has been a very good week indeed. This fact may have brought some comfort to the smartly dressed sixteen-year old who wanted to be an artificer, who therefore took more complicated tests than the other candidate that day, but who at the end of it found that he, too, was advised to come back in another year's time. And he was advised to be ready to consider other branches in the Navy if necessary.

The interview with this younger candidate was conducted by a fleet chief petty officer, a more suave, less blunt man than had conducted the interview with the older applicant. He established that the youth did not know who his real father was, though he had made attempts to find out from relatives. This was the young fellow I mentioned earlier, who 'didn't know' quite a lot. He was asked what he thought of marriage. His answer was inaudible, though the question had been asked with sensitivity and tact.

He was asked roughly the same stock questions about his family and school background, but some of his answers were more positive.

'How did you get on at school, being a prefect?' – 'They didn't mind when I told them what to do. They gave me a lot of lip, but in the end they did it.'

'What was your proudest moment?' – 'When I was presented with my medal for football in the junior school; and last Sunday, when I won a medal for athletics.'

'Why do you want to be an artificer?' – 'Fixing things. I like fixing my bike. I like looking into a car engine.'

'What kind of artificer?' – 'A working engineer; that one appealed to me from your booklet. I dislike the one in the boiler room, on the marine engineering side.'

'Why?' – 'It would be being stuck down there, which would be hot. If you were in the Mediterranean, it would be *very* hot.'

'I have asked you a lot of questions; is there anything you would like to ask me?' – 'Nothing exactly.'

The final result of this sixteen-year-old's application that day was that he was told to go away for a year, as the fleet chief petty officer put it, to 'find out what he would be letting himself in for – we are looking for a chap as an artificer who is doing middle management; and he is far too immature at present. But he is in the top 20 per cent in the country for his basic tests.'

He was indeed: he got 101 compared with my eighty-five, leading me in every one of the four categories except literacy, beating me by eight marks in reasoning. Whether his reasoning in future would prompt him to return to the Navy again in twelve months, or to look for some other employment, only time would tell.

'In another year or eighteen months,' said the fleet chief petty officer, 'he could make an artificer. But he would have to show he has got the potential of middle management. That is what we are looking for.'

If the candidate decides his talents would be better used elsewhere, his report – compiled by the careers advisers without the taking of notes (except on examination results) – will be destroyed in three years, by which time it will have become either totally irrelevant or so out-of-date that a new one would have to be made in any case if the man came back again.

Officer selection, I was told, was 'a different ball game'. It was also, I found, a rather less depressing one. Questioning tended to be more intelligent and lively. But the standards can be even more exacting. One careers adviser, who would of course see only a small percentage of applicants, confided that the result of his eighteen months in the job had been only three men actually installed into the Navy as officers – the rest either having fallen by the wayside or being still under consideration.

Officers, unlike ratings, are not selected by the careers organization in the field. They are referred from them to the Admiralty Interview Board at HMS *Sultan*, Gosport – if they meet the entry criteria.

'What they want to know from us,' said the lieutenant careers information officer, 'is if the candidate is academically qualified and they want us to see that he knows what it is he is being asked to do. We initially counsel the man and then pass him over to the next man in the chain whose title is misleading – the Area Schools Liaison Officer. They are wrongly titled in my view – they should be known as office recruiters or counsellors; they have outlived their original title.'

The lieutenant-commander who was the area schools liaison officer concerned with the officer candidate whose interview I saw was a small active man, who had previously been captain of six ships, a course officer on the commanding officer-designate course in the School of Maritime Operations, HMS *Dryad*, and had obviously always been a general stickler for standards.

'A lot of the boys I see now, not to put too fine a point on it, are drongos,' he said. 'I cannot see them becoming the same calibre of officer as I was dealing with years ago. I think the quality of officers we had then was infinitely higher. We are getting a lot of rubbish presenting themselves at the moment. I am saying that an awful lot of the boys, by and large, are not of very good quality. But the standard maintained by the Admiralty Interview Board is still fairly high, and we see good chaps coming along. I have recently seen one who has got academic scholarships; but academics are not the end of it. He must be a quality lad – for a start, in appearance. If they dress like yobbos they will be treated as yobbos, almost.'

He produced from his desk drawer a list of qualities he had jotted down as being required by the officer candidate. It was a long list. He must have seen me looking at it with trepidation, because he quickly explained: 'Training a helicopter pilot costs £500,000, a Harrier pilot £2 million. We have to be thorough.'

Then he read out his list: academic ability, intelligence, motivation, knowledge, alertness, stamina, dynamism, enthusiasm, sense of humour ('Because things don't always go terribly well.'), decisiveness, articulateness, team spirit ('In a ship you can never get far away from your colleagues; if a guy is an isolationist he is not going to succeed.'), personality, maturity and leadership potential ('Self-confidence plus knowledge, an elusive quality. Someone like Mrs Thatcher oozes self-confidence and doesn't think for one moment she is wrong.')

It would be nice to think that all these qualities are discovered in all social classes. But the Navy maintains that it has discovered that, in practice, they can be more readily found in middle-class communities like Brighton or Guildford.

'Without being class-conscious,' said the lieutenant-commander, 'recruiting in Brighton and Guildford tends to be more productive. Perhaps the chap we are looking for is someone not exactly from a middle-class family, but someone who will *encourage* those values.'

People who came from very poor families might be at a disadvantage in several ways, he said. Perhaps they just didn't know about the sort of things the Navy was looking for. But candidates could be disqualified also by being too smugly sure of themselves.

'I saw one chap,' said the lieutenant-commander, 'who had about fifteen "O" Levels, had represented his school at seven different games, took four "A" Levels, was totally physically fit and wanted to join the Royal Marines. He was so confident and smug, but he failed.'

The officer candidate being interviewed that afternoon was not smug. He knew all about the value of the self-deprecating remark or laugh, and he used it with considerable confidence on his interviewer – a woman, a second officer WRNS, who was only a few years older than his own twenty years.

The Navy's unusual habit of using women officers to interview men, if they happen to come from their allotted geographical area, is a socially interesting one that 'progressive' opinion would approve. But it has its humanly funny side if, as with the twenty-year-old applicant, sex appeal and charm is shrewdly exerted on the professional interviewer. It must seem a long hour to a professional woman determined to remain uncharmed and detached – and officer interviews do take some sixty minutes compared with the forty or so accorded to ratings.

The second officer WRNS established where the candidate had gone to school and the results of his examinations. Then: 'What I want to do over the next hour or so is to get you to talk about yourself, so that I know as much as I can about you.'

The candidate, six feet tall, with well groomed hair, a smart but inconspicuous dark blue suit, and a very clean white collar, explained his family circumstances. He had gone to a number of schools, ending up in a secondary modern one.

'I was ahead of my contemporaries,' he said. 'There was lenient discipline. I think I wasn't very ambitious. I put very little effort into my "O" Levels. I was very pleased and surprised to get such good grades.'

Had he ever been a prefect? – 'I was a prefect once or twice when it came round to my house's turn. I think I was chosen on the basis of, "It was him last week, so it is you this week."' (And he used his self-deprecating smile.)

'What did you feel about being a prefect?' – 'Quite often, as you had this little book to write names in, your friends thought you were a bit of a grass.'

'And did you rat on your friends?' – 'Oh yes! Otherwise it would have been my name in the book.'

The candidate quickly established himself as a gregarious person who could thrive in group activities – *if* he was interested in the subject. He had helped form an astronomy society at school. But he played little cricket, and football didn't particularly interest him.

'That is heresy for a young man, isn't it?' – 'Oh, yes!' (And another self-deprecating smile – he was not at all thrown by the accusation of not sharing mass taste, which was surely a good sign.)

'Have you ever applied to the Navy before?' – 'No, I haven't, but I have applied to the RAF, only my "A" Level results told me I had failed the RAF qualification. I could have gone to a polytechnic, but a supermarket chain offered me a job as trainee manager, and I took that.'

'Why did you accept that management training?' – 'Because the RAF had said, "Apply in two years' time" – I failed on the exercises for officers, assault courses, that sort of thing. Although the management training isn't officer training, being an officer is basically being in charge of men and being able to co-ordinate those men. I took it, really, as a good chance to be trained in man-management.'

'So why did you not want to stay there?' – 'I find it rather boring and not too challenging. Although I believe I am doing a good job, I still want rather more.'

'How do people of the same age react to being given instructions by you?' – 'Some people seem not able to manage them properly and they react by being cocky, but I think of the reason *why* I am asking them to do something, and my staff are very happy with me; they will do what I want when I ask them.'

The questions were not presented in a predictable order. Why had he decided not to reapply to the R A F? – 'I have always wanted to fly. I saw an advertisement in the *Daily Mail* for pilots and observers; I reacted on impulse. But since I have read the literature, I have realized the Navy could be a more interesting career than the R A F can offer. There is a better opportunity for travelling the world.'

After the fairly standard questions to discover what the candidate knew about the Navy and N A T O, he was asked how he kept in touch with what was going on in the world.

The answer appeared to satisfy the interviewer: 'I watch the news at most times of day and watch "Breakfast Time" on the B B C. I occasionally read the *Daily Telegraph*. I think I am probably biased towards conservative politics, and it seems to be the most conservative paper.'

'Did you read it today?' – 'Yes.'

'In order to be ready for this interview? – 'Yes' (and the same playful smile).

'Have you given thought to the fact that you are now applying to join an armed fighting service, and that a few years ago, in the Falklands campaign, young men were being shot at and killed, and were shooting at other people?' – 'Oh yes! I feel that I don't relish the thought of being shot at, or shooting someone else, but it has to be done. It is a subject I have thought about.'

'Any girlfriend?' – 'No.'

'Any questions for *me*?' – 'Yes, the chances are about one in ten of being a helicopter pilot. What would they be for a fixed-wing aircraft pilot?'

And there were many other questions eagerly put about his personal prospects, ending the hour-long interview on an affable note spoilt only by his referring to his possible coming 'induction'. That was more than his charm could persuade the interviewer to overlook.

'*Induction?*' she said edgily. 'You *must* stop talking like an RAF officer!'

While the candidate watched a video film on the Admiralty Interview Board, the second officer WRNS explained to me what they were looking for in a future officer. 'Someone with a fair range of interests, leadership potential and initiative – all that, yes, but someone who is interested in the organization he wants to join, and in the world in which he lives. He must try to make the effort to read the *Daily Telegraph*, *The Times* or the *Guardian* every day if he can, or every other day if that is all he can do.'

Four out of five of the people she interviewed, she said, knew less about the world than this particular candidate: 'He is definitely going forward to the Admiralty Interview Board. He knew how to use his charm, didn't he just? But one or two have said, "What is NATO?" He was comparatively well informed.'

Ideally, said the second officer WRNS, candidates were interviewed by officers of the branch of service they aspired to join, which meant that Royal Naval interviewers faced Royal Navy candidates, Royal Marine personnel faced Royal Marine candidates, women interviewed women and men interviewed men. That was the theory. But in practice Royal Navy candidates, who make up the majority, are often interviewed by a Royal Marine or WRNS officer. So she spent a lot of her time interviewing men.

'Could there be an initial resistance to being interviewed by a woman?' – 'Oh yes.'

'I have come across, though not as the norm, instances of an attitude of "What are *you* doing, interviewing me?" It is never said out loud, but that is the attitude. One feels a certain resistance, and such candidates split into two categories. Either they stiffen up, so that I have to do a lot of work to get results, or they come the old male chauvinist and invite me out to dinner. On balance, most of them want to take me out to dinner. Very often they are initially antagonistic and, being a woman, I still have to get information out of them without being too friendly. It is a fine line which the WRNS officers in this field are faced with, which we all learn to deal with in time.'

I asked the second officer WRNS if she could remember her most difficult interview. Yes, she said, she certainly could. It was her first interview – the one in which the man who wanted to be a Royal Marine broke down and cried.

'It is very difficult with Royal Marines,' she remembered, 'because they are very selective. He was a very young seventeen-year old, very immature, and perhaps – it being my first interview – I was a little heavy-handed. He burst into tears. It was right at the very end of the interview, and I was deferring him for a year because, knowing the standard set was above the norm, and that he didn't meet it, I had to counsel him on those lines – to present himself again later. And he was so disappointed he cried. As far as I am aware, he never came back.'

Would the very act of crying put him out of the running for the Royal Marines? Well, said the second officer WRNS, if he could not take positive criticism at that stage, it did rather tend to support her decision to defer him. 'According to policy, we should have chased him up, but I am not sure he ever did come back. Because the Royal Marines are taking so few, the Royal Marines can afford to be very selective.'

And so, she said, could the WRNS. They recruited a limited number. Policy decreed that women be interviewed by women. What was the main stumbling block when interviewing women candidates? 'Possibly the majority of women would prefer to be faced by a female interviewer, but perhaps not all. With the direct entry candidates the main problem is that we have very many very high-quality applicants for so few places. These are all undergraduates, or girls

with other acceptable professional qualifications in the sec-
retarial and catering fields, and I have to question them intensively, even to the extent of ascertaining how often they played
sport in their school teams.'

Women candidates are interviewed in depth because the
interviewer is in a position to refuse them, whereas with men
she can only advise them to defer their application for a limited
period to give them a chance to improve on their weaker
points before going to the Admiralty Interview Board.

Yet interviewing women could be easier than dealing with
male candidates. With men, she often had to try to make a
conscious effort to put a candidate at ease by using humour to
overcome his nervousness. 'I suppose one tries a few innocent
women's wiles, just to settle him down and get him to realize
that he can express himself, and by smiling and trying to turn
it into a conversation rather than a "What is your name?" sort
of interview. With women I tend not to have that problem at
all. They are usually older than my male candidates, and tend
to be much more mature, because of the sort of things they
have done: they were Guides from the time they were young
girls, they did sports and leadership activities at university, and
consequently they tend to be able to relate to others that much
more easily. They also know the steps they are going to have
to go through, and are mentally better prepared.'

Which is not to say that women candidates cannot sometimes
strike an antagonistic chord in the interviewer. The interviewing
officers are taught how to put this in the background, and how
to give the candidate the benefit of any such personal doubt.

The previous month, I was told by the Royal Marines
warrant officer in charge of the officer statistics, there had been
one hundred and twenty-two inquiries from would-be officers,
of which thirty-nine had applied to the Admiralty Interview
Board. In the whole of the past year, there had been 1,164, of
which 203 had gone on to the Admiralty Interview Board;
seventy-one of these had passed.

The commander in charge of the South-East region chipped

in at this point. He said that typically 75 per cent of all the officer intake in recent years had spent at least some time, or all their school lives, in a comprehensive school. Perhaps he spoke defensively. There is an organization, *not* under his control, called the Senior Schools Liaison Officers, who go into what are called the 'traditional officer-producing schools'. These officers visit schools they know have in the past produced a large proportion of the officer intake, and they are concerned purely with officer recruiting. Four retired captains go round this sort of school – which in practice are mainly public schools – singing the Navy's praises and reporting back not to the Navy Careers Headquarters but direct to the director of naval recruiting.

'It is not the case,' insisted the commander who was the South-East regional careers staff officer, 'that we have first division and second division schools. But in practice, because that is where we get a large proportion of our material, that is where they go. Other services go into these sort of schools on the same basis and at that level – and so we also need to.'

The lieutenant careers information officer for the London area also came smartly to the defence of the Navy. 'I can actually give you examples of schools in our area where you get *more* recruits for officers than in what we call the "Sizlo" or Senior Schools Liaison Officer schools; but let us say that these schools should *be expected* to produce results, although only 33 per cent or so of the officer intake have been to public school.'

My own feeling (that the Navy, in common with the Army, by looking to the public schools as a special category when searching for officers, might make the whole social bias of officers self-perpetuating) was not entirely removed by these assurances. But it did appear that a young man attending an ordinary careers service office without benefit of a public school education would be able to make the best case for himself he could manage – and he would do it before interviewers more than ready to listen and to appreciate what qualities he had to offer.

~~~~~~~~~~~~~~~~~~~~~~~~~~~~~~~~~~

13

RALEIGH'S LADS

'Some of the youngsters turn up with funny underpants, the briefest of briefs, which aren't going to last long in an environment like this. Some bring only a hand towel, which is going to be no good if they are going to be showering several times a day. And if they have dandruff, you know that up to now they haven't been having even one shower a day.'

– Chief petty officer, HMS *Raleigh*, training school for ratings.

'These guys join us as civilians, and mainly go on to further training. It is important to let them know they are in a disciplined service without, at the same time, putting the fear of Christ into them, so that they sign on out of fear. We don't want that.'

– New entry training officer, HMS *Raleigh*.

The new rating recruit has just arrived for training, but could not bring himself actually to sign on the dotted line. He hung back from the contract room, where all the others who had arrived on the same day were busily writing their signatures. He knew he couldn't face it. He would not be able to go into the showers with the rest. A vital part of his anatomy was too small.

In vain did the new entry training officer, puzzled behind his fair and friendly philosopher's beard, reason with the seventeen-year old. First he tried humour. Was there some sort of competition, and who was he trying to beat? How was he in the position to know what the average was? No change of mind rewarded the efforts of the new entry training officer of the new entrants training centre just across the River Tamar from Plymouth. He tried physics. Didn't the chap know that hot or cold water in the showers, or anywhere else, could influence the vital statistics?

The young man who had arrived as a recruit didn't budge, and saw no humour in the situation. 'By the time I had finished with him, after talking to him for twenty minutes, there was no way I would have signed him on, as the mental blockage would have been as large a handicap as a broken leg,' the new entry training officer told me, wincing at the remembered experience. 'Other lads, faced with the contract to sign, say they don't want to lose their privacy. Often it really boils down to the one big problem – homesickness.'

The young men in their teens and twenties, who are met off the train at Plymouth and bussed to their first experience of the Royal Navy in action, may be excused a sense of strangeness and disorientation. The very name on the notice-board of the establishment through whose well guarded gates they are passing defies easy assimilation and comprehension: Royal Navy, Queen Alexandra Royal Naval Nursing Service and Women's Royal Naval Service New Entry Training and Royal Navy Supply School. Even experienced hands shorten it in their minds to 'Raleigh'. The fact is that HMS *Raleigh* has in recent years, following defence rationalization, taken on so many different and varied jobs that visitors are given a sort of printed menu setting the jobs out in full, plus a guide to take them round the multiplicity of red brick and white plastic blocks that form the 'ship'.

The young men who arrive for their first training – called Part One in the trade – need not concern themselves with any other thoughts; but the physical evidence of the other activities surrounds them, from the first moment, like a new town. Instructors say the five thousand or so young men who enter the establishment every year for their first training are not allowed out unsupervised for a week because if they *were* allowed out they might lose themselves.

At first I greeted this explanation with some scepticism. Eventually it took on extreme plausibility.

The total establishment, in any one year, may reach 24,000 people since Wrens and sailors in mid-career also come to it. There are eighty-eight different courses. The staff consists of about seven hundred people. On any one day there can be two and a half thousand people in the place.

'Our training task is 20 per cent up on last year, and next year it is going to be slightly higher,' I was told by the captain of HMS *Raleigh*, a brisk veteran, who had been in the Navy thirty-two years, including time spent as a pilot in the Fleet Air Arm and as the First Sea Lord's secretary. He didn't think there was much more sensible scope for further rationalization: the place couldn't hope to take on any more major tasks *and* still operate efficiently.

'From the captain's point of view, we are at the limits of what we can sensibly take into this establishment,' he told me. 'From the new rating's point of view, the basic introduction to the Navy hasn't changed much since 1884: team work, discipline, co-ordination and pride in themselves, and their service. The essence of *Raleigh* is firm discipline, friendly discipline, and extreme cheerfulness and enthusiasm.'

One can see how teenagers fresh from home can find this positive mood rather difficult to discover in themselves during that first cloistered week of the six-week initial training course. They have just said goodbye to a tearful or – even more demoralizing – relieved mum. They have had time to get more and more apprehensive as their rail warrant has whisked them nearer and nearer to Plymouth. From the moment they have stepped off the train, they have been enclosed in the naval machine, from which they will not be able to take even a five-minute breather until the first long week has passed. Even for the enthusiastic, the adjustment is understandably difficult. For the ones who have had their doubts from the start – perhaps having been hard-talked by someone else into applying – it must be alarming.

The modern Navy is aware of this. Centuries back, it used pressed men. Now it is most careful to *un*-press them as much as possible. It *wants* overwhelmingly reluctant members of the hundred or so new recruits who arrive every week (usually on a Monday) to fall out of the picture as quickly and comfortably as possible. Better do it at the Torpoint establishment than in a ship in action.

All new recruits are asked their motives for wanting to join. Travel, at 28 per cent, is the single most popular reason for wanting to sign on. Then comes career prospects (19 per cent of applicants), father in Navy or other armed service (17 per cent), was Sea Cadet (14 per cent) and job security and good trade training (13 per cent each). Further down the list are community lifestyle (10 per cent), unemployment in home area and liking for sea (both at 9 per cent) and, last, long-standing ambition (8 per cent).

These statistics blur but do not conceal the fact that a high proportion of young men are putting themselves forward because of parental influence or factors which can flow from it. If one adds up those who have come because of family connections with the Navy, those who were in the Sea Cadets (possibly because at a young age they were influenced to join) and those applying because of unemployment in their home areas, one gets a figure of 40 per cent, compared with the ones who say they have acted out of a liking for the sea or a long-standing ambition (17 per cent between them).

It therefore says something for the greeting they get in the Navy that the number who leave voluntarily, or are asked to do so, amounts to only 10 per cent.

Possibly in their first hours in the Ganges division – the block of eight messes, each with twenty-five men in which recruits will be quarantined for a week – many young men feel the 10 per cent will include them. It is the function of the new entry training officer to allay these fears while weeding out recruits who are genuinely unsuited.

Ganges division, which took its name from the former boys' training establishment H M S *Ganges* at Shotley, near Ipswich in East Anglia, is a square block like any of the others, except for a notice prominently screwed on to the front wall near the doors: 'These Buildings Are Out of Bounds To All Except New Entries and Staff.'

This is the first real intimation the recruit will have that he is now in the grip of what the staff call the 'Process', which will convert him from a perhaps untidy civilian into a trained sailor. I asked the new entry training officer what was the reason for this isolation: 'We explain that if they go out of the building they will get lost, they will get challenged. But we don't want them to think they are being kept separate to prevent people talking to them and telling them it is all rubbish. The majority of them are really keen to get here. It is the week *before* he leaves home that the real doubts start.'

The Process will tell a would-be sailor from the start, without the need of words, that he is now part of a community rather than an individual unit. He will be escorted from the bus which has brought him from Plymouth railway station, and into the reception room. It is not until fifteen are in this room that the Process can start. Young men can sometimes wait for a considerable time, coping with their doubts or containing their enthusiasm, before there is a group big enough to enter the system. At peak times, the staff keep the Process going at the rate of five or six groups an hour.

A lecturer sent by that august disciplinary figure, the master-at-arms, gives them instructions about what they can do and what they can't do. They can't smoke in the corridors outside messes, or in their rooms. All medicines being taken must be produced.

In what must be to any newcomer a blur of intense activity, the young men are then handed a kit bag with their name at the bottom, and their kit, with the instruction that they put their names on everything with an old-fashioned indelible marker. Then they assemble in an ante-room of the Contract Room, where the intricacies of the contract they are about to sign are explained to them. It is at this stage that shuffling feet, or glazed eyes, or trembling hands indicate that doubts are surfacing about the legally binding step – perhaps the first contract of any kind the young man is signing in his life.

The Navy recognizes these doubts and today seeks, with some subtlety, to filter out the substantial from the passing ones. To sign the contract, the new recruit has to take a positive physical action – he has to get up from the ante-room and move into the Contract Room to sign. It is the reverse of having the pen thrust into his hand and being told where to sign. It enables him to keep his seat in the ante-room without losing too much face with his fellows – who are now out of sight in the Contract Room itself. All the young men have been left alone, without staff presence, while they have studied the contract. All the pressure they may have felt upon them since they arrived is neatly removed. If the young man signs on the dotted line, it is by his own positive and uncompelled act.

Once the new entry training officer has attended to the formalities of those who have signed, and only then, does he go through to the ante-room where the one or two doubters are still sitting. Falling into his friendly uncle, as distinct from administrator, role, the new entry training officer takes the men individually to one side and asks them why they have apparently changed their minds.

'I certainly don't persuade him to sign,' said the new entry training officer, 'because the guys who really don't want to sign, we are better off without. Some of the reasons are amazing. All the excuses we get! We have to separate the wheat from the chaff. Remember that some of these lads have been just about in tears from the moment they have got off the bus and saying, "I want to go home." Practically everything is based around homesickness. If he is crying, he is not crying because he doesn't like the look of the buildings, he is crying because he is homesick. And whatever he says, the first thing we have to do is to *get him to admit it*.'

Sometimes the veneer the recruit puts over his real feelings is a thick and unlikely one. One doubter on a Monday night who had been told to 'sleep on it', changed his mind on the Tuesday morning. He was being escorted to the pay office when another cloud of doubt overwhelmed him, but he was not candid about it.

'What are all the others doing now?' he asked.

'They are having their blood tests,' said the instructor with him.

'Just as well that I'm not joining then, because I have smoked pot, taken acid and sniffed glue.'

The new entry officer prudently did not take this at face value. He telephoned the recruit's mother. She said: 'He has never sniffed glue or taken acid, and he hasn't smoked pot for two days.' This lad was one of those sent home.

On the Tuesday morning, having either resolved his doubt or departed, the new recruit will get up early (5.30 am) for a 6.45 am haircut. The Navy believes that recruits' hair should start off summarily short, further to emphasize that recruits are now in a disciplined service – though it is noticeable that experienced ratings and officers tend to allow their hair to grow slightly longer, provided always that it looks more like a helmet than a mop.

Also on Tuesday, the recruit will take back to the stores any kit and equipment which did not fit him properly, and exchange it for something that does. He will receive instructions on how to iron his naval suit and other clothes – an expertise to which many young men manage to remain remarkably resistant.

On Wednesday there will be physical fitness training and medical checks and on Thursday there will be a fifty-minute period of instruction on marching. Senior ratings say the time isn't enough – a refrain I was to hear fairly consistently throughout the Navy. Recruits are told to 'forget the videos and the glossy magazines – you are going to be given the run-around here and it is going to be bloody hard'.

Being overweight starts to create difficulties from this point; and the Navy reckons that about three in ten recruits, officers and ratings, *are* overweight. One large man, with a shirt collar almost big enough for a horse, was so overweight that there was a temptation to reject him. *Raleigh* resisted the temptation and, instead, sent him prematurely over the assault course, to see whether he was carrying fat or muscle. Though overweight, he managed just as well as those weighing much less. Officers at *Raleigh* say that muscle weighs more than fat, and that it is *good* to have extra weight as long as it is in the form of muscle. This particular man stayed in the Navy.

'If they're overweight with fat when they get here,' said one of the senior ratings at HMS *Raleigh*, 'they usually lose it in three weeks. The life here is quite brisk.'

On Fridays the recruits appear for the first time in full Navy dress uniform – their 'Tiddly Suits' – and are formally welcomed by the divisional officers of whatever division they have been allocated. The officer tells them the division is the greatest, which is thought to help men settle in on the Saturday.

The remaining six weeks of the training at HMS *Raleigh* are a careful balance of one hundred and one topics of training and talks. By this time the young recruit will have got over the worst of the culture shocks and will accept more equably a few rockets from the instructors. But the instructors are still careful, even after four weeks of the seven-week course, to mix a suggestion of understanding helpfulness with any dressings-down that must be administered.

In Revenge Squadron at the establishment, I watched the divisional officer and a chief petty officer of formidable experience and height – about six foot six – doing one of the regular kit inspections. A roomful of twenty recruits were supposed to lay out their kit on the tops of their beds, with each item of clothing folded neatly into a rectangular shape that would precisely cover the *Naval Ratings Handbook*.

The procedure evidently had an almost religious significance. Perhaps for this reason, the visibly flustered assembly continued to find it an awe-inspiringly difficult technique. 'I try not to be an ogre, but I do try to put some ginger into it,' the six-foot-six chief petty officer told me. 'One young man the other day called me Lofty. I told him he was a very brave young man. Needless to say, he suffered for it.'

The chief petty officer approached a young recruit with the face of a solemn Mr Punch, a face sad and weather-beaten before its time, and regarded the kit laid out on the bed with displeasure. 'General presentation, one out of ten,' he said disgustedly. 'And I think I am being generous there.'

He picked up the young sailor's white-topped naval cap. 'You have got the rim wet, and it will go all limp. Wash the white top of the hat with soap and water, but hold it *that* way up, white rim toppermost, so the water doesn't run down into the blue rim, right?'

He picked up a sea jersey and smelt it. 'Dirty!'

He held aloft a pair of overalls. 'Creased. You haven't ironed these overalls at all, have you? And you've left them hanging up wet, so the crotch is halfway down to your knees. Some of you have crotches in your overalls down to your ankles. *Not* the right way to do it!'

He looked at a shirt. 'Not ironed this recently, have you? Collar dirty, not washed. You can see the black in the creases of the collar.'

He picked up a white shirt. 'Look at the fluff on that.' He gave it a violent flap. 'You see? Just by doing that you could have shaken that fluff off.'

He held aloft a sports shirt. 'Irish pennants! Look at them! Loose bits of cotton hanging out.'

He grabbed a towel. 'You'll have a bit of difficulty folding that. Bulky! Every item must be folded to book size.'

He waved a pair of socks. 'Dirty! Dirty because you haven't bothered to wash them.'

He held a green and red pair of brushes between finger and thumb. 'Take that stuff away and get some good ones.'

He whirled a lanyard. 'Grubby round the knot. And that is because your hands aren't clean when you handle it. Get them clean!'

He threw a pair of underpants back on the bed. 'You've been wearing these for more than a day. Wear them one day only and wash them.'

He seized a wire coat-hanger, of a type given away by dry cleaners, as if it had threatened him, bent it into intricate shapes and threw it to the other side of the room. 'Get rid of that, it harms your clothes. That thing belongs on the side of a Cortina!'

After these successive hammer blows, the recruit looked no more surprised than I was when the divisional officer delivered the final verdict to an accompanying subordinate: 'There is a lot of work to go into that kit between now and Friday. Fail it!'

The point, however, was that many of the devastating judgements were delivered in a helpful tone of voice, suggesting more sorrow than anger; sorrow that the recruit hadn't come up to the high expectations entertained of him.

The divisional officer who had watched the chief petty officer do the inspection took me to one side. 'There you saw the main problem of adjustment at that stage – youth. They do have a problem of adjustment initially. The biggest problem is mum. Most youngsters come in suffering from what I call the "Day-and-a-half syndrome". Whatever it is, they will put it on the floor; and a day and a half later it appears in the drawer, washed and ironed and folded, and they haven't got a clue as to what has happened in that day-and-a-half. And we have five weeks to teach them, the time between the end of their induction week and the end of the six-week course.'

The chief petty officer, who had slipped into an ordinary

conversational tone as if taking off a fearsome mask, agreed. 'If they fail their official kit inspection, they are given another week. After the second week, they are proposed for discharge as "Unsuitable During Training". Mind you, we have had one or two that went out and then came back in again; and we hope that some of these will go home and practise it and perhaps make the grade.'

Such are the very basics of naval life. In Fisgard Division, I saw artificer apprentice training, a rather more sophisticated business, going on for the benefit of the Navy's young technicians, a third of whom will ultimately finish up as commissioned officers of one sort or another.

The course was re-organized from the one year of the original HMS *Fisgard* course to one term − an induction course prior to the young men going on to further training at HMS *Sultan* and HMS *Collingwood*. The Navy tries to avoid young men spending more than half their time at Fisgard Squadron in a classroom − after all, their natural technological habitat will be afloat. I did spot one class of about twenty-five men in a classroom, sitting in pairs.

Pairing up in the classroom is deliberate policy. A bright young man is paired with a slower one; each is supposed to help the other with different aspects of the course. The surprising thing about the class was that it was not in the least possible, when merely looking at the pairs, to decide which was the bright one and which the less bright. All the class members looked reasonably bright and intelligent, the sort of faces one would see in any day of civilian life. In the present Navy, there is no room for the *really* dim.

The young men, judging from the atmosphere in the room as they worked on their papers, could have been sixth formers of any school or college that had a sixth form. 'They don't spend too much time like this though,' said the apprentice training officer, almost apologetically. 'They do systems engineering and fire-fighting and ship visits. There is a sixteen-kilometre walk and a forty-kilometre all-night hike. Part of the problem is that we want to see whether they will make senior ratings. If successful, they will be chief petty officers at the age of twenty-three or twenty-four. They have to be worthy of their rate on that basis.'

By week six, about halfway through the term, anyone falling behind is given extra study. At the end of ten weeks, if there is no improvement, the young man will probably be asked to leave. There are four examinations, in Maths, Mechanical Engineering Science, Electrical Engineering Science and General and Communications Studies. If the candidate fails one subject, he re-sits the examination. If he fails two, he either repeats the term, or withdraws from apprentice training but not necessarily from the Royal Navy.

To enter as an artificer apprentice, the young man must have had 'O' Levels in Maths, Physics and English Language, or have passed a Naval Entrance Examination. In practice, one in five also have 'A' levels. They are expected to achieve about the equivalent of 'A' Levels in terms of technical qualifications, or a Technical Education Council Diploma by the end of their apprenticeship. Most pass the examinations after a term at Fisgard Squadron, an achievement perhaps made more likely by the fact that normally over 90 per cent have been placed in the technical categories that were their first choice.

The wastage rate is therefore modest. In the year before my visit, 544 young men had entered; forty-five had been given Premature Voluntary Release. One officer estimated that of these, at least half were 'self-select failures' and that of the forty-five, there were less than ten that the Navy would have liked to keep.

The apprentice training officer said that officers and senior ratings at Fisgard regarded themselves as 'the final part of the recruiting process'.

'The recruiting officers have done the best they can, but in the limited time available they can't know a man completely,' he explained. 'In this first term we carry on the process of the examination of the man and see if we can find out a bit more.'

Of the intake of 544 that year, only ninety-one in all had gone – 15.6 per cent, or roughly one in six.

In minimizing the wastage rate, Fisgard Squadron does not easily accept excuses for premature departure. One recruit said, 'My hobbies include ferreting, falconry and working on motor bikes, and the first two of my hobbies aren't going to be practical in the Navy.'

'Actually,' recalled the lieutenant-commander who commanded Fisgard Squadron, 'we didn't agree with him there. We maintained that we had some people who did those things and I have come across one chap who had a motorcycle folded in his cabin.'

Whether they are going to be seamen or technicians, the young men are given a few intimations of the possible shocks of naval life well before they get their first ship. None of the shocks can better the physical shock they get when, as a brief but compulsory part of their schooling, they get their fire-fighting training.

This is no matter of setting a few logs alight and then playing a hose on them, as they gruellingly find out at the fire-fighting school in the HMS *Raleigh* complex. Outside the main building of the school are a number of steel-walled large rooms, built to resemble the compartments of a ship. Each room has a door which is closed behind the stalwart lads who are following in Nelson's footsteps. A smoky oil or wood fire is alight in the room, and the students have to conquer the fire with the available equipment. The clouds of black smoke pouring from the buildings testify to all and sundry that the young men are having a remarkably lifelike experience of what a fire can be like in a ship.

But the fire-fighting instructor at the school, a lieutenant on an extended period of service with the Navy, professed himself not completely satisfied.

'It is all a bit artificial at present because it doesn't *really* prepare people for what happens when their ship catches fire,' he explained. He showed me the plans of a new and enormous piece of equipment he had designed, which would cost £1¼ million to build. Not only would it have steel compartments that could be realistically set afire or flooded as might happen when the 'ship' was hit by the enemy, but it would also produce a horrible noise, and rock violently as if with the movement of the sea. And he would like to see a replacement of the old units outside by new computer-operated ones using propane instead of wood fires.

At the time when I paid my visit, young men were having to be persuaded through the existing smoke-filled rooms by petty officers. The conditions were contrived not only to be as realistic as then possible, but to give the young sailor a good chance to display his moral fibre.

A fifteen-gallon tank of diesel fuel was set alight and the young students stood watching it from behind a curtain of sprayed water, whose effectiveness as a protection was being demonstrated. A member of the staff tipped a bucket of water by remote control on to the blaze. The result was that the water rapidly expanded by a ratio of seventeen thousand to one, which vaporized the fuel, producing an enormous fireball that shot a hundred feet into the air.

'Nothing will protect you from this fireball if you are in it, and it can last up to ten seconds,' the fire-fighting instructor commented to me. 'This demonstration proves two things: the marvellous effect of a water wall, and the folly of pouring water on to a fire.'

All the fire-fighting gases, foams and blankets used in fire-fighting aboard ships were demonstrated to the recruits. The roaring of the flames was very real and would help prepare the young men for what happened in the Falklands in 1982, when noise of 'only' ninety decibels drove some men to distraction in view of the other psychological pressures put on them at the same time.

I asked the fire-fighting instructor if real injuries were common during fire-fighting instruction. He answered immediately with a frank: 'Yes. Mainly minor burns. I have had two chaps hospitalized in the four and a half years I have been here, one of them only four weeks ago. The chap was in hospital for three days. He was too keen. He rushed into a unit when it was still too hot. Hot water from the ceiling came down on his back, scalding him. He had worked with me for three months, he was cocky, he thought he knew it all.'

The instructor, a bald and bespectacled old hand whose specialist skills were eagerly hung on to by the modern Navy, felt that improvement would come with modern and more realistic simulators such as the one he had designed, which he wanted to replace the present ones – which at the time of my visit included one steel room in which recruits were put before about forty tons of water was pumped through a jagged hole in the side of the 'hull' in some twenty minutes. Recruits had to stop the hole up with the aid of a steel bunk frame, a mattress, and a few lengths of wood.

His other complaint was the familiar one heard in the Royal Navy after the defence cuts of the 1970s and early 1980s – lack of time. 'One thing I hesitate to mention to you,' said the instructor sombrely, having obviously thought deeply before he spoke, 'but I feel I should. It is the amount of time my young men get under the courses for actual fire-fighting and wearing of breathing apparatus. Retained firemen in civilian life spend fifty-five hours under instruction, and are supervised for the next twenty hours. Ours get much less than that, but that is supposed to turn him into a fire-fighter, which is crazy.'

The captain of HMS *Raleigh* himself put the general point succinctly. 'In the old days when the young boy seaman went to HMS *Ganges*, he was there for a year. Twenty years ago at *Raleigh*, he was here three or four months. Now we do it in six weeks. We have been squeezed. That means ever-greater demands on the motivation and expertise of the staff. My goodness' – and I was surprised he did not use a more naval expression – 'the old British taxpayer has got his pound of flesh out of the Navy today, in terms of value for money.'

In lean times the training of officers, too, can mean that flexible ingenuity has to augment tradition.

14

BOARD OR RACK?

'A lack of steel about him, I would say. He became rather smarmy. He told me he always gets on well with women. He told me I must be very clever to do my job. It was a very childish attempt to manipulate the interview his way.'

– WRNS officer member of Admiralty Interview Board, describing a candidate (failed).

'I see fair potential, perhaps five out of ten. Did he *have* to have a crumpled suit? We see boys who slave on a paper-round to pay for a new suit to come here. There are rough edges – he bites his nails.'

– President of Admiralty Interview Board (a captain) of another candidate (passed).

Gale, the twenty-four-year-old would-be naval officer who had done rather badly in the gym, was visibly proud of his intellectual reading habits – and visibly sure that his naval assessors hadn't got any. Perhaps later he thought the Royal Navy was guilty of the arbitrary manners of the Nelsonian quarterdeck when it told him to his face that he gave an impression of intellectual arrogance and flippancy; and that perhaps he might like to apply again when he had thought about it.

It was just as well that the Navy's selection officers, far from being crudely insensitive, did not relay to him *all* that had been said about him behind the scenes. One of the members of the Admiralty Interview Board, the Navy's officer-selection body, gave her verdict (yes; *her* verdict – the Navy does use a woman as one of the assessors) in very blunt terms indeed.

'I thought he was pompous and with a somewhat casual manner,' she said. 'He began the interview with a swear word about his father, though he quickly corrected himself and realized he had made something of an error. He talked down about other people he had come into contact with, including his parents. I think he sees the social side of life as more important than the professional side. I put to him points about discipline: what if an eighteen-year old gave him orders? He said he would laugh, though he would carry out the orders. I think he is very self-centred. His status-seeking came out when I asked him why he went to the university he had done. He replied, "A better question would be why not Oxford or Cambridge?" In my view he has limited leadership potential.'

Bull, on the other hand, a young would-be officer of the same age as Gale, perhaps suffering more than was immediately visible from sad family problems, but with a habit in the tests of giving a firm and courageous lead (often in quite the wrong direction) may have been equally surprised that he was accepted for training at Britannia Royal Naval College at Dartmouth as one of the successors of Nelson.

His assessors hadn't liked his rumpled suit, and they noticed that he bit his nails. But they were quite sustained in their view that he deserved a chance to prove himself as a potential leader of naval men.

It would have been possible for an average civilian sitting-in on the whole proceedings (with the exception of the deep exploration of personal details) to come to the firm conclusion that, in their selections, the Admiralty Interview Board's priorities were not the same as those of a civilian organization. But it became very apparent to me, as a fly on the wall, that, right or wrong, the Royal Navy *does* know what it is looking for, and that it is prepared to be far-seeing and sensitive in the way it handles those to whom it gives a thumbs-up, those it rejects entirely and those it suggests might like to do some hard thinking and come back for another try.

If on occasion the Royal Navy can give the impression of a mirror image of Gale's superciliousness about naval values, by displaying short shrift to *civilian* inadequacies, it can be very patient with the vulnerabilities of youth and inexperience when assessing its own future material.

At first I admit I regarded with some scepticism the Navy's pretensions to an open-door policy for its would-be officers (did it *really* tally with some of those public school accents and manners I had encountered in high places?). But if social standing can be of some advantage in the upper reaches (in what profession, including left-wing politics, is this *not* so?), it is undeniable that in choosing its basic officer material, the Navy does try to keep open house.

In selecting men and women who think they may be officer material, the Royal Navy first of all prides itself on its *accessibility*. It claims to be the only one of the uniformed services in which *all* candidates are seen by the principal selection body, without previous pre-selection, except by entry requirements.

The claim may or may not be a clever put-down of the other services; but it is unquestionably a decisive factor in the way that the principal selection body, the Admiralty Interview Board, operates – scrutinizing candidates with a thoroughness that seems to include everything except a psychiatrist's couch. In the Admiralty Review Board's literature about the system, there is a cartoon showing how the candidate sees himself – as an unkempt medieval prisoner being stretched on the rack. It is not quite as bad as that.

The Admiralty Interview Board is not really centred in Spain like the Spanish Inquisition. After a spell near Southampton and at Britannia Royal Naval College, Dartmouth, it is now based at Gosport. It occupies a handsome brick-built wardroom block surrounded by new buildings which, at the time I visited, were due to become the biggest naval engineering complex in the United Kingdom. In these dignified but fairly informal surroundings, the Board assesses about two thousand candidates a year. It recommends about seven hundred from which the Second Sea Lord's Department in the Ministry of Defence makes the final selection to fill quotas. It turns some of the rest away with finality, and some with the helpful suggestion that they might like to try again in a year's time, after attending to stated points of behaviour, appearance or habits.

I saw the whole process of 'boarding' a specimen group of four candidates. Unlike the Army and the Royal Air Force, the Navy appoints civilians as full members of the four-person boards who assess the candidate. It has a roster of seventy headmasters, fifty of them still working, twenty of them retired. The people on the roster are prepared to do a week or so's boarding once in a while. They will do it because, as Admiralty Interview Board members will quickly tell you, 'In the Navy we want *brains*, and we don't rule out any man finally just because his tests in the gym weren't all that good.'

It is in the gym, after a preceding day of psychometric and other written tests, that the candidates meet their first practical challenges, watched by the four members of the board. The board I watched consisted of a Royal Naval captain of trim and classless appearance and voice, acting as Board president; a commander; the headmaster of a college in the South of England, and a W R N S second officer, a pleasant young lady who nevertheless proved herself to be a formidable cross-examiner in some of the later, more intellectual, tests.

The board was fairly typical, the four candidates slightly less so. They were all older than average, at least in chronological terms.

I have given them all fictitious names and have further obscured real identities by juggling with some points of fact; but the total picture will be a true one. There was Bull, the twenty-four-year-old product of a comprehensive school, coming before the Admiralty Interview Board for the second time, this time in search of a short-term (eight-year) career. There was Gale, the same age, also an ex-comprehensive school pupil and wanting to be an instructor officer. There was Black, another comprehensive school product, but only twenty and wanting a full career as an engineer. And there was yet another comprehensive school product, Fay, who was twenty-two and hoped to get a degree from his polytechnic so that he could succeed as a direct graduate entry for a short career as a seaman officer.

All but Fay, who wore a blue pinstripe, were dressed in identikit single-breasted grey suits, Bull's rather rumpled (which drew unfavourable comment from some members of the Board) with matching grey shoes (which drew further criticism). Gale and Fay wore beards, Black and Bull were clean-shaven. All four were reasonably well spoken, except that Black, as time wore on, lost audibility. When he later revealed his medical history, it came as no surprise.

As the four candidates lined up in the gym (actually an enormous aircraft hangar equipped with ropes, planks and an artificial pond the size of a small swimming pool), the board members explained to me the aim. No one went on to Dartmouth for officer training with less than four hundred and fifty marks out of the maximum one thousand. Supply officers had to get five hundred marks.

Though it is comparatively difficult to recruit officers, even at a time of high civilian unemployment, senior officers make it plain that standards will *not* be significantly dropped. Even the 'physical' tests in the gym were 90 per cent *intelligence* tests, evaluating the capacity to think quickly in the face of hard physical tasks and to get strangers to work with you and for you in a joint enterprise.

In the gym the four candidates were faced with their first 'dry' task – getting a timber across a padded floor space about twenty feet by twenty feet. They had to do it by using another timber suspended from ropes, and without once touching other pieces of equipment or the floor. Like Army officer candidates, these naval ones wore large numbers on their sweatshirts and were addressed by number only; *un*like Army candidates, who are allowed to have a leader who 'emerges', the Navy candidates each acted as group leader in turn. Bull, as Number One, was the first leader. He gave his orders crisply and audibly, even when they were plainly wrong and led nowhere. He also tended to give orders in the second task. This was a 'wet' one, in which an oil drum had to be taken across the pond with only short planks and ropes as equipment. And he gave the orders despite the fact that Gale, as Number Two, was *supposed* to be in charge. Already personalities were beginning to emerge. Bull might lack judgement, but Gale was a follower, albeit a wordy one, allowing himself to be dragged along in Bull's wake instead of taking charge himself.

A heavy oil drum is not the easiest thing to get across a small pond, even when there is a tiny table placed helpfully in the middle of the pond itself. In all these gym tests, only the leader is allowed to see in advance a photograph of the setting and the equipment to be used – thus testing his ability to make his exclusive knowledge clear to the other three candidates.

Soon Bull, from a table in the centre of the pond, was busy disputing points with Gale. At one point, Bull asked Gale, 'Would it not be better to get the barrel itself across now?' and got the sarcastic answer, 'Yes, that might not be a bad idea.' In the meantime, Black had got on to the central table, only to fall off it into the pond; while Gale and Fay were busy arguing on the side of the pond on which they started, and from which they were supposed to extricate themselves, and get to the other side, in the time allowed.

'One minute left, gentlemen,' said the senior rating who accompanied the candidates through the gym tests, and who then spent the rest of the day chatting with them in the waiting-room as they waited for other tests – producing additional intelligence which would be communicated to the Board members in due course.

It was by now obvious that the team under Gale were not

going to get the oil drum over the pond in the time available. It became even more obvious when, with Bull instead of Gale shouting exhortations from the bank, Gale, Black and Fay (all trying to stand on the small table at once) cascaded abruptly into the pond.

'Time gentlemen, please!' called the senior rating.

'They are all overweight,' said the president crisply. 'They need a good run on the moors. And the teamwork was poor.'

The next task was a 'dry' one. All four candidates changed into dry clothes before they tried it. It consisted of getting the oil drum over 'an electrified fence', actually a horizontally hung ladder hung from ropes. For this test, Black was leader. While he was being told more than once by the Board members to speak up, Bull was busy telling the candidates how and when to lift the drum over the 'wire'. This task *was* completed within the time. It seemed that, even if Black was a recessive sort of character, he could at least get other people to work with him, and didn't resent it when they used their own initiative.

The next test was another 'wet' one, with Fay as leader, involving taking two small but rather heavy 'acid' drums across the pond.

'Remember you've got acid in these,' shouted the senior rating, as Fay grabbed a canister, overbalanced, and grabbed one of the available ropes.

'That rope you're holding is out of bounds, Number Four!' pointed out the senior rating.

Fay attempted to make up for this reverse. He tried walking on one of the planks. He fell in.

'One minute, gentlemen!' said the inexorable senior rating.

In that minute both Gale and Fay managed to fall in.

'Time, gentlemen, please!'

'This was rather wetter than usual,' the headmaster told me as the candidates went off to change again, and the board walked into the board room to mark up the candidates.

Sitting in their fixed places at the lozenge-shaped mahogany table (I was soon to sense the confusion that could have arisen if they had ever switched places), the four board members gave their personal marking on a scale of zero to nine for each of the candidates in turn. To Bull, the commander gave five, the headmaster six, the WRNS officer five and the captain four. To Gale, each of the board gave only one. To Black, the commander gave three, the others two, three and three respectively. To Fay, the commander, the headmaster and the WRNS officer each gave three, while the captain gave two.

The board members then gave reasons for their markings in turn, and arrived at a final agreed mark. For Bull, five. For Gale, 0.75. For Black, 2.5. For Fay, 2.75.

Although I was assured that the gym test would not necessarily damn a candidate for good, the pattern of marking that was to apply that day was already showing itself. This to some extent confirmed what I had been told about the gym tests: that they were tests of practical intellect as well as strength and endurance. Gale, the candidate who was to be accused of intellectual arrogance, was doing very badly indeed. Both the self-defeating Black and the rather vague Fay were doing poorly. Only Bull, the candidate who was not afraid to give a lead (even when it was totally misconceived) was gaining marks at pass level.

The Board then went on to discuss the personal records of the four candidates.

'Reads women's magazines,' noted the captain of one of the candidates.

'I'm a bit worried about that,' said the commander.

'Well,' said the Captain fairly, '*I* get forced to read about new kitchens in women's magazines. Shall we have the candidates in?'

Enter Bull, Gale, Black and Fay for their theoretical exercise. This involved their presence in the West Indies in a boat, with a storm approaching and various priorities to be attended to. What would their plan of action be, in the light of all the stated constraints? The WRNS officer, who conducted the exercise, gave the candidates fifteen minutes to discuss and form their plan, and then another five minutes to put it to her. They could either choose their own spokesman, or all present their case as a team.

No prizes for guessing that it was Bull who emerged as spokesman, or that the plan he put up was soon shot full of holes by the WRNS officer. She told the team to think again. They thought again, and Bull changed his tune under individual questioning rather better than Gale, who seemed willing to agree to anything, Fay, who seemed unable to change his mind at all, and Black who was silent unless positively canvassed.

After the candidates had been sent from the boardroom, the Board did another assessment of marks, called the 'wash-up'. Bull, with four, four, four and two marks, had dropped slightly behind. Gale had fared much better with three, four, three and three. Black had slumped badly with four marks of one. Fay was still below the pass line with three, two, two and three. The marks agreed by the Board as a whole after full discussion were Bull 3.75, Gale 3.25, Black 1 and Fay 2.5.

While the WRNS officer began interviewing the candidates about their personal records in another room, the three remaining members of the board gave individual interviews in depth to each of the candidates. Again, Bull came up with replies which were visibly pleasing to representatives of a disciplined service. He told the headmaster that he thought he had suffered at sixth form college because he had been used to a grammar school, where the discipline was strict and formal, and had been thrown too quickly into a relaxed atmosphere.

To the commander, he readily admitted that he had got bored with jobs behind counters in civilian life, and that he had left the Royal Navy previously because he had wanted to be a pilot and had been told he could not be one.

'What are your ambitions now?' the captain asked him.

'To get to be a seaman officer, plumping for aviation.'

'Do you think that aviation is still possible?'

'Yes, sir.'

'Don't you think it is a pipe-dream?'

'No, sir, I will get my training in the Navy, and then for the air.'

The captain looked at him speculatively. 'If I told you that there was no chance of becoming connected with the air service, would you still want to join the Navy?'

'Yes, sir.'

Bull, like the other candidates, was probed about his views and attitudes to current affairs. The captain asked him how much more he thought the government should be doing about the unemployed.

'Currently, sir, they want to spark investment in industry, and they can do that with promised tax cuts. I agree with the government's aim of making industry more competitive, but it does cause unemployment. Hopefully we are going to be employed eventually in new industries, and until then we must grin and bear it.'

Did Bull see signs that unemployment was creating disorder? 'Not among the unemployed,' said Bull. 'But there are certainly disruptive elements on the left and right. They are using unemployment as a political vehicle. The unemployed could be manipulated by subversive elements.'

These answers obviously struck the Board as well balanced, as had Bull's reply to the commander's question on whether he would have qualms of conscience if he had to involve himself in the taking of human life: 'No sir, but only if it is absolutely necessary.'

Bull made way for Gale. If any personality among the four candidates screamed, 'Civilian!' to the heavens as well as the Board, it was Gale's. At college, he said, he had once told a lecturer to make his lectures more comprehensible. He had run a school magazine. He had joined the Officers Training Corps, but not put in as much time at it as he should have done.

'What about these women's magazines you read?' asked the commander.

'I just enjoy reading the stories, and some of the recipes in there.'

'You cook?'

'I think I can cook better than most people I know, certainly my mother.' This remark, it was to emerge later, did Gale no good at all.

Neither did his mention, on his application form, of liking J. R. Tolkien-*type* books. His explanation of the phrase (that the Board might not have heard of the authors he really meant) made *me* breathless with its condescension; and I was only a spectator.

Asked what he would feel if he were required to become involved in the taking of human life, Gale replied sensibly enough that he hoped it would be a member of the enemy's armed forces, but that he would not enjoy even that.

'Yes,' said the commander, 'but would you have great qualms of conscience?'

'No great qualms, no. I am certainly not a conscientious objector. I think you were going to ask me if I could manage to die for my country?'

His accompanying laugh went down very badly. 'We don't go into it *that* deeply,' said the commander dismissively, and later made the remark that seemed to represent the board's general view of Gale: 'He is too flippant, that guy.'

As a civilian, I had not found Gale's attitude outrageous: it was that of a basically nervous young man striving for an air of worldliness but unable to provide enough content to justify the attitude. Gale, it seemed to me, was a classic case of a young man who, because he was more intelligent than his humble mother and father, assumed himself to be an intellectual giant when actually he was just an ordinarily intelligent person. A shrewd civilian – say a tutor – should have pointed this out in a kindly way years ago. Perhaps it was not the board's business to be that analytical, but I was not surprised when, later, the board told Gale, in terms slanted to the Navy, about how bad an *impression* he made.

Candidate Number Three, Black, was treated with visible kindness. It was already obvious that he was not officer material. And it was obvious to a civilian spectator (and, I later discovered, the board) that a mere exhortation to change his attitude would not suffice. Black, with a history of depression, was suffering the obverse error to Gale: the intelligent son of a father with high expectations of him, and a passively nervous mother, he visibly found the strain of life intolerable but – and this was the clincher for the board – could not *see* that he had a specific problem.

The more Black talked about himself, the more his voice faltered and grew more faint. He agreed he had twice pulled out of university courses, but he still didn't know what happened. 'It seemed that virtually everything I attempted didn't quite work,' he said. When he was asked a question about specifically naval knowledge, he was more often right than wrong, but the *way* he delivered the answer undermined the impression of being right. His reply to the inevitable question about how he would react if he had to become involved in the taking of human life was, in fact, sensible. 'Um . . . I suppose I wouldn't have qualms, but obviously if it was at all possible to avoid it . . .' His voice trailed off, distracting attention from the fact that his answer had been essentially sound.

'What should the government be doing to help people like you, with "A" Levels, to get jobs?'

'I don't know – there are arguments all over the place. I don't know who to believe; whether it really is best to get inflation down as the top priority; but at the moment it doesn't seem to be working. As for "investing in jobs", it strikes me as a very short-term solution. I am not entirely convinced it is not a Catch-22 situation.'

In print, all these comments appear intelligent and admirably balanced. But the faint-hearted delivery negated any favourable impression – and in an armed service instructions are given in crucial situations by word of mouth, not in the form of transcribed notes.

After Black left the room, there was an uncomfortable silence.

'I am now feeling sympathy for him,' said the commander, voicing the general view.

It was by now obvious that Black would not be joining the Navy; but it was also obvious that the men judging him were no mere automata devoid of human understanding; and that when Black was inevitably told that he was not naval officer material, it would be done in a sympathetic way. It seemed to me that just *because* the needs of the service had to be ruthlessly served, the members of the board were compensatingly anxious to be considerate to the candidates as human beings.

The final candidate, Fay, was like Bull in at least one respect: he professed to prefer a college in which he was not entirely free, but was encouraged to work.

Fay admitted that he was disappointed with his 'A' Level results. He spoke about his water sports and his chess, but not in particularly enthusiastic terms.

The commander pounced on a point that worried him. Why was Fay wanting to opt for only a short-term career?

'If I was selected and I enjoyed it, I would extend it,' said Fay.

'Have you ever been aboard a warship?'

'I have seen HMS *Belfast*.' (The naval museum moored in the Thames.)

On the walls of the boardroom were four pictures of warships. Fay was asked to identify one, and got it right. He was asked to identify another, and got it wrong.

'Where is Dartmouth?'

'Near Woolwich on the Thames.'

It was possible that, in his nervousness, Fay had simply thought the question referred to *Greenwich*; but the elementary mistake in placing Devon alongside the Thames would obviously do him no good.

'Where are the Navy's principal air stations?'

'Lee-on-Solent. Apart from that I am not quite sure.'

Then the commander asked the question about qualms in the taking of human life.

'Yes, I have. Of course I have. But it would not stop me from doing it.'

The captain took over. At his polytechnic, had Fay ever joined a students' picket line? No, but he had once walked past one. There had been an emergency meeting of the students union, but hardly anyone had turned up.

Which of the two political extremes had made itself most heard? The left side had always been heard. Was that sowing the seeds of the destruction of democracy in this country?

'It is wrong, what they are doing,' said Fay. 'But there is nothing you can do about it, especially with the one man, one vote system.'

'Why is it, that no one is prepared to speak up for the right?'

'I was not prepared to; I had other things to do. It didn't involve me where I was working; the students' picket was in a different site, five miles away.'

'What are your views on the abolition of the Greater London Council?'

'I have got mixed feelings. I think we should get rid of it, but then it will only be replaced by another bureaucratic system. The reason I want to get rid of it is the amount of money it wastes on grants and subsidies to minority groups, some of them so silly. There are other things you can put money to, like housing.'

'Do you think if you offered housing to some of the people wandering the streets of big cities, they would take it?'

'Some would. Maybe in the winter you would get a positive answer.'

After these questions (which appeared to be designed not to establish a candidate's political views, but only to see if he was able to discuss difficult issues in a balanced and even-handed

way), the last of the candidates was released and the next –
short and sharp – phase of the boarding took place.

This consisted of the senior rating, who had been with the
candidates all day, coming into the boardroom to give the
board *his* impressions of the men. There are those who see
something sneaky in this arrangement. But members of the
board told me that the senior rating's observations were usually
helpful to the candidates; often he was able to bring an additional shaft of human and professional understanding.

'As a group they get on well together,' reported the senior
rating. 'Number One, Bull, did a lot for them – a bit of a
father figure. He is a very pleasant young man, with a lot of
confidence. Number Two, Gale – I found this young man
very poor. He had a lot to say, but when he talked it was about
trivia, nothing that would help. The others got bored with
him talking little bits of nonsense. From the way he talks, it
sounds as if he is academically extraordinarily intelligent; but
he didn't come over as that. I can't put my finger on it.
Number Three – Black. He was a quiet young man, probably
very nervous. The impression was of a little boy lost. Number
Four – Fay. A pleasant young man, very keen to get a naval
career. He said he was flummoxed by the naval questions in
here, but sounded very knowledgeable about ships when he
was talking in the waiting-room. A bright young man, but
hasn't got a lot of confidence in himself. That is what came
over to me, sir.'

The senior rating left. It was only at this point that the
results of the previous psychometric tests of the candidates
were given to the rest of the board by the personnel selection
officer – the WRNS officer. Bull's results were good and his
answers diligent.

The headmaster articulated a civilian's reservations about
Bull: that his essay marks were rather low and that he was too
addicted to commas and semicolons.

'Up to it on paper, no more,' said the headmaster.

The 'intellectually arrogant' Gale's intelligence tests were only average; and it was obvious that the WRNS officer had not exactly been swept off her feet by him. 'He has a very supercilious and superior attitude to his parents and describes the relationship as "tolerable". He has not told them he is applying to come into the Navy because he "doesn't want superfluous advice" from them. His family do not really mean much to him. No girlfriend. A three-month relationship two years ago is the most lengthy relationship he has been involved in.'

Nor was the headmaster impressed by Gale's essay: 'Muddled in argument, irrelevant and didn't answer the question.'

The self-extinguishing Black, on the other hand, won very good psychometric test grades, and produced what the headmaster called a 'very good' essay. There was general regret that he appeared to have a health problem, and particularly that he did not seem to be aware of that fact.

Number Four, Fay, had results that the WRNS officer called 'a mixed bag'. In some respects his intelligence tests had been good, but he had worked inaccurately. The headmaster said his essay had been 'adequate', but not a systematic analysis of its subject.

Having completed this round of observations, the Board then repeated their process of awarding around-the-table markings, correcting them in negotiation and discussion to a generally agreed figure. The markings came under four headings: effective intellect, leadership, character and personality, and commitment. And in practice (cutting out the extremes at each end of the excellence scale), marks brought candidates into three main bands: pass, borderline (of which two thirds fail) and fail.

The only candidate to be given a fail by all four members of the Board was the young man with problems, Black. Gale attracted two borderlines and two fails, as did Fay. Bull got two borderlines and two passes.

The eventually agreed markings were no surprise, except

perhaps in their tolerance to Gale and Fay. Both were on the borderline-fail boundary (and therefore a long way from the pass mark), but were told they could apply again later if they wanted to. Black was rejected as quite unsuitable. Bull, the 'father figure' who was always confident if sometimes wrong, was passed – but only just.

I was not allowed to sit in on the sessions in which the captain, alone with each of the four candidates in turn, told them the results. It was apt to be, it was explained to me, a rather emotional and private moment. I could quite believe it: the board had been taxing enough for a spectator, let alone a candidate.

But the captain who was president of the board did tell me afterwards how the four young aspirants to the Royal Navy had taken their news. Bull had been pleased but not surprised. Gale had been very surprised he had failed – it had probably been, said the president, the first time he had failed at anything in his life; he had now perhaps learned a little about himself and the impression he could give to other people. Black had been dejected, but had been tactfully advised to seek a polytechnic course near home, and not to waste a quite good brain by trying again for the Navy. And Fay had greeted his rejection in dull silence, having probably 'got the message' during the day and realized that, when the pressure was on, he panicked. He had been told he could come back for another try, but the president was not sure he would.

As a visitor I was asked – as are all visitors – if I had any comments about the system, which encompasses three or four boards on any one day, each dealing with up to five candidates, would-be Royal Marines and WRNS as well as would-be Royal Navy officers. I said I wondered whether it was entirely fair for the board members to know all about the candidates' educational and personal history *before* they met the board face to face. Was there perhaps a case for having an observer sitting-in on the boards who had absolutely no previous knowledge of the candidates, but who could judge purely on the impression given at the time? In other words, could human intuition be given more of a role in the choosing process? An intuition that could by-pass possible prejudice about a young man's social background or school?

But the commodore of the Admiralty Interview Board, who bade me a civil goodbye from the establishment, thought it might be difficult to orchestrate. And in any case, the failure rate of candidates passed to go to Britannia Royal Naval College at Dartmouth – 8 per cent – was about the same fall-out rate that would apply in any organization, and did not suggest that the process was wrong.

'We are not complacent,' said the commodore, a tall red-haired officer with bushy eyebrows and a submariner's background. 'But if we had *less* than an 8 per cent failure rate, we would be uneasy. It would mean we had been failing people we should have been passing – we would be failing good people.'

On the strength of what I saw, the Admiralty Interview Board does not miss good people, and is patient with those who have only fair potential. Perhaps one day, with the humility of forty-year olds inside or outside the Royal Navy, the youthfully flippant Gale and the youthfully panicky Fay will testify to the tolerance and open-mindedness that caused them to be told they could have a second try. They might also testify to the fact that, having eventually passed, their ordeal was only just beginning.

15

COLLEGE CHAPS

'My aim is not to break them down and build them up again. My aim is to show them that they can cope, that if a person gets organized he will – hopefully – manage.'

– Chief petty officer in charge of a division, Britannia Royal Naval College, Dartmouth.

'It is not as physically demanding here at Dartmouth as it ought to be. The physical training sessions need to be much more formal and demanding. It is too easy for us *not* to do things.'

– Petty officer in training to become a commissioned officer at Britannia Royal Naval College, Dartmouth.

The steep steps are a symbol. There are some three hundred of them standing between Britannia Royal Naval College and the water's edge. In the bad old days would-be officers, aged from thirteen upwards, had to run up and down them at the double. It was a rather heavy-handed, if unintentional, way of showing the young salts that the difficult transition from the theoretical life of an educational establishment to the practical life of the ship at sea was precisely the transition they were there to make.

Nowadays, the six hundred or so embryonic officers who pass through Dartmouth at any one time are allowed to *walk* up and down the steps, while the plaster figures of bearded

Neptunes on either side of the gate at the foot of the steps stare morosely out across the mouth of the River Dart to the sea a few yards further on – as if in lament at this mollycoddling, while each still keeps one foot firmly on top of a globe depicting the world.

Only a generation or so ago, when Dartmouth still took boys destined by birth or wealth to become the leaders of the Royal Navy, the place was a public school; and, according to those who survived it, *felt* very much like one. Now the young men of seventeen-and-a-half and upwards who go to the Britannia Royal Naval College find a unique example of that British capacity to compromise and change while remaining essentially the same. It has met the needs of an age which is infinitely more technical, and theoretically more egalitarian, by retaining its naval discipline while using twenty-eight civilian tutors. They walk about the place in parson's fleck or check suits rather as if they were lecturers at a polytechnic smartened up a little for a job application.

The presence of a director of studies in the form of a civilian ex-headmaster who 'runs parallel to, and below, the captain', might have horrified some of the crusty old salts who experienced the original system. But it is welcomed by the newer breed of naval officers, who rather like to think that modern naval men can hold their own in modern techniques, ideas and disciplines.

I met the director of studies within a few minutes of driving through the massive black iron gates with the gilded 'E R I I' crests, and up Prince of Wales Drive, to the long graceful Edwardian palace overlooking Dartmouth town and the sea beyond. It certainly felt more like being back at school than being called up. I found a bespectacled academic in a sober grey suit whose voice would be more suited to the assembly hall than the barrack square, and whose penchant for naughty ambiguities would be more often heard in the senior common room than in the wardroom.

'The whole lot of us,' said the director of studies in describing the staff of Dartmouth, 'get together in the lecturers' common room, and you will find lecturers and naval officers lunching together in the naval wardroom. We like to think we are very well integrated with the Navy, and that the Navy are very kind to us civilian lecturers. Because the Navy quite like us, we are always being asked, "Are you coming out for dinner?"'

The truth of this point was brought home when I was invited later to have lunch with the captain of HMS *Dartmouth*, a very naval figure with penetrating grey eyes. I found myself sandwiched between him and one of the most senior civilian lecturers. Yes, the civilian in the country checks *had* been invited to lunch – though perhaps he was more often silent before the captain than a lecturer in a public school would have been before his headmaster.

The civilian diffidence, I was soon to see, epitomizes the relationship of civilian learning to naval discipline at modern Dartmouth. The civilian element, as organizational jargon might have it, is second among equals, though dependent on the individual personalities involved. It is, in other words, treated as an equal or near equal as long as it serves the purposes of the Navy.

The young would-be officer who arrives at Dartmouth, sometimes as young as seventeen, finds the civilian lecturers are there to do rather more than give him a smattering of the sciences if he has studied arts subjects, or a patina of general knowledge if he has been science-orientated. From the moment he arrives, the young officer with his obligatory two 'A' Levels finds himself in a strange world which is determined to convey to him in the first week that he has to learn to dress himself properly, to be where he is supposed to be on time, and to jump to it when he is told to jump to it. Boys destined to be ratings who arrive at the Royal Naval and Women's Royal Navy Service New Entry Training Establishment at Devonport may sometimes break into tears in their first days there; but for an officer to display such feelings, modern age or no, would be *inconceivable*.

The young officer needs someone who can give his previous identity a boost while saving his face in his new and strange identity. The civilian lecturer is that person.

'The civilian lecturer,' said the director of studies, 'provides a sort of familiar background to the young man who has never been away from home before. When the young man arrives here, I might say to him, "Where do you come from?" And when he tells me, I can say, "Oh yes, I know your headmaster." The look of relief across his face as he realizes that he is faced with someone dressed as a civilian, who knew his headmaster, and is connected with his past, not someone beautifully dressed in blue and gold! It is a very useful thing. The Navy realizes that.'

Dealing with the midshipmen (the would-be officers) was relatively easy, said some of his colleagues, because you knew what you were doing. The people they had difficulty with were those occasional admirals who appeared not to want the midshipmen to do any *thinking* at all.

'Most understand what we are trying to do,' said one lecturer. 'Some may look upon us as a relic, just like the original schoolboys we had here. They may think we are doing the same job as the schoolmaster was doing forty years ago. And of course we are not. What I worry about is that in the first few weeks here the midshipman is inevitably told to do as he is told and jump to it; but later, when they become commanders or captains, they are going to be the men who are going to have to *say*, "Jump!" They are going to have to *think*. That is what we are here for, whether it is computer studies or strategic studies.'

The academics may provide a psychological cushion for the midshipmen, as well as a link with the town of Dartmouth, a mainstay of the cultural activities of the college, and a thread of continuity while the naval personnel change every two or three years. But some young men facing the college for the first time can still find the first month a shock.

This first month is called the 'New Entry Period'. It is the nearest the midshipmen will get to smelling the breath of Captain Bligh. First, the midshipman is allocated a division from among four, rather as if he were being allocated a house at a public school. The four divisions are called Blake, Cunningham, Hawke and St Vincent. There is also a division called St George for senior ratings who are hoping to come up through the ranks, and a division called Talbot for WRNS. Each division will have almost a hundred officers under training divided into four groups under an assistant divisional officer, who may be a young officer scarcely older than the midshipmen themselves and who is described in the Navy as 'working at the coal-face'. They are there to act as a model to the young midshipman, to lay down the law as and when necessary, and, say officers, 'to guide and care for him, develop his character and leadership qualities, teach him professionally and assess him'.

The young midshipman will be left in no doubt of what the formalized objectives of Dartmouth are. They are 'to develop qualities, personal standards and conduct required of a naval officer; to provide a broad foundation of personal knowledge; and to provide an environment in which officers can learn to lead.' Nor will he be left in any doubt about what the objectives mean in practice.

Whether he is going in for a two-term career; whether or not the midshipman is a graduate, he will be put through the hoop physically and mentally during the first vital month. Nor will he escape the onerous first days if he is one of the overseas midshipmen, of which Dartmouth had seventy-five from seventeen countries (mostly the Middle East) when I visited.

Officers explaining the system will say drily, 'The midshipman will hear horrible stories about what it is like here at first, and of course when they get here they find it is much worse.'

Hardly an exaggeration. The midshipman will get up at six, wash and shave and then go out for what is called 'Early Morning Activity', which may be physical training on the parade ground, activity on the river or a run lasting twenty-five minutes. He showers and changes into the rig of the day, and then has 'After Breakfast Activity' until 8.40 am. Six instructional periods of fifty-five minutes each, plus further periods in the afternoon, go on for most of the day, ending at about eight in the evening. This means a working day of about eighteen hours, every day. After this, the midshipman is expected to shave again before he comes down to dinner in either the senior or junior dining-room. In the first term, dress for dinner tends to be battledress uniform. But seniors (those who are doing the extra third or fourth terms) will have black trousers, the traditional bum-freezer jacket and black bow tie.

Weekends are *not* for idling. On Saturday the midshipman will go to sea in picket boats, on Saturday evening he will do a night march of ten miles or so and on Sunday morning, to help him recover, he will be sent on a twelve-mile day march in a group with no leader, to see who and what emerges.

Nor is the new midshipman pampered back in his living accommodation. I was shown one or two living cabins by a chief petty officer in charge of a division. He seemed proud of the cabins, including the 1954 desks, the grey iron chairs, the old green carpet and the 'soft' armchair.

'We *do* give the good boys the good cabins,' said the chief petty officer. 'That is recognized. As people leave, other people go to the better cabins. You don't need soft beds. The new entrants step into bed, blink, and get out the other side: that is what it *feels* like to them, they are so tired.' The official Navy line is that new entries are put into multi-berth four to six berth cabins or small dormitories 'so that they can give each other support'.

I was shown another senior's cabin. This one was occupied by the midshipman who was working out duty rosters for the whole division for two weeks ahead. On the walls were a number of posters and colour photographs cut from magazines, including one of a gorilla saying, 'Patience my ass – I'm gonna kill something.'

It was pointed out to me that this cabin had the new type of wardrobe, but, said the chief petty officer (in case I should think they were being pampered), all midshipmen had to clean out their own cabins for the first month. Only when they became seniors, whether they were graduates or not, would they have stewards to clean up their cabins for them, and this only after the first hard month as seniors.

'This is the first floor,' said the chief petty officer proudly. 'Only seniors come here. The juniors are up on the second floor.'

Right, I said, I'd like to see one or two juniors' cabins. There was no objection (although a viewing had not been volunteered). I found two midshipmen working in a rather bare cabin for six. Every week, they said, they had to air the bedding and change the sheets.

'It is the start of the team spirit,' explained the chief petty officer quickly.

For the students at Dartmouth who are coming up through the system as senior ratings, the perception of the college is possibly a rather different one from that entertained by the young gentlemen straight from school. I met half a dozen such ratings. Some in their early thirties, others in their late twenties (generally they are rather younger), they were in sharp contrast to the fresh-faced youths at Dartmouth whom fate had *always* intended to be officers.

The officer candidates of St George's tended to think deeply before answering questions, and then to give thoughtful, careful answers. They had obviously reached that point in life when, a few disappointments and reappraisals behind them, they were able to look at themselves with sober objectivity impossible in younger, more inexperienced naval men. One man in his late twenties, who had just completed twelve of the fourteen weeks of his first term, said he had been secretary to a captain and for eight years had wanted to be an officer.

'I *could* have come here ten years ago, on the supplementary list [a list which carries more limited chances of long-term promotion], as an upper yardman, but I cancelled my papers when I failed my Admiralty Interview Board,' he told me. 'I think I failed through inexperience – I had only been in the Navy three years. There is a big difference in mental attitude needed between being a petty officer and being an officer. The difference is maturity, I suppose. Whereas you can just get along as a rating, as an officer you have got to be able to think about things, to put them into force, and lead the team. As a senior rate, you don't have to do that. It wasn't the educational side that was the difficulty with me. We need four "O" Levels and I had six, though I went to a county secondary school.'

A thirty-three year old who had been a petty officer engineer mechanic working on Sea King helicopters before coming to Dartmouth, and who looked young for his age, said he had wanted to be an officer for four years. This had been his second attempt: 'I failed the one last year. The reason they gave was that they didn't like my attitude. But if you want my honest to God opinion, I got the impression that *they* got the impression that I was the only one of the applicants with time on his side – I was younger than the rest. I can't honestly tell you what I did better the second time than the first, but I got into Dartmouth.'

I began to gather the impression that the Navy is quite keen on those ratings who, if necessary, try and try and try again to become officers, perhaps believing – rightly – that stamina and a capacity for overriding disappointments are at least as important as academic knowledge. A petty officer meteorologist with a saturnine face and a foreign name said he had tried twice to join the Navy and did not think that the only reason he was turned down the first time was that no one could pronounce that name. He applied to the Navy to be an officer after getting two 'A' Levels and six 'O' Levels at his grammar school in the north of England.

I asked him why he thought his attempts to join the Navy as an officer had so far failed. 'I didn't know anything about the Navy as such, coming from a really non-naval background,' he answered. 'I was totally inexperienced about life, I would say, although I was nineteen at the time. I was living at home. Anyway, I joined as a rating, and then found that within three months of joining I was rushed here with an officer's place.'

All the St George's candidates I met agreed that the Navy appeared to treat them as full equals of the younger men who were coming straight to Dartmouth from school as potential officers. The only complaint came from a petty officer physical training instructor. He thought that the regulations and standards about physical fitness were not hard *enough*. 'If you can inject a certain amount of determination to get over hurdles into your personality, it will stand you in good stead,' insisted the square-jawed petty officer. 'Navy fitness is all wrong. It is too irregular and, because of that, unfair on the men. We went for some competitive heats with the Royal Marines in training. Without exception, all of us from Dartmouth found it difficult; some of the chaps couldn't handle it. They had to make allowances for us. That should not have happened.'

His colleagues at St George's Division did not agree with him all the way. One said the Navy was trying to train more men actually aboard ships (usually the attack ships *Fearless* or *Intrepid*) and on board it was more difficult for men to keep fit. Another pointed out that the Navy was now trying to link physical fitness to promotion; but it was still a new scheme and should be given a chance to prove itself before being dismissed. Yet another said that extreme physical fitness was not the chief point, and that the real problem was getting officers coming straight from school to know something about what life was actually like aboard a ship. 'Guys coming straight from school know nothing,' he said dismissively. 'They think the Navy is Dartmouth, which it isn't.'

He had a point. But perhaps Dartmouth and the rest of the Navy have close similarities. Of the dozen or so St George's candidates who had arrived at Dartmouth that term, *none* had had to drop out. This spoke well for the mature men coming up from being ratings; but it also suggested that Dartmouth was close enough to what they had already been used to in the Navy generally not to trouble them unduly.

All candidates, be they direct from school or up from the ratings' mess, are warned early on to 'be themselves' and not try to impress with a false front, because it would not stand up to the shocks it would receive. If they have a North Country accent, they should keep it. If they came from a comprehensive school rather than a public school, they should not hide it. Performance, not background, was what mattered.

The training staff officer, a lieutenant-commander with a sailor's beard and schoolmasterly glasses, assured me that candidates often tried to impress in the early stages, but soon found the act collapsed. The staff were used to midshipmen arriving back from a group task 'like an Irish Parliament – all talking at once and all wanting to be leader'. But at least that gave the staff a valuable insight into their characters. So did the three-day exercise on Dartmoor, when the would-be officers had to carry fifty-pound rucksacks and sleep in bivouacs. Affectations tended to fall apart under such stresses, which were deliberately introduced. Those who appeared confident sometimes cracked when the pressure and the spotlight was on them. Others, quiet at the start, asserted themselves more and more as the exercises progressed and emerged in the final stages as very strong leaders.

Snobbery by officers in the face of ratings is a waning asset, candidates are warned. 'It is true to say,' the training staff officer told me, 'that the divisional officers, which men will model themselves on, are told that the standard of recruits now coming into the Navy is very high, and that they are going to have to deal, as officers, with ratings that aren't going to be so far removed academically or socially from them. They can find that they have ratings in their division who went to the same school and got the same results as *they* did.'

There seems to be a general regret that, almost without exception (only one exception around the time of my visit) the black faces at Dartmouth are those from other countries rather

than from Britain itself, though there is a small trickle of
Asians. The training commander, the man who equates
roughly with the civilian director of studies, but is a naval man
through and through, assured me in his tastefully decorated
office (ebony head of a black woman and a telescopic golf club
on his desk) that there was no prejudice against black faces as
such.

'It is very difficult to say why there are so few black faces at
Dartmouth and in the Navy, because I don't know how many
British black people apply to the Admiralty Interview Board
to join,' he said. 'They are steadily increasing in numbers.
There certainly aren't many. But we have internationals here
and one loses sight of that particular aspect. All the internationals are fully integrated within their division – another
good reason for multi-berth accommodation – though because
of their different academic backgrounds they may be doing
some of their professional studies separately. They certainly do
their leadership training with the rest of the midshipmen.'

Evidently reading my thoughts – to the effect that accepting
a black man as a guest was perhaps different from accepting
one as a permanent colleague – the training commander added
crisply: 'As a navigator on a frigate, I had in a navigator
yeoman's job, working next to me, a second generation
Liverpudlian black whose views on life were thoroughly British; the colour of his skin was completely incidental.'

One of the few pieces of social discrimination to be found at
Dartmouth occurs in forms of address. The senior ratings who
are on the staff of Dartmouth address those midshipmen
coming straight into the Navy as would-be officers as 'Sir',
while they address the ratings striving to become officers as
'Mister'.

This, they say, is to save the ratings' faces if they have to go
back to being ratings again: losing the greeting of 'Sir' might
be painful for them. Perhaps. What is certain is that being
called 'Sir' does not insulate the midshipmen of Dartmouth
from the (sometimes openly expressed) opinions on their

performance held by members of the staff who happen to be ratings.

In the staff general rates mess I found the master-at-arms, a mild, bearded figure more like the young George Bernard Shaw than the disciplinary ogre who, in the old days, one would have expected to bear that title. He said there was no disciplinary procedure against officers formally vested in him, but there were unofficial ways in which midshipmen could and would be told if they were off-course.

'Like that?' I asked. 'Would he be shouted at?'

The master-at-arms gave this some thought, and said at last: 'He would be given very firm advice as to the right way to do things; and if he fails, he will be put on what is called corrective training. But 99.9 per cent get through the first difficult period without traumas. Their main problem is lack of knowledge of whether they are, or are not, allowed to do this or that.'

And what were they *not* allowed to do? They were not allowed, said the master-at-arms, to smoke in class rooms or corridors or public areas; only in the bar or their cabins. There was no restriction on the amount of drink they consumed; but on the other hand their bar bills were checked (they could not go outside the college itself for drink or anything else in the first month); and if the bar bills were thought excessive they would be advised to cut back. And women? 'They are given guidance on correct social behaviour, shall we say? They do not get all-night leave whilst they are in the junior gun room (which in practice means the first year at the college). They can request an all-night pass if they are married and a wife is visiting. Fortunately, Dartmouth as a town is not a place where the local damsels can lead a sailor too far astray, because there aren't too many of them.'

I got a diplomatic answer when I asked whether having to tick off an officer would be an embarrassment for a master-at-arms – who was, after all, a rating, though a senior one. Sometimes yes, he admitted – though it depended on personalities.

'There are cases of saying to a superior officer, "Sir, you are a twat," if that is what needs to be said,' said the master-at-arms slowly. 'They are officers under training; they do not become officers until they *leave*. I perhaps wouldn't say, "Sir, you are a twat." But I would say, "Sir, you aren't getting it quite right." It doesn't pose a real problem, and I haven't come across anyone who resented it. Only once has it happened that I have said to a chap, "Sir, one of us should be feeling a bit of a wally at the moment, and I feel all right; how are you feeling?" Usually it doesn't come to that.'

The young gentlemen are firmly instructed in the purely social niceties while they are at Dartmouth, including how to dress while off duty. The captain, a man with wide naval experience and a relaxed social manner, said that today, precisely *because* the Navy was trying to be more egalitarian, Dartmouth had to give such guidance. The officers under training came from all sorts of educational and home backgrounds, only about 30 per cent from the public schools. It was no longer to be assumed they had followed the same etiquette.

The result was that little playlets were arranged, illustrating how the future naval officer should dress in his spare time. 'If you are going into the town, you wear a sports jacket and worsteds,' said the captain. 'After all, if you had people going down there in earrings and jeans, it would cause comment, wouldn't it? Not merely among the locals but also among the ratings, who are supposed to be given an example by officers.'

Perhaps anticipating that I might go away thinking that young officers were encouraged to be conformist Philistines, the captain pointed out that the college was far from culturally dead: a couple of officers would occasionally be heard singing duets on the quarter deck (translation: in the assembly hall), with officers under training and staff listening; and there was a flourishing music and arts society.

It is possible, perhaps, that the young men at Dartmouth find the instruction on welfare, discipline and dress less onerous than the duets. One twenty-year-old midshipman said the instruction on the social niceties lasted only for the first term. 'What they really are telling you,' he said, 'is that they expect a little more of you than you would have displayed before you came to the college. In the bar, it is always jackets and ties. And when you go ashore you can always tell a midshipman in the town; they are the ones with jackets and ties. You don't blend in with the background at all; it is expected of you that you maintain that little bit higher standard than anyone else. I didn't mind this, not even at first.'

This officer under training was the son of a chartered accountant and the product of a local comprehensive school in the north of England. He was midway in that grey spectrum between the 'young gentlemen' who would automatically have become officers in the old days, and the technical meritocrats who rise up through the ranks. As such, he said he had no difficulties because of the differences of background.

'Relating to people of different background is something you have to learn to do,' he told me. 'On a ship, after all, you have got to get on with anybody. When I joined, we had Randolph Churchill, the great-grandson of Sir Winston, in Blake Division. We also had a lad from Lancashire, certainly from a less well-off home. He had problems; but they were academic ones, not social. If there is a snobbish side to the Navy, it is perhaps because of the press the Navy sometimes gets, emphasizing the glamorousness of the life.'

There have been those who would have liked to see Britannia Royal Naval College change even faster than it has. The commander – the man who is second only to the captain and who, at least theoretically, outranks anyone on the civilian side – acknowledged that he was aware of this.

'We have just grown from a public school,' said the commander. 'Some other people may think we should have been more aggressive in change. But we have evolved steadily, and I am a great supporter of it.'

Not all the time of midshipmen at Dartmouth is spent either on fairly sophisticated academic study or on gruelling marches and climbs which are conceived to beat all but the really fit. Some time is spent in a way many a civilian would regard as the height of luxury. At Sandquay, just below the college and on the Dart's mouth, there are ninety-four sailing, power or rowing-boats available to educate the young midshipman in the ways of what will be both his friend and his enemy throughout his career – the sea itself.

Dartmouth's bosun, who runs this formidable fleet, told me he estimated the value of the boats available to the midshipmen at £1½ million. When I visited the quay, there were a handful of 'Bosun' dinghies in fibre-glass, four 'Contessa' thirty-eight-foot ocean-going yachts at £65,000 each – one for each division – an 'Oyster' class yacht called *Amaryllis* which cost £42,000 and which the college used for competitive racing, a number of whalers, and *Bluebottle*, the Duke of Edinburgh's sailing boat. 'It gets used half a dozen times a year and we tart it up twice a year,' said the bosun, as he showed me round the ships' workshops that would make any civilian sailing enthusiast's mouth water.

There was a workshop where engines can be taken to pieces, put together again and tested in safe conditions before being fixed back into their respective boats. There was a covered slipway for the four Contessas and a high, covered repair shed which could take two Contessas easily, plus many small craft like the 'Blue Skiff' the midshipman-maker actually declined to paint the regulation blue because he was so pleased with the smooth, now merely varnished wood that showed off his handiwork.

In the middle of the River Dart's mouth, a number of midshipmen were manoeuvring a 'Cheverton' ship's boat – one with a single propeller – while others were aboard a twin-screw picket boat costing £200,000, its fibre-glass hull protected from youthful bravura by a wood sheathing over the bows. The bosun watched one picket boat that appeared to be about to ram another in the stern, ground his old salt's teeth, and said to me out of the corner of his mouth, 'If we have got to make a mistake, we will make it here, so that when we get to sea, we don't make it. These chaps will be *teachers* next term: they learn fast. The easiest mistake is this: they think the boat is a car and has got brakes. That is to put it bluntly. And they fail to realize that a boat can go at various speeds. They think it has only two speeds: fast and stop. You can get lads here who have been on boats on the Broads. But it's not the same, doing it in the Navy. There are routines, rules and regulations. Look at that man trying to come alongside! He should have had his men doing boathook drill, to start with. There should have been a fellow there pushing the boat off with a fender. But notice the officer aboard hasn't said a word; he's just letting them stew. Would you care to go aboard?'

It would have been impolite to reveal my hesitation. I agreed to watch a 'Man Overboard' drill from one of the picket boats; observed one of the international midshipmen tripping over a coiled hawser and politely declined his assistance in getting aboard; and took up a position safely inboard, where even the heftiest collision would not have tipped me into the water.

Once out in the mouth of the river, the bosun engaged me in informative conversation. 'I have got boys out at sea much of the time. They do exercises after dark, acting as British boats and the enemy, or trying to stop smugglers. They go across to France, sleeping ten aboard, always under supervision. They go away for a week on summer leave . . . MAN OVER-BOARD!'

Without pausing in his remarks, the bosun had reached forward, seized a thick wooden post with a rope loop on one end, and thrown it overboard.

I have to say appreciatively that had it been me who had gone overboard, the midshipmen would surely have hauled me back aboard again before the cold water finished me off, though I would have preferred more finesse with the boat-hook than was shown to the wooden post. And as the crew – two of them internationals – did bring the boat alongside

Sandquay without the aid of brakes and without an audible bump, the bosun's confidence that next year they would be teaching their juniors was vindicated.

In such demanding and sometimes pleasingly spacious ways does Britannia Royal Naval College at Dartmouth foster in human beings, who are little more than boys when they arrive, a feeling and instinct for the life of an officer in the Navy. It is an intimation that the life of a naval man, even in the late twentieth century, can be gentlemanly as well as efficient.

There is another ubiquitous intimation, and he is called Mr Pook. Mr Pook is the tailor to the college, a man well-seasoned over the years in how to custom-tailor a uniform (currently costing £250) to please both the young man's legitimate vanity and the Navy's regulations.

'Have you seen Mr Pook yet?' is one of the reassuring cries that midshipmen receive from their senior officers in their first days at Dartmouth. It is arguable that England will always be England, and the Royal Navy always the Royal Navy, as long as there is always an attentive Mr Pook binding up fragmented social standards with his deft tape measure.

And, after all, young men being shaped up for possible future command deserve a few refinements.

16

WHO COMMANDS?

'They have a hell of a lot of dealings with one another at the top. They know who thinks what. If you have made a professional misjudgement, it may well be the final nail in your coffin. In other words, as applies elsewhere, if you are a dogmatic man, you must be right and seen to be right.'

– Officers Planning Section officer handling naval promotions.

'I think it is probably an advantage to have had a family background in the Navy, a father in the Navy, because it washes off on you and you fit in with the Navy. But after that you are batting on your own performance. I don't believe those who say that birth and privilege are the deciding factors.'

– Naval commander.

'Okay, there was one case where people may *say* they *did* rig the result to give a man a command – the Prince of Wales! But it can't be rigged. You have so many officers required to be promoted, and the individuals are promoted on their records and their merits.'

– Naval commander.

The bearded captain with the watchful eyes was insistent that the Royal Navy was not an élitist organization, giving promotion because of smooth social connections. He was personally in an unusually powerful position to know.

He had been conscious when he first joined at twenty-three that he was 'a little different'. The son of a coal-miner, he had been invited to leave university because, he remembered, he had been more interested in horse racing and bookies' shops than in academic theory. He had then spent over two years as a miner at the coalface.

It must be said that none of this showed in his appearance, which could have passed as patrician; and I wondered whether he would have become a captain if he had *looked* like a caricature of a miner. But all he had been conscious of at the time he joined the Navy, he told me, was that 'with my background you possibly know a bit more about life than a thirteen-year-old entrant to Dartmouth'.

He said that he had quickly been disabused of the notion that he might be treated differently from other young officers. 'I was accepted without question. People didn't give a rat's arse about where I came from. All they cared about was how I did my job. It has always been a matter of pride to me that I have got as far as I have, and as far as I *would* have done if I had joined Dartmouth at thirteen – which is now an anachronism. It now no longer takes boys at thirteen.'

He and his contemporaries were the first of the new short-career officers introduced in the early 1950s to beef up officer strength. The Navy created an eight-year career structure, and gave the men a bonus of £1,500 at the end of it – sufficient to buy a decent house in those pre-Suez, pre-inflation days.

'Then the Navy looked at some of us and said, "These guys aren't half bad,"' remembered the captain of humble origins (but confident and cultured manner). 'They started transferring officers like us from the short-service list to the general list. We have had a significant success rate, really. We have had a large number of captains, and some notable flag officers, who have come up through that stream.'

All well and good. But only about one in twenty of the Royal Navy's captains of ships actually striding the bridge have experience of that other, equally formidable, bridge – the professional one between being a rating and becoming a commissioned officer. Public school accents are common on the bridge.

These two facts combined might seem to be convenient ammunition for those who would like to caricature high-ranking naval officers in Gilbert and Sullivan terms: as grace-and-favour popinjays who rise not through the ranks but through a slippery exploitation of birth, nepotism, the right clubs and useful social connections.

While not going as far as that, there are some men in the Royal Navy who believe that, at the higher levels of officer promotion, a man's face has got to fit the required image; and that the image is that of an alert, socially accomplished, clean-cut, privileged son of the traditional ruling class.

One officer who *had* come up through the ranks told me in a burst of candour, 'You will find that people with the right background and connections will get the promotion. Nothing is written down about this; but you will find they are reported on in such a way that they get through. I am not a socialist, I am non-political, but I think these things sometimes go on.'

Even he, who did not at all fit the personality mould he was talking about, said that such things happened only *sometimes*. But I weighed his remark against a B B C television series on the selection of submarine captains under punishing ex-aminatory exercises. Candidates fell out of the running one after the other for a number of operational reasons, sometimes getting badly flustered about it. And at the end, lo and behold, who were we left with? Officers who almost exactly fitted the personality mould of privilege and social accomplishment. No doubt all of these men were in fact competent professionals as well as having faces that fitted. But some viewers must have asked themselves whether there had been an *atmosphere* that helped these men to perform at their best, whilst others performed at less than their best because they felt themselves to be fishes out of water. In other words, the fine-toothed comb through which officers must pass may be perfectly fair in that it brings forward men who *are* competent professionals, but may be unfair in *not* bringing through other men who could have been just as competent if given a chance in a more egalitarian atmosphere?

Human nuances are inaccessible to exact evaluation; but the Navy as a whole certainly does not see it in that light. When I put the point to one officer who had spent some time on matters connected with officer promotion, he promptly hit me with the bludgeon of history: 'No, no! We no longer buy our commissions and we don't get them by grace and favour. As a matter of fact, it was in 1860 when the present system started; only before that did officers get where they got through grace and favour.'

No one, of course, had thought that the present system could *formally* be based on grace and favour, but the officer insisted it wasn't based on an informal version, either.

'The important change was introduced in 1860 because they had had a run of bloody wars and sickly seasons,' he said. 'I mean they got lots of diseases and died – and the officer corps had major problems. They had an admiral of the fleet who was about eighty; if they were midshipmen they might be aged between eight and forty. It had been very difficult to get promotion apart from grace and favour or dead men's shoes. Since then we have had an officers corps as it is now, more or less, with its laid-down ranks and promotion rates and promotion boards and all things like that. Fourteen committees have sat on the question since 1860, so I think we are up to date.'

Promotion in the Royal Navy, I was told, is no longer a game of chance in which the highest counters are wealth or privilege (though a gracious wife may still be a great asset). It is now more true to say that a man's career is planned carefully like a map, and that the very title of the department under the naval secretary which handles promotions – the Officers *Planning* Section – indicates a career structure which naval men will say is infinitely superior to anything found in either the civil service or local government. They will add that several large civilian companies have modelled parts of their own appointing and career planning on the system in use for the Royal Navy.

Officers maintain that a man is carefully watched and evaluated at almost every moment of his naval career – so that there is no feeling that all one has to do is stand on a moving escalator.

The administration of promotion is the responsibility of the naval secretary and much of the donkey work is done by four hand-picked officers in the Officers Planning Section, one for the seaman branch of the Navy, one for the engineers, one for supply officers and one for the instructional branch. The one for the seaman branch has the largest job, dealing with 40 per cent of the total number of officers rising, or failing to rise, through the system; and my search for its Officers Planning Section officer took me into the old Admiralty building, around a courtyard off Whitehall, where a white stucco figure of Nelson, mounted impressively high in a niche in the sea-blue wall, greets visitors – the original for the one surmounting Nelson's column.

The officer was a commander, a submariner who had been driving a Polaris submarine before doing his present desk job: perhaps a suitable preparation, I thought to myself, for a man having to handle explosive issues about a man's advancement in his chosen career. He was wearing a plain navy-blue suit with no trace of gung-ho about it, and he told me the key to the whole system of promotion was a map.

The present system has in fact been followed since 1956, under a provision called AFO 1/56 which devised a general list of officers, known as the 'Central Pillar', and giving the individuals on it the opportunity for promotion all the way from joining the Navy as an officer to flag rank – i.e. admirals of various degrees. There are two smaller pillars on each side of this central pillar, called the 'special duties list', composed of officers promoted from being ratings, and the 'supplementary list', which comprises officers on short-service commissions, who may have anything from three-and-a-half to twelve-year commissions on joining.

Both the special duties and supplementary list officers have an opportunity to transfer into the general list (which is really the mainstream list for men who can go straight to the top), but only under certain conditions.

I was anxious to raise this point with the Officers Planning Section officer, since one of the main routes by which a rating becomes an officer is through the special duties list (upon which I was, however, assured he was fully on a par with an officer who had come up through Dartmouth College) although there are several other avenues by which a rating can reach the general list.

First, let us consider the mainstream of promotion, the general list, and a mythical young man who will be called Sub-Lieutenant Jones. Jones would come out of Dartmouth training as a sub-lieutenant, and go to sea in the fleet, in submarines or the Fleet Air Arm.

His first steps forward are assured. Five years after joining, subject to satisfactory performance, he would be promoted lieutenant, automatically. He then serves eight years in the rank of lieutenant. During this time, reports on him and his progress are drawn up annually. At the end of it, he is promoted lieutenant-commander – again subject to satisfactory performance.

This is the last automatic promotion that Lieutenant-Commander Jones, probably now in his early thirties, will have; for the available jobs are thinning out and there is need for distinctly fewer commanders than lieutenant-commanders. Annual reports continue to be written on him in his new rank. When he has three years' seniority as lieutenant-commander, he moves into what is called the promotion zone, the period during which he is considered for further promotion. He may stay in it for another six and a half years if he is not promoted, making nine and a half years in all, at the end of which he can consider his chances of future promotion to be virtually nil.

Lieutenant-Commander Jones will then carry on in the Royal Navy in that rank until he retires at the age of fifty. His only chance after the 'zone' expires is to get what is called an over-zone promotion. This depends on the good opinion of his reporting or commanding officer, probably the captain of his ship. The commanding officer may say the man is 'worth another shot' and that the promotions board has made a mistake in Lieutenant-Commander Jones' case. But he may well be told for his pains that Lieutenant-Commander Jones, like all other lieutenant-commanders, has not only had six-monthly reports written on him since he entered the promotion zone, but has also had what the Navy calls a 'shot' at promotion every six months and that thirteen failures covered by the period between his three years and nine-and-a-half years seniority may say something about the man that is difficult to argue against.

But Lieutenant-Commander Jones can also be partly a victim of the numbers game. The promotions boards will select, at the end of any one six-month period, only the number of commanders they actually require, and they will do it from what is called a 'batch' of contenders.

The batch system is central to naval promotion, and the Navy has become conscious that it must be varied on occasions to be fair to both the Navy and to the individual officer. It was invented in 1931. Naval officers still tend to talk about it with enthusiasm, as if it were newly minted. Under the system, officers of similar seniority are put into a batch of about fifty men in the seaman branch, perhaps less than half that number from the more specialized branches. In effect, each officer is therefore competing with, and only with, men of almost precisely the same seniority.

In a very obvious way, this seems fair and also makes for easier administration. But there can, equally obviously, be occasions when Lieutenant-Commander Jones will find himself in a batch of high flyers against whom he hasn't a chance, whilst in the batch six months ahead of, or behind him, there is a dearth of promotable officers, let alone high-flyers.

What, I asked, happens then? In such cases, I was told, the promotions board – chaired by the Second Sea Lord – might consider transferring a promotion to Lieutenant-Commander Jones' batch from one of the less able batches contending for promotion. Each batch covers a six-month period, from January to June and from July to December.

I asked the Officers Planning Section officer if a sly word from a senior officer could affect the promotion chances of Lieutenant-Commander Jones.

'It is all done through the collection of reports – that is all,' was the answer. 'The man is not personally interviewed or anything like that. It is done purely on the history in the paperwork. The reports, in particular, comment on an officer's suitability for promotion to the next rank and his potential for the next rank above *that* as well.'

A man singled out as a high-flyer under this system would probably get his promotion to commander at his first available opportunity, after three years as a lieutenant-commander. In practice few achieve this – probably an average of one out of a batch of fifty. Most men have several shots before they get promoted and some will not get promoted at all.

The document that will condition Lieutenant-Commander Jones' career is called S206, and a collection of these over the years constitutes a man's biography – at least in naval terms. The observations can be almost totally impersonal at the start and then perhaps get more personal, more fleshed-out with personal detail, as the promotions enter higher and higher stratospheres.

The captain of the ship is the man who will write these reports as reporting officer, and they will then go to the squadron commander – possibly the captain of the frigate squadron in which Lieutenant-Commander Jones is serving. Jones' captain, every six months, will fill in his S206 and give markings for qualities such as initiative, alertness, intelligence, reasoning power, power of expression, leadership, professional ability, tact and social attributes. 'Social attributes' is defined as an ability to get on with people, both senior and junior.

Can things like a sense of humour be registered in Lieutenant-Commander Jones' accumulating naval biography — since one imagines it to be a prime necessity when several hundred men are confined in one ship together for perhaps weeks or months? 'Things like a sense of humour will not be in the standard markings but in the written section of the report,' said the Officers Planning Section officer.

But personal whims of a single reporting officer would play no part in Lieutenant-Commander Jones' career, it is claimed. The reporting officer, too, is being reported *upon* in his own promotion process. The squadron commander makes notes not only on the man being reported on, but also on whether he considers the report of the reporting officer to be a fair one.

The squadron commander might write, 'I support this well-written report, a very observant report, and I endorse the recommendation for promotion.' This of course is what Lieutenant-Commander Jones is hoping for.

Perhaps he would instead write, 'I believe this report is guilty of over-egging (praising) this man and have marked the man down by three points.' Or even, 'I believe this is a harsh report, and I have marked this man up.'

From the squadron commander the report would go to the flotilla flag officer, who also has an opportunity to put any remarks down on paper. He has probably visited all the ships in his flotilla while they are at sea, and has his own views not only on Lieutenant-Commander Jones but also on the captain of the ship, *and* on the squadron commander. 'Flotilla staff officers go to sea as well,' pointed out the Officers Planning Section officer, 'and when they get back *they* will feed into the admiral how that ship is getting on.'

Everyone, in other words, is so busy reporting on everyone else, and signing their name to it, that a merely spiteful remark on Lieutenant-Commander Jones is likely to be more trouble than it is worth to anyone reporting who happens to dislike him personally.

Of course the professional and personal aspects of likeability can be linked, especially at the higher levels of promotion – though this is probably no more so in the Royal Navy than in any civilian company boardroom, where having clubbable qualities and being acceptable to colleagues are necessary parts of the personal equipment for the job.

It is certainly very much the case in the Navy at the level of captain; but the hurdle Lieutenant-Commander Jones faces before he gets into this more rarefied territory is being made up to commander. If he is of average age, he will have become a lieutenant-commander at thirty-two, and has until he is forty-one and a half to be promoted commander. If he doesn't make it, he is rather in the position of the 'passed-over major' in the British Army: he is a competent and useful man at that level who may go on at the same pitch of dynamism because he happens to be that sort of man, or he may become disgruntled and look forward with eagerness to his retirement at fifty. It is a sad fact that any organized force of men, certainly an armed force, relies to a certain extent on the work of conscientious people who know they will climb no more rungs of the ladder. The compensations are stronger in the specialist branches, especially the engineers, who can normally find highly paid jobs in civilian industry when they retire.

Let us assume that Lieutenant-Commander Jones is eventually successful in being promoted commander. He will not assume the rank at once. He will wait six months while his 'papers are shovelled around' and plans are made to relieve him at his present post. In June or in December, six months after his promotion was announced, he will find himself serving as a commander. He will hold this position for five years before he moves into the next promotion zone – the one for captain. This zone will last four and a half years, which gives Commander Jones ten shots at being selected for promotion to captain. Exactly the same criteria are used, and the same batch system. The only noticeable change is that the batches have tailed off in numbers: from the fifty hoping to be promoted to lieutenant, there are now perhaps only twenty contending for further promotion.

If Commander Jones is not made a captain, he will have fifteen years as commander, before retirement at fifty-three, going to sea, working in the Ministry of Defence, or shore establishments, or training schools, or the diplomatic service as naval attaché.

The average age of promotion to captain is forty-five. Surely by now Commander Jones bears little resemblance to Sub-Lieutenant Jones, that far-distant fellow whose reporting officer may have denounced him as immature for his age, or over-assertive for his brains, or under-active for his potential, or over-fond of a nip or two of Scotch while ashore? Yet all that distant paperwork may still be there to tell against him.

The Navy, I was assured, had thought of that. 'Some of the earlier reports on the man have been ditched,' explained the Officers Planning Section officer. 'They are now more interested in the man's skill in middle management than what he was like as a young lieutenant. Only his performance as a commander would be considered. All the rest stays in the official records with the whole of a man's reports; but that is *not* the record that is put before the promotions board at this point. And the promotions board's members have not been there long enough to remember for themselves what the man was doing earlier in his career. Men will serve two and a half years on the board, chaired by the Second Sea Lord, and will not know about the things said about the man's early career.'

Captain Jones, if things have gone right with him so far, will serve nine years in the rank, or up to the age of fifty-five if this is earlier, when he may be considered for promotion to rear-admiral. At these levels, the air is getting thinner. While there may be a need in the Royal Navy at any one time for over four hundred captains, only about twenty-eight rear-admirals are required.

Only about one in five of the now-depleted batch of captains will go on to reach rear-admiral after nine years as a captain, or at age fifty-five. This point in Captain Jones' life is not a promotion zone, it is a fixed promotion *point*, at which he will either be promoted or retired. But the Admiralty Board, which handles promotions at this level has permission to 'dip down' the list of captains it would like to see made admirals *before* their nine years' seniority as captains. A high-flyer would probably be made rear-admiral at about forty-seven or forty-eight.

If Captain Jones becomes Rear-Admiral Jones, his life thereafter will be dictated rather more by chance and mysterious considerations than could be put down neatly on the six-monthly reports of his past career. The Navy line is that it will be dictated by the service requirement, his specialist skills and his performance. It is likely that unless he is very accomplished Rear-Admiral Jones will fill only one appointment as a rear-admiral. About 50 per cent retire after one appointment.

'They might say – the Admiralty Board – that he was going as Flag Officer, Portsmouth, and he may then be told there is no other job for him,' said the informative commander, confessing that these matters were really beyond his ken. 'Or he may be told that he will be appointed later to another job. It is very personal by this stage; and it is really the First Sea Lord who decides, guided by reports on the flag officer's performance and taking into account the views of the Admiralty Board, the Commander-in-Chief Fleet and Commander-in-Chief Naval Home Command. These great men get together every six months, studying reports written on Jones' performance, having promotion meetings and considering appointments to be filled and the talent on the flag list, and then considering who to promote to vice-admiral. And who to give a second job as a rear-admiral and who to retire.'

Did this mean in practice that the First Sea Lord could ditch any officer if he did not like the cut of his jib? 'If the First Sea Lord disliked a man,' said the commander cautiously, 'it would not be his decision completely; other members of the board might say, "He is exactly the man we want for this particular job and there is no other man who can do it as well." Then I am sure that the First Sea Lord, being a sensible man, would put his personal feelings on one side and sign his approval. The test always is – who is the best man for the job?'

I asked the commander if there was really a strong system of checks and balances at this point. An unfair question, perhaps; and he regretted that he had his ideas, but did not feel like sharing them with me, because they might not be the official answer. He thought the right answer might be that the abilities of the various people being assessed were known, and *well* known, by this time and that a fair outcome would emerge from round-the-table discussion. The men who got to the top in the Navy, he said, got there on outstanding merit – merit which was recognized and highly sought after by industry when the men retired.

That is the promotion system from top to bottom; and of course it is likely that Jones' personal interest in the proceedings may stop somewhere short of the top. The system does evolve with the passing years but not, it seems, in major ways; the main outlines date back to 1956, the year of the Suez reverse, when it became obvious to the sharp-eyed that Britain might still be a world power, but no longer a major one. Naval officers who have studied the promotion systems in the British Army and the Royal Air Force, and in the civil service, have come to the conclusion that their own system has little or nothing to learn from these; and that the six-monthly reports in the promotion zones are a frank and efficient way of updating the assessment of a man's capability. They insist that these reports by captains are written with extreme care and coolness of judgement, and that personal pique would stand out a mile on the foggiest day.

Perhaps; but I thought it fair to put a few more questions.

Was the candidate shown the reports the captain was preparing on him? The answer was no; the Navy had a 'closed reporting system'. But the reporting officer had to have a 'performance assessment discussion' with him, which would be based on the report which had been written. The reporting officer was not required to show him his opinions, but he *was* required to inform the junior officer of how the captain saw him matching up to the job. The captain *might* read out selected bits from the report, or he *might* read out the full report if he so wished. Then the captain, as reporting officer, *might* mention things – possibly adverse ones – that he had *not* mentioned in his report. He *might* say, 'Look, Jones, unless you stop getting pissed every night, I am going to have to start making comments about your drinking habits, or your habit of crashing your motor-bike.' In this way, I was told, dangerous habits might be headed off without having to appear on an officer's record.

In the dealings between the captain as reporting officer and the junior officer being reported upon, there are certain complications of definition. The captain is required to inform the officer of any adverse comments he has made *which he considers to be within the power of the officer concerned to remedy*. Seasoned officers say that this means that if you pick your nose and have it reported, it will be read out to you; whereas if you have a nervous tic in your eye, it won't be mentioned, since presumably there is nothing you can do about it, poor fellow.

This is known to be a grey area, since even the cleverest psychiatrist could hardly come to a scientifically established conclusion about what facets of human behaviour are re-mediable and which are not. There is an even greyer area around another topic that may enter an officer's reports – certainly the higher he goes up the scale.

That topic is the officer's wife. What behaviour of a wife is 'remediable' and what isn't? This can be a poser for the con-scientious reporting officer when considering whether an officer should be promoted to captain and above. Every re-porting officer, it is said in the Navy, has a bad dream: he is reporting on an officer who is a super chap, who would make a first-rate 'representational' naval officer if sent to the USA on an exchange; but unfortunately he has a neurotic wife, and it is considered that 'representational' duties require the wife to 'pull her weight as a member of the team', as one officer put it. The reporting officer may find himself writing down something like 'But for the fact that his wife is a dipso-maniac/neurotic, this officer would make a particularly fine naval attaché.' In such a case, it would be thought that there was no point in showing the comment to the officer, since the only remedy would be for the officer to divorce his wife, a course which even a disciplined force like the Navy does not consider it suitable to advise.

To civilians, the appearance of the wife's character and shortcomings in a report about the husband may strike a jarring note. But senior naval officers point out that even if an officer is not a 'representational' figure, and that the only ambas-sadoring he will do for Britain is receiving civic or national dignitaries when the ship is in a foreign port, the existence of a wife with problems may create problems for *him* in the performance of his vital duty; and that these problems, if likely to be significant, should be officially known. The more senior the officer, the more his wife is likely to affect his career chances.

The Officers Planning Section officer said he thought the wife became a factor at senior commander or captain and above levels, because it was realized that the trauma of a diffi-cult marriage could affect an officer's performance, which could itself affect other men's lives. Was the wife on a bender, crashing the car and killing the children? An officer could worry about that. I took the point, while reflecting that perhaps it was just as well that the same reporting system had not applied to Admiral Nelson and Lady Hamilton.

Not that wives pose the only problem about which a man may be reported on without knowing; if he has a bad stutter, the Navy will probably consider that incurable, too, and not mention it to him, though it may have gone down on his report – but only, the Navy insists, if the impediment is actually affecting his performance. There have been, the Navy points out, officers with various disabilities, including stutters, who have risen to the highest ranks. This I found to be true in the officers I met.

Is the system paternalistic and almost pre-arranged, in the sense that the things the report writers are looking for will be most often in practice found in their 'own sort of people' socially? Naval officers deny the paternalism; but concede that in practice it is quite difficult for a man who has been a rating to get to be a senior officer, and *very* difficult for him to become a captain – hence the figure of one in twenty captains who have come up from being ratings. But it must be said that officers I came to respect pointed out that the education system had only reached a rough equality in recent years, and claimed that the Navy had led social change in its promotion procedures.

At one end of the professional social scale is the naval officer whose father is a high-ranking naval officer, who starts at Dartmouth, takes easily to the Navy as the Navy takes to him, and who achieves speedy and sure promotion. Naval officers concede that he *is* lucky and he *does* have an advantage, but that the advantage is not nepotism. One officer pointed out that in any case there were currently more sons of naval officers at Sandhurst with the Army than at Dartmouth with the Navy.

Another officer, a commander, put it this way: 'It is most unusual for a son to be in the same ship as his father, so it is impossible for him to be the reporting officer on his own son, and the son is on his own. There are lots of passed-over lieutenant-commanders with very senior fathers, and some sub-lieutenants have been discharged from the Navy as being unsuitable who are sons of very senior officers, either serving or retired. And some sons are a damn sight better than their fathers, don't forget that. No, nepotism is no problem.'

The rule that fathers and sons cannot serve on the same ship is an unwritten one. But some rules about promotion are written; and some that are written definitely affect the chances of promotion at the other end of the social scale: the lad who starts off as a rating.

Though the general list, which is the central pillar of naval promotion, goes up to flag rank, the pillars that stand to each side of it, the special duties list and the supplementary list, go up only to commander. Ratings have access to both of these lists. They can become lieutenants on either list and they can become lieutenant-commanders on either list. After either of these promotions, they can offer themselves for selection to go on the general list, which is one hurdle; and on the general list, they will be competing for further promotion with the officers who came up through Dartmouth College – another hurdle. If they do not get on to the general list as either a lieutenant or a lieutenant-commander, they can advance one more step, to commander, on either the special duties or supplementary list; but then their promotion stops. They cannot become a captain on either of these two lists because, as commanders, they cannot be transferred to the general list, irrespective of how good their service has been. Only by getting transferred to the general list *earlier* can they go on to become a captain or a flag officer.

To those in civilian life – where promotion tends to be more unpredictable but also more flexible – the Navy system might appear to restrict unfairly the promotion chances of an ex-rating. But naval officers point out that such a man is a known quantity for many years; and that if he really has the stuff of an admiral in him, he will have been transferred from the special duties or supplementary list on to the general list well before the time he *must* have done so to continue getting promoted.

I asked the Officers Planning Section officer about the mechanism by which a man was transferred from the two 'side' pillars to the central general list. 'Transfer boards are made up of four officers in the same way as the promotions boards. It is all based on the reports of his reporting officer rather than personal interview. They look at the representations of those who have applied for transfer. Then they transfer according to a set quota.'

Wasn't the 5 per cent of captains who have come up from being ratings rather low?

'In comparison to what?' asked the Officers Planning Section officer deftly.

'In absolute terms.'

'Well, I would say it demonstrates how difficult it is to get promoted if they have started off as ratings. There are five hurdles. You have to have the educational qualification; you have to be promoted from a rating; you have to be transferred to the general list; then you have to be promoted to commander, and then promoted to captain. You have five lots of doors to get through.'

'Is that healthy?'

'I am not sure healthy is the right word. I think it indicates that if the man has the ability to be promoted to the rank of captain, then he will get there. But it indicates that the special duties officer, having transferred to the general list, is in competition with everyone else and treated in exactly the same way. No special consideration is given to the fact that he was a special duties officer. He is taking his chances, and the competition is pretty stiff.'

In any case, pointed out the Officers Planning Section officer, the Navy now had a system under which keen and qualified young men could change their minds after joining as a rating, if they experienced the life and said to themselves, 'Not for me! I want more than this.'

Such a young man, under the upper yardman scheme, could – between the ages of eighteen and twenty-four (twenty-five for engineers) – go over to Dartmouth College either on the general list at that stage or, if with not quite so many GCE passes, on the supplementary list. In the latter case, once having got the required qualifications, he could later transfer to the general list. In this way quite a lot of ex-supplementary list (short-service period) people got promoted to captain. But the list was comparatively new, and would take thirty-five years to work through the ranks completely to the highest levels. In the meantime, there were many special duties list commanders who kept to their present rank, which required highly specialist skills. Perhaps in any civilian system they would not rise to the top in the boardroom, but remain as production directors.

At the higher levels of the Royal Navy, it is possible to visualize promotions as dealings among gentlemen – objective and fair dealings, no doubt, but still choices among gentlemen who understand the requirement and have to make decisions based on the proved abilities of their more junior colleagues as understood in their own terms.

At the lowest end of the scale, involving ratings, the process is differently located geographically (no cosy corridors in Whitehall) and far more impersonal. And (at least when I inquired, and probably still) largely administered in a day-to-day sense by a *woman*, though a Royal Navy officer has the final responsibility. In this light at least, let no one say that, where a job can be done equally well by a woman as by a man, the Navy refuses to move with the times. One man at HMS *Centurion*, the shore establishment near Gosport which houses the administration of ratings, said he had been there five years and, in his experience, the job had *always* been done by a woman.

I found the advancement and promotion officer, ratings, in a suite of three modest offices, no bigger than small living rooms, in a stone-rendered building in the *Centurion* complex. A tall, laughingly pleasant first officer, WRNS, of under forty, with striking blue eyes, she was in the process of telling someone over the house phone that if they thought *that* (whatever it was) wouldn't cause confusion, they were being beautifully naïve, and would they do it some other way? Plainly ratings' promotions were in the hands of someone not likely to be intimidated even at the peak times of the year – summer and autumn – when personal forms come in by the thousand and have to be sifted and presented coherently to a multiplicity of promotions boards.

The three offices of the advancement and promotion officer, who reports directly to the captain, naval drafting, are a sandwich. She sits in the middle one; on one side is the office that handles the first steps of a sailor's career, the advancement office, and on the other is the office that monitors his progress from petty officer level, the promotions office. This, when I visited it, was in the charge of a very seasoned fleet chief petty officer who could and did put in a tactful, 'Also, Ma'am . . .' if Ma'am did not have every tiny fact at her fingertips at any given moment.

Ma'am plainly knew very incisively what she was about. She cautioned me not to take her too literally when she said she was responsible for *all* advancement and promotions because at the very first level there was such a thing as a time advancement. An ordinary rating could be made up to able seaman at the gift of the captain of a ship or shore base, and it was arranged according to time served, with other qualifications.

Apart from time advancements, all advancements are handled at *Centurion* on a roster basis. This means, as the fleet chief petty officer put it, 'seniority tempered by merit' and distinct from the later stages of career growth, where it was a case of 'merit tempered by seniority'.

The first stages are purely non-selective – there is a roster of men available; and when Ministry of Defence statistics show there is a vacancy the man at the top of the roster gets his advancement. There are in fact three rosters – what is called the 'Dry Roster', of men for whom there are vacancies, and who can move up straightaway if they have the necessary qualifications at that point; the 'Intermediate Roster', with men in date order showing their potential for the next rating level when a vacancy occurs within a two-year period; and what is called the 'Normal Roster', composed of men past this point who, on a six-month basis, have merit points recorded against their names: the names then go into a merit-point order, and the man at the head of the list is advanced when Ministry of Defence statistics reveal there is a vacancy at that level. This process goes on until a man reaches the rank of acting petty officer. Then the next move – to petty officer – will cause his papers to be moved to the office on the other side of Ma'am's – the one that handles promotion.

At the advancement level, the candidate is reported on at yearly intervals, and so is he at promotion levels. This is unlike the promotion system of officers, who are reported on six-monthly – not because, I was told, they are regarded as a more interesting élite, but because they are much fewer in number, and so do not entail the same vast amount of administrative time. At both advancement and promotion levels, the rating is marked at these yearly intervals on eleven aspects of his character and performance: (1) professional knowledge; (2) effectiveness at his job; (3) energy and initiative; (4) intelligence; (5) management and organizational skills; (6) leadership; (7) cooperation; (8) adaptability; (9) integrity; (10) courage and stamina; and (11) personal qualities.

The system is applied in the same way with ratings in promotion as in advancement. The man's divisional officer awards the marks, the head of department approves (or disapproves) them, and they are then sent to *Centurion* under the captain's signature. But with ratings in the promotion process, a new element is added: the written word. Ratings are not merely awarded marks out of a hundred under eleven headings. Three quarters of the two-page report are left blank for a written report by, first, the divisional officer, then the head of department and finally the commanding officer's report. As the report goes up the scale, the reporting rating or officer can see what the man lower down the scale has written, but he is not obliged to follow it: he can, to some extent, argue against it if he is so inclined.

There is only one restriction on the reports that are written on a man at promotion level: the observations have to be related to the eleven markings at the head of the form. In all other respects, the reporting officer is free to write as he pleases, and points may be made bluntly or subtly, according to the requirements of the situation and the personality of the reporting officer. The commanding officer makes a firm recommendation for promotion or a firm recommendation for denying it or postponing it, and signs his name.

And so it goes on, up to chief petty officer at which point – probably when the man is in his early forties – his twenty-two-year period of service in the Navy will be coming to an end.

Unlike officers, ratings are not faced with promotion zones – age bands where in effect they are expected to get on or get out: the rating who has been a petty officer for years can, in theory and sometimes in practice, be promoted to chief petty officer years after most of his age group have been promoted, and towards the end of his own service. The only stipulation is that no one can be advanced or promoted if they have already completed twenty-two years of *pensionable* service (the first year or two's service in the teens is not pensionable). If he is to be appointed fleet chief petty officer, it must be before he has completed twenty-two years' pensionable service, and he must be prepared to sign on for another five years. With these stipulations, the system of ratings' career growth seems to be rather kinder to the late developer than the officers' system, where a man is either definitely up with the hunt at the appointed times, or definitely out of the race – a system based on a philosophy which is certainly not so harshly applied in civilian life. The only time zone to bother the naval rating bears hardest on the brightest. There are *minimum* times for promotion; the rating must be three years a petty officer before he can become a chief petty officer and three years a chief petty officer before he can become a fleet chief petty officer.

Before the advancement and promotion officer went on to

explain how the promotions boards met and operated in the final adjudication process, I had a few questions that exercised my cautious civilian mind. With the first ten qualities on which a man was judged being so comprehensive, what could the eleventh, 'personal qualities' mean – except an invitation to the reporting officer to air his personal prejudices? Surely all the previous ten had already dealt with any relevant factors about the man's personal qualities?

Ma'am did not agree. 'I think a naval person would know what was meant. You can have a crashing erk who has dandruff round his shoulders, who is badly dressed, droops, and doesn't walk around in a positive manner. But if you have a particularly upright young man, who walks in a positive way, is immaculate in appearance, charming, gets on with everyone, well mannered and personable, then I would suggest he was a man of high personal qualities. You have a norm, and you know where they range in that. In other words, if a chap is a good ambassador of the Royal Navy. I would not put it down purely to clothing and demeanour.'

'It means behaviour *as well* as clothing and demeanour,' put in the advancement and promotion officer's experienced fleet chief petty officer.

'It is a management view of the whole man,' said his lady superior. 'It may not be the most important thing. If a man's leadership marking is well down, that factor will *certainly* be taken into account in deciding whether that man is suitable for the next higher rung.'

What about educational qualifications? 'The only level where educational level bites is from chief to fleet chief petty officer, where they are required to have two "O" Levels, including English Language, for selection to fleet chief petty officer. At the lower level, there is a special Navy arithmetic and English test, but it is a fairly basic requirement, a basic level of numeracy and literacy. We would have no knowledge of where they went to school . . . well, that is not *quite* true, but where they went to school is not relevant. Things like having parents or uncles in the Navy or other services have no influence at all.'

So what is made available by way of documentation to the selection boards who each sit at H M S *Centurion* for one week, considering promotions for each specialized section of the Royal Navy from petty officer to chief petty officer – eight tribunals spread over the months of September and October?

The essence is the full reports and a tick by one of three boxes – 'NOW', 'NOT YET', or 'NO' (on the lower end of the advancement scale, it is merely 'YES' or 'NO'). Each of the reports to be seen by the selection board will have been read personally by the advancement and promotion officer, and returned to source if there are inaccuracies, discrepancies or omissions. As this applies to around six thousand reports each year, it quickens the pulse of the promotions office considerably. The reports arrive in the middle of July. Between 5 and 10 per cent have to be returned for amendment. Here the principle enunciated by Ma'am – 'Our aim is always to look after the individual' – must always be kept in mind.

'We have got our little babies, and we must always remember that,' said Ma'am. The briskness of the tone did not disguise the evident sincerity of the sentiment; the more sincere, perhaps, because the lady had no children of her own.

Whether the selection boards can have the same maternal spirit is problematical. They must certainly have a strict eye to the rules, and they must, on fairly numerous occasions, call in the advancement and promotion officer or her staff for clarification or memory-prodding. On such occasions, the staff will consult a manual as thick as two telephone directories, known officially as the BR 10-66, and unofficially as the 'Boards' Bible', and relay the information to the particular board. The Bible contains all the rules, and all the exceptions to the rules, and all the exceptions to the exceptions to the rules; and it is updated from time to time, which provides further challenges to memory if concentration slackens.

Ma'am waved the Bible at me, thus incidentally proving

that she had a strong wrist. 'I came here ten months ago and we have received three amendments since then,' she said. 'I see it was revised five times in 1983 and five times in 1982. I gather another amendment is due to be issued, so we must familiarize ourselves with that.'

The end product is a choice made very strictly within the existing rules, and possibly as sensitive as the volume of work allows. It is certainly more in accord with the times (and in advance of most civilian practice) than the system which operated until 1971.

Different ranks sit on the selection boards, each perhaps bringing a different point of view. There are always three members, so deadlocks are impossible. Two commanders and one lieutenant-commander sit on candidates going from petty officer to chief petty officer, and one captain and two commanders sit to decide who goes up from chief petty officer to fleet chief petty officer; all are of the same specialization as the men due for promotion.

All selection boards are what the Navy calls 'Paper Boards'. They look at the reports, not the men. No individual ever appears before a board.

I asked the advancement and promotion officer whether excluding an actual sight of the rating involved was fair, since the man himself could not explain or add to anything in his written record. Perfectly fair, thought the advancement and promotion officer: 'Perpetual assessment under our system extracts the best people from the system. If you are an actor or actress, and convincing as anyone can be for half an hour, and you swot up with the *Daily Telegraph* or *The Times*, people may say, "We have got a star here." While in practice they can no more make a decision than fly to the moon.'

Personal interviews might possibly cripple the administration. During the spring and summer, *Centurion* handles ten thousand or so dossiers on the promotions side and probably more on the advancement side, advancing between fifteen hundred and two thousand a year, and promoting about five to six hundred from petty officer to chief petty officer and a few more – less than a hundred – from chief petty officer to fleet chief petty officer.

Such a vast system, to be fair, must clearly have checks and balances, means of ensuring that injustices are not perpetrated under the deadweight of catering for sheer numbers. What, I asked, were they?

'I think the checks and balances lie basically in the fact that you are comparing man to man at the same rating level, and therefore Instructions S-264 Delta [which lay down guidelines, so that a man's nature can be related to a numerical assessment] mean that you are not going to have a chap who is absolutely spiffing and give him only fifty-five out of a hundred,' said Ma'am briskly.

It does seem that if there is *de facto* injustice, it is not through the workings of the advancement and promotion officer, but through the statistics of the Ministry of Defence, computerized at HMS *Centurion*. These cover the *demand* for ratings at various levels. In recent years this has gone down rather than up in line with defence cuts that – at least until the Falklands war – tended to be regarded as of overwhelming importance.

Each ship or shore establishment has a laid-down manning level. There is an additional number to cover sickness and welfare losses to the Navy and the need to have some men engaged in higher training for their future careers and the Navy's needs. But the final number of vacancies at the end of the Ministry of Defence's calculations *is* final and may allow through men who would not get through except at time of active need, or exclude, at least for a time, perfectly able men because at a particular time there were no vacancies for them in a higher rank.

No system of course can be completely fair, but as they say in the corridors of *Centurion*, 'Let anyone who wants to find a fairer one go ahead and try.' At any rate, the people I met at *Centurion* had all the hallmarks of caring people; caring in the brisk naval way, perhaps, but still caring. Perhaps there was sound good sense in delegating a woman to look after her 'babies'.

Once on active service, of course, there is rather less room for the protective approach, either to officers or ratings (though there are some sectors of that active service that provide ample compensation).

17

ELECTRONIC AND OTHER BRAINS

'Our business is brains. We are separate from the School of Maritime Operations because we have a different job. We all operate in support of the fleet, but 50 per cent of my life is to be a think tank in the medium or long term – to look ten to fifteen years ahead.'

– Captain in charge of the Maritime Tactical School, HMS *Dryad*.

'But there has been a revolution in modern warfare. The pace is such that we cannot afford to stick by the old specializations.'

– Captain of School of Maritime Operations, HMS *Dryad*.

'It is probably a boy of about eighteen who will spot the enemy missile first.'

– Lieutenant-commander at School of Maritime Operations.

In Nelson's day there was no doubt about the location of the nerve centre of a warship: it was where the captain was. It was so for a long time after Nelson died. The bridge was the holy of holies and the only one. But in the last few years the effective nerve centre of the Royal Navy's ships has descended a deck or two, to that windowless part of the ship that has become the new holy of holies. It is the electronic and mechanical brain known as the operations room.

In this smallish room, chock-a-block with electronic equipment, panelled with cathode-ray tubes, it would be all too easy to regard the human beings in it as mere appendages to the technology. Easy and dangerous for, as we shall see, in the Royal Navy the first detection of trouble may still rest with the quick wits of a human being – and one who may be no more than eighteen years old.

A nerve centre in the electronics age must be based firmly on an education system that has all the atmosphere of a disciplined service while meeting all the academic requirements of a polytechnic or university. The operations room virtually has its very own educational system.

Take the high road from Portsmouth, overlooking the naval base and the coast, drive seven miles, sweep down into the little and unremarkable Hampshire village of Southwick and you will come upon a remarkable symbol of the Royal Navy's present identity as a hybrid of seafaring tradition and modern technological grip. It is within the shore establishment called HMS *Dryad*, and is called the School of Maritime Operations. This sounds, to a civilian, like a very wide generic title but in fact refers to the specific sort of 'operations' that go on in an operations room.

The wardroom, where the officers live and socialize, and the accumulation of silver and gilt memorabilia, are in Southwick House, once the stately home of a Mrs Borthwick-Norton. It is a handsome white stucco building with an imposing colonnade and a distinguished military, as well as civilian, history. In 1944 it was the headquarters of Admiral Sir Bertram Ramsay, the Allied naval commander-in-chief for the invasion of Nazi-occupied Europe; General Eisenhower and General Montgomery had quarters in the vicinity, and Eisenhower went into Southwick House itself to take his decision to launch the Normandy landings on D-Day, 6 June 1944.

Southwick House was the third house on the site, built in the mid-nineteenth century on a site originally used by an Augustinian Priory. Dryad, too, has an historical resonance, the word being Greek for a wood nymph – a mystical creature who could no doubt find its way as expertly as the modern ops men who pass through HMS *Dryad*. Between 1795 and 1873 four ships with the name were built, the last being finally used as a tender to the old navigation school. The name was adopted by the school when it was evacuated from Portsmouth Dockyard to Southwick in 1941.

During and since the war, different departments and different buildings have been added, ringing Southwick House with the concrete and steel buildings that give HMS *Dryad* the appearance of a rather daunting polytechnic campus. When I went there, two old wartime concrete prefabricated huts were still in use as instructional areas, though I was assured they would soon be gone and yet another modern building would soon be in their place.

But the atmosphere was as if a film of a civilian polytechnic had been speeded up. Everyone seemed addicted to doing things at the double. On my walk of a few hundred yards from the car park to the captain's study, I passed several two-legged testimonials to the seductiveness of constant movement. Some men ran in track suits, some men carried squash rackets, some ran *and* carried squash rackets. The courts were excellent, I was assured by the lieutenant-commander who whirled me round the campus like a tornado; so was the 'cinemasium', a gymnasium which could be turned into a theatre; and so was the all-weather cricket pitch.

'All thanks to rum, really,' said the lieutenant-commander. 'When we abolished the rum ration in the Navy – because you couldn't have people handling complicated electronics when they would have been over the legal alcohol limit for driving a car – we put the money saved into sailors' welfare. It goes to buy facilities for sailors, like the golf course which, true, is also used by others, but is cheaper for sailors. There is a lake with fish and the Royal Navy Equestrian Association have the stables.'

The captain of HMS *Dryad*, a clean-shaven officer with piercingly dedicated eyes, about to leave to take up a senior job in the Ministry of Defence, after commanding the carrier HMS *Illustrious* a few years previously, received me in the captain's office. This had even more naval insignia and impedimenta than books.

'There has been an enormous change in the past ten years,' said the captain. 'The Navy used to be full of the traditional specializations. When we established the school as the School of Maritime Operations in 1974, we set out with a view to making the art of warfare cohesive. We are now over ten years down that road, and we have seen the enormous advantage in bringing together all the different aspects of warfare – communications, underwater warfare, anti-air warfare, surface warfare, the use of radar and electronic warfare and so on.'

In the Army, said the captain, there was an enormous *esprit de corps* within the regiment and the battalion; it was the strength of the British Army. Up to the 1970s, the Navy had its old distinctive skills – and these all had their own corporate spirit, and there was a great sense of belonging to the old specializations. But because warfare had become so complicated, it had become necessary to draw all the original specialists together.

'And because of that, to a certain extent each specialization loses its sense of identity,' added the captain. 'But I believe the operations branch of the Navy as a whole is at last beginning to have a sense of corporate identity, while still preserving to some extent the individual identities – underwater, above-water, radar, and so on – to give people an individual sense of identity and competitive spirit. It will take another five or ten years before we have that overall sense of identity that the separate naval skills had in days gone by. But we are at last dealing with a new generation of sailors, so it is happening that warfare as a skill is successfully coming together, and that is a great naval achievement.'

Could the school accelerate that process? The captain said he regarded that as his main task. His main duty was to set up the various seaman branches as a cohesive warfare branch which was able to fight a modern warship. That was his biggest task: to make people feel they belonged to the concept as a whole, while still retaining their pride in their separate skills.

'But there has been a revolution in modern warfare. The pace is such that we cannot afford to stick by the old specializations,' he insisted. 'We are in the lead in that. Within NATO, the Americans are fascinated to see how the School of Maritime Studies is developing; the Dutch and Germans are watching with great interest, and are still bringing together different skills into the operations room. People are impressed by the fact that we have taken the bull by the horns and stepped into the twenty-first century.'

It is easy for any civilian to understand that in modern warfare the old definitions – and skills – break down. Can a submarine launching a nuclear missile at distant land be said to be confined to 'underwater' skills? Can a pure radar man be comfortable and useful in a modern operations room, in which radar will be only one of the ways in which a target or an enemy can be detected? Obviously not.

Hence the emergence of a newly-defined officer called the principal warfare officer, an operations room officer who may have his own old specialist skill, but is also able to fight his warship on his own initiative if time is too short to involve the captain – a further reminder, one would have thought, that in modern warfare the captain's personal grip on his ship at all times cannot be as great as it could be in the days of Nelson.

Producing able principal warfare officers is the purpose of the most important of the 250 different courses that the School of Maritime Operations runs; many of the other courses are geared to supporting and complementing the principal warfare officer training. RAF personnel come to the school, too. The two services tend to get on well with one another – two technicians together – despite the fact that at one stage the decision was taken by the politicians to give the maritime air role to the RAF at the expense of the Navy (a decision later modified).

Officers said they did not notice a difference in social mix of those coming to the school now as compared with a decade ago, but they did notice a difference in professionalism. One of them said: 'There are many social activities going on here and I would not belittle the important aspect of dealing with the whole man, whether it is at officer level, senior-ratings or junior-ratings level. But that is not the main purpose of the Royal Navy. In anything, industry or commerce, social skills count and I suppose that in the services we look to a man's officer-like qualities. There are social attributes which are an enormous help; but we are first and foremost emphasizing professionalism. There are some officers who might be professionals and not care for social activity. Well, it takes all sorts to make a world, and one of the things about the Navy is that it has got a marvellous mix of people.'

This is indicated quite clearly in the mix of people who run the school for the new coordinated naval arts. The captain, I later discovered (he was far too polite to blow his own trumpet when we were face to face), had been equerry to the Queen. He had also been a public schoolboy and could not, by any stretch of the imagination, be mistaken for anything else.

But the commander who was directly running the forty-two-week principal warfare officers' course was a saturnine, quiet-spoken man who had joined the Navy as a rating, become a special duties list officer, transferred to the general list, got into the warfare officers' stream, did a principal warfare officer's course himself at *Dryad*, went to sea, came back to *Dryad* for an advanced warfare officer's course (which no longer exists), went to the guided missile destroyer HMS *Fife*, then drove an offshore patrol vessel, HMS *Lindisfarne*. When I met him he had almost completed his three years' service at

Dryad and would be, he said, going to be officer in charge of the Operations Evaluation Group at Northwood, working for the commander-in-chief.

Obviously he was a professional of quite a different type to the captain, one whose technical skills gave him a quiet confidence among ex-public schoolboy officers; and one who perhaps understood more about the fears and difficulties experienced by less socially exalted or less immediately confident types than could be understood by his public-school colleagues.

'The person who comes out of the course best,' he told me, 'is the one who has had previous operations room experience prior to the course – normally an aircraft controller. Frigate navigation officers and ex-small-ship commanding officers normally succeed. Officers who haven't served in frigates or haven't had operations room experience tend to come off worst; but personality, as distinct from technical experience, does play a part in this. The quiet introvert has to work harder to complete his course successfully, because he is the leader of the whole operations room and has to get these men to work for him – it is all communication.'

Students on the principal warfare officers' course, those who will be the leaders of the ship's electronic brain, have their course divided into four 'modules'. First there is eight weeks of technological training, a major part of it on computers, then twenty-one weeks of common training for all warfare officers, then nine weeks of streamed-time training for above-water, underwater, or communications specialists, and finally four weeks of common training and assessment.

The failure rate is about 10 per cent. It used to be lower than that. I asked the commander why more people now failed. 'Because we have changed the course from all-common training to partly streamed training, which is more specialized. There are two mid-course assessments before a final assessment at the end of the course; failures are taken off the course. We are producing specialists earlier than we previously produced them – three years earlier. It *is* altogether a good thing. You don't really lose anything in terms of being a basic sailor.'

The commander said he supervised the training of eleven courses over a two-year period, taking a maximum of sixteen students and a minimum of eight. All were seaman officers with about eight years' experience, ranging from those with four years' service as a lieutenant up to two years as a lieutenant-commander. The object was to train a man who could be on watch and was able to take all necessary action if the ship hit trouble.

'Unless you carry out the *initial* reactions correctly, the ship will stand a fairly good chance of being sunk,' said the commander. 'In the old days, you may have had six different officers in the operations room, but none of them with the overall experience and knowledge to fight the ship if that was necessary before the captain could be summoned.'

The lieutenant-commander who was whirling me through the school underlined the point. 'Queen's Regulations were changed to give the principal warfare officer the authority to open fire without telling the captain. This change was introduced in 1974. They *inform* the captain of what they have done, rather than asking his permission to do it. We are talking about people who are lieutenants, occasionally lieutenant-commanders.' Some of his colleagues insisted that in an emergency an officer of the watch could always have acted first and asked permission afterwards *in practice*; it was just that in 1974 the Queen's Regulations had made the specific point and regularized the position for the principal warfare officer.

Officers come to the school in four main categories. First, sub-lieutenants aged twenty and over if non-graduates, twenty-four or over if graduates, come to be trained as officers of the watch, who need to know what is going on in the operations room; second, warfare officers who will fight the ship; third, warfare officers acquiring additional knowledge before a second principal warfare officer job as specialists and, fourth, commanding officers who need a thirteen-week warfare refresher, perhaps because they have been, as the lieutenant-commander put it, 'pushing a desk somewhere while the threat has changed, the equipment has changed; *this* course is slanted to the specific ship to which the commanding officer is going.'

The school trains 1,200 officers and 4,600 ratings a year, and on any particular day there are probably in the school some two hundred officers and five hundred ratings on courses. They are taught by a staff of 140 officers, including two Americans, three Canadians, two Dutchmen and one Australian; and some five hundred ratings, of whom one hundred and fifty are Women's Royal Naval Service. The school has trained many Australian officers and some New Zealand officers.

The young ratings' career course at the School of Maritime Operations comes after the first basic training at HMS *Raleigh*, where they have been taught about living in a warship, sailing and discipline. The young ratings first come for their basic operator's course, which teaches just enough to get them to sea quickly – most, after all, have joined to see the sea, not the inside of more classrooms.

'Within six months of joining they will be in their first ship,' said the lieutenant-commander. 'They will do one or two jobs at sea, and their final examinations at sea. Providing they have satisfied their ship's officers that they are up to the standard required and passed a written examination, they come here again for leading-seaman courses, and then they go into the dummy operations room.'

There are in fact half a dozen dummy operations rooms at HMS *Dryad*, or were at the time I was visiting; such is the pace of change in the Navy that there may be even more by now. There was an exact replica of the operations room of a Type 42 destroyer; a 'Leander' frigate (the one with Exocets), an Ikara 'Leander' frigate, a Type 21 'Amazon' frigate and a Type 22 'Boxer' frigate. And there was an empty room, which will eventually be the dummy operations room for the new Type 23 frigate, which at that time was not due to be at sea for another four to six years. But the School of Maritime Operations was making its plans already – an example of the foresight now necessary.

Officers had warned me, 'We are heavily into computers here.' And so it proved.

Even at the most basic layer of training, young ratings have to learn what are called basic injections – requests for information and instructions to the computer, fed into the electronics through a simplified keyboard. The rating is expected to ask the computer the right questions, and to get the right answers. He may have to ask, 'What is the bearing and distance of that ship on the radar screen?' He may also have a sort of television input, and will have to ask the computer questions about what he sees on that. If he wants to tell the computer to do something more active, the injections become more complicated. Having mastered the basic keyboard, the rating will learn how to compile what is referred to as a 'picture', meaning, roughly, an exact map of what the ship is encountering. If the computer says it is faced with a Drumtilt – a form of Soviet radar with attached guns – the young rating is supposed to *know* what Russian ship has that equipment and to build his picture accordingly.

To watch very young ratings processing the basic information that reaches a warship is a thought-provoking business. 'If you have labelled one of your own fighters as an enemy bomber, you will shoot down one of your own aircraft, so team work is vital,' an instructor told me.

A lieutenant-commander, in one of the two remaining wartime concrete huts, explained to me the thinking behind the Royal Navy's use of very young ratings to process the basic intelligence about what the ship is facing. He was the staff officer, electronic warfare, and he rattled off a string of electronic tasks the rating was expected to deal with, including electronic counter-measures, and electronic counter-counter measures. 'We get a young chap from *Raleigh*, and have eight weeks to teach him how to become an operator. We are talking about the seventeen-and-a-half to twenty age group. We simulate situations in which he might find himself. It is probably a boy of about eighteen who will spot the enemy missile first. It is a very important job, though we have a very young man doing it. He would have all the radar signals of other people coming into his head-set. He would spend twelve hours a day at this, the prime warning aid in electronic warfare.'

My manner must have revealed that, as an inquiring civilian, I was rather cautious about sharing his enthusiasm about the prime warning aid being an eighteen-year old.

'Oh yes,' insisted the lieutenant-commander, 'you are relying on his judgement. The machine is assisting him, but the machine can never replace the human operator in the near future. He will have 120 signals to deal with. On the way to the Falklands, for instance, he would study friendly radar, Argentine radar and Soviet radar. It takes this course, plus six months at sea, before he is a fully operational operator. When in harbour he still does the traditional seaman's work on the upper deck and keeps the ship clean and maintained.'

Not all navies use such junior ratings at the sharp end of the electronics game – the first link between an enemy presence and the awareness of it on his own ship. Some navies no more wealthy than the Royal Navy use senior ratings to do the job, which to the civilian mind must seem a sensible use of the extra pay that must be spent on the senior man. But the Royal Navy does not look upon its use of junior ratings at the sharp end as mere economy; it makes a virtue of it.

'The more you require of a man, the more he can do,' said the lieutenant-commander.

Was there any other reason?

'We have *always* had junior ratings.'

Wasn't this dangerous conservatism in the electronics age? 'No,' said the lieutenant-commander. 'It works. By the time he gets to sea, he is well ahead of other navies, because he has been doing nothing else but study the process. And next to him in the operations room will be a leading seaman in his early twenties, who is co-ordinating the effort of the ship. You are talking about a very educated young man, who has a great deal of ability with audio-visual toys, and who is extremely well motivated.'

After watching a number of ratings in a simulated war in one of a series of dark blue caravans called an anti-submarine universal attack trainer, I saw that most of them were having surges of adrenalin rather than the headaches I might have expected. The ratings had already acquired their keyboard skills and were facing a 'simple' war environment as an intermediate stage to the practice in the dummy operations room itself. The trainer simulated two ships, two helicopters, two submarines, four sunken ships and five different sorts of Russian submarines – Juliet, November, Victor, Foxtrot and Yankee as they are known in NATO parlance.

The ratings were doing an anti-submarine exercise, tracking a submarine notionally off Portland in Dorset, scrambling the Wasp helicopters from their own notional ship (an Ikara-fitted 'Leander' frigate). Next week they would be doing a limited war exercise. And if that went well, the following week they would be doing what is described as a 'Free Play War'. Even now they were visibly excited by the atmosphere, as if every one of their senses had been speeded up as they plotted five ships, a submarine moving in and intense electronic activity going on all the while. A lieutenant-commander watching with me assured me that the adrenalin on these occasions would flow almost as strongly as in the real thing.

But such pressures do occasionally create problems for ratings at the School of Maritime Operations, which is one of the reasons why they are given an uncle figure while they are there.

I met him in a part of the school unsympathetically called Flint Block – a bearded lieutenant-commander with a gentle voice and a background which included rising from being a rating. Stuck above the window of his office, facing his desk so that he could always see it, was a cardboard sheet with a maxim written on it in permanent and prominent blue ink. It read: 'It is wrong to coerce young people into opinions, but it is our duty to impel them into experiences.'

The lieutenant-commander evidently had a sense of humour as well as compassion. 'I talk to their mums and dads if necessary,' he said. 'I allocate them to their particular courses, and send them off when they have finished their courses. They have been in the Navy only six to eight weeks and they come for a ten-week or eight-week course. Sometimes they come from their basic training when there is no course immediately available here, so we send them to other places to use the time. Perhaps to the Royal Tournament. They look over HMS *Victory*, they look over the War Museum. They go to other ships, and some have the opportunity to sail in sea-training yachts. They are all eager to get the experience, so we have little trouble.'

What did he find himself talking to mums and dads about? 'Sometimes mum rings up and says, "Is he getting his food?" And sometimes they ring up and say, "My son says he is a bit homesick." It is not a common occurrence. Sometimes *I* ring mums and dads when the ratings are not doing very well, and say, "Can you give him some encouragement?" I am a housemaster, basically. I talk to their bank if they have financial problems. If their grandma dies, we arrange things so they can go home to the funeral, if possible. We do have occasional ones with more than two grandmothers, but it is very rare.'

Plainly the lieutenant-commander was a seasoned professional rather than a young high-flyer. He thought that anyone doing this job needed to be older than average, so that they knew a lot about naval life, and a lot about the dodges that some ratings could try on.

'Some of the young lads today are really fly,' said the lieutenant-commander. 'I mean that in both the good and bad senses of the phrase. Most of the lads these days are well educated – certainly more so than I was when I joined in 1952. You get more questioning, obviously, of basic facts; the main premises of the job. They look at these more carefully than I would have done.'

But, added the lieutenant-commander drily, intelligence and academic ability didn't always go hand-in-hand with common sense. That was very much the case: 'I find the more intelligent some of them are, the less common sense they have. I put it down partly to the fact that at home they have attention; for some time they have been molly-coddled. Mum has done all the ironing and so it is more of a culture shock for them. Probably some of the officers are the same.'

Some officers feel that though officer selection is tough enough, it is too easy for ratings to take the step into the Navy. The official view is that they are wrong, but I did hear the view expressed.

Flint Block itself is purely residential and administrative much of the time. The entrants are reminded about pay, hygiene and discipline. This takes a week and they then go on to courses if such courses are immediately available. Flint Block will hold between 140 and 170 young ratings, all of whom are personally addressed by the captain, who tells them that a modern warship depends on the junior seaman on the operations room keyboard, and that they must get it right first time.

Perhaps surprisingly, the failure rate is encouragingly low. It is between only 0.5 per cent and 1 per cent.

There are two main reasons for dropping out of the courses. The first is that the rating can't stand being away from home, wants to grow his hair longer and generally comes to the conclusion that the grass is greener in the next field. The next, unsurprisingly, is that he can't stay on top of the technological processes.

'They can't see something from other people's point of view,' put in a lieutenant-commander sitting in on the conversation. 'This is a barrier to communication. The Navy gets rid of them.'

The gentle-voiced lieutenant-commander did not reproduce this rather sharp note in his further comments. 'Occasionally we do have a lad who can't hack the technology. Or he is, to put it plainly, unhygienic and cannot maintain a standard of personal and kit cleanliness. Or he can't maintain his financial affairs, and becomes an embarrassment as he runs up debts. After talking to the bank several times, we may get to a point where it simply is not cost-effective to put any more time or effort into the lad. Usually that point comes when the bank has withdrawn its facilities. The worst ones are those who have all these problems combined. We are rather cutting our own throats by having them in the Navy.'

But, said the patient lieutenant-commander, it was always necessary to remember that one was dealing with people who were very young – the age range being between sixteen-and-a-half and twenty-six, with most aged between seventeen and twenty.

In conversations with officers generally at the School of Maritime Operations, pride in the technology they were teaching such young men to handle cropped up time and time again. 'The US navy has 600 ships, only thirty per cent computerized,' said one instructor. 'The United Kingdom has 200 ships, of which seventy per cent are computerized. We tend to be up to date. I remember reading, even ten years ago, that while ships of the Russian navy were on average fifteen years old, and those in the US navy fifteen years old, those in the Royal Navy were only nine years old.'

And the instructors were also vocal in praise of the invention of the principal warfare officer. Time and time again, the point was hammered home: that in the electronic age, the power to respond to a threat must be instantaneous, or as near instantaneous as electronic and human brains can make it.

'In the old days,' said one instructor over a 'Russian' service lunch in the wardroom (you help yourself from the vegetable dishes, which are brought around by ratings, instead of being helped), 'it was accepted that your ship would only fight when it was already at action stations. But with the new speed of the threat, it was recognized that you might be in a position where you had to fight your ship *before* you were at action stations, with the captain probably not there. Specialist officers on the old lines were not competent to do it. So the principal warfare officer takes in the skills of the many types of officers, including the gunnery officers, the torpedo and anti-submarine officers. A gunnery officer trying his best to hunt a submarine on his own until the rest of the team got to the operations room just didn't work well. The change in practice recognized a situation that already existed, and which we had to face.'

And he went off at the double, saying over his shoulder (I think) that he was off to play a game of cricket. I wouldn't have liked to have to face his bowling.

★

It is entirely appropriate that the School of Maritime Operations, being a temple to the god of the electronics age, should play host (as it were) to another school with an even more measured and considered atmosphere than the School of Maritime Operations itself.

Among the other concrete and steel buildings, and indistinguishable from them except for the words on the fascia, is the Maritime Tactical School. It is a rather plain name for a building which is at once a place of education and a think tank that supplies the fruits of high-calibre brains to the fleet at various times, especially in times of emergency.

The captain in charge of the school was a clean-shaven white-haired man who would have looked as much at home in a university as in the Navy. He told me that the school's business was brains, that it was separate from the School of Maritime Operations because it had a different job – it operated in support of the fleet, but 40 per cent of its life was spent on being a think tank in the medium or long term, to look ten to fifteen years ahead. 'Because the level of education we have is at the commanding-officer-and-above level, we are used here as a forum for symposia involving the fleet staff,' he said. 'We are really a sort of college of maritime warfare business and not in the mainstream of training as such.'

The captain regretted that I could not sit in on a wargame that was going on at that time in the school with some of the Navy's best brains: security forbade it. But I could go into the school theatre and be thoroughly briefed by the captain's number-two, a commander with a bright manner and a long pointer.

Tactics, pointed out the commander, were defined as 'disposing ships and aircraft for and in battle and the employment of their weapons and sensors'. That was what the school was all about. Under the captain as director, there were twelve 'executives' of every sort of command experience, all subspecialists in their own right, plus a support team which enabled the team to be self-sustaining. They worked and functioned as one unit.

'But we are educated from the top,' said the commander. 'We are not really a school as such; it is more like a college of learning. Hopefully, we have intellectually stretching debate, and that is how we play a lot of our alleged instruction. It doesn't make sense merely to stand up and pontificate, as I am doing now.'

Evidently shades of gentle *self*-mockery were permitted in the Maritime Tactical School. Perhaps a degree of humour is an essential in a school which includes among its 500 students a year officers of all ages and experience, from junior lieutenants in their early twenties to flag officers of vice-admiral rank. Ceaseless seriousness in such assorted circumstances, one feels, would produce intellectual constipation of a very uncomfortable and unrewarding kind.

The general aims are to monitor the sea experience in the NATO alliance, to study the requirement, and to evolve guidance on the form and spread of forces. There are four courses a year, each of four weeks' duration. Within each course, the students have a formal lecture; what is called a 'Tactical Floor Problem' (in which a sort of deadly chess is played out on a squared floor surface) and then a game, in which rival plans are produced, carried through and compared.

'We are hanging our hats on the pegs of the separate warfare disciplines,' said the commander. 'The first week, it is command principles – for example electronic warfare. Then we go on to anti-submarine warfare, surface warfare, anti-air warfare, the inshore battle, rules of engagement, and then the multi-threat battle in the north-east Atlantic, with a final game from rising tension into war.'

The school has become quite an intellectual powerhouse of NATO and the West as a whole. In the ten-year period from 1973 to 1983, 1,682 British officers passed through: including 1,230 from the Royal Navy, 395 from the Royal Air Force, sixteen civilians, twenty-five from the Royal Naval Reserve, three from the WRNS, and one from the WRAF. But there was also an impressive number from countries outside the United Kingdom. Top of the list was the Netherlands with 179, next Germany with 142, then Australia with ninety-seven, Canada with ninety-six, Denmark with eighty-eight, Norway with eighty-six, the USA with thirty-two, New Zealand with twenty-eight, Portugal with twenty-five, Belgium with twenty-two, Greece with sixteen, Turkey with seven, and France (unsurprisingly, in view of her generally ambiguous attitude to Western defence) with a modest three.

At the invitation of the Navy Department of the Ministry of Defence, the school discharges what is called its tactical development function. The school's instructors go every year to the US War College at Newport, Rhode Island, where they contribute as analysts, and monitor a major NATO paper on some aspect of defence. The USA is said to be extremely interested in the atmosphere and methods of the Maritime Tactical School; and, at the time I visited it, it was expected that the USA would in fact set one up on rather similar lines. Later the USA established several.

I asked the director what ideas produced by the school, acting as a think tank, had been actually taken up. I got the tart answer, 'Unlike with Number 10 Downing Street's think tank, the naval staff tend to introduce what is recommended. They produce a report which is then issued by the naval staff. All we do is prepare it, think it through and suggest proposed actions. Last year's study produced a number of recommendations on how long-range operations should be conducted. We provided a fleet instruction on how to conduct ships and issued the captain of the squadron with a copy of that. It is now coming out as doctrine. What communications ships should have now and in the future. What priority for procurement of equipment. And so on.'

In the Falklands conflict, he told me, the school adopted its war role. This was to move up to the Commander-in-Chief's headquarters at Northwood and support the Commander-in-Chief as a planning staff.

Decisions and the intellectual analysis behind them have to be made (and re-made) in the real world, after they have been made at the Maritime Tactical School. Everyone who is going to command a ship comes through the Maritime Tactical School and faces threats in theory before he faces the chance of having to confront them in practice.

'The prime student is the commanding officer going to sea,' the director told me. 'It is viewed as an essential part of his preparation. I don't find anyone ever saying, "I don't need it." I have been a student six times myself. It is the only time in your career when you have the opportunity to spend a month thinking about war and preparing your mind for what you would do; how you would dispose your forces in such a way that you would win. We are not teaching men to drive a ship or fire a gun – that is the School of Maritime Operations' problem. We are talking about where to dispose your ships, where to deploy them to win. It is a wargame, if you like. We are gaming.'

What could a wargame consist of specifically, I asked. 'Oh, the Battle of the North Atlantic, the Persian Gulf problem, the Lebanon; these sort of operations. We discuss factors that affect decisions in the use of our forces and the relative importance of various assets. Occasionally we discuss a whole catastrophe in the NATO area – the most complex one that could be envisaged. Not Northern Ireland, except when we patrol there; but in the early 1970s we looked at the Cod War and did a lot of work on the best way to handle it. We made recommendations. They went to the Ministry of Defence, and they were implemented.'

I was admitted only briefly to the tactical floor, so the exact nature of the proceedings remained unknown to me, except in very general terms. The floor, about twenty feet by twenty feet, consisted of a blackboard which was in fact blue, with squares made up of white lines – rather like a one-colour chess board. It was a lecture theatre, in which the seats were distributed round the walls – except for one line of ten which was directly alongside the board itself. On this line of chairs sat ten commanding officers, rather like a jury, except the answers they were expected to come up with in the course of a two-hour session were concerned with how to dispose aircraft and other 'assets' in responding to a threat.

The session was in the charge of a Phantom expert, a man who happened to have been a warfare officer on HMS *Glamorgan*. On the blackboard were yellow and pink cut-outs of planes and other assets, to be moved on the suggestion of the 'syndicate' of ten men, while the Phantom expert made chiding but helpful remarks: 'What we have here is a threat, but we don't yet know what it is. If I keep four of my fighters airborne now, I am putting all my eggs in one basket.'

'We are encouraged to set the solutions of the syndicate against other syndicates,' said the director, politely edging me away from the wargame. 'A syndicate would be between six and ten, balanced for expertise. Don't forget, our business is brains.'

It would not be easy to forget. As I left HMS *Dryad*, the captain in charge of the School of Maritime Operations underlined the point for me. 'We turn away four out of five at the recruiting office, but the boys we *do* get never cease to impress me. They were brought up in the computer age.'

Then, with a burst of inter-service rivalry, he added, 'It is professionally and technologically pretty high grade stuff in comparison with the equivalent in the British Army. It is difficult to make a direct comparison, which you should try to avoid from now on. When it comes to fighting a ship, it is so different to the threat in Europe, that I find it difficult to make comparisons at all.'

The pride of the Navy had spoken. As I bade my final farewells, in turn being warned that *Dryad*'s activities changed so fast that what was true one day might not be true the next, I made politic promises never publicly to imply that the modern Royal Navy was comparable with *anything* else. In view of what I had seen, the promise was not total hypocrisy.

PART III

MAKING CONTACT WITH THE REST OF US

18

CIVILIANS OF THE SEA

'Our main role is minesweeping – we are trying to remove an offensive instrument that someone else has put down. I think there is no doubt it is much easier to put over a defensive organization to men and wives than a gung-ho, fix-bayonets-and-give-them-one-in-the-guts sort of thing. It is a different ethos.'

– Chief staff officer (Reserves) to the Commander-in-Chief, Naval Home Command.

'Reserves are paid. If you didn't get paid, you would lose a lot of people now. If you pay people in the Reserve, you get better people. If you don't pay, you get people who just want to wear some sort of uniform.'

– Lieutenant in Royal Naval Reserve.

It takes all sorts – even the most unlikely – to make the Royal Naval Reserve. As the fast patrol ship HMS *Hunter* left Portsmouth naval base, lifted her bows and sped into the choppy Solent at over twenty knots, the radio operator was up on deck shifting the ensign to the sea position on the bridge. A few hours ago he had been busy putting stainless steel acupuncture needles into the arms of two of his Harley Street district patients, in an effort to cure their sinus trouble.

The professional acupuncturist's appearance, given his gold-framed National Health spectacles, was rather studious. He would have passed more easily as a polytechnic lecturer than a naval man. But already he was at home in this grey centre of spray, whose commanding officer had only just torn himself away from his insurance broker's office in the City, and whose coxswain was more used to sitting behind a Whitehall desk.

The thirty-one-year-old acupuncturist was one of the 5,300 people forming the Royal Naval Reserve, now in the process of being increased to 7,800 in a reversal of past winding-down philosophies. He was under training in HMS *Hunter* for a fortnight, sharing a cabin with three other Reserve seamen and confessing to feeling a bit cramped.

'Cramped?' shouted the coxswain above the thudding sea, as the ship hurled itself towards the Isle of Wight. 'We have to accept the fact that for the fortnight we are aboard, we will be living out of a suitcase. As a matter of fact, *I* am living out of an OHMS envelope – a big one, admittedly.'

Respectful silence reigned. The coxswain had been in the Royal Naval Reserve for twenty-one years, the acupuncturing radio operator for only four months. Both men, in their different ways, had obviously been equally keen to join the naval force whose main role in war would be to man the minesweepers and control Merchant Navy convoys.

The object of training aboard HMS *Hunter*, a 'Tracker' class ship, was less ambitious: it was to give the four newcomers to the Reserve their basic training in seamanship. They were working from Southampton but made a detour to Portsmouth to pick me up. The detour had also, said the commanding officer, given the men practice in the proper procedure – piped salutes and so on – which was more important at a place like Portsmouth naval base than at Southampton. I was glad to hear my own contribution to Reserve training had been positive rather than merely passive.

Having got the ship well clear of Portsmouth, the commanding officer, a lieutenant RNR with a cheerfully alert face, a Rolex watch and a commuter's house in Chislehurst, was more free to talk about the chain of circumstances that had led him into adopting the recruiting slogans of the Royal

Naval Reserve: 'Make Your Time Maritime' and 'Add Navy To Your Life'.

'I was in the Royal Navy, training to be a helicopter pilot,' he shouted above the roar of the engines, the thudding of the waves and the hiss of the spray. 'I joined when the Conservative government was in. Then a Labour one said there would be *no* Fleet Air Arm after 1982. So they took only 60 per cent of those on my course, and I wasn't among them. They said, "You can continue your commission as a seaman officer or go outside." I decided to go outside. And then a different government got back in, and it all changed again.'

But by that time, the lieutenant had decided that his connection with the Navy would be through the Reserve. This would be demanding enough for a man now in middle management, and with a wife and two children to consider.

'The strange thing,' shouted the lieutenant, 'is that at the very time the Navy are expecting more and more of you, even requiring you to captain a ship, you have more responsibility in civilian life, too. My wife reacts very well to my Reserve activities, but then I was doing it before I met her – it is part of what she married, really.'

HMS *Hunter* was now going at the maximum permitted speed, with the coxswain – the man from a Ministry of Defence desk – at the wheel. He had jammed himself firmly against the grille beneath his feet and the vertical grille behind his back, but he had not actually tied himself in with the webbing belts. He said it was rough, but not *that* rough.

The coxswain was a man who could easily have impersonated the playwright Samuel Beckett: a hawkish face made more steely by black metal spectacles. The hands gripping the ship's wheel could have been lined with steel.

Only when he had been relieved at the wheel by one of the four beginners could he explain his route into the Royal Naval Reserve. 'I couldn't get into the RAF. I wanted to go in an aircrew, but I was about seventeen or eighteen and I had a terrible stutter. Same thing when I applied to join the Royal

Navy. I haven't still got the stutter – I think the Royal Naval Reserve cured that.'

He had seen attitudes in the Reserve change greatly in the twenty-one years he had been involved. It was nothing like as casual as it used to be. More professionalism had come into it, which was good; but a lot of the fun had gone out of it, which was not so good. Exercises were now more professional in the range of evolutions – practices – carried out. He had once been in the Mediterranean in the hot weather when the ship had been closed down in chemical warfare defence. He had spent the whole morning, some four hours, in a protective suit and respirator. He couldn't hear the captain on the bridge and the captain couldn't hear him in the wheel-house. Four hours of that had been enough – 'we each lost half a stone that morning'. And at the time of the Falklands crisis, their ship had been near Sicily and he had wondered, 'Do we go left to Ascension Island or right to the United Kingdom?' In fact the ship turned right for the UK – the Reserve was not mobilized for the Falklands though some individuals were used – but the excitement had been intense.

The coxswain had a distinctly military background. His father had been in the Army, his mother had been in the Army and some uncles and cousins had also been in the Army. It was easy to understand how that stutter must have affected his morale and how he had fought back against it by joining the Royal Naval Reserve.

But what about his wife and children? Did *they* understand?

'They think,' said the coxswain, 'that it is terrific. I used to do a lot of sailing and mountaineering. When we got married, I couldn't afford mountaineering and sailing. With the Royal Naval Reserve, it doesn't cost you anything, and you get paid. Admittedly the payment is not high, but shall we say I am not running at a loss. My wife actually wanted to join too, but I'm not going to let her become involved with a lot of *matelots*!'

If the latter sentiment might be described by some as

chauvinism, the point about the modest pay was incontestable. Opinion is divided in the Reserve about whether the pay is a significant factor in the motivation of the men and women of the Reserve; but no one regards it as a lavish waste of the taxpayer's money.

The Reserves are divided into five lists. List One is for professional sea-going Merchant Navy officers, who are required to do fourteen days a year with the Reserve. List Two is the air branch, who do seventeen days a year. List Three is the main one, for control of shipping officers, seamen and communications officers, who do fourteen days a year, plus one hundred hour-long drills. Completion of this earns them a tax-free bounty of £450 plus a uniform allowance. List Four is for professionals such as doctors and dentists, who do a fortnight's paid training a year, plus fifty hour-long drills. They get only *half* the £450 bounty. List Five covers people from any of the previous lists who are either fully trained or cannot afford the time to spend more than a fortnight every two years – for which they get a bounty of £150.

Some senior officers say that whatever the motivation that makes people join the Reserve, it is certainly not money. But the commanding officer of HMS *Hunter* said he thought money *was* important; without it, you would get an inferior sort of recruit, one in love with a uniform rather than wanting to do a serious job. 'But I can't say I did it for the money,' he said as the ship took a bearing from Yarborough Monument on the chalky skyline of the Isle of Wight, 'though the money helps. There is a great social side to it. If you get paid, it is a bonus.'

Only one man aboard cheerfully admitted that money was *very* important to him. This was the eighteen-year-old midshipman, the son of a Trinity House pilot who had joined the Royal Naval Reserve four months previously, and was now officer of the watch in HMS *Hunter*, busy with his maps and charts on a fibreglass sloping desk on the port side of the upper deck. 'I wanted to join the Navy when I was still at school,' he

said. 'But I failed, so I joined the Reserve instead. I am in my
first year at University College, London; I wanted to go to sea,
and the money might come in handy as a supplement to my
grant.'

Eighteen-year olds seeking to augment their modest grants
are plainly *not* to be evaluated as mercenary. It was quite clear
that this cheekily smiling young man was doing it for the fun
rather than the cash.

It was rather demanding fun. H M S *Hunter* had now reached
Sandown Bay, where the main business of the day would be
done. This was practising how to let go and weigh the anchor,
an evolution which is not as easy as it appears, especially when
those taking part are trying it for the first time. The ship eased
back from the twenty knots or so which had been deliberately
maintained so that the usual speed of a minesweeper – fifteen
knots – would seem *slow*. Two of the tyro seamen went
forward to the anchor winch as the ship took up its bearing on
a building on Sandown Bay.

'Captain,' demanded one of the young officers, 'is this a
dummy run or the real thing?'

'You don't need a dummy run, do you? No, this is for real.'
The commanding officer turned to me and said wryly, 'If this
works, since it's the first time they've tried it, I shall be
amazed.'

He was to be amazed; but only after a slight expenditure
of time. To make the anchor hold properly in the seabed,
the seamen had to bounce on the cable more than once, winding it out and then in again repeatedly. Time visibly began
to hang heavily for the hawk-faced coxswain. 'With all the
difficulties of Reserve life,' he said, 'especially the cramped
conditions on a ship like this, you can do two things. You
can either throw your hand in, or have a bloody good laugh
about it, and press on. You can't take some things too seriously or you would end up throwing granny down the
stairs . . . Ah! Hallelujah! We've arrived! Bloody good for a
first time, sir!'

'Yes,' riposted the commanding officer drily, 'but the trick is getting the anchor back again.'

While *Hunter* was at anchor, there was a brief pause for lunch. I sought out the acupuncturist, improbably in the ratings' mess, to explore his naval motives. For a man who looked like an intellectual, he was surprisingly defensive about his acupuncture techniques, surprisingly at ease about his new naval connection.

'In civilian life,' he said, 'I am treating small intestines and hearts, lungs and colons, sticking needles in the arms and legs, the head, the neck. I read the colours in people's faces and their smell. With my last two patients before I came here, I stuck the needles in about one millimetre deep and turned them clockwise, for tonification treatment as opposed to sedation. What are you going to write about this, because I *am* rather defensive about it?'

I assured him that I was not all against non-conventional medicine and had no desire to ridicule it. But what had persuaded him to take a step in an entirely different direction for a part-time activity?

'I joined the Royal Naval Reserve for the adventure,' he said. 'It means breaking away *and* getting paid for it. There aren't many hobbies which are so different. I have a girlfriend, and she is a bit blasé about it. She would not join herself but has no objection to my doing it. She is not CND, but perhaps a bit arty, shall we say? As far as I am concerned, I am doing it for the adventure and excitement. As far as service in the Navy itself is concerned, if I were called upon to serve, I would; but I hope it would not be necessary. I do not particularly want to go to war.'

The man sitting next to the acupuncturist was an eighteen-year-old London bus conductor who had volunteered to act as chef for the fortnight. He thought the Royal Naval Reserve was something he 'got more out of' than conducting a bus, though some of his mates kidded him that he'd joined because the Army wouldn't take him. Red-faced and overweight, the

chef cheerfully admitted that the Army wouldn't take him. 'I
wanted to be a paratrooper, but the doctor advised me not to
go into the Army. My eyes are okay, but I would probably
fail the eye test, and I did have chest problems when I was
younger.'

The chief of the boat – the engineer-electrician – was the
oldest man aboard. He was forty-four. He was philosophical
about the corned beef and salad he was eating. He was still
single, he said; he had been thirteen years in the Royal Navy
and had then joined the Royal Naval Reserve. That was ten
years ago.

Why had he wanted to carry on with the naval connection?
'I had a five-year break before I came into the Royal Naval
Reserve,' said the small, barrel-chested veteran. 'At first when
you leave, you are glad to get away from it. But then you miss
the life. I think what I missed most was the travel and the life
of the mess deck. Once you get over the newness of civilian
life, it is not quite as good as service life in many respects. You
tend to be a lot more friendly in the Navy than you would be
in civilian life. You tend to rely on someone in the ship in a
way you wouldn't do in a civilian job.'

The chief bosun's mate – the senior seaman on board – was
described, as always, as the 'Buffer'. He was a man of twenty-
six with a fair beard, gold spectacles and a civilian job as a
systems analyst for a bank. He was responsible for safety on the
exposed upper deck, for which his spectacles were not regarded
as being a disbarment, as they had been when he had tried to
join the Royal Navy itself.

Soon he was busy bouncing on the anchor chain again, and
the first lieutenant, a thirty-two-year-old employee of the
treasurer's department of an American firm of commodity
brokers in the City of London, was doing the navigation because the midshipman was still regarded as rather too green to
cope with every eventuality.

The shore authorities had told me there would be no time
for man-overboard drills as well as anchoring drills; but the

ebullient commanding officer demonstrated one for my benefit. A blue buoy was thrown overboard. One of the seamen
put the ship about. After ten minutes of stopping, starting and
circling – accompanied by much thrusting of long and short
boat-hooks – the blue buoy was retrieved. It was a fine if cold
May. Had it been an icy December, the 'man overboard' would
have been dead from the cold twice over. But the coxswain
pointed out that most of the time had been used in trying to
spear the eyelet on the buoy with the boat-hook – a problem
that would not present itself with a real man overboard.

The commanding officer, taking control himself as HMS
Hunter eased her way back into the Solent at the end of the
exercises, professed himself fairly satisfied with the new intake.
The thirty-one-year-old merchant banker whom the commanding officer had just relieved at the wheel said philoso-
phically that even as an able seaman in the Royal Naval Reserve, you met a greater variety of people and situations than
you did when drawing up currency-exchange agreements.

'What does it feel like,' I asked him, 'as a manager in your
firm, when you have to call people "Sir" in the Royal Naval
Reserve?'

'It depends on the person you are calling sir,' was the immediate response. Plainly such a man would *not* be likely to be as
philosophical if he considered the men of the Reserve to be
overgrown schoolboys playing with boats. His presence was
testimony enough – if any had been still needed – that the
Royal Naval Reserve is a serious part of Britain's defences in
time of peace and war.

There is testimony of a different sort. The Royal Navy is
making a very tangible sign that it takes the Reserve seriously
by giving it eleven brand new and highly sophisticated ships
for its minesweeping tasks. The 'River' class Fleet Minesweeper
is capable of sweeping deep-laid mines which the former ships
could not handle. All eleven are due to be in action from the
end of 1986. They take account of the enormous strides in
minelaying techniques since the Second World War. Now-

adays mines are not necessarily near the surface, ready to strike a ship's hull. They can be laid deep to explode not necessarily under the first ship to pass, but possibly under the tenth or the twentieth. Mines can be laid by aircraft or merchant ships. All these sophistications mean that the task of minesweeping is both more difficult and more important.

One new 'River' class minesweeper will go to each of the eleven divisions of the Reserve, all situated by the sea with the exception of London. A twelfth will be manned by the Royal Navy, who will use it with what officers call 'a buddy-buddy system of training' with the Royal Naval Reserve. It is hoped that the experience of the Royal Navy will rub off on the Royal Naval Reserve in this training.

The new 'River' class will replace the old wooden 'Ton' class, which have served the Royal Naval Reserve well in the past. But the new ships and equipment are expected to be a major attraction in recruiting people into the Royal Naval Reserve and keeping them. The head of the Reserve, the Chief Staff Officer (Reserves) to the Commander-in-Chief, Naval Home Command, who is head of the Reserves, a bearded and businesslike man who found it easier to talk in civilian terms than many naval officers, told me that recruiting had in the past been made more difficult by the economy measures of the 1970s and the talk of reducing the number of minesweepers.

'All that doesn't help recruiting or retention, because no one wants to join an organization which is demonstrably reducing in scope,' he told me. 'We are talking here about a volunteer ethos – the bounty is a maximum of £450 a year. We have recently done a survey on why they join and why they go. They join basically because they feel they would like to do something for the country, though they don't want to join the service full-time because of professional or other commitments. They like to be part of our maritime heritage. This was the reason this country was able to attract men off the streets of the heartland of Birmingham, and turn them from butchers to fore-topmen in the Napoleonic wars.'

There was objective evidence for the captain's optimism. At the time I met him, the Reserve had just completed one of a new series of twice-yearly recruiting campaigns. It had received more inquiries than it had received for a decade. The number of replies was 4,500. Although the captain said he would be surprised if they recruited more than one in twenty of the people who had replied, it was counted as an encouraging victory. Two hundred and fifty people would be a satisfactory crop from one half-yearly campaign: greater numbers would be welcome but would require greater short-term investment in training facilities.

The fact that minesweeping is involved as the main objective of the Reserve is thought to make recruiting easier: it is a completely *defensive* operation, designed to save lives, not take them.

'It is certainly easier to sell to wives,' said the captain. 'A recruit will say to his wife, "What we are trying to do is to make sure that, if there is a war, the shipping routes to bring food and supplies to this country will be kept clear." And that is very true. It always has been true. Nothing has changed. It has always been the name of the game, keeping the shipping routes clear – 90 per cent of our food comes to us by sea. If I were a civilian, I believe I would be able to sell to my wife the concept of actually trying to *save* lives. Unless you can carry your wife with you, you have got nothing.'

But in the past, even if their wives were convinced, some men have chosen to leave the Reserve. There has been the inevitable fall-out of those who recognize they have made a mistake and simply don't like naval work. But there has also been a fall-out of those who cannot be kept motivated. And officers estimate that possibly the most important factor in this waning motivation has been the limited and rather old machinery they have had to use – especially when their private reading must have told them that much better machinery was available on the market.

'I am sure,' said the captain, 'that the new ships and

equipment will sustain motivation. It is an *expanding* business now, and I am very sanguine about the outcome. If response in the last few months is anything to go by, there is a large upsurge of interest in the Royal Naval Reserve. They can see, with modern stuff coming in, that they are taken seriously.'

The theory is that, from the declaration of an emergency, it would take two or three days to get the Reserves into their ships. In a nuclear age, a civilian might be tempted to think that either the war would be over by then, or that many of the men would find it impossible to leave their families and make for their ships.

I put the point to the captain, and got a thoughtful reply. 'Let's be honest about this. We recognize that for all sorts of reasons some people will not be able to turn up. Some people with responsible careers will be travelling outside the United Kingdom for their companies. They may be in Nicaragua or Alice Springs, in the middle of a business conference of crucial importance to their businesses when someone hits the red button. They may not be in a position to join the colours. The manpower of the Royal Naval Reserve makes allowance for that – there is a 10 per cent manning contingency, which is realistic.'

It is estimated that 10 per cent would not meet the call. Some might be sailors reluctant to leave their families for their ship with a war in the offing, some might be surgeons in the middle of London, who thought they were more likely to be needed there. Others might have their own reasons. The Reserve is made up of many civilian occupations, from coalminers to hairdressers, from lawyers to business tycoons. There are many local politicians, though few Members of Parliament, who might be expected to be en route for a nuclear shelter. There are young men with young families, and older men with ailing wives. A 10 per cent fall-out would hardly be surprising.

Normally the age of fifty is goodbye time for men and the Royal Naval Reserve. But the Reserve has to adhere to the principle that rules are for the guidance of wise men and the obedience of fools, by allowing some sprightly volunteers to stay on past this age.

In at least one group, the aviation branch, due to be expanded from fifty strong to one hundred strong in the next few years, the restrictions on age will be rather more strictly applied. At one stage the number of aviators available went down to twenty, partly because the medical standards were so high, partly because recruitment was difficult. The Navy and Whitehall saw the danger in time, and went for a policy of expansion rather than contraction.

'The aviation branch is a marvellous asset,' said the captain. 'They cost us peanuts, they are fully trained men, and they are civilian helicopter pilots in the helicopter industry, all ex-Fleet Air Arm officers who come back to us to do their seventeen days' training a year.'

Naval control of shipping by Reserves is equally important, and involves far more people than the aviation branch, as I discovered when I visited the largest of the eleven regional divisions of the Royal Naval Reserve. London Division was at the time located in two old warships, dating from the First World War, and placed alongside the Embankment at Kings Reach – though the expectation was that headquarters would soon be shifting to shore premises at St Katharine's Dock near Tower Bridge. When I visited the venerable H M S *President* and H M S *Chrysanthemum*, I climbed over the Embankment river wall with businessmen bearing brief cases, trendy City men carrying Harrods plastic bags, and girl secretaries with stylish handbags. It was 6.30 in the evening, the time training starts on Tuesdays and Thursdays.

There was laughter and joking among the five hundred or so members of the London Division. It would have been re-pulsively inhuman in peacetime if this had not been so. But the underlying spirit was serious and the adrenalin was obviously flowing. This was proved by the fire drill, which came only a few days after a fire in Bradford Football Club's stand had killed fifty-six people, and which cleared both the ships in exemplary time.

About one hundred of London Division's personnel are involved in Naval Control of Shipping, which would mean the control of merchant shipping in time of war (when such shipping would not be allowed to wander the precarious oceans at will). The Naval Control of Shipping officer was a forty-nine-year-old ex-Royal Naval man, now running a small company making sectional timber buildings such as sports pavilions and conservatories. Tall, bald and bespectacled, he was giving sober attention to the programme of lectures which is a special feature of Thursday evenings.

'We also have three weekends a year on which we do paper exercises,' he told me. 'We set a scenario and go through the whole gamut of message writing, preparing the sailing orders for merchant ships.'

In time of war, the Naval Control of Shipping personnel would not be at London headquarters. They would be sent to ports round the country, or to alternative sites where control of shipping could be managed if port facilities were not available. In NATO exercises, Reserves are sent out to the billets they would occupy in wartime. These are spread virtually all round the world. Some control personnel remembered with enthusiasm being sent to Hong Kong and Singapore.

Didn't it all seem a little artificial in peacetime, controlling ships that weren't actually there? 'No,' said the Naval Control of Shipping officer emphatically. 'We are able to maintain motivation, because we can do it for real on occasional exercises. From time to time we charter merchant ships, and shove them in convoys. And during peacetime exercises in the actual ports, we go on board merchant ships and brief the masters for a wartime situation. We get a very good reception.'

From the point of view of civilian expertise, the Naval Control of Shipping branch of London Division was an interestingly mixed bag. The second-in-command was a solicitor, the man below him was a local government officer and the administration was done by a Women's Royal Naval Reserve who in civilian life was an air hostess.

The five hundred civilian men and women who nationally make up the Naval Control of Shipping Branch do the work themselves, with hardly any Royal Naval involvement. The only exceptions are the Maritime Trade Faculty, based in H M S *Vernon* at Portsmouth, which conducts two-week courses on shipping control, and the Director of Naval Operations and Trade's department, which concerns itself on a continuing basis with the planning of exercises. The heads of the Reserve try to keep their personnel at the peak of the knowledge obtained at the Maritime Trade Faculty at HMS *Vernon*, and at the peak of efficiency required by the exercises planned by Naval Operations and Trade.

The real difficulties of nautical life help to keep Reserves on their toes. When I was with London Division, the propellers of a tender *Oliver Twist* had snarled up with some loose rope.

The answer was the divers. All divisions have a team, who do practically all that Royal Naval divers do, with the exception of bomb disposal. The London Division's team was in the charge of a lieutenant-commander who, in civilian life, was a curator in the Science Museum at South Kensington, responsible for administering grants to help provincial museums buy old ships and the like.

The diver who went down under the *Oliver Twist* was a laboratory assistant to an education authority, having just graduated. While he was freeing bits of green and blue plastic rope, looking rather like a punk's wig, from the propeller, I talked to his back-up, a British Rail engineer. 'I have always been interested in the Royal Navy, and I began diving when I joined the Reserve two years ago,' he said. 'We have to do a commitment of one hundred and twenty minutes' diving per quarter, but you can do far in excess of that. *All* dives are difficult because of the dangers, but probably the most dangerous I have done were night dives in Portsmouth Harbour, to a ship's bottom. The longest I have ever been down was the fifty-five minutes we have to do as a training dive.'

A sense of responsibility is inculcated very firmly in the Royal Naval Reserve, whether it is on technical matters or the elementary business of deportment. There is no room for amiable asses. Certainly those personnel I came across in London Division were all in responsible jobs in civilian life: the captain ran a firm of silversmiths and cutlers, the liaison officer was a chartered surveyor, and the solitary Royal Naval man involved, a commander whose role was principally advisory and who, in appearance, was indistinguishable from everyone else, told me of the other human professional assets enjoyed by London Division.

'It is the most incredible value for money,' he enthused. 'We have twenty-two doctors and four or five dentists. They familiarize themselves with the Navy. For very little outlay, we then have some tremendous experience we can call on in the Navy in time of war. In the Falklands campaign they were not recalled, but they did two or three weeks of filling gaps the Falklands had left in our hospitals and other establishments.'

Women Reserves play many responsible roles. They form London Division's Degaussing Department, which is responsible for calibrating the degaussing circuitry in ships – the circuitry that modifies a ship's magnetic signature, making it less likely to be picked up by a magnetic mine.

I did not see a male black face in London Division, but I did find a black female one, dodging in and out of the tiny classrooms and the main signal office of the communications department below decks. She was twenty-seven years old, a librarian in civilian life and a signal processor in the Royal Naval Reserve. She said she had no naval family background; and she thought that the general lack of naval background among West Indians was probably one of the reasons why there were comparatively few volunteers for either the Royal Navy or the Royal Naval Reserve.

'Probably most people join because of some family tradition,' she said. 'It is not really traditional with West Indian families.'

I asked her if she had experienced any prejudice against her because she was black. 'Not really. Most people here don't meet a lot of black people, in view of their backgrounds and where they live; and perhaps that makes it easier. If you think of somewhere like Hackney, where I live – my father works for a motor firm – race is one of the topics of conversation, and you get comments about it. For some of the neighbourhoods where there aren't a lot of blacks, it is a distant problem they don't have to worry about.'

Some of the equipment aboard HMS *President* and HMS *Chrysanthemum* was decidedly ancient – including the telex machines, the typewriters and the morse keys. But there were some modern intrusions, including cassettes for morse instruction. Since morse became a back-up rather than a chief method of communication in the Navy, standards have slipped. Morse is now taught up to sixteen words a minute, whereas in the 1960s it was taught up to twenty-five words a minute. As in so many other aspects of defence, it is to be profoundly hoped that the complex modern machinery works under fire, and that the back-up is never needed.

In the time I spent with London Division, it was quite clear that the *people* were intensely aware that one day they might be needed. There were only slight signs of that essentially civilian fever in relation to things military: the excitement in ceremonial and display. It was true that London Division of the Royal Naval Reserve was thinking of inviting, to the commissioning of a new training ship, more VIPs than the Royal Navy would have invited. It was also true that the lieutenant-commander in the Naval Control of Shipping branch was trying to re-establish two defunct traditions: the use of the two historic but now never used silver bugles for sounding Sunset, and the organizing of recruiting banquets at the very grand Fishmongers' Hall. Perhaps *both* initiatives could be placed under the heading of blowing one's own trumpet. And in an over-communicated age, where modesty can often lead to self-extinction, a modestly paid but very necessary defence force is surely entitled to its little frills and vanities.

19

RESETTLING IN CIVVY STREET

'You don't actually see ex-naval officers walking around on their uppers, do you? It is amazing the jobs they take on once they leave the Navy, and the way they succeed at them.'

– Ex-naval officer, now director of a directors' employment agency.

'You mustn't be frightened, as an ex-naval officer, of where you sit or what they call you once you go into civilian life. It can be a hard lesson to learn.'

– Ex-naval captain, now working for an organization handling naval equipment.

'I say to civilian employers, "Why do you want specifically ex-naval electricians?" And they say, "Because they are well motivated." And I say, "Then perhaps you require security guards who are also well motivated and have integrity?" That is how you find jobs for ratings.'

– Resettlement officer (commander), HMS *Nelson*, Portsmouth.

The moneyed lady with a large house told the naval resettlement officer at Portsmouth – the head of the department which helps settle naval men and women back into civilian life

– that she wanted an ex-naval houseman/parlourman. There was only one stipulation. He must be homosexual.

At first the resettlement officer, a retired commander who had heard a lot in his time, thought he must have misheard this proviso. The lady assured him he had not misheard. He pointed out that the Royal Navy was not expert in finding jobs for homosexuals: 'We don't have too many of those.'

Still the lady was insistent. 'My husband and I spend a lot of time out, and we have teenage daughters. The last parlourman we had, they were afraid to be in the house with him. And in any case homosexuals are usually good at dusting, and we have lots of *objets d'art* we don't want broken.'

The resettlement officer proceeded to do his best to oblige, since a satisfied employer is one who may well then employ other naval men in quite different capacities. He rang up the Regular Forces Employment Association, which exists to help ex-servicemen find work, and which is always informed when people are leaving the Navy.

One of its officers promptly replied, 'Oh, I know about her, she wants a homosexual. We don't have many of those.'

Undeterred, the stalwart resettlement officer thought again. He remembered a petty officer who had been discharged from the Service for reasons which would not have constituted an offence in civilian life, but which might constitute a recommendation in the eyes of the lady. The man was traced to a provincial town, where he was living with a relative.

'I asked him whether he would be interested, and whether he would mind my telling this would-be employer something about him,' remembered the resettlement officer. 'He said, "Go ahead," so I did.'

The resettlement officer, by now perhaps feeling that this was not the least bizarre piece of advocacy he had ever been called upon to deliver to secure an ex-serviceman a job, tactfully assured the lady that the ex-petty officer had been discharged for an offence that would not have been an offence in civilian life.

'Yes, but is he a homosexual?'

The resettlement officer agreed that indeed some attributes of the man's character might not entirely rule out that possibility.

'He got the job and wrote me a nice letter,' the resettlement officer told me.

Humour and humanity are clearly prerequisites of the Resettlement Office of the Royal Navy, housed in one of the matchbox blocks of HMS *Nelson* at Portsmouth, not far from the main naval base. The modern Navy, it would appear, is ruthless about its own rules, determined that its members shall toe the necessary behavioural lines, but unvengeful towards those who cannot stay the course.

Generally, said the resettlement officer, he thought the Navy recognized that people who were kicked out with no notice – as with the parlourman – and who were left with their families and lives in ruins, sometimes needed *more* assistance than the man who was leaving normally.

'We don't condone this situation,' said the resettlement officer, 'but we are faced with the need to try to assist people. And if we help them not to become a drag on the community, we have done a public service.'

Of course most of the service done by the resettlement officer is private rather than public, and involves citizens of more usual personality and potentiality. At the time I spoke to the retired commander in the resettlement officer's chair, two hundred and twenty ratings a month were being released from the Navy in the Portsmouth area, men and women. The figure is subject to much fluctuation because of the changing social climate. In 1978, when all the services still had a gripe about low pay, the number was up to four hundred a month. In 1980, with the recession biting hard on civilian employment, the figure was only one hundred and fifty. By 1985 it was between that and two hundred; and in 1985 the average per month was expected to be well over two hundred, with some months rising to two hundred and fifty.

The Navy does not want a static force. It welcomes a reasonable outflow of personnel. The trouble is that, while the majority of ratings passing through the three naval release depots – at Portsmouth, Plymouth and Rosyth – are predictably leaving the service at the end of their contracted period, about thirty a month leave at short notice for a variety of reasons. Often the ones who leave voluntarily are the ones the Navy would like to keep; just as some of those who would like to stay on for a renewed contract are not the ones the Navy wants. Sailors who wish to terminate their contracts prematurely have to give eighteen months' notice. For various reasons, some have to leave before this – creating minor imbalances in the system – though many prefer to stay on to complete twenty-two years, after which they become eligible for a pension.

I asked the commander (a paternal figure with gold half-moon spectacles suspended from a cord, and a face always contriving reasons for a smile) to explain the underlying philosophy of the Royal Navy's system for resettling into civilian life men who might have spent less than half their recent years on dry land, and women who have become used to the demands and protection of a disciplined service.

'The aim,' said the commander concisely, 'is to motivate them to do things for themselves.'

Both officers and ratings are encouraged to attend interviews at two specific points in time before they leave. The first interview is two to two and a half years before they are due to leave, when they are encouraged to talk to a resettlement officer about planning their future. If they are officers or senior ratings they are encouraged to do courses at that stage. The basic course is called the Second Careers Advice Course.

The commander pointed out that the Navy recognized that it could be only a first career: 'This is so whether they are junior ratings or admirals.' Men and women were encouraged to start thinking early about their experience and their suitability for civilian jobs. And they were encouraged to take as many as necessary of the courses that made up the first phase – the so-called 'Advice Courses' (later to be followed by more specific training courses). Each Advice Course could take one or two days, and people could do as many as they liked – though it was *not* an entitlement, but was at the mercy of operational needs.

Such courses are held, deliberately, *not* on naval premises but in hotels, clubs or colleges of further education: it helps people to start thinking in civilian terms. The advanced sort of Advice Course is called 'How to Apply For a Job'. It tells men and women how they should make a job application and conduct themselves in interviews. It is usually held six or seven months before the man or woman is due to leave the Navy.

There are then a number of career briefings, which take place at various centres in Britain and abroad. The *Services Resettlement Bulletin*, issued regularly, is an eighty-four page magazine which normally has nearly ten pages of dates and venues, followed by a few more pages of specialist briefings, concerning financial aspects of resettlement and, in particular, house purchase. The career briefings consist of one- or two-day courses. Men and women leaving the Navy can take as many as they like in their last two years of service.

'Generally speaking,' the resettlement officer told me, 'people are sensible. They will ask to do three or four, and will fit them in with their ship's programme. They don't ask for more than they think is reasonable. Because of that, they are usually spared. But in a ship, it is sometimes awkward.'

The Navy is perfectly well aware of this. Every ship and shore establishment has someone who is nominated by the captain to oversee resettlement matters. He is not expected to be an expert; he *is* expected to keep the administrative wheels turning for all the men or women involved and to know what book to consult if he does not know all the answers himself. Even small ships like minesweepers, with a limited crew, have a resettlement man. So have submarines.

But the nerve centre of the whole operation is in Portsmouth, where the resettlement officer publishes, for the whole Navy, what are called 'Naval Resettlement Notices'. These are virtually a sale and mart of job vacancies. Once a week, the bulky publication goes to every ship and shore establishment.

In one issue, it may be advertised that Lord Blank has a vacancy for a butler, and is also a *potential* employer of accountants and security staff. When such an employer is first diagnosed, he is sent a letter and a Blue Book – a guide to the training of naval people calculated to be helpful to the employer. It is often assumed that there is no longer, in the present state of society, a demand for domestic servants or a desire to do the work. The Navy has discovered that both suppositions are false: there is a steady demand for house-management personnel, handyman gardeners and the like.

'Would-be employers, however, want people of integrity, so that they can push off to Monte Carlo and be reasonably confident that the silver will still be there when they get back,' said the resettlement officer.

At the time of our conversation, a peer actually *had* asked for a butler; a school popular with the Royal Family wanted a porter; and the Commonwealth War Graves Commission wanted a driver/messenger.

These are the sort of job notifications that delight the re-settlement officer: 'The technicians have really little difficulty in finding civilian employment – particularly the electronics people. They should be able to market themselves, if appropriately motivated and directed a bit. It is the others who can have more difficulty. The people to worry about are those with service skills that aren't required outside the Navy. I encourage employers who want these sort of people to use our services. And I try to get the ear of employers who are *not* looking for electronics wizards, though we still run courses for the technical people.'

Courses tend to be well attended, whether for technical subjects or not. One on insurance attracted sixty naval personnel; one on the Metropolitan Police drew eighty and one on the Prison Service one hundred and fifty. All were held in the Portsmouth area, and all dealt with employment possibilities in their particular line of territory rather than with specific training.

Some possible second careers are so esoteric that they are not on the list of activities for which courses can be run. In such cases, the Navy permits the man or woman concerned to spend a few days with an employer of their own choice. One man wanted to take up loss-adjusting, and was found a suitable firm. Another wanted to be a broadcaster, and went to the BBC. Yet another wanted to be a coal-miner and was found a suitable mine.

In their last year, naval personnel have what are called 'Living and Working' courses, and take part in a 'Jobs' Fair'. Big employers in the area are invited to these. As many as ninety employers may each send a couple of representatives to explain and discuss employment prospects.

During the last six months of their service, ratings and officers have at their disposal a large number of specialized courses of training. If they want to do an outside course, they are free to take one lasting a month, if it does not conflict with their service duties.

Some officers think they are not so well cared for as the ratings when it comes to these courses. Ratings need to serve for a minimum of five years above the age of eighteen to be entitled to this four weeks. Officers can also have the four-week courses, but the eligibility rules are more complex. An officer *may* have served five years and get a course. But most officers in practice contract to go on for much longer than five years in the service. If an officer leaves early – before the age of forty – he is not entitled to this pre-release training. He may have served for twenty years; but if he is only thirty-nine he is not eligible. When I put this point to the resettlement officer, he diplomatically declined to comment. 'That is the situation at present,' was all he would say.

He was more forthcoming when I asked how much the

system had changed in recent years. 'I think there has been much more awareness among services people of what is available to help them. Because of the recession people recognize it is pretty chilly outside and they are looking at every possibility to help them with their resettlement. Many people come in here wanting to use our facilities and advice. The range of careers is changing all the time. If we put on a course – say about buying a business – we quickly get a hundred names down for it.'

The image of the modern sailor about to leave the Navy hardly squares with the Nelsonian image of the jolly Jack Tar who can think no further than his next grog. It is that of a disciplined man who realizes clearly that in civilian life discipline helps, but is not in itself enough; and that thought, rather than pride, may offer the best solutions for the future. One chief petty officer wanted to run an old people's home. The Navy attached him to a reputable home, run by an ex-RAF man. In the course of five days he learned some of the essentials of the job. One of the things he learned was that old people tend to have problems with their feet because they have difficulty cutting their own toenails. So the Navy was happy to see him arrange a private course in chiropody for himself.

Officers are left to shift for themselves rather more, possibly because, at some deep subliminal level, the Royal Navy still regards officers as *gentlemen*; and gentlemen confer favours, not receive them. But officers can sometimes face bigger problems than ratings in adjusting to civilian life.

Civilian employers who are being recommended an ex-naval officer for a job almost always put one crucial coded question: 'Is he a status person?' If the answer is 'Yes', the employer is more likely to offer polite regrets than a job.

The question means several things, all of them adding up to a potential thumbs-down. Will he be pedantic and grumpy to those beneath him in the civilian hierarchy? Will he be happy working in an open-plan office, instead of having a sanctum of his own? Will he insist on being called 'sir'? Will he continue to refer to himself by his naval rank, and expect others to do the same?

If there is a 'yes' answer to any of these questions, it is unlikely that a job will be offered. Employers know that a great adaptation is necessary for civilian life, and that any man who is set in his ways will probably make for trouble in the organization.

One retired naval officer I addressed as 'captain' quickly shushed me. 'Call me Mister or call me Jack,' he said. 'I find I do more business in civilian life that way. You could say that a test of suitability for a civilian job is a willingness to renounce the naval rank.'

Even the adaptable are prone to cling to some aspects of naval thinking. Another retired captain told me he had endeared himself to the first civilian employer after he left the Navy by saying, 'I don't care a damn where I sit or what they call me.'

But the retired captain admitted, 'I retired on half pay at fifty-five. I had the feeling I could have been made rear-admiral, but it didn't happen. So I said to myself that I would get a civilian job which, with my pension, would give me an income as big as I would have got if I *had* been made rear-admiral.'

He eventually succeeded. He joined a firm making ball bearings, on the external relations side. For the five and a half years he stayed there, he suppressed his rank in favour of plain 'Mister'. It was only when he was made redundant by this firm, and joined an organization connected with naval equipment, that he resurrected the 'captain'. The rank then had direct relevance to the job he was doing, and opened more doors than it closed. Firms liked employing ex-naval officers, he thought, because their knowledge of technology was often translatable into civilian life, and because the ex-naval officer was used to working in confined spaces with men of all ranks and types, and probably had more concern for them as individuals than the average executive in civilian industry or commerce.

'I interested myself in ball bearings,' said the retired captain. 'I read all sorts of books on the subject. Did you know that a ball bearing can be made to relative tolerances of one inch to the height of Mount Everest – about a 30,000th part of its own size? Hearing that nearly brought tears of appreciation to my eyes. Then a director of the firm said to me: "You do realize, don't you, that we aren't trying to make ball bearings, we are trying to make *money*?"'

That is the point that retired naval men find most difficult to take: the absolute difference between the Navy and private industry is that in industry nothing is of value that does not make a profit.

One captain not yet retired – he still had another two years to go – told me that he was already rehearsing in his own mind to make this essential transition. 'If a course of action was suggested to me in business, it would be motivated by the need to make money, and have no value outside that,' he said. 'Whereas I would probably instinctively try to give other values to my decisions, including the care of the workers. I shall have to adapt.'

Some jobs can have a direct connection with a naval man's service life. Makers of weaponry, and other equipment which they hope to sell to the Ministry of Defence, have an obvious interest in employing former naval officers, because their knowledge and their rank opens many Whitehall doors. In such cases the final rank is taken out and dusted, perhaps after many years of disuse.

In such cases, the value of the ex-naval man to the firm may be generally conceded by the rest of the executives. But occasionally the placing of an ex-naval man into a slot in a firm which has been coveted by the civilians who have worked there for years can cause friction.

'I can understand that,' said the captain two years away from retirement. 'If you have been toiling away for years with your eyes on a particular job in the organization, it is quite natural that you would resent it when some military person is brought into that slot.'

Specialized employment agencies say that the very existence of such a sentiment in a naval man is interesting and significant – because few people in civilian life would care tuppence about the feelings of people they pipped to a particular job.

'You must remember,' said an executive of one agency, 'that, in private industry, you are appointed for one thing and one thing only. That is that you will be able to make money for that company. That is the sole criterion, and that is what retired naval men find it so difficult to condition themselves to. The only reason the firm will take you on is that they think *you* will make money for them. That is why you are there, and that is why thinking about the people who *didn't* get the job is irrelevant. The company simply thought you could make more money for them than the other candidates.'

There are a number of organizations handling the re-settlement of ex-naval men and women. They work principally on the old boy network. One agency appointments director told me, 'In fact we don't canvass, we rely on them coming to us.'

Hence the importance of the old boy network. Naval officers connected with phasing naval men into civilian life all have their own contacts, who can suggest names of retiring officers or ratings who could be interested in their services. At one lunch I had with head-hunters in their West End of London offices (egg mayonnaise, veal with cheese and spinach, fruit or cheese, two sorts of wine) I found the other guests of the agency to be two ex-captains.

I asked one of them how the agency got to know suitable names. 'Like *this*,' he replied – and handed one retiring officer's curriculum vitae to the head of the agency.

If they had been flies on the wall, many naval men facing retirement, at fifty-three in the case of commanders or fifty-five in the case of captains, might have been reassured. There is no doubt that even the most clipped and incisive naval officers do become distinctly nervous when the time approaches at which they must exchange the cloistered atmosphere of the ship or the shore base for an unpredictable civilian world which has its own values and worries, and does not believe – at least in peacetime – that it *owes* ex-Navy people a living.

For some ex-naval men, the difficult period spent in writing numerous job applications is soon forgotten in the demands and satisfactions of a new job. I met one captain who had just come back from the Falklands as captain of a frigate, who told me he was about to leave the Navy two years ahead of the age of fifty-five. He was attending a business studies course at the Polytechnic of Central London, and he struck me as being a little apprehensive about the future.

A year later, when I asked him how his retirement had developed, he insisted that though he may have *looked* apprehensive, he had not been especially so. He had expected to have six months to a year of applying for jobs. He had in fact got a job with British Aerospace in just over six months, after nearly a hundred letters and inquiries for jobs.

'My background operationally in the Navy, with torpedo and anti-submarine work from way back, helped me,' he told me. 'As it happened, British Aerospace had just started up a new underwater division; and I just fell into a job in forward planning.'

The captain thought that the business studies course had been useful, although it might have been even more useful had he known what job he was going into before he took the course. 'But,' he said drily, 'as I had spent the previous six months down in the Falklands, I couldn't do much hunting for jobs then.'

His major fear had been that he would end up in a static desk job. In fact, in his new job, he commuted every week from his home in Hampshire to British Aerospace in Bristol, a two-hour car journey. He also spent quite a bit of time in London or at the research centre at Weymouth, returning home for Friday, Saturday and Sunday nights.

One of the satisfactions he found in his civilian job was the thought that he might be able to get more good equipment into the Navy as a civilian than he would have been able to do had he stayed in the Navy. The services now relied more on outside industry to provide equipment, and to think about what the services might need. There was not so much central control. There was more opportunity for private industry to think about what things the Navy might require, and to produce them.

With his pension, his new salary left him better off than when he was in the Navy: 'I seem to have a lot more to spend, and I seem to be able to spend a lot more time with my family than I did during my last few years in the Navy.'

Despite his successful naval career, this officer had no sense of bitter deprivation at leaving the Navy. 'I don't miss it at all,' he said. 'I don't regret my period in the Navy, and I have no bad feelings about it, but I just don't miss it. It surprises me, actually. Of course, I might miss it later; but the job I am doing is interesting and worthwhile.'

The memory of the numerous job applications before he struck oil possibly rankled more than the clipped-voiced captain would admit. Still, he had kept his nerve, and did not go through an employment agency. He had tried one agency, but they had wanted a lot of money to arrange a job – between £4,000 and £6,000. The agency was a good one. But he still thought the fee was a lot of money, though if he had been unable to get work for himself, and they had found him a job in the £20,000-a-year salary bracket – which was what he had discussed with the agency – he supposed the fee might have been worth it.

Naval officers have their nerve steadied at this crucial moment in their lives by the philosophy of self-help prevalent in the service. It was epitomized by the First Sea Lord when this particular captain went to see him to say farewell at the end of his naval career.

'Well,' said the First Sea Lord, 'as far as I can see, most of those who really *want* a job get one.'

When he was doing the business studies course at the

Polytechnic of Central London, they indoctrinated the captain
with the same idea: that a man who really wanted a job would
get one, even if it took nine months or a year, and a lot of
application letters. So the six months it actually took the captain, some of it taken up with the business course, and some of
it with a sailing holiday, seemed not as fearsome as it might
otherwise have done.

But the plain fact remains that a modern naval officer had
better have *some* savings, because he may well be still twiddling
his nervous thumbs when ratings who have called him 'Sir' for
years are long settled in their civilian second careers. Times
may have changed, but ex-officers of the Royal Navy do *not*
see themselves as parlourmen or butlers.

In Conclusion

The Royal Navy approaches the twenty-first century in a state of some flux. Perhaps because of this it clings the more tenaciously to traditional practices and habits as some sort of safe harbour amid the surrounding squalls. It never goes to the lavatory, only to the heads, and presumably always will. It 'goes ashore' from any ship, even a shore establishment. It has traditional toasts to accompany the Loyal Toast to the Queen for each day of the week, including Saturday's jocular 'Wives and sweethearts – may they never meet'. And so on.

Sometimes in my travels around the Royal Navy, talking to some of the Royal Navy's 63,000 men and women, and some of the 7,500 Royal Marines, it has struck me strongly that naval men and women fight for these little observances with the fanaticism of human beings who have the underlying feeling that the central core of their lives is not under their direct control, but is at the mercy of political and social trends, conflicts and cross-currents.

The Navy has lately become very much a football in defence politics. 'We must maintain the British Army of the Rhine, so we must cut the Navy,' has been a siren song frequently heard in Whitehall. Indeed it is arguable that BAOR cannot be cut without fear of encouraging a rash invasion from the East; but neither can the Navy be cut without the fear of national starvation by sea blockade. And naval officers say, 'Cut the Navy, and you won't *have* a BAOR for more than a week.' The difference between cutting BAOR and cutting the Navy is the difference between the guillotine and the electric chair. Neither can be enthusiastically recommended.

But in practice, and especially at a time when the enormous cost of Trident as a replacement for Polaris has given the pacifist lobby much ammunition ('Twelve weeks of Department of Health and Social Security expenditure spread over fifteen years,' replies the Navy) the Navy has been put into a position of constantly having to justify itself. And this at a time when its complicated technologies defy sympathetic understanding from the ordinary voter; when, indeed, the public is used to coping only with facts and issues which can be explained to them far more simply and clearly than the Navy thinks can, or perhaps should, be done.

The naval man's natural taciturnity has been complicated by this increasing use of sophisticated technology. Technology is daunting to the average civilian: the first sight of the operations room on a modern warship will quickly bear this out. It is a jungle of keyboards, screens, dials, instruments and paperwork.

Naval men will say, 'We do tend to man equipment rather than equip men.' And they tend to justify their worth under questioning by blinding the questioner with technology. In terms of their perhaps now more vulnerable relations with a public which has *traditionally* had a soft spot for its Navy, it is rather like responding to a possible shipwreck by clinging to the anchor.

Naval men argue, with reason, that they are very good value for money. Of the £18 billion Defence Budget for the year 1985–6, the Navy got around £6 billion, some 33.6 per cent, or the third one would tend to expect for one of the three Armed Services. But since the number of its *people*, some 70,000 (including the 7,500 Royal Marines) was less than *half* those in the British Army, it is fairly obvious where the lion's share of the Navy's money is going: to high technology rather than people. In fact, the Ministry of Defence pays about £2 billion a year for naval equipment.

Given defence cuts and the shortage of personnel, both men and W R N S are now expected to be something in the nature of jacks of all trades, or at least master of two – their own main speciality and any other duties that can conveniently be lumped with it. These may entail a bit more paperwork for a first lieutenant of a ship or a bit of cleaning and cooking for the communicators.

Officers and men emphasized to me again and again that the little refinements of naval life were usually privately paid for. Officers pointed out that if they wanted better food than the standard £1.20 (at the time) daily allowance, they had to make up the difference from their own pockets. The Royal Marines in particular, perhaps the most directly combative men of the Royal Navy, told me that – though the basic kit they were provided with was adequate – in fact many men bought better items of equipment privately. This state of affairs may or may not be satisfactory; but if taxpayers really wish to complain, they could perhaps do it most effectively by putting their money where their mouth is.

The Navy has had the benefit of distinguished and even Royal patronage. Prince Charles, the Duke of Edinburgh and Lord Louis Mountbatten were all serving naval officers. Perhaps, paradoxically, that gracious and obviously useful connection may have also given ammunition to those who would prefer to think that the Royal Navy is a collection of high-born people who like dressing up in smart blue uniforms with a lot of gold braid. The modern age is geared to respect professionals and workmen rather than well-connected dilettantes. *Are* there any of the latter in the Navy? Men who had worked with or heard of Prince Charles in minesweepers said that he had been a professional, doing a good job despite being afflicted with seasickness (an uncomfortable indisposition in any ship, sheer hell in a minesweeper). Lord Louis Mountbatten was sometimes thought to be venturesome, but never a fool. And the well-connected men who sometimes appear on the bridges of the most prestigious ships were also visibly the sort of men capable of displaying leadership in cerebrally taxing circumstances, as well as physically taxing ones. Any honest observer, even one with a mistrust of public school accents, would have to admit to finding such men personally and professionally impressive.

How pervasive is the old school tie influence? Over a recent two-year period, of those officers entering the service, 26 per cent were from public schools or their equivalent. In the case of the Royal Marines, it was a remarkable 68 per cent. Are public schoolboys more *used* to hardship? It could be. Perhaps the proportion of naval officers who have come up through the ranks are a balancing factor. Over a recent period of four years, the proportion of ex-rating officers was 21 per cent for the Royal Navy and 23 per cent for the Royal Marines. It appears that, except in the case of the Royal Marines, half of the officer corps consists of products of the state school system who go straight into officer training, topped and tailed with a quarter of public schoolboys and a quarter of ex-ratings. The Navy would not express it in quite those crude terms. But it does appear that it has tried for some sort of balance in terms of personal background and professional experience; though it remains a fact that the proportion of ex-ratings who rise to the top in the *combat* role of commanding ships is much, much smaller than the proportion who become other sorts of officer.

Yet, it appeared to me that there was less of a *personality* difference between senior ratings and officers than in the corresponding grades of the British Army, where the social divide can be a rather big one, especially in the Guards and some infantry regiments. On several occasions, with the Navy, I found senior ratings able to explain in simple and direct terms professional details over which officers had faltered, breaking off and restarting sentences, shifting their ground and generally torturing the rules of grammar and syntax. In officers, adrenalin may be a very necessary accompaniment of thought; it is not a substitute for it. Senior ratings, in this respect, were generally impressive.

I found that much of the personal resentment among senior ratings within the Navy was directed at university graduate officers where the adrenalin (some might have said bumptiousness) had not yet been conditioned by enough experience of practical matters. But this is certainly not exclusive to the Navy; civilian employers in industry and commerce are gradually becoming bolder in proclaiming that some of the results of keeping a young man in academic cloisters until he is biologically old enough to be the father of school-going children can be asinine. It is just that in a disciplined service, where the asininity cannot be greeted with two fingers by the lower ranks, the pent-up tensions produced may be greater. With senior ratings who were thinking of leaving the Navy, pay was hardly a factor and the increasingly hard work in the Navy only a secondary one: the real irritation (perhaps as much as the long periods of separation from families) was young university officers who did not understand other people's problems. I tend to the belief – it was one of my reasons for writing this book – that the man of action has been unwisely discounted in the present age in favour of the cerebral and passive observers: the economists, market analysts, commentators, lecturers and consultants who can all swim wonderfully on the beach. But immature bossiness is not the same thing as effective action.

Officers and ratings in the Women's Royal Naval Service were confident of the maturity of young women in the Navy. I saw much evidence to support this. Young girls training to be ratings were well spoken and sure of themselves. This could have been a reflection of the increase in the confidence of women in society generally. But it did seem to me that the standard of WRNS recruits was high, possibly even higher than for the women of the British Army. I was not surprised to hear that the Navy could recruit three times the number it actually took on. As far as the WRNS are concerned, it is still a buyer's market for labour.

The Navy has taken the decision to use many WRNS officers in the public relations field, acting as go-betweens between the Navy and the media and public. All of those that I encountered were exceptionally good at their job, reacting to the professional demands put upon them with remarkable resource and diplomacy. I was told that there were only five male naval officers concerned full-time with public relations. There could be a case for having more public relations officers who are male and, therefore, for the rest of their service, actually concerned with the seagoing life of the Navy. It would give an immediacy, a sense of talking to the actual men who do the job and take the decisions. But the WRNS who are the spokesmen for the Navy do a remarkably good job, from a position of essential disadvantage created by the fact that everyone knows they do not actually go to sea and fight.

Wives of naval men have sharply differing stories to tell of their lives. I met many wives whose separation from their husbands for regular periods of time had produced obvious maturity and self-reliance. I also met some who were angry because they felt their husbands were being called upon to do too much in a pruned Navy, and who obviously would not be sorry if their husbands decided to leave at the earliest opportunity. It was some wives rather than husbands themselves who were angry because of what they saw as the brusque manner of some young officers towards experienced ratings: they felt their menfolk would not have to stand this degree of arbitrariness in civilian life (possibly thanks to the trade unions); and they plainly felt vicariously demeaned themselves. This was an occasional grumble. More consistent was the view that the Navy should allow more freedom to wives living in quarters to choose their own decorations, and more personal dignity by treating them as individuals in their own right instead of characterizing them by the rank of their husbands.

But any disciplined service (perhaps any bureaucracy) tends to slip with gratitude into neat rather than tactful systems for docketing people. Viewing how the Admiralty Interview Board selects young would-be officers for training, I was struck by the humanity and perception with which the system was applied.

But the system itself? The selectors know before the young

man faces them what school he went to and what that school thought of him. I believed the members of the Board I watched in action when they told me that they were interested in finding officers from *all* types of school. But the fact remains that the Navy has a system whereby it has special recruiting campaigns in 'good' schools – usually boarding schools in the independent sector of education – and also has a system where would-be officer assessors know from the start what school the candidate comes from. The way is smoothed for the élite while it is merely not actively barred to those from humbler homes and schools. It is just as well the system *is* used with imagination and flexibility. Otherwise it could favour those with youthful confidence rather than those with innate intelligence. In decision making, it is good to be confident: it is better also to be right.

The Navy's confidence is especially evident in the Fleet Air Arm, that élite that prides itself, when compared with the Royal Air Force, on being prepared to tackle anything, and damn the red tape (but not the safety rules). It may be just as well the Fleet Air Arm has great confidence: its role has been threatened and whittled down in recent years. Its fixed-wing flying role has been taken from it, fortunately leaving it the revolutionary and formidable vertical take-off Sea Harriers as well as the more conventional helicopters. Both enemy surface ships (from the Sea Harriers) and submarines (from helicopters) still have much to fear from it.

If only on the grounds of encouraging healthy competition with the RAF, there is an obvious case for maintaining a strong Fleet Air Arm as part of the Navy. There is the same case for maintaining the Royal Marines as part of the Navy, though in personality and thinking they more resemble men of the British Army – men who are unconsciously always bracing themselves for direct hand-to-hand combat. It might well be the Royal Navy that delivered Royal Marines to a conflict; it *would* be the Royal Navy that delivered the Fleet Air Arm to a conflict. The Fleet Air Arm has an obvious link with the Navy that goes beyond empire building, and the occasionally heard arguments for hiving them off to other services seem unlikely to bear fruit.

Some of the question marks hanging over the Navy of the future are not concerned with cash. There are several that are. Few officers and men I spoke to doubted that the financial pressures on the Navy in recent years had been unhealthy. I take their point.

What sort of pressure is it that (for example) forces the Navy to call its new aircraft/marine carriers *Invincible* and *Illustrious* 'through-deck cruisers', because aircraft carriers were at one time (before the Falklands) ideologically unacceptable on grounds of cost? What sort of pressure is it that persuades reasonable men to put into warships, because they are cheap, mattresses which give off black, lethally toxic smoke in a fire? Plainly it is a pressure that has persuaded sane men to cut corners in the equipment of ships rather than risk reducing their number. It may be argued that on balance they were right – on the basis of the knowledge and expectations at that time. It now seems clear that they should never have been put in the position of having to take such a 'cyanide or arsenic' decision in the first place. It was unfortunate that it took the Falklands war to make it clear. But some naval people now believe there are signs that, with the Falklands receding in public memory, the financial pressures are closing in again, and that they could hurt the Navy.

Perhaps if Nelson, the imaginative innovator, were alive today he would give a new order to augment 'England expects that every man will do his duty.' It would be: 'England expects every naval man and woman to acquire the persuasive arts which can make the essential nature of the Navy and its people alive and real to the taxpayer.'

For want of such an order, Nelson's heirs could suffer – to the detriment of us all.